JENNY UGLOW

· A YEAR WITH · GILBERT WHITE ·

The First Great Nature Writer

faber

First published in 2025
by Faber & Faber Limited
The Bindery, 51 Hatton Garden
London ECIN 8HN

This paperback edition first published in 2026

Typeset by Faber & Faber Limited
Printed and bound in the UK by CPI Group (UK) Ltd, Croydon CRO 4YY

A CIP record for this book
is available from the British Library

ISBN 978–0–571–35419–1

Printed and bound in the UK on FSC® certified paper in line with our continuing
commitment to ethical business practices, sustainability and the environment.
For further information see faber.co.uk/environmental-policy

Our authorised representative in the EU for product safety is
Easy Access System Europe, Mustamäe tee 50, 10621 Tallinn, Estonia
gpsr.requests@easproject.com

2 4 6 8 10 9 7 5 3 1

A YEAR WITH GILBERT WHITE

Jenny Uglow writes on literature, art and social history. Her books include award-winning biographies on Elizabeth Gaskell and George Eliot, William Hogarth, Thomas Bewick and Edward Lear, as well as group studies including *The Lunar Men* and the panoramic *In These Times*. A retired editorial director of Chatto & Windus, and former Chair of the Council of the Royal Society of Literature, she grew up in Cumbria, and she and her husband Steve now live in Borrowdale.

Further praise for *A Year with Gilbert White*:

'A wonderfully fresh perspective on a fascinating man, place and time.' Tristan Gooley

'Charming . . . What makes this book so joyful is Gilbert's wonder at the natural world. *A Year with Gilbert White* is gorgeously illustrated and strangely comforting in its seasonal rhythm of daily entries – it is like Radio 4's shipping forecast for naturalists.' Andrea Wulf, *Financial Times*

'The author brings her subject endearingly alive . . . [an] enriching book.' Gareth Thompson, *Nature*

'A fascinating mosaic of biography, ornithology, ethnology, horticulture and weather . . . Tenderness, along with humour and generosity, predominates here . . . *A Year with Gilbert White* glows with the combined enthusiasm of two brilliant natural historians recording the minutiae of the world around them: the budding of wild flowers, the arrival of migrating birds, the sex lives of snails. A feast of a book, it is beautifully illustrated and compulsively readable.' Norma Clarke, *Literary Journal*

'Uglow creates a captivating picture of the man, his milieu and his age.' *The Economist*

'Uglow has paid White the great compliment of looking at his journals with the same loving curiosity as he lavished on Selborne.' Kathryn Hughes, *The Times*

'A glorious celebration of a year in the life of an eighteenth-century curate and his English country garden.' Philip Hoare, *Observer*

'An absolute joy . . . [Uglow] writes about [White] with a fondness you would typically find only with friendship.' Kate Bradbury, *Gardens Illustrated*

'In *A Year with Gilbert White*, Jenny Uglow traces the pioneer naturalist's life through 1781 and reanimates the man, his beloved Hampshire countryside and his age.' Boyd Tonkin, *The Spectator* Books of the Year

'Jenny Uglow expands upon White's diary entries for 1781, brilliantly bringing the modest Hampshire curate to life.' Jonathan Self, *Country Life* Books of the Year

by the same author

GEORGE ELIOT
ELIZABETH GASKELL: A HABIT OF STORIES
HENRY FIELDING (Writers and their Works)
HOGARTH: A LIFE AND A WORLD
CULTURAL BABBAGE: TIME, TECHNOLOGY AND INVENTION
(with Francis Spufford)
DR JOHNSON AND THE CLUB (National Portrait Gallery)
THE LUNAR MEN
A LITTLE HISTORY OF BRITISH GARDENING
NATURE'S ENGRAVER: A LIFE OF THOMAS BEWICK
WORDS & PICTURES
A GAMBLING MAN: CHARLES II AND THE RESTORATION
THE PINECONE: THE STORY OF SARAH LOSH
IN THESE TIMES: LIVING IN BRITAIN THROUGH NAPOLEON'S WARS
MR LEAR: A LIFE OF ART AND NONSENSE
SYBIL & CYRIL: CUTTING THROUGH TIME

For Steve

'Annus Mirabilis, or the Natural History of the Twelve Months.'
   GILBERT WHITE

These are brand-new birds of twelve-months' growing,
Which a year ago, or less than twain,
No finches were, nor nightingales,
        Nor thrushes
But only particles of grain
And earth, and air, and rain.

   THOMAS HARDY, 'Proud Songsters'

CONTENTS

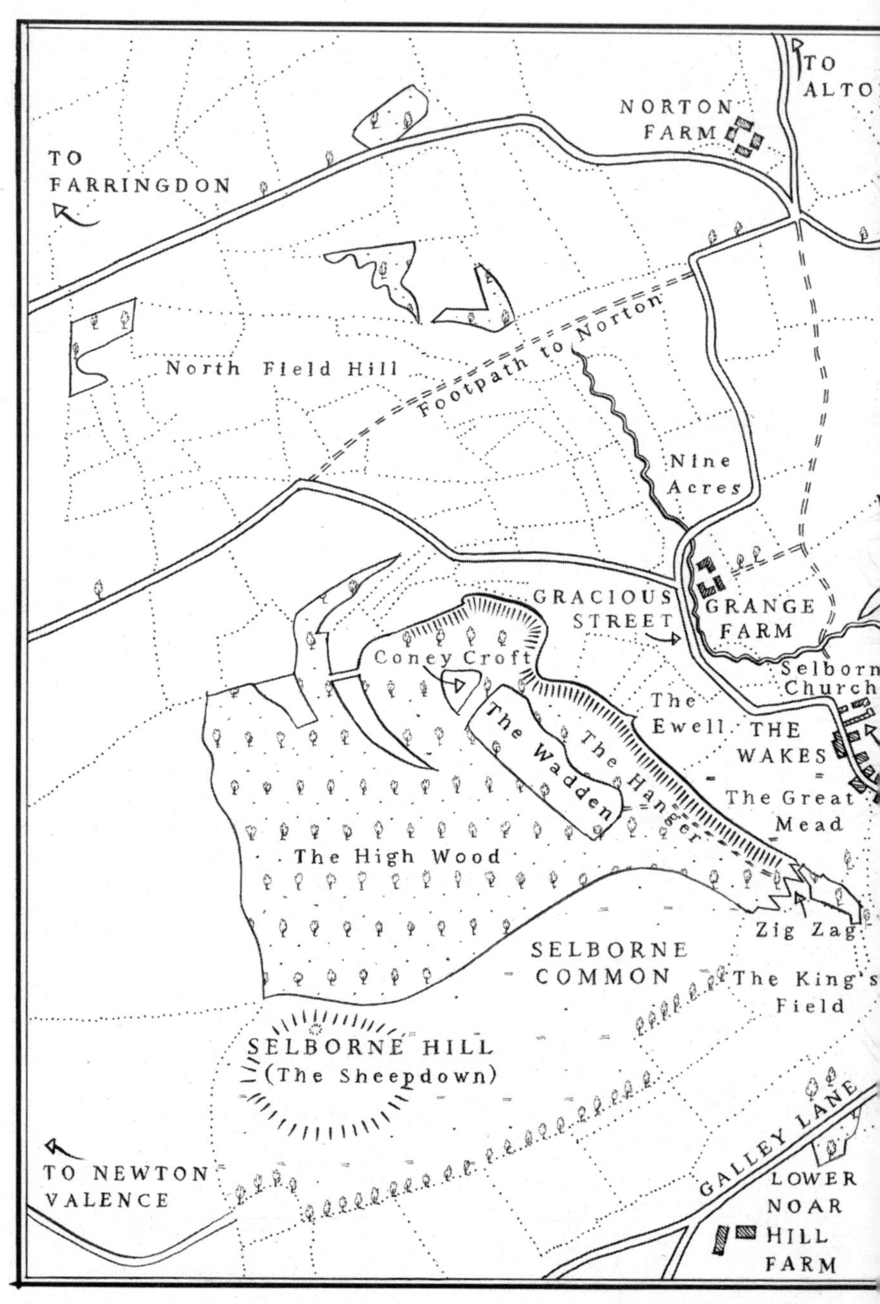

TO ALTO
NORTON FARM
TO FARRINGDON
North Field Hill
Footpath to Norton
Nine Acres
GRACIOUS STREET
GRANGE FARM
Coney Croft
Selborn Church
The Ewell
The Wadden
The Hanger
THE WAKES
The Great Mead
The High Wood
Zig Zag
SELBORNE COMMON
The King's Field
SELBORNE HILL
(The Sheepdown)
TO NEWTON VALENCE
GALLEY LANE
LOWER NOAR HILL FARM

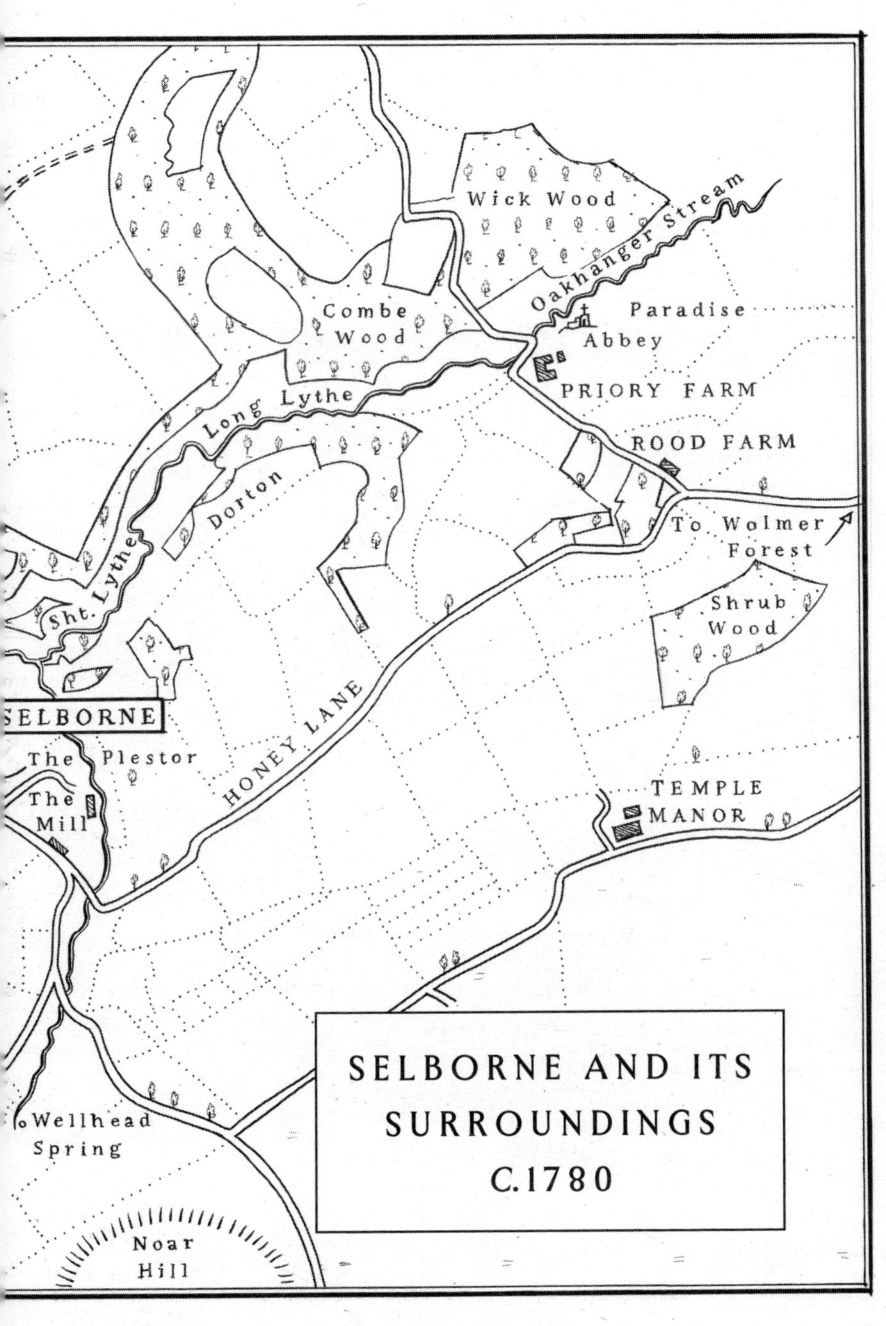

Wick Wood
Oakhanger Stream
Combe Wood
Paradise Abbey
PRIORY FARM
Long Lythe
ROOD FARM
Dorton
To Wolmer Forest
Sht. Lythe
Shrub Wood
SELBORNE
The Plestor
HONEY LANE
The Mill
TEMPLE MANOR
Wellhead Spring
Noar Hill
SELBORNE AND ITS SURROUNDINGS
C.1780

TIME & PLACE

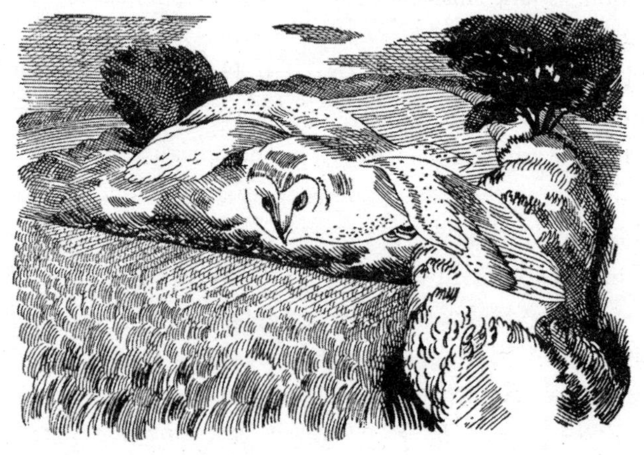

John Nash, *The Natural History of Selborne*, 1951.

I N 1781, the year this book spends with Gilbert White, he was sixty, a country curate in Hampshire, comfortably off but not rich, living in a village he had known all his life, surrounded by friends and constantly in touch with his family. All that remained to complete his satisfaction, as Jane Austen might say, was the publication of his book, *The Natural History and Antiquities of Selborne*. He had planned and worked on this for the past seven years and would spend a further seven polishing and revising it, so 1781 was the midpoint in its long gestation. But in fact the year could have been picked out with a pin, a typical year in the life of a man who was watching the natural world and the goings-on of his village, while slowly creating a wholly remarkable work.

The main part of Gilbert White's book is a personal evocation of the birds, insects and other animals in a single parish, and of the people who lived there. The second part, about the parish history – the '*Antiquities*' of its title – is often dropped from later editions, so it appears simply as *The Natural History of Selborne*. 'Scientific' in its detail, it is also intimate and informal in tone, open to speculation and amazement. No naturalist – or 'natural philosopher', as they were then called – had written like this before, with a vivid, flowing style that brings out the author's own enquiring, warm personality, as well as his loving record of the life around him. This is what has made *The Natural History* a treasured work, never out of print since it was first published in 1789, a book that nineteenth-century emigrants and soldiers fighting in the trenches of World War I took with them as a vision of the country they had left behind, an emblem of 'home'.

The book's core is made up of two sequences of letters that White wrote to his fellow naturalists Thomas Pennant and Daines Barrington. He kept copies of these letters, and over time he played with them and edited them, putting in new details and stories, and finally adding extra, invented 'letters', which were never sent, to give a frame for the whole. Letters are by their very nature open-ended, occasional and immediate, and this structure allowed him to jump from topic to topic, so that readers could follow him as he roamed through a wood or dissected a bird, sharing his feelings as he watched an owl swoop or recoiled from a foul-smelling bat, or pondered the reproduction of eels and chats about hops and hay.

As he worked, he turned constantly to the journals that he had kept for many years, using them to compare dates, to chart the slight variations in the flowering-time of wildflowers or the arrival of migrating birds. He mined his journals, too, for striking examples and incidents, like the nuthatch wedging nuts in a gate or the adder shedding its skin like a glove. The journals let him keep his finger on the pulse of the year, recording the small things that sum up a day. His jottings were quick, shorn of adjectives, curious, cross, delighted, awestruck, sharp as his watching eye.

WRENS SCUTTLING UNDER hedges, mist across fields, owls chasing swallows nesting in chimneys and falling down in clouds of soot – Gilbert White made these come alive for me when I picked up *The Natural History of Selborne* in my teens. The bald opening worked like a children's book, telling you exactly where you were:

> The parish of Selborne lies in the extreme eastern corner of the county of Hampshire, bordering on the county of Sussex, and not far from the county of Surrey; is about fifty miles south-west of London, in latitude 51, and near midway between the towns of Alton and Petersfield.

I liked the way he circled above the map like a hawk, before swooping down to the village street, to birds in the bushes and crickets in the grass. I liked the letter form, with its vivid digressions ('first I must mention, as a great curiosity . . .'), turning blithely from ancient oaks to stubborn ravens and unearthed fossils. Back then, I didn't read all of *The Natural History*, dense with detail, or appreciate White's discoveries and arguments. He sprang into focus as a man and a naturalist when I read Richard Mabey's biography, first published in 1986 (a perfect life, as far as I'm concerned). I then became intrigued as to how he fitted into the interest in natural history that blossomed from the mid-eighteenth to the early nineteenth century. This was shared among all classes, from Midlands industrialists collecting minerals and fossils to Thomas Bewick in Northumberland engraving birds; from women botanists dissecting bulbs to the workers of Manchester a generation later in Elizabeth Gaskell's *Mary Barton*, 'who know the name and habitat of every plant within a day's walk from their dwellings'.

That spreading interest was something different and democratic. It drew on scholarly studies, but it was born from people's contact with the natural world in the course of their daily lives. Its beginnings coincided with the vogue for the 'picturesque', which was not only an appreciation of landscape as a picture, but a valuing of an emotional response, the ability to admire, to be delighted or moved by the odd and the irregular, to see a familiar landscape in a new, personal way. A copse was no longer an economic fact – 'a fine stand of timber' – but a reminder of home, or of lost love, or of a sense of place so intense that the felling of an oak or a line of poplars could feel like a personal grief.

I wanted to understand this new kind of writing, which is imbued with such feeling and links scholarly knowledge to simple daily watching. It seemed to demand a new way of approaching Gilbert White. Was it possible, I wondered, to follow him through the year, writing day by day myself, alongside his *Naturalist's Journal*?

The overarching narrative is the passing of the year, in which each month has its distinctive character. Following a journal, however, means surrendering continuity to serendipity, abandoning a straightforward account and accepting the wayward and random. The sequence may jump from poetry to potatoes, from sermons to swifts. Some days in 1781, Gilbert – I call him by his first name because there are so many Whites in his spreading family – has nothing to report except the weather. This lets me look at entries from other years, following the track of his life, forward and back and sideways, exploring the way that his thinking was coloured by his experience and milieu and the ideas of his time. It's like meeting someone in late middle age, learning about them not in a chronological stream, but bit by bit, at first in a rush, then in sporadic bursts. Our lives are linear, running on through the years, but they are also layered, like strata, or a tangled hedgerow, where branches, fed by unseen roots, shelter an abundance of life.

IN THE CENTURY after Gilbert White died, his admirers developed an image of him as an unworldly clergyman exploring some pre-industrial idyll. To the American writer James Russell Lowell, he seemed 'to have lived before the Fall . . . his volumes are the journal of Adam in Paradise'. Yet Selborne was no lost Eden and Gilbert no solitary idealist. In many ways he was typical of clergy families and country gentlefolk: classically educated, generous to the poor but complacently sure of his place and proud of his country. In 1781, the year of this journal, George III had been on the throne for twenty-one years, with no serious sign yet of his later madness. For most of that time, from the end of war with France in 1763 until the start of the American War of Independence in 1776, Britain basked in its dominance in Europe, and in its booming trade and 'polite' culture. Canals and new turnpikes criss-crossed the land, and huge, improved steam engines thumped in foundries and mines; soon steam would replace water power in mills and new 'manufactories'. In the cities, theatres, pleasure gardens and coffee houses flourished. In small towns like Alton, three miles from Selborne, the doctors and lawyers, corn merchants and brewers and their families flocked to assemblies and balls, ordered new novels and set off for musical evenings and whist parties, the men brushing their wigs, and the women trying out new fashions.

The dominant note was the rise in prosperity of the 'middling classes', but such generalisations quickly crumble, as they do in any age. We have to set Gainsborough beauties against boys hung at Tyburn; tea caddies on the table against bloodshed in India; sugar cones in the larder against slave ships at sea. Squires enclosed the land, while homeless vagrants roamed the roads. A London toff could lose £20,000 in one night at cards, while a farm labourer earned 1s 6d a day. There were increasingly fierce demands for democratic rights. Amid all this, thinkers in Britain and America, and the rational *philosophes* in France, argued about society and politics, about knowledge and the nature of the self, and debated issues like the age of the Earth and the ordering of species.

Gilbert followed these arguments, feeling himself to be part of a collaborative hunt for knowledge and a drive for improvement. Yet his brilliance stems not from the pursuit of grand theories, but from his everyday immersion in a particular area, where he knew every field and bank and ditch: his home village, Selborne.

SELBORNE IS A FEW MILES off the main road from Farnham in Surrey, to Winchester in Hampshire. As you approach it from the north, on the bus from Alton, over the downs with their broad, open fields, you can see the curve of the Hanger, a long, wooded hill, but you can't see the village until you are actually there. Suddenly, the road dips steeply down towards a stream, then climbs up again, round a corner, to meet the village street. In Gilbert's day, Selborne was not only hidden, but almost cut off. The modern Alton road had not been built, and to reach the village coaches had to wind through a network of lanes, even driving round the other side of the hill and approaching from the south. Over the centuries, carts had worn the lanes away, sinking them to depths that were sometimes two or three times the height of a man. These ancient, pre-Roman tracks were just wide enough to let a cart struggle through, but faced with sunken tracks clogged with mud, deep in snow or awash with water pouring off the fields, coachmen often gave up. In December 1773, urging Gilbert to get together with the vicar to demand a decent road, his teasing, jovial, hypochondriacal friend John Mulso, whom he had known from his student days, fumed in mock despair: 'Think only of my knowing no Time of ye Year for getting at You *without a Guide*; & seldom with One?'

Once reached, the village was a busy, clattering place. Within an outer circle of farms – Noar Hill, Burhurst, Temple, Priory, Norton and Grange – Selborne was, and is, 'one single straggling village street'. Gilbert's house, The Wakes (originally just 'Wakes', after a family who had lived there), looked across this street, known then as 'the Cartway'. In the 1760s, he planted four lime trees to screen the blood and guts of the butcher's shop opposite and made a new pavement to avoid the mud and puddles: 'Finish'd a paved foot-path from the Butcher's shop to the Blacksmith's, above 70 Yards: it cost just one pound.' The street meanders from north-west to south-east, parallel to the hill in the west whose slopes are covered by the Hanger, a long, hanging wood typical of the area, whose beeches were to Gilbert 'the most lovely of all forest trees'. From the top, 300 feet up, where sheep grazed on open common land, you could see for miles in all directions.

The village feels embraced by the landscape, with the Hanger behind like a backrest and lower ridges running out like arms on each side. Between these ridges, beyond the church, a slope dips down to a green valley, which winds towards wider country and further hills. It is a wonderful place for a naturalist, partly due to the geology. A band of greensand runs north to south, with layers of chalk to the west, rich loam in the valley to the east and, in the distance, the sandy loam and heath of Woolmer Forest. The different soils of the district encourage different trees, plants and crops, creating, as Gilbert noted, a huge variety of habitats: cornfields and scrub; woods and grassy meadows; chalky gullies and open heaths.

Gilbert had known this district all his life. He knew the people of the village, too, with their worries, quirks and oddities, and he saw how a landscape is inextricably entwined with the history and lives of people who have worked it for generations. In the opening letters of *The Natural History of Selborne*, he describes the setting like a travel writer, but he also rolls back through time, from his own childhood memories and those of old poachers reminiscing in the pub to the description of

Queen Anne in the Holt – the great wood east of Selborne – 'reposing herself on a bank smoothed for that purpose', watching gamekeepers drive a herd of deer before her 'with great complacency and satisfaction'. He makes a point of saying that he heard that story from an elderly keeper called Adams, whose father, grandfather and great-grandfather had been keepers before him. 'And thus,' as Virginia Woolf wrote, 'the straggling street is allied with history and shaded by tradition. No novelist could have given us more briefly and completely all that we need to know before the story begins.'

Despite its difficult lanes, Selborne was part of a network of villages and market towns that were near enough to the coast to billet soldiers on their way to embark at the docks and to hear the Portsmouth guns boom. The village looked serene and stable, and so, on the whole, it was. It still had remnants of medieval and Tudor practices. A bit of the old open-field farming system endured, with strip farming for crops and pasturage after the harvest, and it retained the traditional social structure: an overall landlord, copyholders, tenant farmers and cottagers. The copyholders – who included the White family – were the lucky ones, whose possession of land and houses was written into the manorial roll and could be sold or passed on for a small fee to the landlord. The tenant farmers owned strips in different places and tended to live in the village and have their barns out in the fields. The cottagers, who had only a small garden plot and the right to graze livestock on the common, worked as labourers and farm servants. 'We abound with poor,' Gilbert wrote,

many of whom are sober and industrious, and live comfortably in good stone or brick cottages, which are glazed, and have chambers above stairs: mud buildings we have none. Besides the employment from husbandry, the men work in hop gardens, of which we have many; and fell and bark timber. In the spring and summer the women weed the corn; and enjoy a second harvest in September by hop picking.

He notes hardship, too. Only a handful of parishioners received parish relief, but his account books are full of small handouts to the poor, while his journals record terrible epidemics of whooping cough and measles, from which many children died. But the overall picture gave him hope. In a list at the start of the manuscript of *The Natural History*, dated 1783, the heads of all families are named (all men, apart from five women) and the number in their household. In all, there were 313 people in the street, and another 363 in the outlying parish. In a detailed return to the Bishop of Winchester five years later, having looked at the parish record over the sixty years from 1720 to 1780, Gilbert noted that baptisms exceeded burials by a third. The village was growing.

GILBERT'S JOURNALS AND LETTERS bustle with names, ranging from those closest to him – his large and often confusing family – and spreading out to neighbours, Oxford friends, scholars and naturalists in Britain and abroad. He was born in 1720, into a generation that was heir to the quest for knowledge and the surge of experiment launched by the Royal Society, founded in 1660, six months after the Restoration. The Society's motto, *'Nullius in verba'*, was a call to value your senses, to place empirical knowledge and experiment above written texts and ancient authorities. The scope was universal: astronomy, geology, physics, chemistry, mechanics, botany, zoology, everything from the planets above to the beetles in the soil beneath. Interest in natural philosophy boomed, and instrument makers flourished. By the 1740s, when Gilbert was a student, all kinds of people across Britain – dukes and doctors, squires and merchants, girls at home and soldiers in barracks – were collecting plants and shells, measuring rainfall, watching birds, experimenting with electricity. Scholarly clergymen, faced with conflicts between empirical findings, like the existence of fossils, and biblical stories of Creation and the Deluge, worked to accommodate the two approaches, arguing that the workings of God must operate in the physical world through 'natural laws'. The more people understood

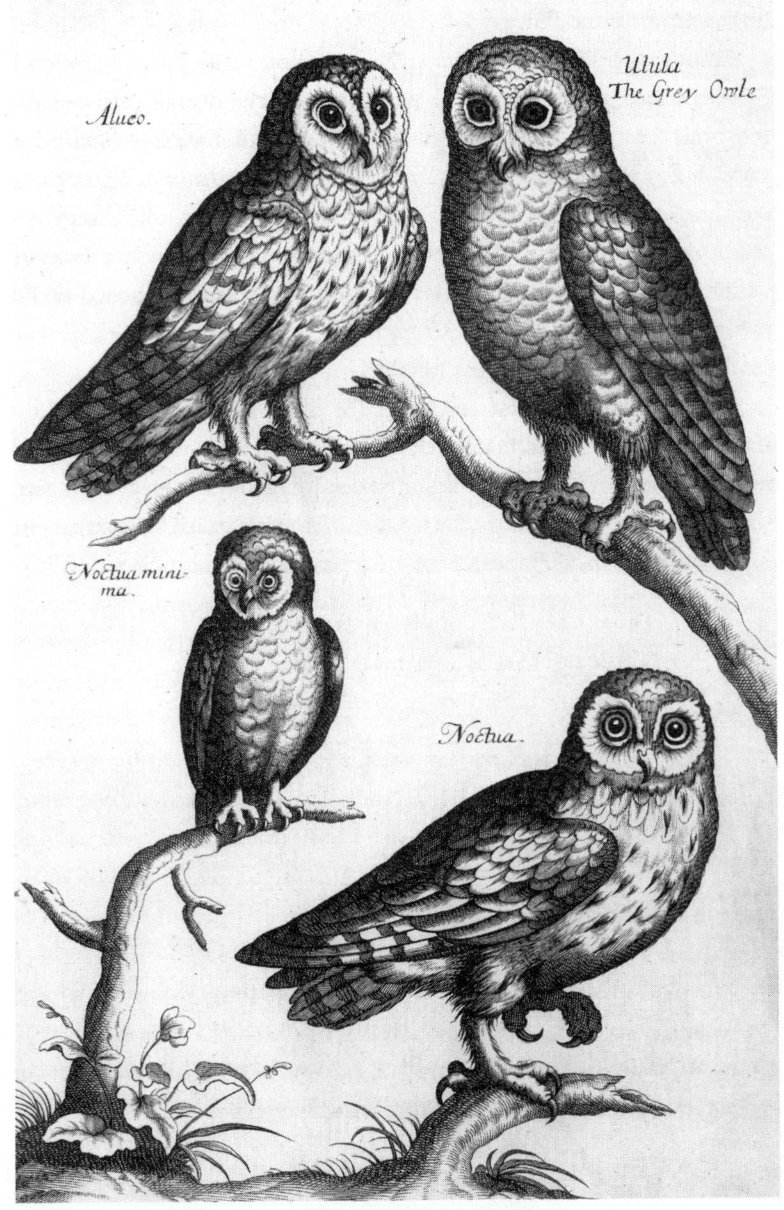

Owls. From John Ray, *The Ornithology of Francis Willughby* (1678).

those laws, these clerics argued, the nearer humanity would come to understanding the Divine.

Among the older authorities whom Gilbert cited with reverence (while diplomatically correcting their errors and wilder conclusions), the most important to him were Francis Willughby, whose much-admired *Ornithology* appeared in 1676, and Willughby's Cambridge tutor and collaborator John Ray, 'our great naturalist', as Gilbert calls him. Ray's studies of birds, fishes and insects were pioneering works of observation, which he drew on to develop his theory of natural theology, arguing for creation by a benign Divinity. Integral to this was the idea of a natural 'economy', with each creature filling its appointed function (thus, slugs may seem like a pest but they feed the birds; bees gather nectar for themselves but also pollinate the plants). This blended with the classical notion of the Great Chain of Being, ascending from the meanest insect, through the reptiles, fishes, birds and mammals, with humanity one link from the top, as Pope put it in 'An Essay on Man':

> Far as Creation's ample range extends,
> The scale of sensual, mental pow'rs ascends:
> Mark how it mounts, to Man's imperial race . . .

Gilbert, however, valued Ray less for his theories than for his scrupulous fieldwork and careful observation. A true empiricist, the more Gilbert looked, the more he questioned both the idea of a static natural hierarchy and the vision of the world as a complex piece of interlocking machinery. What he found was more surprising: evidence of adaptation and change, and behaviour that defied logic – the tadpole's transformation, the cuckoo's opportunism, the longevity of a tortoise. 'Providence' seemed, increasingly, to be a pattern of creation 'not subjected to any mode or rule', and the Divine to be a life force within nature itself, not imposed from above and beyond.

W ITH THE ACCUMULATION of knowledge came the need to order it. The drive of Gilbert's generation was towards arranging and classifying, identifying types or families and their origin. This spirit lay behind projects ranging from the French *Encyclopédie* to Johnson's *Dictionary*, Priestley's *History and Present State of Electricity* and the Comte de Buffon's *Histoire naturelle, générale et particulière*, published in fifteen volumes between 1749 and 1767. (The director of the Jardin du Roi in Paris and curator of the royal zoological specimens, Buffon allegedly sat in his study in full court dress and wrote for eight hours a day, for forty years.) Ruthlessly anthropocentric though he was – believing humanity was distinguished from all animals by the power of reason – Buffon still found it hard to forge 'the Chain of Being' into any coherent order. With such multiplicity and variety, the links were impossible to chart neatly.

Nature, it appeared, defied systematisation. But taxonomy was at a point of momentous change. In 1735, in his *Systema Naturae*, using particular points of identification, such as the sexual system of plants or the different beaks of birds, the Swede Carl Linnaeus proposed a new hierarchy of organic life. This placed 'kingdom' at the most general level – animal, vegetable or mineral – followed by classes, orders, family, genus and species; and instead of descriptive Latin terms, Linnaeus used only two names, the first for the genus and the second, or 'trivial', term for the species. The impact was revolutionary, providing an arrangement and a language that could be used on a global scale – another form of the Western drive to 'own' the world.

Gilbert slowly adopted the Linnaean names, but then he moved on. Taxonomy was useful, he felt, but it was more important to study the behaviour of animals in their habitat than simply to label them. Writers stuck in their studies, he said, could offer only 'bare descriptions and a few synonyms'. The true naturalist must get outside: 'investigation of the life and conversation of animals, is a concern of much trouble and difficulty, and is not to be obtained but by the active and inquisitive, and by those that reside much in the country'.

While he urged investigation in the field, he still welcomed the drive to order knowledge, with its emphasis on measurement, even of an unpredictable element like the weather. Long ago, in 1667, Robert Hooke had proposed that fellows of the Royal Society should make daily weather observations that could be compared to formulate 'Axioms, whereby the Cause or Laws of Weather may be found out'. In the end, the reports were too uneven and lay mouldering on the Society's shelves. Other initiatives proved equally flawed, but many people followed Hooke's lead, including Gilbert's brother-in-law Thomas Barker, who kept weather records from the age of fourteen. Gilbert himself was keen, but for a different reason: 'The weather of a district,' he wrote, 'is undoubtedly part of its natural history.' It was the idea of 'the district' that enthralled him. By concentrating on a small patch – his 'abrupt, uneven country, full of hills and woods, and therefore full of birds' – he knew he was doing something valuable, something new.

Gilbert White kept a series of journals for forty years, until his death in 1793. The first, kept from 1751 to 1768, was his *Garden Kalendar*, which was stuffed with accounts of building hotbeds, planting fruit trees, bulbs and annuals, harvesting cucumbers, cabbages and carrots. The *Kalendar*'s notes are appropriately down to earth, punctuated by delight at a fat melon or rage at slugs. But they are also sociable, embracing the farmers who supply his manure and the friends who share his melon feast. In the garden, he was both scientist and aesthete: while he dug and planted and scoured seed catalogues, he also created a witty variation of a fashionable garden on neoclassical lines, designing it in miniature, on the cheap, with a statue of Hercules cut out of wood and a vista through five-barred gates.

As he brought plants from the lanes and fields into his garden, his interest in botany grew. In the mid-1760s, he compiled his *Flora Selborniensis*, a diary of the budding, flowering and fading of wildflowers and trees, and of birds nesting and fledging. He was interested

  A YEAR WITH GILBERT WHITE

in the proposed idea that sharing accounts like this might in time establish a 'natural calendar', a guide to sowing, planting and reaping. But he knew that for this to be even vaguely reliable, you would have to collect information over a long time, building a huge pile of separate records. What he needed was an easy way not only to note his findings, but to store the mass of information so that it was clear and easy to retrieve, allowing direct comparisons, year on year.

He found this in 1768, when he began using the cleverly organised *Naturalist's Journal*, designed by the lawyer and naturalist Daines Barrington. This used a grid format, with each sheet covering a week. The days ran down the left-hand side, and the page was ruled into ten columns. The first were for such things as air pressure, temperature, wind direction and rainfall; the central columns were for specific notes, such as plants in flower; the wider column on the right was designed for 'Miscellaneous Observations'. Although the order varies between different years, the opening column was either the barometer reading or the temperature, which was the first thing most people wanted to check.

In Gilbert's journal, however, the miscellaneous observations took on a life of their own, spilling into other columns, wandering round the page and eventually leaping across onto separate inserted sheets. They were full of delight and amusement, but accurate recording came first. 'I watched it narrowly' is a common phrase. As his friend John Mulso told him: 'You are more able to see with your own Eyes than any Man I know.' For many years, for example, he watched a pair of white owls (which we now call barn owls) that nested under the eaves of the church. From the hill opposite he could see them sweep across the meadow for prey, dropping suddenly, 'like a setting-dog', into the grass or corn. 'I have minuted these birds with my watch for an hour together,' he wrote, finding that they returned to the nest about every five minutes. As well as observing, he dissected birds found or shot by neighbours, to explore their anatomy and diet, and supplemented his observations with careful measurements: the different lengths of the tail feathers of a male and female swallow, or the weight of a tiny harvest mouse.

He was keen not only to record, but to understand. Why, and when, does a bird change its song? Why should a hedgehog dig holes in the grass? He was not always right: in September 1768, he wrote, 'Hedge-hogs bore holes in the grass-walks to come at the plantain roots, which they eat upwards.' He worked out that they could bore under the plant with their upper jaw, eating the root upwards and leaving little round holes. This, he thought, was 'very curious' – and indeed it was, as hedgehogs eat slugs, beetles and worms, and the little round holes were probably made by caterpillars. But while his deduction was wrong, he built up a picture of hedgehogs in which his own life runs alongside theirs. When he comes across a nest of baby hedgehogs, his fascination increases:

> No doubt their spines are soft and flexible at the time of their birth, or else the poor dam would have but a bad time of it in the critical moment of parturition: but it is plain that they soon harden; for these little pigs had such stiff prickles on their backs and sides as would easily have fetched blood, had they not been handled with caution.

At five or six days old they are blind, like puppies; they have 'little hanging ears'; they can draw their skin down over their faces but can't yet curl into a defensive ball – perhaps, he thinks, because the muscle hasn't yet fully formed. We see him turning them over, noting every detail, drawing his conclusions, a certain tenderness lurking in the phrase 'these little pigs'.

Sometimes his journal entries are comically abrupt; at others they read like miniature lyrics, distilling the essence of a scene – the flight of a bird, the ripening of fruit, the gathering of a storm. Here are some, taken at random:

> Ice bears. Boys slide.
> Wood-larks hang suspended in the air, and sing all night

Swifts copulate in the air, as they flie.
The water shines in the fallows.
The Ring-dove hangs on its wings, and toys in the air.
The boys at Faringdon play all day in their shirts.
Larches turn yellow: Ash leaves fall: the hanger gets thin.

The rhythm of that last line evokes movement as well as a moment. And similar trios of phrases or short sentences appear right from the start of his journal, as here, on 5 April 1768:

Gold-finch, *carduelis*, whistles.
Cucumbers shew fruit in every light.
Tadpoles swell in the frogspawn.

A season comes to life. We are reading a poet as well as a naturalist.

HE IS WRY, FUNNY, generous, often amused; he can be prickly, restless, alarmed. Endlessly curious. A lover of music, gossip and travel writing, as well as nature. There's no need to bring a newspaper, he tells his brother Thomas somewhat testily, as they have four delivered – but he records the news rarely. He has no sentimental illusions, describing labourers' frostbitten fingers and land cursed by drought. He writes of a boy obsessed with bees without judgement, simply as a strange phenomenon, unexplained. He adds to his local knowledge by wide reading and correspondence but sees no need to venture far. I thought of him when I heard the elderly writer Ronald Blythe talk about living all his life a mile or so from the farm where he was born. 'My world seems to be so enormous where it is,' he said. 'There's so much work to do where we are.' Really, there was no need to go anywhere else.

Gilbert's journals bring us slap up against that local immediacy. Reading them today is startling, not because so much has changed – which I expected – but because so much is still the same. His entries bring this home to me, although my comparisons are confused by place as well as time. Gilbert lived in the south, and I am in the north, in a hamlet at the top of a Cumbrian valley. He gardened on alkaline chalk and clay, while I struggle with acid slate and granite. But he makes me look and listen and hunt to find out more, all the time conscious of how inadequate my knowledge is.

The relative richness of the world that he describes is astounding. Yet this is no settled past. He already mourns disappearances, like the 'heath-cock, black game or grouse', shot to extinction around Selborne, and laments the decline of familiar birds. An old sportsman told him that the beech woods were once so thick with wood pigeons that he could shoot seven or eight at a time as they wheeled overhead. Musing on this, Gilbert notes that a hundred or more could still be found in the Hanger in the 1760s,

> but in former times, the flocks were so vast, not only with us but all the district round, that on mornings and evenings they traversed the air, like rooks, in strings, reaching for a mile together. When they thus rendezvoused here by thousands, if they happened to be roused from their roost trees in an evening,
>
> Their rising all at once was like the sound
> Of thunder heard remote.

It seems apt for him – and for us today – to summon up *Paradise Lost*.

JANUARY

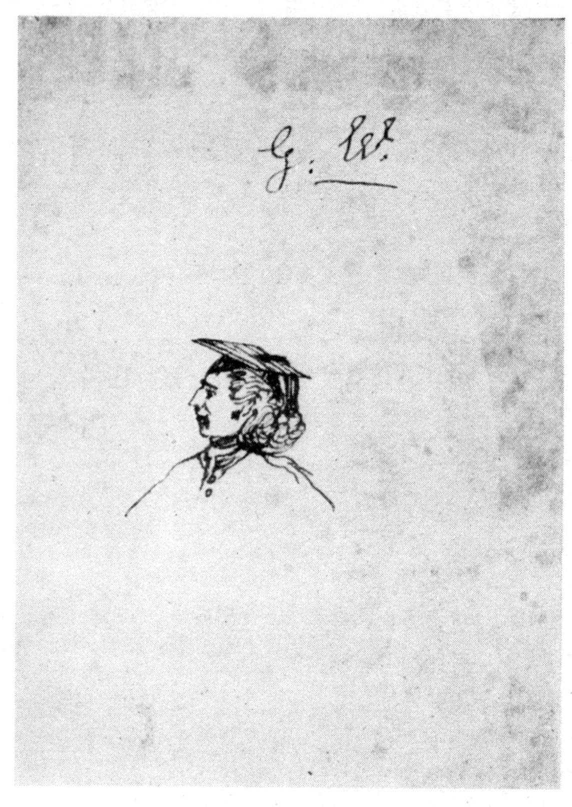

A pen-and-ink sketch of Gilbert White as a student, *c.*1744.

WHAT DOES HE look like, waking on New Year's Day? The only authentic portraits of Gilbert White are rough pencil sketches in his copy of Pope's *Iliad*, drawn by an Oxford friend, which show a slight young man with a thoughtful expression. Portraits of his brother Thomas suggest he had a brawnier build, but if Gilbert shares the family colouring, he has brown eyes and brown hair, perhaps greying slightly now. He is slim, wiry and short, only 5' 3" in his boots, slightly less than the average height for the 1780s, and he is always astonished by the way his nephews – of whom there are many – grow taller each year. 'Jack is very tall indeed!' he had written fondly to Jack's father, his brother John, five years before, 'but if he continues healthy it will be esteemed an advantage to be a well-grown man.' Did he mind, then, being not so well grown?

In the January cold, in this long-familiar house, he feels close to his family, a web of siblings and uncles and aunts and cousins, nephews and nieces and relations by marriage, almost all connected in some way with the clerical life. He pushes aside the heavy curtains round his bed, embroidered long ago by four of his aunts with flowers and fruit against a pale wool background. Three years before, when he built a large new room on the ground floor, he told his sister Anne Barker that he had moved his bedroom from his 'little red room' and 'have put my old white bed in my late drawing-room, where I lie, as you ordered me'. This was on the first floor, looking across the garden to the sloping fields and the beech woods of the Hanger.

He dresses: undershirt, linen shirt, breeches and hose; a long waistcoat, with his clergyman's white stock round his neck; a clerical topcoat, stout shoes. Perhaps he is grateful for socks like those a Selborne girl is knitting for his brother Thomas, 'a fine ribbed one and a pair as thick as a jack-boot'. Downstairs the maid lights the fires. The kitchen is warm and the kettle on the boil. He likes his coffee and tea, expensive though they are, often asking his niece Molly, Thomas's daughter, to send coffee and chocolate or 'half a pound of *Break-fast green-tea* at 10s and half a pound of *best tea* at 14s'.

Monday 1
46½. 29 3/10. S.   *Dark, rain, rain.*

Today, as on every New Year's Day, he brings out the new set of pages for *The Naturalist's Journal*. He usually bought these from his brother Ben for 5s, 'half-bound and interleaved', but this year he was frugally using up a copy from the earlier set, published by William Sandby from 1767 to 1775, when Ben took over publication. This set had lain unused, marred by a printing error, so that the columns on one side of the page begin with the temperature and on the reverse with the barometer reading. Gilbert was entirely unfazed by this (and to avoid confusion I have simply put the temperature first). The columns thus run across the page, beginning with temperature readings, which Barrington decreed should be made at 8 a.m., 12 noon, 4 p.m. and 8 p.m.

I was puzzled by the numbers and letters at first, but this is what they mean:

46 ½ – temperature, in degrees Fahrenheit
29 3/10 – barometric air pressure, measured as 29 inches of mercury,
  plus 3/10 of an inch
s – wind, from the south, as shown on his wind vane

Today, Gilbert leaves the temperature until noon and starts with his barometer, tapping it in case the mercury has got stuck. By the mid-eighteenth century, barometers were absolutely the thing to have, luxury goods announcing a familiarity with the latest 'philosophical' interests of polite society. The *Gentleman's Magazine* carried a flurry of articles on their use, and countless jokes and satires linked the rise and fall of the mercury to the rise and fall of lustful passions. They were relatively new: London makers had developed portable commercial barometers in the 1690s, fifty years after Galileo's pupil Torricelli had experimented with a mercury tube (mercury has a far higher density than water, so can show pressure in a much shorter column). The basic

          A YEAR WITH GILBERT WHITE

principle was simple: when air warms, it rises; when it cools, it falls, increasing its weight, or pressure. If the mercury fell, maybe showers or storms were on the way; if it went up, it promised to be fine; if it stayed steady, the weather was stable.

For the first time, it seemed that an instrument might actually predict the weather. Some barometers had a 'wheel' attached, a dial linked to the tube by a pulley, so that as the mercury moved, a hand pointed to labels: 'Fair', 'Very Dry', 'Much Rain'. Barometers measured atmospheric pressure in inches (usually between 28 and 31; the mean pressure in eighteenth-century England was 29½), showing the value on a scale, either on paper or engraved on a backing plate protected by a hinged glass door. One side showed inches, the other tenths of inches, hence Gilbert's complicated-looking figures. His brother-in-law Tom Barker's barometer was even more precise, with a sliding scale that let him read the tiniest movements of a hundredth of an inch.

Fashionable though they were, some people thought barometers confusing as they registered change rather than the weather outside; the dial might say 'Fair' while rain fell. They could go wrong and give false readings: 'Reduced my barometer to the true standard of 28 inches, lowering it about two degrees,' Gilbert wrote tetchily on 11 February 1773. Furthermore, with little understanding of how the atmosphere related to the gravitational pull of the Earth, no one could agree exactly how, or why, pressure rose or fell. Were the variations due to different concentrations of 'vapour'? Or perhaps to the force of the winds? The arguments went on.

A bow-fronted stick barometer by Peter Dollond of London, *c.*1760.

Tuesday 2
40½. 29 2/10½. SW. 11.   White frost, sun, sun, rain, snow.

Frost coats the grass, and ice on the puddles splinters into glassy triangles under his boots. The barometer has fallen very slightly, and the temperature is lower. Most British thermometers, including Gilbert's, use the scale proposed by Daniel Fahrenheit in 1724, which runs from 0 to 180 degrees; the temperature at which water froze is set at 32°F, blood heat is 100°F – later adjusted to 98.6°F – and 'fever heat' 110°F. On this day, the temperature is 40½°F in the noonday sun, just under 5°C. (The US still uses Fahrenheit, but most other countries have adopted the Celsius scale, developed by the Swede Anders Celsius in the early 1740s, which set the freezing point of water at 0°C and blood temperature at 37.5°C.)

Gilbert keeps one thermometer indoors on a shady staircase. When he takes it outside, he writes 'abroad'. In years of severe frost he hangs it indoors, in a small room without a fire, and over several years, in times of snow and ice, he compares the temperature in the yard to that in the wine cellar, where he stores his provisions. 'Frost begins to come in a door,' he writes in January 1770. 'The thermometer abroad sunk to 25; & in the wine-vault rose to 44.' In Celsius, that would be −4°C outside and 7°C in the cellar – quite a difference. Some years, the journal records the temperature before daybreak as 11°F, a freezing −12°C.

The wind is 'SW' – from the south-west. The most important figure today, however, is the final one, measuring the rain that fell the day before – 11 hundredths of an inch. Lack of rain was frustrating, as he joked to his niece Molly, asking her to thank her father Thomas for his present of a 'rain-measurer' in April 1779: 'There *was* a time when rain-measurers were very entertaining; and doubtless there *will* again: but now we have seen no rain for four months!' So far the winter has been dry, but this morning, at last, a tiny amount of water swirls in his rain gauge. His measurer is the latest design, like the one that the physicist John Dalton would describe a few years later at the Manchester Literary and Philosophical Society, insisting that 'A strong funnel, made of sheet iron, tinned and painted, with a perpendicular rim two or three inches high, fixed horizontally in a convenient frame with a bottle under it to receive the rain, is all the instrument required.' Dalton's talk was about experiments to find 'whether the quantity of rain and dew is equal to the quantity of water carried off by the rivers and raised by evaporation; with an enquiry into the origin of springs'. Theories about springs and rivers were vague. In the previous generation, these included the idea that salt water was driven upwards to mountain tops by the pressure of air on the sea – like mercury in a barometer – where it issued as springs, somehow remarkably salt-free; or that all springs came from a huge 'orb' of water in the bowels of the Earth, linked to the sea by chasms. It took time to accept the cycle of evaporation from seas, springs and rivers, followed by condensation and then rainfall.

Gilbert's concern was more practical. In Selborne, the rainwater trickled down through the chalk until it met the hard greensand. To catch this, every house and farm had its own well. Those in the village were around 60 feet deep, but up on the downs, where the greensand sloped further down beneath the chalk, they could reach 350 feet or more. The village also had two streams, one running from the spring known as 'Well-head', to the south of the Hanger, the other starting at the north end of the hill. The site of this second spring moved according to the level of the aquifer, and sometimes the water ran underground, surfacing in the ponds by Gracious Street. In Dorton, the two streams met, flowing east past the old Priory and eventually becoming a tributary of the Wey, joining the Thames and gliding out to the North Sea. South of the village, however, the streams ran down to join the Arun, flowing down to the Channel. The clear chalk waters spread out like ribbons, linking the village to the wider map.

Wednesday 3
38. 29 6/10¾. NW. 33.   *Some snow on the ground.*
Frost, sun, frost.   *Vast halo round the moon.*

When Gilbert looks up at the moon, it is encircled by a misty disc, enclosed in a brighter ring. 'Vast,' he writes, with a tinge of awe. We know now – I can find it just by googling the phrase – that this optical illusion is caused by ice crystals in thin cirrus clouds in the upper atmosphere, which act like a lens, refracting the moon's light. The ring is always the same size, sometimes with a second, 'vaster' ring outside.

In folklore, the rings marked the marriage of earth and heavens: moon haloes were thought to be signals from the sky warning of storms. Still, in this supposed age of reason, old beliefs lingered. To shake off superstitions 'is the hardest thing in the world', acknowledged Gilbert; 'they are sucked in as it were with our mother's milk'. A century before, John Ray had listed proverbs concerned with weather and husbandry, in a collection often reprinted during Gilbert's lifetime, although, Ray warned, 'These prognostics of weather & future plenty &c., I look upon as altogether uncertain, and were they narrowly observed would, I believe, as often miss as hit.' His list included many that we still use: 'March comes in like a lion, goes out like a lamb,' or 'An evening red and a morning grey, is a sign of a fair day.'

The days were past when good weather was thought a reward from heaven, bad weather a rebuke, storms and disasters signs of divine wrath. But if treated warily, popular culture could still supplement rational enquiry. Studying the weather, Gilbert took folk wisdom into account, just as he learned from the long experience of the farmers around him.

Thursday 4
36. 29 8/10. NW.   *Halo round the moon.*
Frost, grey & mild.

Friday 5
34. 29 9/10. N.   *Hard frost, rime, sun, thaw, grey.*

Halo or not, the early days of January 1781 are free from gales. It's colder today, almost freezing. There is always an overall pattern to the winter months, with frost and snow at some point, but no one can predict the weather week by week. The earth is closed down, waiting. The birds are silent, apart from the nuthatch, Gilbert notes, which chatters as it flies. Yet, in many Januaries, he sees hosts of chaffinches and buntings in the stubble fields, while 'linnets congregate in vast flocks, & make a kind of singing as they sit on trees'.

I am writing this on 5 January 2024, in Borrowdale, 330 miles north of Selborne. The temperature is −1°C, with white frost on the grass and the roofs of houses, sheds and barns. There's no point putting the washing out as the ice will stay all day, and by mid-afternoon it will be freezing again. The fallen leaves, sodden with rain, are suddenly crisp, their edges sparkly and curling. Beneath them, I learn, are worms and bugs and, especially, nematodes – or eelworms. I put my glasses on, but I can't see them. Maybe I need a magnifying glass. But I know that these tiny, almost invisible, hair-thin worms – 'the most numerous animals on earth' – are everywhere, hundreds in every handful of leaf mould, billions beneath the soil, recycling debris, remaking the world.

Saturday 6
38. 29 9/10. SE, S.   *In the churchyard at Faringdon are two male*
Grey & mild.   *yew-trees, the largest of which measures 30 feet*
                             in girth.

In the eighteenth-century church, benefices or 'livings' – appointment as a parish vicar with a home and guaranteed income for life – were granted by patrons. These were usually aristocrats or local landlords, but the government awarded some as rewards for service or support, and about 5 per cent were controlled by Oxford and Cambridge colleges – in Selborne's case by Magdalen College, Oxford.

A country clergyman's income was modest, but vicars could add to this by holding more than one living, without actually residing in the parish. In their stead they hired a curate, an ordained clergyman who would take the services, officiate at baptisms and burials and oversee the needs – the 'cure' – of the parish, including supervising local charities and visiting the sick. Curates were usually young men at the start of their careers. Their pay was poor, their future uncertain and their reputations variable: some were diligent, some were lazy, some were sober and some perpetually drunk. Gilbert – one of the sober ones – turned down several offers of livings and took curacies instead, chiefly to avoid leaving Selborne. By 1781 he had been curate of All Saints church, in the nearby parish of Farringdon (which he spells 'Faringdon'), for twenty years; his handwriting first appeared in the parish register among the baptisms for 1760. He took the services, gave the sermons and wrote down details of weddings, baptisms and burials in his firm, clear hand. It was a peaceful routine, broken once or twice by a rare sense of shock, which was reflected in his notes in the parish register: 'A young woman, a vagabond, who died in a barn was buried 1st Nov. 1769. She was stark naked.'

If the weather looked doubtful, he often went over the day before. Farringdon was less than three miles north-west of Selborne, and to ride or walk there Gilbert would follow the old medieval roadway up the hill from Gracious Street, crossing the fields until he reached a group of thatched cottages and long, low barns. All Saints church, with its twelfth- and thirteenth-century nave, squat tower and fine windows, stood slightly apart from the village, flanked by great yew trees.

It seems odd for Gilbert to make a note today, in 1781, of trees that he had known since he was a boy, but yews are on his mind. This year, he is working on the second part of his planned book, the *Antiquities*, dealing with the human rather than the 'natural' history of the parish. Looking back at the distant past, he writes of the old yew in Selborne churchyard, 'whose aspect bespeaks it to be of a great age: it seems to have seen several centuries, and is probably coeval with the church, and therefore may be deemed an antiquity'. He puts the yew in the *Antiquities* rather than *The Natural History*, as a sign of ancient settlement, as venerable as any abbey or church. In Selborne churchyard, he gets out his tape measure, rolled up in its leather case. 'The body is squat, short and thick,' he writes, 'and measures twenty-three feet in the girth, supporting an head of suitable extent to its bulk.' Measuring the trunk

      A YEAR WITH GILBERT WHITE

of a yew, three feet or so from the ground, is still a way of guessing its age. When a yew is three or four hundred years old, the heartwood begins to decay, and the hollow centre prevents one estimating its age by counting the rings; the trunk's circumference is the sole guide. If the Selborne yew's circumference was 23 feet and it was the same age as the church – probably an underestimate – the Farringdon yew, at 30 feet, was much older. Several British yews are thought to be between two and three thousand years old, regenerated by new roots piercing down into their empty centres. One or two may have reached five thousand years, 'older than Stonehenge, older than the pyramids'.

The Selborne yew is a male tree, 'which in the spring sheds clouds of dust and fills the atmosphere with its farina'. In February and March, different flowers will appear on the male and female trees. On the male trees, small whitish globes release clouds of pollen, filling the air, as Gilbert says, with a dust as fine as flour. This is blown by the wind and pollinates the female trees, whose greenish buds develop into cup-like, rosy berries enclosing the seeds. Why, Gilbert wonders, are churchyard trees so often male? Why are there so many yews in churchyards? Were they burial places, shelters or 'emblems of mortality by their funereal appearance'?

As emblems of rebirth and immortality, yews had been sacred since the Celts. Anglo-Saxon and Norman churches were built near the old trees, and churchyard yews provided the springy wood for longbows. But, as Gilbert notices, they mix the promise of new life with the threat of death: cows die from eating the toxic berries; herds of cattle perish after grazing on the poisonous needles; horses tethered to yews collapse within minutes. So, he asks, how is it that hogs can eat the berries in the street, and sheep, deer and turkey can crop yews without harm? How can blackbirds and thrushes eat the rosy cups, while avoiding the poisonous seed within?

The old Selborne yew had a bench circling the trunk for churchgoers to rest on. When it finally blew down in 1990, around thirty skeletons, the oldest dating back to 1200, were found among the roots. Villagers prayed among the tangled branches, trying desperately to winch the tree back into place. When this failed, craftsmen carved the wood into souvenirs, like the relics of a saint. The shorn-off trunk is still there today, wreathed in brambles and spattered with fungi, a shelter for insects and birds.

Sunday 7
42. 28 8/10½. W.   *Grey & mild, sun, grey.*

Thirty years before, on 7 January 1751, when he began his *Garden Kalendar*, Gilbert had been hard at work in the garden. He had helped his father John for some years, and in 1747 he had bought a new edition of the standard reference work, *The Gardeners Dictionary*, compiled by Philip Miller, director of the Chelsea Physic Garden. From then on, he took up gardening in earnest, planning an orchard, making hotbeds for cucumbers and melons and digging vegetable beds and 'basons' – round beds in the chalk filled with manure and good soil – on the slope of Baker's Hill. In brisk notes in his *Garden Kalendar*, he recorded January's work: earthing up celery, sowing radishes, turnips and lettuce, planting crown imperials and passion flower – and 250 cabbages. Did he give them away? Or perhaps he pickled them?

Monday 8
42. 30 1/10½. NE.   *Sun, brisk air, grey & mild.*

Gilbert had known the garden and the house from childhood. He was born on 18 July 1720 in the vicarage, just down the road. His grandfather was then Selborne's rector. Also a Gilbert White, he was the fourth son of Sir Sampson White from Whitney (twice mayor of Oxford and knighted by Charles II in 1660 for loyalty to the Crown). Selborne's living, in the gift of the village's landlord, Magdalen College, had been badly neglected during the Commonwealth and Restoration, and perhaps, Gilbert mused, it was because the college authorities thought so little of the parish that they granted it to his grandfather in 1681, when he was only thirty-one and a junior fellow at the college.

Families of Whites had lived for many years in the surrounding district, on the borders of Hampshire and Surrey. The Revd Gilbert married Rebecca Luckin, the daughter of a farmer from Noar Hill, in the next-door parish of Newton Valence, whose family had been in the neighbourhood for generations, so the couple and their six children were soon firmly embedded in the community. An active, much-respected man, the reverend restored the church and turned the old Elizabethan vicarage, with its great hall and slate floors, into a comfortable house. As well as building a new brewhouse and barn, he 'removed the hovels in the front court, which he laid out in walks and borders; and entirely planned the back garden, before a rude field with a stone-pit in the midst of it'. This garden, with a grassy terrace on a promontory above the stream, was always a magical place for his grandson Gilbert. From here, in a summerhouse set into a high beech hedge, the young boy could look across the valley of Dorton, gold with buttercups in summer, in winter white with snow, to the woods and fields beyond.

Tuesday 9
38. 30 2/10. NE.   *Sun, frost, harsh wind, frost.*

The Revd Gilbert's will was full of bequests for church repairs and for buying land whose rents could pay for 'teaching the poor children of Selbourn parish to read and write, and say their prayers and catechism and to sew and knit'. (The old spelling of Selborne often varied, as it does in this will.) His son John – our Gilbert's father – carried out these provisions, including a bequest of £200 for improving the roads, which he used to build a firm causeway to replace the 'miry and gulfy lane' towards Woolmer Forest and Farnham, the nearest local market.

In temperament, John was very different to his forceful, energetic father. A quiet man, happy to play the harpsichord, read, garden and ride out into the countryside, he qualified as a barrister and was briefly a Justice of the Peace, but gave up the law in 1719, when he married Anne Holt, daughter of the vicar of Streatham. When Gilbert was born, they were living with John's parents in Selborne, but they soon moved away, first to Compton, in Surrey, then to East Harting, in Sussex, where Anne's family had a farm. Anne was almost constantly pregnant, and after sad years when three babies died, children arrived like clockwork every autumn.

Since Selborne vicarage was tied to the Revd Gilbert's living, as insurance for the future he bought The Wakes and the land around it. When he died in 1728, Rebecca moved across the road from the vicarage with her two unmarried daughters, Elizabeth and Dorothea. The following year, the girls were married, on the same day and both to vicars – Elizabeth to her cousin Charles White, from the nearby parish of Bradley, and Dorothea to William Cane, her father's successor in Selborne. The pattern was so common as to be almost expected, creating a wide network of linked clergy families.

With The Wakes empty and echoing, John and Anne came back to Selborne. With them came Gilbert, who was ten in 1730, plus five children under five – Thomas, Ben, Rebecca, John and baby Francis. Two more arrived: Anne in 1731 and Henry in 1733. The house was a squash for eleven people, with a parlour and kitchen downstairs and two bedrooms above, one for the grandmother and one for the parents, with their latest baby in its cradle. The children and toddlers squeezed into three attic rooms under the roof. When Gilbert was small, his father taught him, and he may have gone to school in Farnham at some time. On stormy days, he was pent up in the house, reading or trying out tunes on the harpsichord, but one can imagine the relief he felt at rushing outdoors – a skinny, springy boy exploring the woods, ditches and fields, picking up snails, hunting for birds' nests and coming back breathless, with grazed knees and muddy shoes, grass on his shirt and twigs in his hair.

Wednesday 10
33½. 30 1/10. NE.   *Hard frost, sun & clouds, sharp wind.*
                            Full moon.

In the bitter December of 1739, Anne White died, aged only forty-six, after a bout of measles, at the time a deadly disease that could ravage a village. John lived on in The Wakes, still working on the garden, laying out walks and hedges. When Gilbert began gradually to take over, his gardening was guided by affection for his father, and when John was ill in 1757, he took great care with the borders that his father could see from his window:

> Took up the yellow lilies & a fine large Martagon under my father's window, & planted them in a bason in the field; the two Xiphiums [Spanish or Persian iris] were encreased to a great number; planted some of them in the Basons round the lilies & some in a row under my Father's window; planted my Tulips in the same place & a few Ranunculus, & Fritillarias.

A few weeks later, he added narcissi, so that their scent would waft indoors, and fifty snowdrops, which happily 'turn'd out double'. The snowdrops, he knew, would flourish in the coldest winter, the sharp tips of their leaves piercing through the snow. Their sap contains proteins that bind with ice crystals and stop them from freezing, and the air inside the bell-shaped flowers is warmer than outside. When the temperature rises, the outer petals move upwards, letting the bees come in. In March 1758, during John's last illness, Gilbert planted more clumps of snowdrops, still in bloom.

Thursday 11

34. 29 8/10½. NE.   *Hard frost, dark sky, harsh & severe wind.*

As the wind sets in from the north-east, Gilbert's adjectives darken: 'harsh', 'sharp', 'severe'. He can work out the wind's direction easily by peering at the wind vane on his roof. The universal design was – and still is – simply a pole onto which is mounted a crossbar with a flat 'rudder' at one end and a point like an arrow at the other: as the wind hits the rudder, the bar spins so that the arrow points to the direction the wind is coming from. Sometimes British wind vanes have an indicator below the arrow, marking the compass directions 'N', 'E', 'S', 'W'. Weathervanes like this were known in Greece and Rome, Syria and Byzantium; the Anglo-Saxons made riddles about them, and the word 'vane' is said to come from their word *fane*, meaning 'flag'. By the late Middle Ages, they topped church towers and spires across England, their rudders often shaped like a cockerel with outspread tail, an emblem of Christ's warning that St Peter would betray him before the cock crowed thrice, telling people to watch and be wary.

In Selborne, the maypole on the Plestor, the open space in front of the gate to the church, was blown down in a gale one New Year's Day, and once it was mended, painted and hauled back into place, the villagers proudly replaced the vane on top. 'We talk of gilding the Vane,' wrote Gilbert with amusement. He had at least improved its movement: 'If I had not interposed, the vane would have rested again on a *shoulder*; but now it is to turn on a pivot on the top.' He had no way, however, of recording the wind's force: there was no accepted system until the naval commander Francis Beaufort developed his scale in the early 1800s. Gilbert's only assessment was adjectival – 'severe' or 'brisk' or 'mild'.

Friday 12
32. 29 9/10. NE.   *Hard frost, dark & sharp.*

Frost glitters all day. A dry spell like this, with no snow to provide cover and insulate plants from the icy wind, was dreaded by gardeners and farmers. Every few years, Selborne experienced this freezing drought, with the frost penetrating deep into the soil. On 12 January 1780, 'For want of snow to cover, the garden things suffer; cabbages, spinage, celery &c.' The thermometer fell to 18°F, then 16½°F (−8 to −9°C). Frost alternated with thaw. Towards the end of the month, turnips exposed to the air froze, thawed and then rotted. The farmers who did best 'pulled their turnips, & stacked them up in buildings, & under hedges'.

When the snow fell, the laurels and laurustinuses on Gilbert's walks

                                    A YEAR WITH GILBERT WHITE

shrivelled and browned, as if scorched by fire. But much as he disliked the cold, Gilbert was excited by extremes. At the end of January 1776, his journal announced: 'Below zero!! 32 deg. below the freezing point. At eleven it rose to 16½. Rime. A most unusual degree of cold for S.E. England.' (In terms of the Celsius scale, it was swinging between −18°C and −8°C.) In such winters, Gilbert and his great friend Richard Yalden, vicar of Newton Valence, shovelled the snow off the path between their houses and compared their thermometers. Put side by side, they read the same, but they found that when Richard's thermometer was used at Newton Valence, a couple of hundred feet higher up the hill, it was always two or three degrees lower than Gilbert's at The Wakes. Following Gilbert's example, Richard kept his own 'Journal of Weather & other Occurrences' at the back of his leather-bound book of accounts, which contained everything from parish tithes to 'Burbey's bill for News, Paint, & Butter'. His journal started out as two fairly neat columns, but soon became a blotched scramble across the page, suggesting how difficult it was to make a clear record without the structure of Barrington's grid: 'Jan 25 Much Snowfall 26 Bright sunshine but very cold 27,28 tremendous Frost, 29,30 wet Feby 1,2,3,4, Much fog 6,7,8 Cloudy and little sun . . .', and so on, mixed up with notes of family visits, progress of crops and 'dined with Mr White'.

By contrast, Gilbert's records were impeccable, or as near as he could get. His thermometers were from good makers: one from John Dollond, whose customers included James Cook and Thomas Jefferson; and one from the skilled instrument maker and lecturer Benjamin Martin. Yet in icy weather the latter was not good enough. In the bitter winter of 1784–5, Gilbert would write in his journal with some annoyance:

My apples, pears, & potatoes secured in the cellar, & kitchen-closet; my meat in the cellar. Severe frost & deep snow. Several men, that were much abroad, made sick by the cold: their hands & feet were frozen.

We hung-out two thermometers, one made by Dollond, & one by B: Martin: the latter was graduated only to 4 below 10, or 6 degrees short of zero; so that when the cold became intense, & our remarks interesting, the mercury went all into the ball, & the instrument was of no service.

Saturday 13
34. 29 7/10½. NE.   *Hard frost, dark & harsh.*

How did animals and birds fare in extreme cold? January 1781 was not as cruel as many winters, when chamberpots froze under the beds. When he started *The Naturalist's Journal* in 1768, the snow had lain nine inches deep. On 4 January that year, he had written:

The birds must suffer greatly as there are no Haws.
Meat freezes so hard it can't be spitted.
Several of the thrush-kind are frozen to death.

Eight years after that, on 14 January 1776:

Rugged, Siberian weather. The narrow lanes are full of snow in some places, which is driven into most romantic, & grotesque shapes. The road-waggons are obliged to stop, & the stage-coaches are much embarrassed. I was obliged to be much abroad on this day, & scarce ever saw it's fellow.

The poultry stayed in their hen houses, skylarks and bramblings appeared in farmyards with the chaffinches, and cats caught the birds as they came for shelter. Blue tits and nuthatches pulled off mosses and lichen in search of grubs. Driven by hunger, hares came into the garden and nibbled the pinks, and early lambs fell frozen to the ground. Rooks flocked to dunghills: 'What drops from horses is immediately eaten by crows, & rooks: so strict an economist is Nature, that the most refuse matter is turned to some use; nothing is wasted.'

The ground is hard as a rock.
The roads & fallows are dusty.

The cold drought continues. It's impossible to plough or sow wheat. On Sunday, as Gilbert goes to preach in Farringdon, dust swirls in an icy wind across the stubble. He often looks up at the rookery by Farringdon vicarage, watching the birds rise and swoop and return to their posts. Rooks were rarely bothered by the chill, but on 20 January 1775, he had inserted a note about a tragedy involving the birds:

> Mr Hool's man says, that he caught this day, in a lane near Hackwood-park, many rooks, which attempting to fly fell from the trees with their wings frozen together by the sleet, that froze as it fell. There were, he affirms, many dozens disabled! It is certain that Mr H: man did bring home many rooks & give them to the poor neighbours.

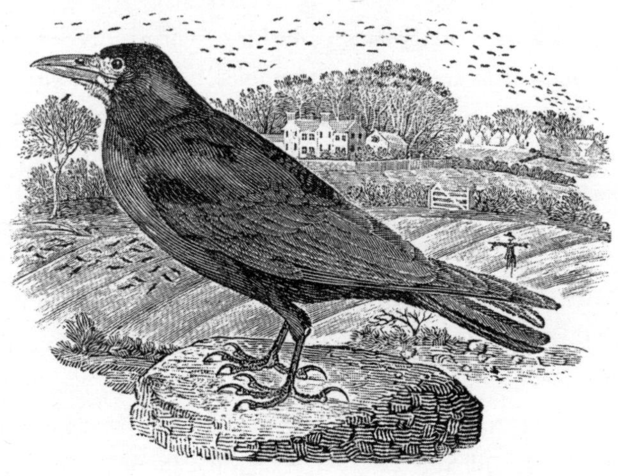

'The Rook' by Thomas Bewick, in *A History of British Birds. Vol. I: Land Birds* (1797). A working engraver, Bewick, like Gilbert, was an 'outdoor naturalist' and a careful watcher who believed in showing a bird's habitat and life, and its relationship to the human world.

Rook pie for all.

It's miserable weather, but still, the rooks are feeding in the bare fields and gathering on their nest trees. The wood engraving by Thomas Bewick, a great admirer of *The Natural History*, shows this, with a single bird, the dominant 'sentinel', keeping watch from a tree on the left. But while the landed gentry – like the squire who may have lived in the small manor house in the print – were proud of their rookeries, farmers thought the birds pests. Gilbert had doubts about this, and some years ago he had suggested a rather ruthless test:

> A rook should be shot weekly the year thro', & it's crop examined: hence perhaps might be discovered whether in the whole they do more harm or good from the contents at various periods. Tho' this experiment might show that these birds often injure corn, & turneps; yet the continual consumption of grubs & noxious insects would rather preponderate in their favour.

The argument goes on today. Rooks do damage young cereal crops, but in fact they eat pretty much anything: worms, beetles, slugs, insects, grain, acorns, seeds, fruit, vegetables, carrion and kitchen slops – and other birds' eggs. They hide their food, storing it in caches, in holes or under stones, and apparently even dunk hard bits occasionally, like a biscuit in tea.

Monday 15
34. 29 ¼/10. NE.   *Millers complain for want of water.*
Hard frost, dark, &
misty, sun, bright,
hard frost.

The water levels sink and waterwheels can hardly turn the grindstones in the mills. There is no meal for livestock and little flour for bread.

Tuesday 16
33, 34. 29 5/10. NE.   *Hard frost, rime & fog, dark & harsh.*

'As intense frost usually befalls in Jan:' he had written five years before,
'our Saxon forefathers call'd that month with no small propriety wolf-
month: because the severe season brought down those ravenous beasts
out of the woods among the villages.'

Wednesday 17
35. 29 3/10¾. E.   *The dew on the windows is on the outside*
Rain, rain, deep fog.   *of the glass.*

The condensation shows how cold the early morning is. It had been
cold, too, on 17 January 1739, when Gilbert was eighteen and pack-
ing his trunk, setting off to study under Revd Thomas Warton, sixteen
miles away, in Basingstoke.

Warton had held the living there since 1723, arriving with a col-
ourful reputation after years in Oxford. Staunchly royalist during the
Civil War, university and city had remained supporters of the Stuarts
after the Catholic James II fled and the Protestant William and Mary
took the throne in 1688. Tensions grew with the accession of the first
Hanoverian king, George I, in 1714 and the failed Jacobite rising a year
later, and Warton was roundly cheered when he published a satire on
George I and gave an implicitly Jacobite sermon. His popularity was
such that in 1718, he was elected Professor of Poetry, holding the post
for ten years. His time at Basingstoke was altogether calmer. The three
Warton children – Joseph, Jane and Thomas – were all slightly younger than Gilbert, but he came to know them well. In time, Jo would
become a satirist, critic and teacher, while Thomas – a close friend of
Samuel Johnson, until they fell out – would follow his father as Oxford
Professor of Poetry. Jane, who wrote anonymously, was one of a group
of feminist writers arguing for better education for women and attacking the double sexual standard. It was a lively, scholarly household.

When Gilbert set off for Basingstoke, he made a list of the books he took with him. The classical texts and grammars (two borrowed from his uncle, Charles White) included editions of Horace's *Odes*. His love of Horace was challenged only by his admiration of Virgil, particularly the *Georgics*, with their celebration of the rhythms of the rural year. The sole contemporary book on his list was James Thomson's long blank-verse poem, *The Seasons*, published between 1726 and 1730. Thomson had borrowed the *Georgics'* four-part structure and sometimes wrote in direct imitation of Virgil, yet to Gilbert and the Warton brothers he felt modern. He touched on the movement of the planets, 'Firm, unremitting, matchless, in their course.' He wrote on the 'secret, strong, attractive force' of gravity; on optics and the refraction of light; on insects 'Evading even the microscopic eye!' His British pantheon embraced Bacon, Newton and Locke, as well as Chaucer, Spenser, Shakespeare and Milton. Above all, his verse felt immediate and impassioned. In 'Winter', for example, he caught the changing days of thaw and frost that Gilbert saw in the streams and ponds of Selborne:

> The loosen'd ice,
> Let down the flood and half dissolv'd by day,
> Rustles no more; but to the sedgy bank
> Fast grows, or gathers round the pointed stone,
> A crystal pavement, by the breath of heaven
> Cemented firm; till, seiz'd from shore to shore,
> The whole imprison'd river growls below.

The Seasons was admired and quoted by eighteenth-century readers and by the Romantics of the next generation: Clare saved his pocket money to buy a copy; Wordsworth thought Thomson a genius, while damning his classical style; Burns called him his 'sweet poet of the Year'. Thomson showed Gilbert that 'Nature' itself could be the heart of a work.

Nature! great parent! whose unceasing hand
Rolls round the seasons of the changeful year,
How mighty, how majestic are thy works!
With what a pleasing dread they swell the soul,
That sees astonish'd, and astonish'd sings!

Thursday 18
38, 44. 29 2/10½. E, W. 32.   *Gnats come out from the laurels, & dance*
Dark & mild, wet & foggy.   *in the air.*
                                   Earth-worms lie out.

In two days of thaw, the thermometer has leapt to the low forties Fahrenheit (around 6–7°C), and a little rain sits in the rain gauge. Signs of life appear. Against the dark background of the laurels, Gilbert watches the gnats swirl and shimmer, catching the light. In the late afternoon sun, these delicate winter gnats, looking like tiny crane flies, form a spiralling cloud, billowing like smoke. Their lifespan is as short as five days, but they are there in the coldest weather, even hovering over snow; in summer, lost in the clouds of other insects, they are hard to see.

While gnats dance round his head, worms poke up by his feet. Contrary to contemporary belief, he insists that they are far from torpid in the dead months. They come out every night in a mild winter, he says, as anyone who would 'take the pains to examine his grass-plots with a candle' – as he clearly did himself – could see. Intrigued by creatures often overlooked, he declared:

> The most insignificant insects and reptiles are of much more consequence, and have much more influence in the oeconomy of Nature, than the incurious are aware of; and are mighty in their effect, from their minuteness, which renders them less an object of attention; and from their numbers and fecundity.

They might appear 'a small and despicable link in the chain of Nature, yet, if lost, would make a lamentable chasm',

For, to say nothing of half the birds, and some quadrupeds which are almost entirely supported by them, worms seem to be the great promoters of vegetation, which would proceed but lamely without them, by boring, perforating, and loosening the soil, and rendering it pervious to rains and the fibres of plants, and, most of all, by throwing up such infinite numbers of lumps of earth called worm-casts, which, being their excrement, is a fine manure for grain and grass.

A good monograph on worms, he felt, would open a new field in natural history. That study would appear a hundred years later, in 1881, as *The Formation of Vegetable Mould Through the Action of Worms, with Observations on their Habits* – the last book of Charles Darwin, a keen admirer of Gilbert White.

Friday 19
43. 29 7/10. N. 19.   *The* Antyrrhinum Cym: *still in full bloom.*
Sun, mild, frost.   *[Antirrhinum cymbalaria: ivy-leaved toadflax.]*
        Snow-drops bud for bloom.

Snowdrop buds gleam in my own garden, slivers of white. I expect these in January, but not the ivy-leaved toadflax, which normally flowers from April to November. I think of toadflax as a weed, smothering warm brick walls, pretty but negligible, to be pulled out in armfuls. Gilbert's delight makes me look again. To him, it was still an exotic, introduced in the early seventeenth century, arriving, so one story said, with marble sculptures that had been brought to Oxford from Greece, thus gaining the name 'the Oxford weed'. Gilbert dignifies it with its Linnaean name, *Antirrhinum cymbalaria* (more commonly today, *Antirrhinum muralis*): its leaves, with their rounded lobes, were thought to look like cymbals, and the tiny purple and yellow flowers like miniature snapdragons.

He had planted his toadflax two summers before, 'on a shady water-table of the wall of my house'. The following spring, on 29 April 1780, he found that it had grown 'at a vast rate & extended itself full *nine* feet'. The mechanism that propels it is magical. To begin with, its stems turn to the light, but once the bees have pollinated the flowers, the long, reddish stems turn back again towards the dark, seeking cracks to push in the seed, toeholds for the next scramble up the wall. Gilbert's toadflax flowered until the hard frost, then seemed to die, before bursting back into life again. It gave him joy: 'When in perfection it is a lovely plant.'

Saturday 20
37½. 29 2/10½. S.   *White frost, sun, rain, rain.*

On rare occasions, Gilbert fiddled with his journal entries. Mulling over the piercing wind before the brief thaw, today he writes a note: 'At the end of the new parlor a box-tree is nearly killed by the current of air; while a laurel in the same circumstances seems not to be affected at all.' Eighteen months later, he will rework this, making it more active and sharpening the contrast: 'At the corner of my great parlor there is such a current of air that it has half killed a box-tree planted for a screen: while a laurel planted in the same draught remains unhurt. This laurel continues to flourish; Octr 1782.' He's playing with style, practising different forms of prose to go in his book.

A shrivelled box tree, condensation on windows, snow 'half a shoe deep' – he measures the weather, as we all do, by the senses, by what he sees and touches and feels. It's a month since the winter solstice, and he judges the lengthening of the days by a domestic 'heliotrope', a primitive sundial measuring the shadows cast by a pole or, in this case, by The Wakes' long chimneys:

My Heliotrope, which is J. Carpenter's workshop, shows plainly that the days are lengthened considerably, for on the shortest day the shades of my two old chimneys fall exactly in the middle of the great window of that edifice at ½ hour after two P.M. but now they are shifted into the quick-set hedge, many yards to the S.E.

His own house and street become his instruments.

Elsewhere, he toys with the idea that the gentry might set up heliotropes in their gardens for entertainment, building simple timber obelisks about 12 feet high, one for winter and another for summer. The summer one could be deep in the garden, to be viewed on a fine summer's evening, but the winter one must be 'within sight of some window in the common sitting parlour, because men, at that dead season of the year, are usually inside at close of day'.

Sunday 21
44. 29 3/10½. SW, NW.   *The roads & paths very miry.*
Rain, rain, rain.

No shadows from his heliotrope today, and the rain makes it hard to travel on the slippery roads. When they were young, the White children often travelled to stay with relations. One frequent stop was Bradley, five miles north-west of Alton, where Gilbert's uncle Charles White – a tall, amicable, scholarly but outdoorsy man who would ride out in all weathers – had been vicar since 1726. Charles was both John White's cousin and his brother-in-law, having married John's sister Elizabeth. He was also, for a time, Gilbert's landlord, as The Wakes had been left to Elizabeth when her mother Rebecca died in 1755. Until Charles's death in 1763, Gilbert paid him rent of £5 7s a year.

His uncle and aunt had always been fond of Gilbert. Charles lent him books, and Gilbert chose Charles's college, Oriel, when he went up to Oxford in 1740, rather than Magdalen. The affectionate relationship continued. When Gilbert started the *Garden Kalendar* in early 1751, he gave Charles four passion flowers, and planted wallflowers from Charles's garden into his own in the autumn.

Gilbert's favourite place to stay, though, was Ringmer, on the South Downs, in Sussex, where his aunt Rebecca was the wife of the vicar, Revd Snooke. Gilbert loved the South Downs, with their sheep-cropped turf and their open views of the Weald on one side and the sea on the

                    A YEAR WITH GILBERT WHITE

other. In 1773, he wrote that he had known this long ridge of 'majestic mountains' for over thirty years, yet still explored it 'with fresh admiration year by year; and think I see new beauties every time I traverse it'.

On other holidays, the children from The Wakes visited their aunt Mary, who had married the Revd Isaac, rector of Whitwell in Rutland. Here, they became friendly with the Isaacs' neighbours, the Barkers of Lyndon Hall. In the Easter holidays of 1736, when Gilbert was fifteen, two brief notes, signed 'GW', appeared in Tom Barker's notebook: simply, 'A flock of wild Geese flew N.,' and on 6 April, 'Cuckow heard.'

Tom Barker grew up to become a strong, eccentric character: a fervent vegetarian, an avid beekeeper, a keen astronomer who produced influential work on comets, an inveterate keeper of weather records. In his 'speculativeness' he took after his grandfather, the controversial theologian William Whiston, writing prolifically on theology, baptism, prophecy and demonology, firmly believing that cattle plagues and locusts were the embodiments of God's wrath at a sinful people. In 1781, Tom's latest book was *The Messiah – Being the Prophecies Concerning Him Methodized*. Thirty years before this, when he married Gilbert's sister Anne in 1750, Gilbert's friend John Mulso clearly worried about what she was taking on: 'I heartily wish your Sister much Happiness in her new State: with her cheerful & easy Temper She will be ye best wife in the world to Mr. Barker, & may manage to her own Content and his Advantage that extreme Abstractedness & Speculativeness to which I hear He is naturally Prone.' Anne, with her sunny nature, was quite able to cope. The Barkers had four girls and a boy, Sam, who would become the recipient of light-hearted screeds from Gilbert on everything from poetic diction to cabinets of curiosities, from the sexuality of mosses to experiments with sponges.

Though fond of the whole Barker family, Gilbert did quail before his brother-in-law's energy. In 1783, describing Tom's arrival at Selborne with Sam, he reported that Tom had ridden 118 miles from Rutland in only two days, 'without the least complaint or fatigue . . . and at every dining place while the horses were baiting, walked four or five miles in his boots with his wig in his hand'. As agile and restless as he was when he was young, 'he rises at six, and cannot sit still, but starts up the moment he has dined, and runs away to Hawkley Hanger or King John's Hill . . . This morning, Mr. B. ran around Baker's Hill in one minute and a quarter, and Sam in somewhat less than a minute.'

Monday 22
38. 29 3/10. E. 30.   *Snow, snow, snow, bright.*

Tuesday 23
32. 29. E. 3½.   *Snow, snow, snow.*

The wind veers east, and the snow falls.

Wednesday 24
36½. 28 7/10¾. S.   *Flood at Gracious Street.*
Rain, rain, rain,
rapid thaw.

At times of heavy rain and fast thaw, the field springs rise on the Hanger's northern slopes and the ponds in Gracious Street often overflow. Looking back, Gilbert remembered how in January 1774, it had rained solidly, creating such great floods that he couldn't even get down to the ponds. But the floods had compensations: on 14 January that year, a bittern had been shot in Selborne shrubwood, and two more nearby, and as usual, when an uncommon bird appeared in the district, one was brought to Gilbert.

This elusive member of the heron family stalks silently through reed beds or flies across marshes on its broad, bowed wings, its booming note sounding across wetlands in spring. 'These birds are very seldom seen in this district, & are probably driven from their watery haunts by the great floods, & obliged to betake themselves to the uplands,' Gilbert wrote. He measured the bittern carefully – the four-foot wingspan, the feathers

          A YEAR WITH GILBERT WHITE

of the tail and neck – weighed it and made a note of the saw-like beak and the serrated claw on each middle toe – 'very curious!' (The jagged beak helps to stop fish and eels slipping away, while the claw is used in cleaning its plumage.) But then his scrupulously precise description segues into admiration: 'Tho' the colours on the bittern's wings & back are no ways gaudy or radiant, yet are the dark & chestnut streaks so curiously blended & combined, as to give that fowl a surprising beauty.'

The bitterns were not done with. He dressed, cooked and ate them, finding the taste like wild duck or teal, 'but not so delicate'. Mention of the taste of a bird's flesh often appears in contemporary ornithology, a 'scientific' observation. Naturalists had no qualms about slaughtering prized specimens: it's been rightly said that their first response to any rare bird was to shoot it – and, often, eat it. It's part of the whole idea of testing everything through the senses: sight, smell, hearing, touch – and taste. Gilbert's favourite authorities, John Willughby and John Ray, were full of suggestions: carnivorous birds, crows and magpies were 'not worth eating'; birds that fed on insects were not much better; those that ate grain were best; and partridges and woodcock beat the lot:

> If the Partridge had the Woodcock's thigh
> Twould be the best bird that ever did fly.

As for bitterns, in the century after Gilbert wrote, their history was bleak. By 1897, they had been shot to extinction in Britain, and after a brief revival in the Norfolk fens, their numbers fell again, to less than a dozen, when the East Anglian reed beds dried up. Yet wetland management is saving them. As rising sea levels make coastal reed beds salty, conservationists are creating new reserves inland, and now their call can be heard from Somerset to Yorkshire; soon, perhaps, in Scotland.

Thursday 25
36½. 29 2/10½. NW, SW. 24.   Frost, small snow, sun, frost.

Gilbert's concern was with the weather outside his own window. But the papers, getting through to Selborne despite the snow, held significant news. Two days before, on 23 January, the twenty-one-year-old William Pitt the Younger had taken his seat in Parliament for the first time. Within a couple of months, after a powerful maiden speech demanding reform and proposing peace with the rebellious American colonies, he would be seen as a leading figure. His father, Pitt the Elder, had been prime minister twice, in the 1750s and 1760s. By the time he was twenty-four, 'Honest Billy' was Britain's youngest-ever prime minister, leading the country throughout the remaining years of Gilbert's life.

Friday 26
50. 28 8/10. NW.   *Great rain, grey, bright, frost.*

Saturday 27
37. 29 7/10. NW, SE.   *Hard frost, bright, grey.*

In these chilly winter days, Gilbert is far from lonely. He spends evenings across the road in the vicarage with the family of the Revd Andrew Etty, who had been vicar since 1758, and he often goes up the hill to the Yaldens', in Newton Valence. That living was almost a family fiefdom: Edmund Yalden senior, vicar from 1717–46, when Gilbert was young, was followed by his sons, Edmund and then Richard.

The Yalden and White children ran up and down between their houses and stayed close as adults. In 1753, Gilbert's brother Ben married Richard's sister Anne. Another of his brothers, Thomas, became partners with Richard's brother Will in a London wholesale business. In 1758, after Will died, Thomas married his widow, Mary. These interconnections, hard to take in now, are like an elaborate dance, making The Wakes and the Newton Valence vicarage homes to an intricate, close, extended family.

Gilbert spent sociable evenings with these friends, talking, dining and making music, a pastime that was immensely popular in the village. 'We have this winter a weekly concert,' he told his sister Anne

Barker on Christmas Day 1778, 'consisting of a first & second fiddle, two repianos [a kind of cornet], a bassoon, an haut boy, a violincello, & a German flute; to the great annoyance of the neighbouring pigs, which complain that their slumbers are interrupted, & their teeth set on edge.' Four years after this, in 1782, when Anne came to stay at The Wakes with two of her daughters, the girls sat daily at the harpsichord, playing 'many elegant lessons in a very masterly manner'. Gilbert enjoyed this, but the tunes ran maddeningly in his head, night and day. Sympathising with his ear-worms, his niece Molly, who knew him well, sent him a quotation from the life of the seventeenth-century Provençal naturalist Nicolas-Claude de Peiresc, written by his friend Gassendi. 'He preferred the music of birds,' ran the quote, 'to that made either by the human voice or by instruments.' Gilbert agreed. It was not that music did not give him pleasure, but the tunes haunted him so. Yet, he wrote appeasingly to his nieces, 'notwithstanding all that, I would give six pence to hear you two maidens perform the *wopses*, the lesson with the jig, and that lovely minuet, &c, &c.'

Sunday 28
42. 29 6/10. SW, S. 28. *Dark & moist, dark & windy.*

Monday 29
47. 29 6/10. S. *Vast condensations on the walls, &c.*
Dark & moist, rain,
rain.

Tuesday 30
47. 29 7/10. W. 118. *Vast rain in the night.*
Rain, sun, clouds & *Snow-drops, winter aconite, & fetid-hellebores,*
strong wind. *blow.*

Despite their battering by the rain, in Selborne the snowdrops glint white, aconites shine yellow as egg yolk and the pale-green flowers of stinking hellebores droop over their broad leaves. For Gilbert, these are harbingers of life in cold, dark days. Like the toadflax, winter aconites were not native plants, but had arrived from south-eastern Europe in the sixteenth century. In the catalogue of plants in his garden, the herbalist John Gerard had described the joy when they 'come forth of the ground in the dead time of winter, many times bearing the snow on the heads of their leaves and flowers: yea, the colder the weather is, and the deeper the snow is, the fairer and larger is the flower'.

Gilbert's other marker, the stinking hellebore, also disdains the snow, its branching stems waving above the drifts, its lime-green cups a trove for early-flying insects and bees. Hellebores like chalky soils, and they grew wild around Selborne, in the High Wood and Coneycroft hanger, on the top of the down. In his *Flora*, Gilbert gives its common names: 'bear's foot', from the smell – a name common to all the varieties; and 'setter-wort', from the root's use in 'settering' abscesses in cattle, like an early antibiotic. The 'good women' of the area, Gilbert said, gave the powdered leaves of the stinking hellebore to children to cure them of worms, but it was a harsh remedy, needing caution. Nausea, vomiting and spasms could follow. As with the yew and the aconite, beauty and danger, life and death come together.

Wednesday 31
39. 29 8/10. W, SW.   *Spring-like.*
White frost, sun,   *Vast halo round the moon.*
grey & mild.

On the last day of the month, the halo still shimmers round the moon, but now rooks head to their nest trees, jackdaws chatter on church roofs and all the smaller birds are busy. In his early journals, Gilbert tried to note the first time he heard each bird sing – another set of 'coincidences' to mark how seasonal events shifted, depending on the weather. In the mild late January of 1769, he had written: 'Soft day. Bunting sings. A snipe appears on the high downs among the wheat.

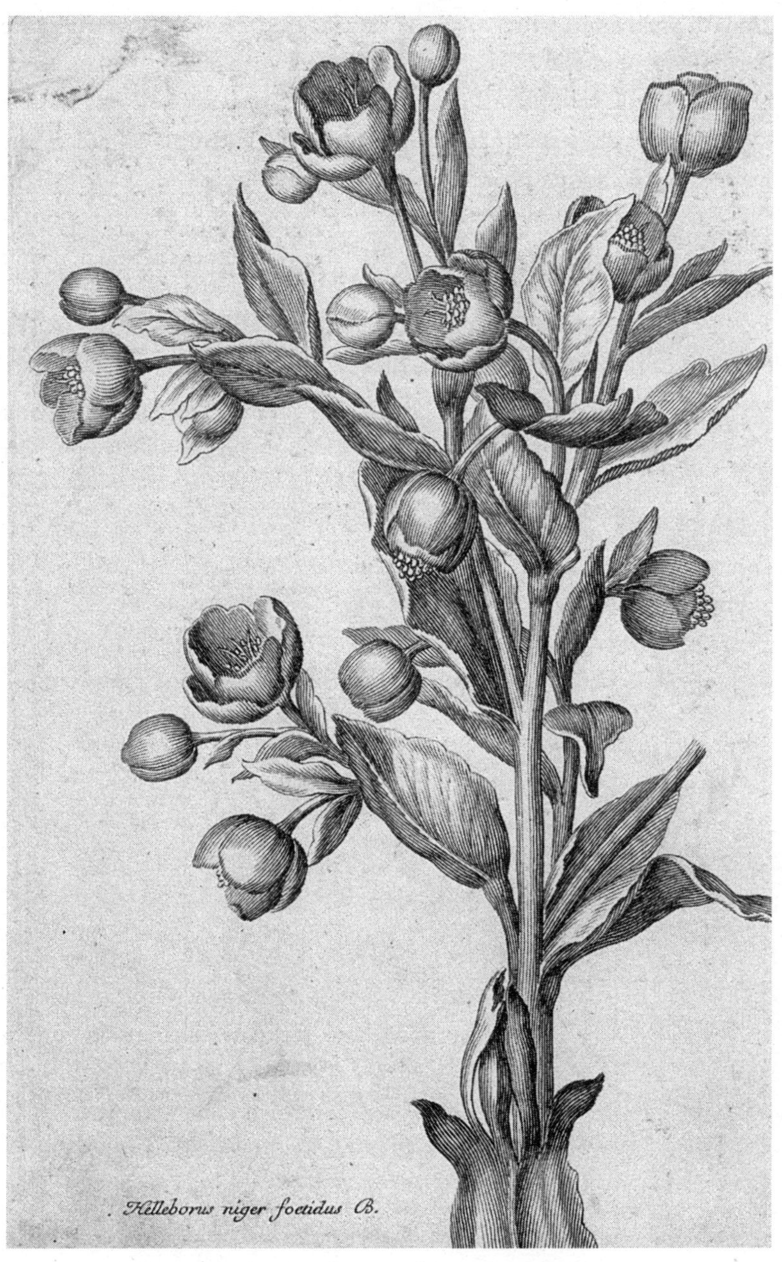

Nicolas Robert, *Stinking Hellebore*, c.1660.

Skylark sings'; and within a week, 'Hedge sparrows sing vehemently.'
A year later, the end of the month resounded with song: 'Woodlark,
great titmouse, chaffinch sing'; 'Blackbird whistles. Woodlark sings in
the air before daybreak. Thrush sings. Missel-bird sings.' Winter is far
from over, but spring is on the way – very slowly.

FEBRUARY

Year Place. Soil.	Therm.	Barom.	Wind	Inches of Rain or Sn. Size of Hail-st.	Weather.	Trees first in leaf. —Fungi first appeared.	Plants first in flower: Mosses vegetate.
Selborne.							
Sunday 8 / 12 / 4 / 8 — *Feb: 4.*	44½	29 6-10½	NW		sun. soft & spring-like.		
Monday 8 / 12 / 4 / 8 — 5.	45.	29 4-10¾	NW.		rain grey & mild.		
Tuesday 8 / 12 / 4 / 8 — 6.	46. 50.	29 6-10.	SW.		grey. sun. spring-like.		
Wednes. 8 / 12 / 4 / 8 — 7.	46.	29 6-10.	S.		sun. grey. sun & mild.		
Thurs. 8 / 12 / 4 / 8 — 8. Full moon.	44½	29 2-10	S.		Grey. rain. rain.		
Friday 8 / 12 / 4 / 8 — 9.	47½	29 4-10.	S.W.	61.	rain. sun & showers. hail. showers.		
Saturday. 8 / 12 / 4 / 8 — 10.	46½	29 6-10.	SW.		sun. sun & clouds.		

A showery week in Gilbert's *Naturalist's Journal*, early February 1781.

Forty-one years before, at the grey start of February 1740, Gilbert was waiting to begin a new stage in his life. The previous December, he had heard that he had been admitted to Oriel College, Oxford, but on that very day his mother Anne died. Instead of going to university, he stayed at home, helping his father. This was one of the bitterest winters anyone could remember, and by February, the great freeze, which had spread across the whole of Europe, still hadn't come to an end. It was not until April that Gilbert finally arrived at Oriel.

Gilbert loved Oxford, its bells and spires, golden stones, coffee houses and inns. In the mid-eighteenth century, the university was no hotbed of learning. Oxford was in one of its laziest, most complacent phases; progressive universities were to be found on the Continent, in places like Leiden and Paris, and in Scotland, in Edinburgh, Glasgow and Aberdeen. In Oxford, student numbers dropped, the Bodleian library's hours were limited and teaching was lax. When his nephews Tom and Henry went to Oriel in their turn in 1783, their sister Molly told them, 'My Uncle White says he remembers two brothers in the same rooms, came round one day to borrow a pen & ink – never having had any since they came to college, though they had been there two or three years.' Gilbert's tutor, Edward Bentham – to whom he paid six guineas a year for his tutoring – was only in his early thirties, and his readable *Introduction to Moral Philosophy* shows that he expected little from his students, reassuring them that they would find nothing in the book 'but such as may be supposed to lie within the apprehension of Common Sense, as distinguished from superior capacity or improvement'. (Bentham, who went on to become Regius Professor of Divinity, married Polly Bates, from Alton, and remained a friend of the family for life.)

According to Edward Gibbon, who arrived ten years later, the Fellows had no time for 'the toil' of reading or thinking or writing: 'Their conversation stagnated in a round of college business, Tory politics, personal anecdotes and private scandal, while their dull and deep potations excused the intemperance of youth.' Gilbert, though hardly intemperate, spent his allowance on port, wine and cider, joined the Music Club and attended concerts, went out on the river and lost money at cards. His little account book, bound in white pigskin, badly scuffed and marked and shut with a metal clasp, shows how he grew in confidence, buying a Nanking waistcoat (which had to be expensively cleaned), as well as shirts and neckties and black worsted stockings. Arranging his rooms, he splashed out on upholstery and the framing of pictures, bought a looking glass, tumblers and '6 drinking glasses', and gave dinners of dressed woodcock and strawberries, and bowls of punch. He may have shot that woodcock himself, as by his third year he was also spending money on his gun, on hiring a horse and on a collar and chain for his dog.

Gilbert often rode out into the country, perhaps missing the fields and woods of home. But above all, he spent time with his friends, especially John Mulso, who arrived at Oriel in November 1740 and whose chatty, teasing, hypochondriacal letters over the years are a revealing window on Gilbert's life, even though his own replies are lost. Mulso had been at Winchester with Jo Warton, who also came to Oriel this year, and William Collins, who went to a different college, Queen's; the trio had been the top three of their final year at school, and now, with Gilbert, they formed a tight foursome.

In his satire of the city's guidebook, Jo's younger brother Tom – who arrived at Trinity four years later and stayed there all his life – painted a tart picture of an Oxford whose 'schools' included billiards, skittles and horsemanship, while 'The Doctrine of the SCREW is practically explained most evenings in the private Rooms, together with the *Motion of Fluids*.' The most-used libraries, Warton proclaimed, were the coffee houses, where magazines and reviews allowed students to pass judgement on books they never read. Otherwise, 'NOVELS supply the

                    A YEAR WITH GILBERT WHITE

place of experience, and give lectures of Intrigue and Gallantry,' and 'Occasional POEMS diffuse the itch of rhyming, and happily tempt many a young fellow to forsake Logic, turn *smart*, and commence Author, either in the Pastoral, Lyric or Elegiac way.' That was an in-joke: both Warton brothers and Collins, and Gilbert himself, were already writing poetry – in a pastoral and elegiac way.

Friday 2
43. 29 8/10½. SW, S. 17.   *Rain, rain, rain, dark & moist.*

It's Candlemas – forty days from Christmas, the midpoint between the shortest day and the spring equinox. In the church calendar that Gilbert keeps to, this is the Feast of Purification and the day of Mary's presentation of Jesus at the Temple, the day when the churchwarden empties the cupboards so that all the candles for the church year can be blessed. But in this rainy, gloomy weather, as people splosh up and down Selborne's cartway they give little thought to festivals of light.

Saturday 3
45. 29 9/10. S, SW.   *Marsh-titmouse chirps.*
Dark, foggy & mild.   *The nut-hatch brings his nuts almost every day*
                              to the alcove, & fixing them in one corner of
                              the pediment drills holes in their sides, & after
                              he has picked out the kernels, throws the shells
                              to the ground.

Two days of rain have softened the soil. It's claggy round Gilbert's boots and lumps of mud fall off against the iron boot scraper at the door. This Saturday, Gilbert can hear the tiny marsh tit, its note insistent, sweet and sharp – 'beep, beep, beep, beep' – modulating into rippling calls and songs. Despite its name, the marsh tit, with its glossy black cap, prefers broad-leaved woodland, like the Hanger and its beeches, spending its winter months in the shrubby understorey. It is its virtual twin, the willow tit, that likes marshy ground and riverbanks.

He watches the nuthatch, beautiful and streamlined, with its blue-grey back and pinkish chest, hanging upside down, its sharp beak going tap, tap, tap. In his shelter by the garden walk – his alcove – it wedges nuts in a crack. He had seen nuthatches do this in a forked branch of his Orleans plum tree as well, hurling the shells on the ground. In February 1775, he had checked this habit with his venerable copy of Willughby's *Ornithology*:

> Saw several empty nutshells with a hole in one side, fix'd in the chinks on the head of a gate-post, as it were in a vice, & pierced, as I suppose, by a nut hatch, *sitta europaea*. Vid: Willughby's *Ornithol*:

Sunday 4
44½. 29 6/10½. SW.   *Sun, soft & spring-like.*

Dripping trees, everything quiet. The gold petals of the aconite are falling, leaving their green cups open to the sky. This is a month of waiting, planning and planting, watching the spears of bulbs poke through the dark mould.

Monday 5
45. 29 4/10¾. SW.   *Made a seedling cucumber-bed.*
Rain, grey & mild.   *Wood-lark, thrush, & great titmouse sing.*
                           Red-breast sings, & the wren.

All week the temperature is mild, in the mid-forties Fahrenheit. While the hard work starts in the garden, the air is full of birdsong. Gilbert's note today reflects this, beginning with a rushing trio of birds, then falling away, like a musical phrase, with a breath-like pause: 'Red-breast sings, & the wren.'

In his mid-fifties in the 1770s, he had begun to worry about his hearing. His gardener, Thomas Hoar, six years his senior, often hears things before him – the rush of wind in the hop-poles and bean-sticks, the first twittering of martins under the eaves. But although Gilbert had bouts of deafness, this didn't seem to affect the higher registers. He could identify every call: the crystal trill of the thrush; the two-note chirp of the tit, 'pee-pit, pee-pit, pee-pit', or 'tea-cher, tea-cher', as local people called it; the piercing warble of the robin. The wren, a brown curve with cocked tail, has a loud song for such a tiny bird, sometimes singing a duet with its mate – 'chirp, chirp, chirp' – then, suddenly, a long, drilling trill – 'chiiiiiiirrrriiipppp'. The thrush and wren are now singing regularly. The woodlark, with its tuneful, falling 'lula, lula', will call from a branch, but like the skylark, it sings most when it flies, spiralling upwards, hanging in the air. Their songs signal the onward run of the year.

Tuesday 6
46, 50. 29 6/10. SW.   *Bees gather on the snow-drops.*
Grey, sun, spring-like.   *Flies come out in the windows. Bat appears;*
                                       & moths flie under the hedges.

Bees, flies, bats and moths – these, too, are markers, the time of their appearance dependent on whether winter has been icy or mild. This year, the air is soft, and here is the first mention of bees. These are honeybees, foraging for pollen and nectar, flying under the arching flowers of the snowdrops and flipping over backwards to tuck their heads inside to reach the pollen. Pressing it into 'pollen baskets' on their rear legs, they carry the bright orange beads back to the hive. Inside the colony, the snowdrop pollen will make 'bee bread', a mix of pollen and nectar or honey, to feed to the larvae for the new breed.

Within The Wakes, houseflies – Linnaeus's *Musca domestica* – come out of their winter 'lurking places' in cracks and corners and the creases of curtains. Attracted to the light, they buzz round the windows, searching for a place to lay their eggs. All insects, as Gilbert notes firmly one February, have a place in the natural economy:

Spiders, woodlice, *lepismae* [silverfish] in cupboards, & among sugar, some empedes [beetles], gnats, flies of several species, some *phalenae* [moths] in hedges, earth-worms, &c: are stirring at all times when winters are mild; & are of great service to those soft-billed birds that never leave us.

At dusk, bats appear – probably one of the little pipistrelle species. Most are still hibernating, but their reserves of fat are running low and on warmer days they venture out for water and food, twisting and turning in the dusk as they hunt for insects. Then they retreat to their roosts in the nooks and crannies of trees, in old woodpecker holes, in the roofs of barns, in cracks in a wall, to sleep until another warm day. And as Gilbert walks down the lanes, moths flicker round his feet. Several kinds, with simple, evocative names – 'Early moth', 'March moth', 'Pale Brindled Beauty', 'Spring Usher' – fly in February, when the air is mild, especially in woodland. Gilbert classes them all simply under *Phalenae* or (his more common spelling) *Phalaenae*, the Linnaean name for the genus in the order *Lepidoptera*, as opposed to *Papilio* for butterflies and *Sphinx* for the hawk-moths. Each year, when the frost thaws a little, he waits to see their pale-brown or speckled grey wings flutter around him, catching the low evening light.

February can mix all weathers in a single day. It's a month of slowly rising sap. Sex is in the air:

Foxes begin now to be very rank, & to smell so high that as one rides along of a morning it is easy to distinguish where they have been the night before. At this season the intercourse between the sexes commences, & the females intimate their wants to the males by three or four little sharp yelpings or barkings frequently repeated.

He learned this, he said, from a former neighbour who 'kept a tame bitch-fox, which every spring about candlemass began her amorous serenade as soon as it grew dark', continuing all through February and March.

A YEAR WITH GILBERT WHITE

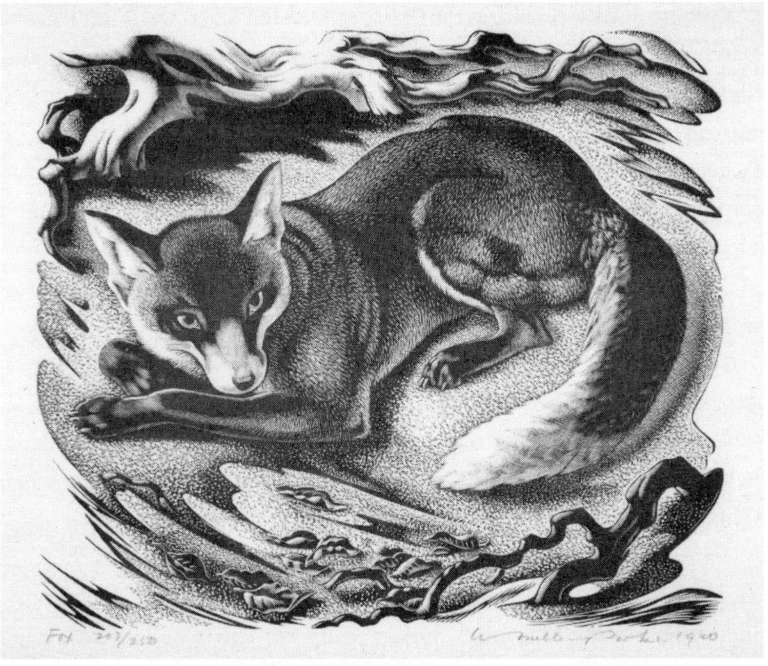

This 1940 wood engraving by the Scottish artist Agnes Miller Parker captures all the sinuous alertness of a fox roused from hiding.

Wednesday 7
46. 29 6/10. S.   *Water-cresses come in.*
Sun, grey, sunny & mild. *People begin to work in their gardens.*

For centuries in Hampshire, people have picked watercress, rich in minerals and vitamins, peppery and sharp. Cresses thrive in the clear water, filtered by the chalk, flowing over the gravel beds. In January, the plants have kept their dark-green leaves low, at water level, but now they begin to rise above the surface, surrounded by a haze as warmth from the water meets the colder air. As soon as the frosts are over, the cress is ready to pick. The spring season begins now, though the cress is at its best in April and May, while a second crop 'comes in' in the late summer months.

Gilbert walks through the village, looking over walls and gates, watching people digging, hoeing and manuring, ready for early plantings. He is busy in his own garden, too. The seedling cucumber bed was just the beginning, and now he works on his vegetable plots on Baker's Hill and in the Field Garden just beyond it, which has room for long rows of peas, beans and spinach. This was a lot to manage, and he needed help. In the early years, the young gardener John Breckhurst planted trees (and accidentally 'scorch'd up & suffocated all the forward Cucumbers'), and later Thomas Hoar took command. Laconic, wary of women, devoted and soft-hearted, Thomas was Gilbert's gardener, groom and general helper for forty years. He slept in the house, looked after the horses, drove the carriage to collect visitors from Alton, helped to brew the beer and read the barometer and rain gauge when Gilbert was away – and worked constantly in the garden.

Farmers brought carts of oozing manure, day labourers did the hard digging and local women came in to weed in the summer. Chief among these was Goody Hampton, hoicking up her skirts and wielding her hoe and her broom, winning Thomas Hoar's grudging respect: 'This is the person that Thomas says he likes as well as a man: and indeed, excepting that she wears petticoats, and now and then has a child, you would think her a man.'

Most years, if February is not too wet, Gilbert and Thomas plant early peas ('Marrow-fat and Hotspur') and broad beans ('Windsor beans', he called them), make a celery bed, trim vines and plant cabbages, spinach and parsley. Occasionally – though this is riskier – they put in lettuces, preferring 'brown-Dutch lettuce', with its rosettes of floppy leaves, and 'green Capuchin', which could be over-wintered under straw. In the flower beds they plant hollyhocks, columbines and sweet william. Across the meadows, they scatter ash, rich in potassium and phosphorus. The ashes come from Gilbert's own wood fires, but he also buys sackfuls from his friend Andrew Etty at the vicarage and orders cartloads from Woolmer Forest, where the furze on the heath has been burned in the autumn.

Cucumbers, which ripen easily in summer, were sneered at in the eighteenth century, widely mocked as the food of the poor; tailors were called 'cucumbers' because these, it was said, were all that was left for them to eat when the quality left town for the summer. A repeated quip was that cucumbers should be thinly sliced, dressed with vinegar and salt and pepper, and then thrown out. But when they were forced into growth, early cucumbers became one of the 'novelties of the spring'. This 'unnatural' gardening, upsetting the seasonal rhythm, had long been the butt of jokes, as in Gulliver's meeting with the ragged philosopher of Lagado, who 'had been eight Years on a Project for extracting Sun-Beams out of Cucumbers, which were to be put into Vials hermetically sealed, and let out to warm the Air in raw inclement Summers'. For upper-class estate owners, however, an early cucumber was a sign of their status, showing that they could employ the most knowledgeable – and expensive – gardeners.

Gilbert built his own cucumber frames, insulating the outside with ferns or straw to keep off the damp, and filling them with dung; usually, he 'borrowed' this from farmers, who came back to collect the spent manure each autumn to scatter on their fields. In 1780 and 1781, he paid Farmer Parsons for the carting of dung, peat and ashes, as well as cords of wood and sacks of coal. Once the frames were filled, Gilbert covered them with glass lights – broad panes of glass – adjusting them to avoid too much steam, wiping away the condensation every morning and cloaking them with mats or pea haulm if a cold spell struck. He grew his plants on 'hills', tumbling downwards – more like courgettes today.

Another cucumber fan, William Cowper, ten years younger than Gilbert, devoted a whole section of his much-loved poem *The Task* to their cultivation, describing how to build a frame, fill it, fork it, plant the seeds in 'pots of size / diminutive' and then plunge the small plants deep into the bed, a skill he thought sadly ignored by poets:

> To raise the prickly and green-coated gourd,
> So grateful to the palate, and when rare
> So coveted, else base and disesteemed –
> Food for the vulgar merely – is an art
> That toiling ages have but just matured,
> And at this moment unessayed in song.

Cucumber competitions were held in late March, with good prizes and strict rules: 'No person shall be permitted to shew cucumbers raised in hot houses or stoves; they must prove the cucumbers to be of their own raising.' Gilbert would have been too late, as he cut his first cucumbers in the spring, but he took great pride in them: one April, staying with his brothers in London, he had thirteen 'large well-grown cucumbers' sent up by coach, as they cost two shillings apiece in town. That month alone, he got forty large cucumbers from his frames.

Friday 9
47½. 29 4/10. SW. 61.   *Rain, sun & showers, hail, showers.*

When a letter arrives from his brother Thomas, Gilbert tells his niece Molly that it's a surprise to see that her father has written it himself, 'for it was indeed a long time since I had seen any such thing'.

Molly usually wrote on her father's behalf. She had been four when her mother died in the autumn of 1763, a fortnight after the birth of twins Thomas and Henry. She grew up as the darling of her bookish father, and at fifteen had come to Selborne to be tutored by the vicar's wife, Mrs Etty ('Molly White is very well; and is stout and large of her age, and a giant to Mrs Etty,' reported Gilbert to his sister Anne). Since then, she had visited often. Tall and fair, warm-hearted and enthusiastic, she was happy to trek up the hill through the mud to a ball at the Yaldens', but she was clever, too, someone Gilbert could write to about

Chaucer or Saxon nouns, as well as salt fish and stockings. In February 1781, he passed on neighbourly gossip. Firstly, Mrs Etty's niece 'Miss Shutter' (Mary Souter) – who had had an adventurous journey from Madras a couple of years earlier, when she was stranded off the coast of Angola – was marrying a wealthy young man from Norfolk. Secondly, he told her, a letter had finally arrived from the Ettys' sailor son Charles, written last July, as he neared the equator on his way to India. Finally, the ponds were dry, and if the twins were preparing their skates, 'they would be troubled to find water to make ice this winter'. He signed it: 'Yr loving uncle, Gil White'.

Saturday 10
46½. 29 6/10. SW.   *Sun, sun & clouds.*

Friday's rain and hail have passed over, and it's warm in the sun. In weather like this, Gilbert sees great flocks of buntings in the fields towards Farringdon, watches the house sparrows 'get in clusters & chirp & fight', and tilts his head back to gaze up as the skylarks mount and try to sing in the wind.

Sunday 11
47½. 29 2/10. S.   *Cucumber plants appear.*
Grey, strong wind,   *Hasels blow.*
stormy, rain.

The first cucumber shoots pop up, and the rising wind twirls the catkins on the hazels, where the short brown stubs of midwinter now 'blow' – bloom – in long golden tassels. These were another of his markers. Every hazel tree has both male and female flowers, but they cannot pollinate each other; the pollen has to reach a female flower on another tree, and for that it needs the wind. The catkins, the male, pollen-bearing flowers, are not designed to attract bees, but to launch their pollen into the breeze. (Honeybees do buzz around, but they find it difficult to collect hazel pollen, which is not sticky, but dry.)

Each hanging catkin is a long cluster of around 240 minuscule flowers, formed the previous summer; the slightest breath of air makes them shiver, wafting dusty yellow pollen to another tree, sometimes quite far away. The female flowers appear as a green bud, but though each one contains up to fourteen flowers, only the styles poke out – delicate, brilliant red tubes no longer than a millimetre or two – with a sticky stigma to catch the wind-blown pollen. From these, the clusters of hazel nuts grow. A strange, elaborate magic.

Monday 12

45. 29. SW. 38.   *Thunder.*
Sun, dark, rain with *Sea-gulls appear: in stormy weather they leave*
wind, stormy.   *the sea.*

The gale drives the gulls inland. 'Sea-gulls, winter mews, haunt the fallows,' he had written in 1777. One year, a man brought Gilbert a seagull, still alive, after 'three crows had got it down in a field, & were endeavouring to demolish it'. There was little he could do.

Tuesday 13

47.28 8/10, 29 1/10. W. 116. *Stormy all night. Much thatch blown-off,*
Stormy, sun, strong   *& some trees thrown-down.*
wind, stiller.

In the dark before dawn, the wind booms through the Hanger. When he wakes, the street is cluttered with branches and straw. By evening, the storm calms, but next day, and all week, the wind roars on.

Wednesday 14

43. 29 3/10. S, W, NW. 23. *A pair of ravens build in the hanger.*
Rain, strong gales, bright, rain.

It's St Valentine's Day, the Roman Lupercalia, which is thought to take its name from *lupus*, meaning 'wolf'; it is also linked to the she-wolf that nurtured Romulus and Remus. A festival of blood and ritual sacrifice and random coupling; the time for seed to be sown, nests to be built. Every year, Gilbert looked out for ravens collecting twigs and beginning to build. I think of ravens as birds of high crags, wheeling in the air above ravines, flipping over in curving aerobatics, and it feels odd to think of them settling in a wood, like rooks. Usually, they are solitary or in pairs, yet sometimes they do gather in flocks, and Gilbert writes of seeing forty at a time, playing about over the Hanger all day.

Reading an article by Stephen Moss, I discover that the raven flies through creation myths from North America and Scandinavia to the nomads of Siberia. It is also the first bird mentioned in the Bible, 'when Noah sent one out from the ark to discover if the flood was finally over; true to this bird's independent character, it failed to return'.

Thursday 15
42. 29 4/10. W. 24.   Helleborus viridis *emerges, & blows.*
Sun, strong wind,   *Strong* N: *aurora: very red in the* N.E.
showers, bright.

Wild wind. Washing on the line, shirts billowing, sheets flapping. Hellebore buds open, in the wild and in his garden. Gilbert had discovered a clump flowering in April 1766:

> Bear's foot, or wild black Hellebore, *helleborus niger hortensis flore viridi,* flowers in the stony lane towards Alton: this is a different species from that on the hill; has a much greener flower, & greener leaves. The other has whitish flowers, & blackish leaves.

In a letter to Daines Barrington, he places it still more exactly: 'in the deep stony lane on the left hand just before the turning to Norton-farm, and at the top of Middle Dorton under the hedge'. At the start of September 1768, he had transplanted some to his shrubbery in the orchard. The following year, on 7 February, he noted that the plant brought 'from the stony-lane, begins to spring. It rises from the earth with it's flower-buds formed: & differs from the *Helleborus foetidus,* that it dies down to the ground in the autumn, while that maintains a large hand-some plant all the winter.'

At night, a canopy of light, green and blue, swirling, streaking, waving, arches of colour rising and falling like curtains against the dark sky. At its heart, a glow of red. The aurora, which we associate with the far north and Arctic, spread far south in the eighteenth century – as it did in Britain in 2023 and 2024 – as explosions on the Sun, connected with sunspots and solar flares, sent excited neutrons to collide with the atoms of oxygen and nitrogen in Earth's high atmosphere, releasing energy as light – green, blue, yellow, red. In the previous century, in the 'little ice age' beginning in the early 1620s, there had been no sign of any auroras at all. Then, in March 1716, a huge aurora was seen from Ireland to Italy, rousing old superstitions and warnings of plague, war or the end of the world. In 'Autumn', the poet James Thomson had suggested that 'philosophic' explanations would stop the superstitions that surrounded the aurora, the visions of armies in the sky, 'Thronged with aerial spears and steeds of fire'. But Thomson's own description of 'meteors' retained an otherworldly majesty:

> Oft in this season, silent from the north
> A blaze of meteors shoots – ensweeping first
> The lower skies, they all at once converge
> High to the crown of heaven, and, all at once
> Relapsing quick, as quickly re-ascend,
> And mix and thwart, extinguish and renew,
> All ether coursing in a maze of light.

The aurora took Gilbert's mind across the globe, away from the local. When his nephew Sam Barker asked him if the aurora ever appeared in the southern hemisphere, Gilbert quoted from Johann Reinhold Forster's *Observations Made During a Voyage Round the World*, published in 1778, his account of Cook's second voyage to the Pacific from 1772 to 1775. Forster, he pointed out, noted that though common in the north,

A YEAR WITH GILBERT WHITE

'I never heard or read of anyone who had seen the SOUTHERN LIGHTS (*Aurora Australis*) before us!' (ignoring all local peoples). Cook's party saw the lights for a week in 1773, 'shooting up to the zenith in columns or streams', sometimes extending over the whole sky, sometimes transparent so that you could see the stars through them, sometimes dense and opaque.

Forster's *Observations* also made a point of showing how the flora altered, depending on physical environment and climate, and how animals varied according to the vegetation – a global parallel to Gilbert's intensely local findings of the effects of different soils.

Friday 16
39. 29 8/10. NW.   *A row of crocus's in the field in bloom.*
White frost, sun &
brisk gale, bright & still.

The crocuses, a streak of colour against the frosty grass, made the Northern Lights feel more exotic still. Those lines of Thomson's, imagining the whole sky 'coursing in a maze of light', were typical of the poetry that had excited Gilbert and his Oxford friends, the Warton brothers and William Collins, when they began writing poetry. They had started young. Collins's *Persian Eclogues*, transposing the pastoral to the desert and Caucasus mountains, appeared in 1742; Tom Warton's *Five Pastoral Eclogues* was published in 1745, when he was nineteen and still a student at Trinity; Joseph Warton wrote *The Enthusiast, or the Lover of Nature* in 1740, the year he came up to Oxford, publishing it when he graduated in 1744. Jo was fiery in his rejection of the dryness and abstraction of Dryden and Pope and the 'rational' moderation of Augustan ideals. Instead, he looked back to Spenser, Shakespeare and Milton, and his favourite book, he said, was Longinus' *On the Sublime*. 'I shall read Longinus as long as I live,' he wrote to his father from Oriel, 'it is impossible not to catch fire and rapture from his glorious style.'

That emotional tone marked a new spirit. Up to that point, 'enthusiasm' was a term of disparagement, usually applied to religious fanaticism, and Warton was replying in part to Shaftesbury's letter 'Concerning Enthusiasm', which called for reason, 'sound sense' and cool, calm, impartial judgement, to protect against 'every biasing passion, every giddy vapour or melancholy fume'. Defiantly, Warton's enthusiast yearns, in a spirit that anticipates Rousseau, to return to some primitive Arcadia where passions run free, and he calls, too, for a celebration of nature, not in images of nymphs and dryads, but in the precise naming of animals and birds. What are the 'attic Vanes' of Stowe's classically inspired gardens, he asks, compared to the thrush-haunted copse, where the fawn hides in the rustling leaves and the squirrel leaps from bough to bough?

Gilbert paints his own ideal scene in his 'Invitation to Selborne'. He composed this in his mid-twenties, when he was cold and homesick in East Anglia in the spring of 1746, but he often revised it to suit particular occasions. 'Now climb the steep,' he urges us,

> . . . drop now your eye below
> Where round the blooming village orchards grow;
> There, like a picture, lies my lowly seat,
> A rural, sheltered, unobserved retreat.

Saturday 17
38. 29 6/10¾. NW.   *Frost, sun & sharp wind.*

He makes a general note on a blank page of the journal, as he often did at the weekend: 'The storms in the beginning of the week did great damage by sea, & by land.' Across the country provincial newspapers printed letters from coastal towns: from Plymouth, where ships were smashed to pieces, or from Yarmouth, where moored vessels were blown out to sea and sunk. This was from Aldeburgh in Suffolk:

> We have had for these three days the most violent storm of wind
> that ever was remembered by the oldest man living; our Coast is

covered with Pieces of Wrecks of Ships, and every Tide throws up dead Bodies, inasmuch that it is Employment for Several Men to bury them; Guns from Ships in Distress are continually discharging; but the Wind blows so hard, that we cannot venture to their Assistance; a Vessel from Lynn, which put here for Shelter, was blown out, and lost within Sight of this Town, and the Crew were drowned.

Thatch on the streets of Selborne seemed as nothing.

Sunday 18
37. 29 6/10. W, SW.   *Hard frost, sun, dark, rain.*

A letter has arrived from John Mulso. Though they were both destined for the church, as students Mulso and Gilbert could not have been more different: while Gilbert loved the outdoors and field sports, the plump, lazy Mulso didn't even ride unless he had to. A hard-trotting horse, he wrote, 'you know, with me, conveys the Idea of very terrible Shaking'. After Oxford, in the 1740s, he had plunged into the world of high society, staying in country houses, going to the latest plays, dropping in to Hogarth's studio to see his *The March of the Guards to Finchley*, which showed the soldiers heading off to fight the Jacobite rebellion in 1745. 'I was at ye Races,' he wrote cheerfully, 'ye Assemblies, ye Concerts, ye Plays, the – in short everything that can be call'd gay, & delightfull.'

The well-off Northamptonshire Mulso family were all fond of Gilbert; in particular, John's sister Hester, 'Hecky', who visited him in Oxford and nicknamed him 'Busser' or 'Whitibus' ('buss' being Shakespearian for 'kiss'). She admired his poetry, too, if with some firm criticisms. Hester was a link to a different literary world, a different kind of 'sensibility'. In 1750, she began a heated debate with the novelist Samuel Richardson – who later became a good friend – arguing that the heroine of his novel *Clarissa* was far too passive and subservient. She herself was anything but passive: in 1760, against her father's wishes, she married Richardson's friend, the lawyer John Chapone, but was widowed within ten months, and as Hester Chapone would become one of the leaders of the scholarly women of the bluestocking circle.

Mulso's older brother Thomas was also a writer, and Ben White published his *Callistus: Or, the Man of Fashion. And Sophronius: Or, the Country Gentleman. In Three Dialogues* in 1769 – not with any marked success. Mulso himself had no such ambitions, happy to follow an easy career, thanks to his uncle, who became Bishop of Winchester. He wanted Gilbert, too, to find a living, get married and have a family. But he appreciated his friend's life in his 'rural, sheltered, unobserved retreat', admiring Gilbert's spaniels, Copper and Fresco, and even trying to follow his passion for gardening. In 1750, after rain and easterly winds, he wrote lugubriously, 'I gather but my third Crop of Peas to day; we have had Colliflowers a good while. Your Salsafi makes it's appearance, It is a root which I don't understand. Gooseberries & Currants blighted to death.'

Monday 19
39½. 29 5/10, 6/10. NW. 20. Sun, sharp air, sun & clouds.

In his letter of the previous week, Mulso told Gilbert, as always, about his family and old friends – and his bowels. He kept off politics. 'I will imitate You,' he concluded, 'in your Prudence in saying nothing of public affairs. Methinks, however, I see You shrug up your Shoulders. In all times, be they good or bad, I am, My dear Gil, Your affecte. friend & Faithfull Servt.'

Selborne villagers remembered Gilbert's 'peculiar way of shrugging his shoulders' whenever he was worried or full of foreboding. He rarely engages with political events in his personal letters or his journal, but the times did feel bad. The American war had dragged on since 1775; France had joined the conflict in 1778, Spain the following year, and in 1780, Britain declared war on the Dutch, who were sending the Americans supplies and munitions. Now there was a threat of a 'Northern Confederacy', led by Russia. On 18 January, the British had suffered

    A YEAR WITH GILBERT WHITE

a grim defeat in South Carolina, at the Battle of Cowpens, and on 5 February, the *Hampshire Chronicle* carried a report from London on the mood in the Tory coffee house in St James's:

> Thursday morning, at the Cocoa-tree, the meeting of the ministerial members of the House of Commons was very numerous, on account of the disagreeable news of Lord Cornwallis's disasters in America, and the prospect of a war with Russia. The meeting seemed much clouded, every face wearing a melancholy aspect. It was said to be agreed among them that the present unhappy war, which we are engaged in with so many powers, cannot be carried on without hazarding the total destruction of the kingdom. In consequence of which a peace must be patched up . . .

Tuesday 20
39½. 29 9/10. N. Dark & harsh, grey.

This is an unremarkable day, but eight years before, this date had prompted a surprising entry:

> Saturday 20, 1773. Trufles continue to be found in my Bro: Henry's grove of beeches: tho' the season is near at an end. It is supposed that seven or eight pounds are taken annually in that little spot. My Bro: & the trufle-hunter divide them equally between them.

Henry, the youngest brother ('Harry' to the family), had been vicar of Fyfield, near Andover, thirty miles from Selborne, since 1762. An unabashed pluralist, he also held a curacy at nearby North Tidworth, as well as the Wiltshire living of Upavon. From 1770, he and his redoubtable wife Elizabeth (she was thirty when her first child was born and forty-six when the tenth arrived) ran a boarding school for about a dozen boys, charging substantial fees.

Their family life was always crowded, sometimes literally. Describing their trip one summer to Ringmer to his nephew Sam Barker, Gilbert

reported that 'Harry and his wife (no small personages) and seven children, two canary birds, one aberdavine, 10 parcels, a dormouse, and
a puppy-dog, all went down in two post-chaises.' (The aberdavine was
a siskin; kept as a caged bird, a rival to the canaries, it doubtless sang
all the way.)

Wednesday 21
38. 29 7/10. N. 15.   *The snow melts as it falls, except on the hills.*
Snow, snow, snow.

As the snow drops from the branches, another brother is on Gilbert's
mind. Mulso had written to console Gilbert on the death of his brother
John the previous December. He was only fifty-three and left a widow,
Barbara, and one son, Jack.

John had been a worry over the years. He had gone as a scholar
to Corpus Christi College, Oxford, in 1746, but had perpetual rows
with the authorities, and although he graduated and hoped to become
a fellow, he was sent down in 1750 for his part in the marriage of an
eighteen-year-old student, 'eldest son of a baronet and Heir to a large
estate', to the daughter of the innkeeper at the Lamb, Wallingford,
'a House of no good Character'. John had apparently entertained the
bride and her sisters in his room. This didn't stop his ordination, but
while he scraped a living in odd London curacies, he was living wildly,
gambling and overspending. By 1752, he was deep in debt, borrowing
from relations and, embarrassingly, from friends in Selborne. The solu-
tion – common to all black sheep – was to send him abroad, and in
1756, he found a post as a chaplain in Gibraltar. He married Barbara
before he left, and Jack was born the following year.

Once John was overseas, the family turned their backs. In January
1759, he wrote bitterly to Gilbert, saying that he had only learned of his
father's death 'in the publick papers, as I was casting my eye over them
in a Coffee House'. His grief was deepened, he said, 'by the long silence
of all my relations in England'.

A rapprochement came in 1768, when, Gilbert told his naturalist correspondent Thomas Pennant, he wrote to 'my South country correspondent at Gibraltar', urging him 'to take up the study of Nature a little, & to habituate his mind to attend to the migrations of birds & fishes; & to the plants, fossils & insects' of his part of the world. John responded eagerly, writing reports and sending specimens for Gilbert to identify and compare with British examples. Parcels arrived at their brother Ben's bookshop in London, containing insects, plants, dried and salted fish, and bird carcasses, often decaying and smelly. Gilbert sent some of them on to Pennant, and gave insects to 'Mr Lee, the botanist of Hammersmith to inspect and ascertain them, because he is the best Entomologist that I know'. He waited eagerly for each box, bombarding John with advice on what to look for and what to read. He was pleased when John began writing to the great Swedish naturalist Linnaeus and sending him specimens. Reading a long Latin letter from Linnaeus to John, he told Pennant: 'The old arch-naturalist writes with spirit still: and is very open and communicative, acknowledging that several of the Insects were new to him.'

As a model, Gilbert recommended Giovanni Scopoli's pioneering studies of the flora, insects and birds in Carniola (now in Slovenia). Through John, Gilbert's world expanded:

Your butterfly-like insect with long remiform wings is curious and rare, and proves to be the *Panorpa coa* Lin. You see it is to be found in few places; and Scopoli knows nothing of it, though Carniola lies in a warm altitude. Send some more specimens. Pray observe how and where they breed. I suspect much that they come from the water, where they perhaps are hatched like the *Ephemerae* [mayflies] and the *Phryganae* [caddis flies].

What sorts of Land-tortoises do you find: when do they come forth and when do they hide?

Have you no stone-curlews (*Charadrius oedicnemus*)? They certainly leave us for some of the dead months of winter.

Are not some of your foxes jackalls (*Lupus aureus*)? That animal wants to be better described.

Driven by such urging, John's work swelled into a document of over a thousand pages, his *Fauna Calpensis* (from the Roman name for the Rock, the Mons Calpe).

It was wildly ambitious, if not impossible, for one man to try and cover everything – geology, plants, birds, insects, fishes – and Gilbert knew this. 'There is endless room for observation in the field of nature, which is boundless,' he wrote in 1770, in response to the suggestion that he write an account of all the animals in his neighbourhood. 'Investigation,' he added, '(where a man endeavours to be sure of his facts) can make but slow progress; and all that one could collect in many years would go into a very narrow compass.' It was no small undertaking, he insisted, for a man to write a natural history from his own observations. Yet that is just what he asked John to do, and what he eventually did himself.

As I read the letters between the brothers, it seems to me that their exchange is key to Gilbert's growing understanding of what it should mean to be a naturalist, and to his decision to write his own local study. He was reading widely, in Continental as well as British sources, getting to grips with new techniques and theories. From his Oxford friend William Sheffield, a distinguished naturalist, he learned how to look for the particular details that identified the differences in species, as laid down by Linnaeus and others, although he later rejected this approach as too vague. For Gilbert, identification was not enough; he wanted to know about the whole life cycle of the birds and insects. For example, although John's discovery of a particular lacewing – the 'butterfly-like insect with long remiform wings' – was much applauded, Gilbert kept pressing him for more information, even after John returned to England in 1772.

John came back because he had the chance of a living as a vicar in Blackburn, Lancashire, and after spending the winter in Selborne, he and Barbara moved north. Over the next few years, he revised and re-wrote his *Fauna*. The plan had been that Ben White should publish it, but both Ben and Gilbert, and the readers they appealed to, struggled with John's heavy style, full of Latin phrases, unleavened by anecdotes. Their criticism was searing. Feeling rejected again, John became ill and depressed. In his letter of 1781, however, Mulso remembered him as someone 'who united in himself things which do not commonly assemble: Mathematics & Poetry, Philosophy & Humour. Pray what is to become of his *Fauna*? That work is not, I hope, to be secreted like a certain Person's, whose false modesty will not trust forth a piece really Good, for fear it should not be absolutely Perfect.' Mulso was right. Gilbert's perfectionism, as well as Ben's commercial sense, doomed John's work. Apart from a short introductory section, the *Fauna* vanished from sight for ever.

Thursday 22
35. 29 8/10½. N.   *Hard frost, sun, sun, bright.*

Gilbert was devoted to John's son, 'Gibraltar Jack'. His mother Barbara had brought him back to England in 1769, when he was ten, to go to school at Holybourne, near Alton, and Gilbert agreed to be his guardian while he was there. When his parents went north to Blackburn in 1773, fourteen-year-old Jack stayed on at The Wakes. Here, he acted as Gilbert's amanuensis and also became his pupil, reading Hume's *History of England*, devouring volumes of *The Spectator* 'with that relish that showed he understood them' and forging bravely through William Derham's *Physico-Theology*. By April 1774, they had read 'all the Georgics through' and had started Horace's *Odes*, until, said Gilbert, they 'found many of them so indecent for a young man, that we have taken to the Epistles, which are a fine body of ethics, and very entertaining, and sensible'.

'I should wish to have him stay as long as ever you and his mother can spare him,' Gilbert assured John. Jack was a beloved member of the household. When he had measles, Thomas Hoar slept in a little bed beside him 'to give him balm tea in the night'. But Jack recovered, and a lingering hoarseness was put down simply to his voice changing. He visited the Mulsos with Gilbert and went with him to Ringmer, tramping across the downs under summer skies. When Gilbert had flu, Jack kept his journal for him and gave his own atmospheric account of a huge landslide at nearby Hawkley, where all the ground was rumpled and forced up, as if in waves.

'He is now a real service to me, and a companion in my solitude,' Gilbert wrote. He missed him when he went to join his parents in the summer of 1775. When, after many discussions of possible apprenticeships, he found a place with a surgeon near Blackburn, Gilbert was pleased and amused: 'As to Jack's "venturing to draw blood from his majesties subjects," I do not so much wonder: I rather admire at the courage of the patients who permit him.'

Friday 23
39. 29 5/10½. NW. 11.   *Ivy-berries are full grown.*
Frost, sun, rain, rain.

Gilbert often comments on the value of ivy, which he had summed up on 14 February 1774:

> The ivy, *hedera helix*, blows in Sept: Octr & Novr the berries are full grown, & ripen in April: thus fructification goes on in some Instances the winter thro'. When the berries are full ripe they are black.

In September and October, butterflies, bees, wasps and hoverflies had clustered round the ivy flowers, the richest source of autumn nectar. Slowly, the seed heads appeared. Gilbert doesn't go in for similes, but how to describe these berries? Each one looks like a tiny medieval mace, a miniature globe sprouting prongs tipped with black. All winter the birds flock to them – thrushes, blackbirds, wood pigeons. They last long after other berries and haws are over, and as if they know this, the birds often leave them until they finally ripen and blacken in the spring. They're full of fat. Apparently – so the RSPB tells me – gram for gram, 'The dry pith of ivy berries contains nearly as many calories as Mars bars! In most cases, while the bird digests the pith and juice, the seeds travel undamaged through the bird's gut, and may be dropped many miles from the parent plant.' So their use goes two ways.

Saturday 24
44. 29 3/10½. W, SW. 21.   Grey, shower, rain.

I think of Gilbert White as rooted in Selborne, but as a young man he was restless. His friends had left Oxford when they graduated, but he was back again that autumn, and on 30 March 1744, he sat a brief exam, settled his fees with the vice-chancellor's office and became a fellow of Oriel, paying for a celebratory peal of bells at the university church. A fellowship was a formal appointment, usually seen as a short-term step, but Gilbert kept his all his life, despite a tiff with the authorities when his father died and it was assumed, wrongly, that he would then have a good income.

In the late 1740s, his student friend William Collins was searching for a curacy in London, eventually finding one in Chelsea. Often pursued by bailiffs, he had come back from Flanders, hoping to 'get a chaplaincy in a Regiment. Don't laugh,' wrote Mulso, 'indeed I don't on these occasions: This will be ye second acquaintance of mine who becomes ye Thing He most derides.' Gilbert, too, was looking for a job, in a half-hearted fashion. In April 1746, he became curate in the parish of Swarraton, where his uncle Charles White was the vicar. This brought him only £20 a year, but his duties were light; indeed, he was hardly there at all. For the next year or so, he criss-crossed the country on long trips to Ringmer and Rutland, and shorter visits to Sunbury, on the Thames, where Mulso was now vicar. He also went shooting in the Cotswolds with Tom Mander, an Oriel friend whose passion for science was a standing joke. 'How does Tom Mander's System of Physics go on?' Mulso asked.

Is He Master of ye weight & ye Power? Has he settled Sir Isaac's & Grimaldi's Dispute of ye Refrangibility or Dispersion of Rays? Will He venture down in a diving Bell, or is He yet as distress'd as a Cat in an Air Pump? You may give my love to Him, if his apparatus does not forbid your Approach.

Experiments, Mulso knew, would soon give way to field sports, 'popping and snapping . . . Tom can walk farthest, though You shoot best . . . Tom drinks Cyder longest, but You take ye larger glasses at first.' Yet although research in physics and chemistry does not feature much in his writing, Gilbert remained interested in such experiments. 'As an electrician,' he told his brother John in the late 1770s, 'you should see Priestley's *History of Electricity*. He sets the whole on a pleasing light.'

In the autumn of 1747, Gilbert was back in Oxford, ill with small-pox. This was severe enough for a nurse, 'Goody Marshall', to be sent from Hampshire, and it cost him a weighty £31 in doctors' bills, plus tea, figs and wine, but by Christmas, he was well enough to buy a shooting net and new skates.

When his Swarraton curacy ended the following April, Gilbert went home to The Wakes. A year later, he was ordained and became curate in Selborne itself, standing in for the vicar, Dr Bristow. But in the summer, he was off again, staying with an Oriel friend, Nathan Wells, vicar of East Allington, among the high-banked lanes of the South Hams dis-trict, between Dartmoor and the coast. Addressing him 'in the Depths of Devon', Mulso wrote: 'You live a scambling rantipole Life & have a great Variety of Objects to be painted upon Paper (at which Landscape Painting I think You have a great & masterly Hand) & sent to your sed-entary friends.' Gilbert, he suggested, had enough material for a volume of 'Tours . . . My great Escapes are when I follow You in Imagination', or even a poem, '*ye Progress*'.

Memories of these escapes stuck in Gilbert's mind, and the plants he brought back grew in his garden. On 6 April 1751, he sowed a bed of sea

     A YEAR WITH GILBERT WHITE

kale that he had collected in Devon. The gift of 'Landscape Painting' that Mulso admired stayed with him, too, enriching his writing about Selborne.

Sunday 25
46. 28 9/10. W.   *Showers, hail, showers.*

Sunday, time for a sermon. Gilbert celebrated nature, in all its specifics, not in poetry, but in prose. Like his fellow students, he was alert to the new 'sensibility' and showed this in a place one might not expect: his early sermons. Most clergymen simply read their sermons from a printed collection, but Gilbert, at least for the first few years, seems to have enjoyed composing his own. His sermons were sewn into individual booklets, with a list on the cover of each place and the date on which he gave them. (After his death, they stayed in the family. Molly's son Glyd preached fourteen of them, altering and annotating them heavily, right up to the 1860s.)

When he stood in the pulpit in those plain country churches with their flagged floors and plaques on the walls, a small figure almost swamped by his black robes, Gilbert looked down on a mixed congregation: the landowning families in box pews; the lesser farmers and tradesmen and their families on the benches behind them; the more earnest day-labourers squeezed in at the side. All were turned out in their Sunday best, church being a time to show off a new hat, exchange flirtatious glances or simply to sleep. No one expected originality in the pulpit, and Gilbert just rotated his sermons about every two years, perhaps assuming that his congregations had short memories or had dozed through the first reading. But he was a natural storyteller, and his sermons were vivid and passionate, using plain, direct language. When he wrote them out, he put rows of dashes to mark pauses for thought or dramatic effect, and he used heavy underlining, both single and double, for emphasis, like the markings a musician might make on a score. They were small dramatic performances, their repetition as welcome as the use of a familiar hymn, so that listeners in Farringdon or Selborne could say, 'Ah, it's the raising of Lazarus again,' or 'Oh good, we're getting Mary Magdalene today.'

Lazarus was the starting point for one sermon preached at Selborne in the late 1750s, and then at Farringdon. The text was about Mary's grief at her brother's death: 'When Jesus therefore saw her weeping: & the Jews also weeping that came with her: He groaned in Spirit & was troubled', which Gilbert combined with a text from the next verse – 'Jesus wept.' From this, he argued that 'Grief & Pity, & a fellow-feeling of the miseries of others, & tenderness of heart, & bowels of Mercy & Love, & the rest of human affections, are not inconsistent with wisdom, & Goodness.' He vehemently rejected the Stoics' belief that passions were diseases of the mind and should be cut off, like 'a mortified limb'. On the contrary, he claimed, Christ is shown, 'not as void of passions, but to have been, in the several parts of his life, sorrowful & compassionate, & angry, & loving & desirous & joyful, & under the same affections as other men feel'.

Intense emotions quickened the soul. Love, hatred, fear, courage – all had a place, he said, in the religious life, which could reach an ecstatic intensity, 'For we can never too affectionately love, or too eagerly covet, or pursue our everlasting Bliss.' No anger was too fierce against those who argued against belief; no sorrow too deep at the risk of losing faith; 'nor any despair be too great for the utter loss of it'. Gilbert's sturdy rural listeners may have been disconcerted. The sermon is almost too insistent: it feels like an argument with the self, presenting religion as a realm where banked-down emotions can soar.

Monday 26

39. 29. W, NW. 19.   *Rain & snow, sun & clouds.*

Gilbert added a sermon or two each year during the 1750s and '60s, but at the point when he was beginning to think about a calendar of flora, and the natural world, he stopped. From then on, it seems, all his

                    A YEAR WITH GILBERT WHITE

writing energies were turned to the natural world. But he still gave his sermons at Selborne and at Farringdon.

When Gilbert was a boy, the vicar in Farringdon had been Stephen Hales, who held the living from 1723 until his death in January 1761. Hales spent his summers here but winters in Teddington, where he held a perpetual curacy and was a good friend of Alexander Pope. (Perhaps it was through him that Pope gave a copy of his six-volume *Iliad* to Gilbert when he went up to Oxford in 1739.)

Hales was one of the many distinguished 'parson naturalists' inspired by John Ray. A fellow of the Royal Society from 1718, his gruesome experiments on living dogs, sheep and horses (including opening the artery of dying horses to measure how high the blood would spurt) enabled him to measure blood pressure for the first time and to explore the workings of heart valves and arteries. Such experiments were justified at the time for both benefiting human medicine and showing the wondrous workings of God, but Gilbert was drawn less to this drastic work than to Hales's *Vegetable Staticks* of 1727. Examining decaying vegetable and mineral matter, Hales was the first person to collect gas by bubbling air through a trough of water, a step towards analysing 'good' and 'bad' air, which led to further work on ventilation, improving air quality in places like ships' holds, prisons and hospitals.

By mid-century, he was a favourite at court and honoured across Europe. Gilbert remembered him affectionately as a benign eccentric whose 'whole mind seemed replete with experiment, which of course gave a tincture, and turn to his conversation, often somewhat peculiar, but always interesting'. Writing to Robert Marsham, a friend of his later years, he noted, with amusement, Hales's constant desire to help; his worry about the incrustation of ladies' tea kettles; his advice on showers of water to clean 'suspicious wells'; his suggestion that air holes in the outer walls might prevent floorboards from rotting; his imploring young people 'not to drink their tea scalding hot'; and his recommendation to the housewife, 'to place an inverted tea-cup at the bottom of her pies and tarts to prevent the syrop from boiling over'. The last example of this benevolence that Gilbert saw was of Hales, 'with his paint-pot before him, and much busied in painting white, with his own hands, the tops of the foot-path posts, that his neighbours might not be injured by running against them in the dark'.

<table>
<tr><td>Tuesday 27
40. 28 6/10½. S, W, NW.
Rain, wind, vast storm,
calm & bright.</td><td>ALTON
Had the duration of this storm been equal to its strength, nothing could have withstood its fury. As it was, it did prodigious damage. The tiles were blown from the roof of Newton church with such violence, that shivers of them broke the windows of the great farm-house at near 30 yards distance. This storm blew the alcove back into the hedge & threw down the stone dial post.</td></tr>
</table>

Diligently, for the last time this month, he taps his barometer and writes down the pressure and temperature. Later today, he will ride over the downs to Alton. All the day before, the wind had boomed in the chimneys, rattling the panes and turning tiles into glass-shattering missiles. At The Wakes, Gilbert was thankful, he told Sam Barker,

> to find that I had escaped with the overturning of my alcove into the hedge, the overthrow of my stone-dial, and what grieves me most, because it cannot be repaired, the ravage of my great wal-nut-tree, which, they write word, is almost torn to pieces!

Wednesday 28
W. Sun, delicate day.   SOUTH LAMBETH

The storms have passed. He sets off to stay with his brothers Thomas and Ben in the London suburb of South Lambeth. He never describes his journeys, simply notes that he has gone from A to B. Usually, he preferred to ride, but for trips like this he could take the lumbering, rolling,

Southampton to London stagecoach, which left from the White Hart in Alton and carried him all the way to Ludgate Hill, sloping up to St Paul's. From there, a servant with a cart could take him and his luggage across the river to South Lambeth. This London parish, stretching along the south bank of the Thames, from Battersea to Vauxhall and Lambeth Palace, was an almost rural area, with orchards and market gardens, and Thomas and Ben were among the many London businessmen who moved there after the new Westminster Bridge replaced the old horse ferry across the river.

Thirty years before, when these two brothers began their careers, Gilbert had still hoped for a university life. In 1752, when it was Oriel's turn to appoint the junior proctor, responsible for policing student behaviour, he had resigned his Selborne curacy to take the post. The appointment ran for a year, and he enjoyed every day of it, going to concerts, playing cards in the common room, winning at chess, going shooting with his new spaniel, buying lobsters and olives, strawberries and cream, and hampers of what he calls 'Mountain-wine, very old, & good' – a sweet white wine from southern Spain. His youngest brother Harry was a student at Oriel, and other siblings and friends came to stay. He showed Becky the Bodleian and Christ Church and its Picture Gallery, took trips with Thomas and Ben, and came back to college in the summer vacation to entertain the Mulso family.

The only hint of any early romance, apart from the flirtatious attention of Hecky Mulso, comes from these Oxford years. When he was proctor, cutting a dash in 'a feather-topped grizzle wig', one of his most costly purchases was 'a Large Pier-glass, second-hand, brought from London by Jenny Croke'. Jenny's mother looked after the rents of some Oxford houses that his grandmother Rebecca owned and also ran the haberdasher's shop in the High Street, where Gilbert splashed out on his official proctor's robes. He had been friendly, if not more, with Jenny while he was a student, and in 1752, she paid a long visit to Selborne. After their return to Oxford, Gilbert gave her an expensive 'round China-turene', perhaps a comic apology for the coach sickness that had 'prevented [him] paying for ye post-chaise'. But Gilbert was not sure about his feelings, to judge by John Mulso's teasing:

> Our Girls are clear that the affair between You & *one Jenny* is quite serious . . . but You was so grave with me in the Post Chaise that I dare not add to their Opinion anything but my Applause of the Lady. However that be, I dare say that She is very instrumental in soft'ning the Rigour of your Oxford Confinement, & often prevents your forgetting family Life.

When his proctorship ended, so, apparently, did this friendship. He would have no family of his own. Instead, with amused affection, he calculated the numbers of his 'nieces and nephews', including wives and husbands.

Leaving Oxford when his year-long appointment ended in the spring of 1753, Gilbert was slightly at a loss. He took on a couple of curacies, first at Durley, near Bishop's Waltham, in Hampshire, a long thirty-mile ride each weekend, and then at West Dean, near Salisbury. But despite the attractions of Old Sarum and Stonehenge, where the jackdaws nested on the high ledges, out of the reach of shepherd boys, this was too far from Selborne, and in early 1756, he gave it up and came home. The Wakes was emptying: his grandmother Rebecca had died the year before, and his sister Becky had married Henry Woods and moved to Sussex. Gilbert was alone with his ailing father, unsure of his next move.

While he dithered, his friends moved on. In 1756, after an engagement of eleven years, John Mulso married his fiancée, Jenny Young, her intransigent father having finally given his consent, after being shaken by an accident, when the coach carrying Jenny and her sister tumbled into the Thames. Mulso and his brother Ned had rushed to the rescue, '& to the saving of my Heart, which was almost broke with fright & Running, met ye two deplorable dribbling Misses in the street', finding them unhurt but 'fairly sopped & well frightned'. (As a wedding present, Gilbert sent him a soup tureen – no hint of coach-sickness this time, just a symbol of hospitality. Inviting Gilbert to stay, Mulso wrote: 'We can make You a Bed in the Turene, for it is pure large.')

Meanwhile, Jo Warton began nearly forty years as headmaster of Winchester College, marked by at least three schoolboy rebellions, and soon his brother Tom became Professor of Poetry at Oxford. Gilbert may have envied him. In 1757, when the provost of Oriel died, he applied for the post but lost in the election. The failure hit him hard. Instead, he accepted a living at Moreton Pinkney, in Northamptonshire, with the proviso that he could have a curate and would not have to move there himself. He would have made a good parish priest, but he turned down all the other livings that Oriel offered him. The only one he really wanted was that held by his uncle Charles at Bradley, only ten miles from Selborne. When Charles died in 1763, he put himself forward, only to be turned down by the patron, Lord Chancellor Henley, whom he had offended with his lukewarm support of Henley's candidate for the Oxford chancellorship. Denied his wish, from now on Selborne was where he wanted to be.

He was not well off. He earned about £30 from his curacy, small amounts from rents in Selborne and elsewhere, and tithes from his living in Moreton Pinkney, but his most substantial funds came from interest on government bonds. Thomas, a shrewd businessman, had been investing on his behalf in 3 per cent and 5 per cent consols (government bonds), which brought in around £123 in 1777, rising to £132 by 1781. In total, Gilbert had around £250 a year.

This was meagre compared to most eighteenth-century clergy, but he could live quite well on it: he paid a small amount of land tax and poor rates, but he had no mortgage, utility bills or income tax, which did not begin until 1809. He paid regular wages to Thomas Hoar and the maid, who also cooked for him, while the men who came in to dig or cut and stack wood were paid daily, as was the carpenter who repaired sheds and barns. He grew his own vegetables and brewed his own beer, bought flour and a five-penny loaf from the baker each week, and had an account with the butcher. He purchased breeches and boots for Thomas Hoar and fine broadcloth and cambric for his own coats and shirts, and his carefully kept accounts note sums for malt and hops, postage and parcels, salt fish, spectacles and sealing wax, lozenges and hair powder, brandy and port, newspapers and new shoes. The pages are also peppered with small charitable payments: 'half-year's petticoats to 5 poor women'; 'cloaths to sundry poor' or 'to farmer Keen for his loss by fire'. His most extravagant indulgence by far was buying books: in 1778, one lavish, multi-volume bundle cost him £5 7s.

MARCH

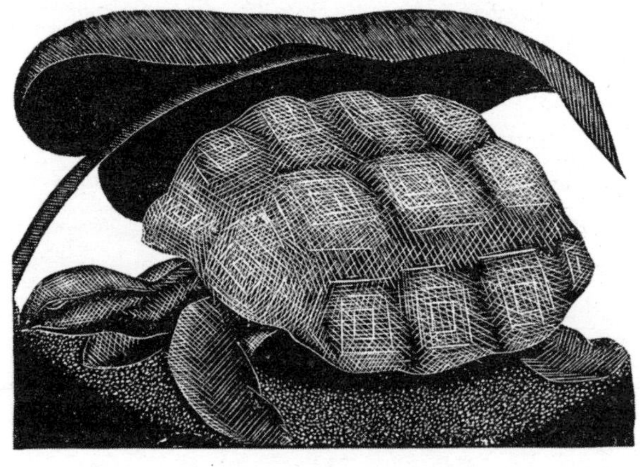

'Timothy Shelters Under a Leaf': wood engraving by Claire Oldham
for *The Natural History of Selborne* (1929).

It's raining in South Lambeth, where Gilbert is staying with Ben and Thomas and their families. Both these younger brothers were far cannier about money and business than he was. Ben, cool and shrewd, with an easy charm, had flourished as a bookseller, and was still running his shop at the Horace's Head, off Fleet Street. In the 1750s, John Mulso already found that he never left Ben's shop without buying something. 'It is very dangerous to go in there,' he moaned. 'I was taken in to buy ye small Warburton's Edition of Pope's Works, which cost me One Pound Seven.' Even if he dropped in only for a chat, 'there stood a confounded Edition of Livy in my Way, which cost me two Pounds before I could get out again'. In 1765, Ben had taken over the business from his former partner, buying libraries sold at auctions and becoming known for fine natural history books.

In the early 1770s, Ben took a long lease on a large plot of Crown land south of the river, the 'Vauxhall Escheat', where he now had a substantial house with a large garden. When he stayed there in 1776, Gilbert, who was planning to add a new room to The Wakes, was mightily impressed, admiring the long drawing room, which Ben's wife Anne, he said, 'has furnished in a splendid manner. In short, they, who have eleven children, shame me who have none, and yet make a pother about building one room.' Their nine-year-old daughter Nanny, who had been ill for some time, 'recovers very fast by living in the country, and my sister looks much the better for being out of town. In short this house will probably lengthen all their days.' It was not to be. Nanny died the following year, and her mother Anne two years later, in 1779. Ben was left with a large family to care for; his youngest son, William, was only eight.

'Respects over the way,' Gilbert cheerily ended a letter to his niece Molly. Her father, his brother Thomas, had also moved to South Lambeth, taking a house opposite Ben's. Changing his name formally to 'Thomas Holt White', in early 1776 he had finally come into the inheritance left to him by his mother's relation Thomas Holt thirty years before. After he graduated, Gilbert had spent months in East Anglia as an executor of Holt's complicated will, sorting out the inventory, selling stock and dealing with tenants in the Fens and the Essex creeks. He remembered it as a bitter, lonely, bothersome time. Laden with annuities and complex bequests, the will ground slowly through the Court of Chancery, until it was finally settled. Once he was financially secure, Thomas began to sell his stock in his large ironmongery business and to think of retiring. Some money from Holt's will came to all members of the family – Gilbert estimated around £300 each. This was serious money, more than his annual income.

In his portrait, probably painted in the mid-1780s, Thomas looks rather woolly – perhaps the artist wanted to show him as thoughtful. In fact, he was bustling and energetic, and when retired, he was hardly idle. He loved figures and statistics, but was equally keen on gardening and botany. His special interest was trees: he apparently wrote a preface (never found) to a new edition of John Evelyn's *Fumifugium* of 1661, which recommended planting trees around London to counter the city's pollution. As if this was not enough, he wrote articles for the *Gentleman's Magazine* on Virgil and Milton, supplied notes for editions of Shakespeare and planned to write a 'natural history' of Hampshire.

Saturday 3
50. 30 3/10. SW.   *Persian Iris blows.*
Grey, mild.

Four years before this, in 1777, Thomas had become a fellow of the Royal Society, where he read out Tom Barker's papers on annual rainfall before they were published in the Society's *Transactions*. These included figures from his own rain gauge and those of Gilbert and their brother Henry. At South Lambeth, he set up his instruments carefully:

Thermometer placed in a shade, on the north side of a wall, abroad. Barometer about twelve feet above high water mark. Rain measurer placed seven feet from the ground. Observations made about eight o'clock in the morning.

During his stay here in 1781, Gilbert jots down the weather measurements and takes careful note of the special plants in his brothers' gardens, including the Persian iris. In warm, sheltered places, this fragrant little iris, about four inches tall with greyish-blue flowers, can flower for weeks in February or March. It came originally from the mountains of Persia, and since the late sixteenth century it had been a staple of London nurserymen, who imported the bulbs from Holland. Philip Miller had included almost fifty species of iris in the 1754 edition of his *Gardeners Dictionary*, and his 'Iris Persica' (listed under 'Xiphium') spread happily in The Wakes' garden, as well as in South Lambeth.

The Persian iris – with a note that if grown indoors in 'a waterglass' or, better, in a small pot of sand, it 'will scent a whole apartment' – was the first plant described in William Curtis's *Botanical Magazine*, founded towards the end of this decade, in 1787. Curtis was a friend and protégé of Thomas White, whose own commonplace book is full of detailed descriptions of plants, with their Latin names. Twenty years Thomas's junior, Curtis was almost a Selborne neighbour: born in Alton, he turned to botany while training as an apothecary (he and Thomas were both members of the Society of Apothecaries). He had then moved to London, where he was so successful that he sold his apothecary business, and in 1772, at the young age of twenty-six, was appointed 'Praefectus Horti' and demonstrator at Chelsea Physic

Garden – the role Philip Miller had held before him. Next, he set up his first botanic garden, to study native plants, at Lambeth Marsh, in Bermondsey – very near Thomas's business – and a few years later, Thomas helped him establish the London Botanical Garden nearby. In 1777, Ben White published the first of six lavish folio volumes of Curtis's *Flora Londinensis*, illustrated with beautiful copperplates.

Gilbert met Curtis in South Lambeth and liked him greatly. In 1776, writing encouragingly to his nephew Sam Barker about the problems of distinguishing between mosses, he reassured him that even Curtis found this difficult. Curtis, 'a very friendly man and always willing to communicate', sent Sam a plate, 'containing representations of the fructification, &c. of his own mosses, such as he uses in his own lectures'. Curtis also reassured him that the Linnaean use of the sexual identification of 'male' stamens and 'female' pistils to create classes – major groups of plants – was impossible with fungi. The web of correspondence was growing.

Sunday 4
30 2/10. SW.   *Frogs begin to appear.*
Dark, still & moist.

People have always looked out in March for snakes in the compost, for insects in the house, for toads and frogs and 'the warm thick slobber of frogspawn', as Seamus Heaney puts it, growing 'like clotted water' in the shade of the bank. Here is Gilbert, in March 1775: 'Snake appears: toad comes forth. Frogs spawn. Horse ants come forth.' And here is John Clare, on 11 March 1825: 'The frogs have began to croke & spawn in the ponds and dykes.' And in Clare's poetry:

> The frog croaks loud & maidens dare not pass
> But fear the noisome toad & shun the grass:
> And on the sunny banks they fear to go
> Where hissing snakes run to the floods below

        A YEAR WITH GILBERT WHITE

The nuthatch noises loud in wood & wild
Like women turning skreekers [rattles] to a child . . .

Frogs croak away in Gilbert's journal, but he confessed that he was no expert on amphibians. 'There is a degree of dubiousness and obscurity attending the propagation of this class of animals,' he decided, which he found confusing. Yet 'the copulation of frogs', he writes, 'is notorious to every body: because we see them sticking upon each other's backs for a month together in the spring'. He never saw the same with toads, he said, although they attracted so much folklore. When the tadpoles grow lungs, they have to leave the pools; they will drown if they stay in the water. He waited for this point, when paths and fields swarm with these 'emigrants, no larger than my little finger nail . . .'

How wonderful is the economy of Providence with regard to the limbs of so vile a reptile! While it is aquatic it has a fish-like tail, and no legs: as soon as the legs sprout, the tail drops off as useless, and the animal betakes itself to the land!

A rare mistake – the tadpole's tail doesn't drop off but is absorbed into the body – and a rare surrender to the old ladder of the Great Chain of Being, where reptiles skulk on the bottom rung.

Monday 5
45. N.   *Wheat looks miserably in Battersea-field.*
Small rain, grey &   *Frogs croak.*
mild.

In South Lambeth, Gilbert and Thomas saddle their horses and ride towards the village of Nine Elms, on the river. From here they turn west, following the dusty, rutted lanes, crowded with carts, builders and workmen, until they reach the broad open space of Battersea Common Field.
A causeway separates the low-lying Battersea Field from the river. On its southern side, the old marshes, drained by innumerable ditches, are

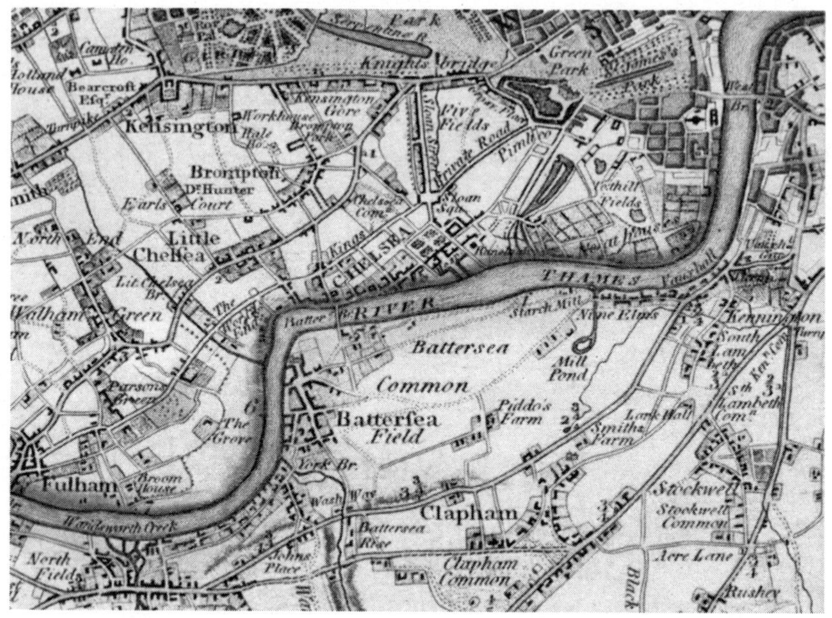

A detail from William Faden's map of London (1790). South Lambeth appears on the far right, between Kennington and Stockwell.

a medley of the market gardens established by the Huguenot refugees a century ago, their soil enriched by horse manure, night soil and ashes rowed across from the village of Chelsea. These gardens are famous for carrots and melons, and for 'Battersea Beans', fat white 'Battersea Cabbages' and asparagus sold in huge 'Battersea Bundles'. Behind them, lavender fields spread out on the slopes of Plough Lane (now Lavender Hill). But the winter wheat on the huge Common Field looks thin and mean to Gilbert's country eye. Sown in November, it should have been showing spikes of green by now, but the soil is dry from the long drought and the air is full of smoke from the corn and sugar mills, potteries, lime kilns and breweries lining the riverbanks. Four years from now, five miles downriver, at Southwark, Matthew Boulton will build his huge Albion Mills, the first commercial steam-powered mill – the prompt, it is said, for Blake's dark satanic mills. Away from the green retreats of Selborne, Gilbert steps into a bristling, growing industrial age.

He does not write about this, but nor does he turn his back on the modern world. When he gets home, he will tell Molly jokingly that soon she needn't suffer dusty roads but could come 'all the way to Alton by water'. An idea was being floated for a canal all the way from Chertsey, on the Thames, via the River Wey, past Alton, to join the River Itchen, flowing down to Southampton. The plan included a daring five-mile tunnel under the hills beyond Alton. 'You may smile at this proposal,' Gilbert wrote, but its promoter swore that the profit from the chalk dug out from the canal's route, burned as lime, and the ashes from the peat, would produce a massive £31,371 (a startlingly precise calculation, equal to over £5 million in today's currency). This was one of innumerable schemes at the height of the canal fever that had spread rapidly since the 1760s. A canal was indeed opened in 1794, running from the Thames via the Wey Navigation. It reached Basingstoke but never went further, and never reached Alton.

Tuesday 6

40. 30 3/10. SW.	*Elms blow.*
Sun, sweet day, red	*Apricot-bloom begins to open.*
even:	*Ants & flies appear.*

Elms 'blow', or blossom, he writes, having seen the green tassels, each stem ending in a tiny dark-pink flower. The elm's single flower contains both male and female parts – a hermaphrodite tree. When pollinated by the wind, the flowers become tiny green fruits with a flattened, papery wing (like sycamore seeds), and these 'samaras', as they are called, lighter than feathers, are tossed far by the breeze.

Elms ruled the landscape from Gilbert's day to the late twentieth century, their tiered branches and heavy crowns towering above the hedgerows. Then, in the 1970s, tree after tree was lost to Dutch elm disease, spreading north from the Channel to Scotland in a mere ten years. Today, older people remember the dread, wondering when each tree would go.

Wednesday 7
40. 30 2/10.   *Fog, sun, sweet day.*

Another 'sweet day', like the one before. The flies and ants are out, and the blossom on Thomas's apricots is on the tip of opening. It has reached that point where you feel that if you look long enough, you will actually see a petal unfurl.

Thursday 8
40. SW.   *Wet fog, dark & mild.*

Knowing how variable spring is – and how our climate is changing – it's hard to imagine what a particular day in March will be like years from now. It might be warm, with bees gathering on the crocuses. Or perhaps, as on the day I write this, there will be ice on the ponds and snow on the hills. Gilbert often looked back through his journals, comparing the current weather, or the date of the arrival of birds, to that of past years, but he, too, found it hard to look ahead. We have the advantage of him: with his journal before us, we can see his future. Here he is, twelve years later, on 7 March 1793, staying with Ben in his new house in the country. Violets are flowering and redwings feed in the meadow. He is so accurate about the dashing, tumbling lambs, who make him think of his old favourite, Thomson's *Seasons*:

> Trouts begin to rise: some angling takes place in this month. My Brother's cucumbers are strong, & healthy. My Brother's lambs frolick before the windows, & run to a certain hillock, which is their goal, from whence they hurry back; & put us in mind of the following passage in the Poet of nature:
>
> > . . . 'now the sprightly race
> > Invites them forth; then swift, the signal given,

                    A YEAR WITH GILBERT WHITE

> They start away, & sweep the massy mound
> That runs around the hill.'

Friday 9
47. 30 2/10½. SW, S.   *Brimstone butterfly.*
Sun, sweet day, red even: *Pile-wort [flower]*

Gilbert sees a brimstone, the first butterfly of the year, emerging from hibernation like a flash of sun playing along the hedge. Brimstones are a rare modern success story in Britain, spreading north in the mild winters, their numbers rising slowly. They are our longest-lived butter-flies, sheltering for the winter in ivy or holly; then first the males come out, with their yellow, leaf-shaped wings, soon to begin hunting for the females, who are paler green, almost white. The brimstones feed on the spring flowers, and the female lays her eggs on the leaves of the buckthorn or alder – good food for the caterpillars.

A burst of yellow comes from the lesser celandine, which Gilbert calls 'pile-wort', adding a small flower icon to show it is in bloom. I think of celandines as taken-for-granted plants, their glossy leaves and starry, buttery flowers covering damp banks and creeping into flower beds, then disappearing in summer. But they are part of the flashiness of early spring, as Gilbert noted: 'The uplands glow with pile-worts, & dandelions; the wet meadows with marsh marrigolds.' The old name 'pilewort' came from their use in treating piles: the nobbly roots look uncomfortably like them, and by the 'doctrine of signatures', which held that plants that looked like particular body parts had a spe-cial connection with them, they were held to be a cure. Piles, noted Gerard's *Herball*, 'when often bathed with the juice mixed with wine, or with the sick man's urine, are drawne togither and dried up, and the paine quite taken away'. Some herbalists still recommend celandines as a salve – they're full of a toxin, protoanemonin, which is slightly astringent – and foragers say you can eat the leaves in salad, but not too many as they burn your mouth.

Saturday 10
47. 30 2/10½.   *Roads very dusty.*
Grey, sun, delicate.   *Rooks build. Insects abound.*
                              Full moon.

Each year, Gilbert watches the rooks make their twiggy nests. They fascinated him because they were so gregarious, yet their colony was a mass of tension. In March 1775, he had written: 'Rooks are continually fighting, & pulling each other's nests to pieces: these proceedings are inconsistent with living in such close community. And yet if a pair offers to build on a single tree, the nest is plundered & demolished at once.' A year later, he watched them set on particular birds like a gang of bullies: 'Some unhappy pairs are not permitted to finish any nest 'til the rest have completed yir building; as soon as they get a few sticks together a party comes and demolishes the whole.' The dropped twigs, he adds, provide kindling for the poor: 'Thus did the raven supply the prophet with necessaries in the wilderness.'

His description of their nesting conjures human stereotypes – the fluttering female and gallant male – combined with an acute observation of bird behaviour, noting the submissiveness and calling common to all corvids during mating and nesting:

> As soon as rooks have finished their nests, & before they lay, the cocks begin to feed the hens, who receive their bounty with a fondling tremulous voice & fluttering wings, & all the little blandishments that are expressed by the young while in a helpless state. This gallant deportment of the males is continued thro' the whole season of incubation. These birds do not copulate on trees, nor in their nests, but on the ground in open fields.

Through all his writing rooks bustle and caw: 'rooks, in the breeding season, attempt sometimes in the gaiety of their hearts to sing', he notes, 'but with no great success'.

At one point, he asks why are their flocks so often followed by a flight of starlings?

Is it because rooks have a more discerning scent than their attendants, and can lead them to spots more productive of food? Anatomists say that rooks, by reason of two large nerves which run down between the eyes into the upper mandible, have a more delicate feeling in their beaks than other round-billed birds, and can grope for their meat when out of sight. Perhaps then their associates attend them on the motive of interest, as greyhounds wait on the motions of their finders; and as lions are said to do on the yelpings of jackals.

This is one of many questions raised, then left aside. Gilbert was a pioneering field naturalist, but not a scientist in modern terms, one who would test his findings and follow everything through. He was more of a philosophical muser. He was curious, for example, about the rooks' tendency to albinism, eager to see such unusual birds. A neighbour, he said, had two completely white chicks in a nest, but 'a booby of a carter, finding them before they were able to fly, threw them down and destroyed them'. Gilbert only saw them nailed against the end of a barn – a farmer's warning to all birds to stay away.

Sunday 11
38. W, NE.
Cold air, sun.

> *The tortoise came forth, & continued to be alert 'til the 25th & then eat some lettuce; when the weather turning very harsh he retired under the straw in his coop. About this time the shell-snails at this place began to move.*

While Gilbert stays on in London, Thomas Hoar, who is devoted to Timothy the tortoise, reports from Selborne that Timothy is now waking after his first winter in The Wakes' garden. (Technically, it should be 'her first winter', as a post-mortem revealed her to be female, but to the White family Timothy the tortoise was 'he', and so he is here.)

The tortoise had belonged to Gilbert's aunt Rebecca Snooke, who had died at Ringmer on 8 February 1780, aged eighty-six. Her husband had bought the tortoise long ago from a sailor in Chichester for 2s 6d, and he had roamed her walled garden ever since. He could not be abandoned. After Mrs Snooke's funeral, Gilbert filled a box with earth and carried him home to Selborne, as he noted in his journal:

Brought away Mrs Snooke's old tortoise, Timothy, which she valued much, & had treated kindly for near 40 years. When dug out of its hybernaculum, it resented the Insult by hissing.

Freed from his box after the bumpy ride from Sussex, Timothy had been carefully placed deep in a flower bed in The Wakes' garden. But it was a warm day, so he 'heaved up the mould, & walked twice down to the bottom of the long walk to survey the premises'. Next day, he came out, then dug himself halfway in again, and finally retreated deeper. In late April he widened his breathing hole, stuck his head out and surveyed the scene. Then: 'Tortoise comes-forth, & walks round his coop: will not eat lettuce yet: goes to sleep at four o'clock p:m.' By 2 May, 'Tortoise marches about: eat part of a piece of cucumber-paring.' Soon he ceased being 'it' or 'tortoise' and was given his name:

17 May: Timothy began to break his fast on the globe-thistle, & American willow-herb; his favourite food is lettuce, & dandelion, cucumber, & kidney beans.

27 May: Timothy the tortoise possesses a greater share of discernment than I was aware of; & is much too wise to walk into a well, for when he arrives at the haha, he distinguishes the fall of the ground, & retires with caution, or marches carefully along the edge: he delights in crawling up the flower-bank, & walking along it's verge.

Gilbert identified him as the *Testudo Graeca* of Linnaeus'. He weighed him, examined his dung and urine, and saw how he disliked

     A YEAR WITH GILBERT WHITE

rain and how he covered himself with dead grass when the sun was too hot. In July, with his friend Richard Chandler, he dunked him in a tub of water to see if the species was amphibious. Although Chandler – and John White, writing from Gibraltar – had heard that some tortoises like ponds and lakes, Timothy did not. He sank and walked on the bottom, and 'seemed quite out of his element, & was much dismayed'.

Monday 12
36. 30 3/10. NE.   *Ice, grey.*

Gilbert enjoyed staying with his brothers, with their gardens and books and different family life, but although South Lambeth was almost in the countryside, it was nothing compared to early spring in Selborne, where the trees were budding and the spring bulbs, grasses and wild-flowers were leaping up.

In the late 1750s, Gilbert had begun to bring wildflowers into his Selborne garden. In the following decade, his interest in botany grew. It was spurred in 1765 by his reading of the second edition of Benjamin Stillingfleet's *Miscellaneous Tracts Relating to Natural History, Husbandry, and Physick*. In this, Stillingfleet included a calendar of the 'Flora of Uppsala' in 1755, made by Linnaeus's follower Alexander Berger, plus his own 'Calendar of Flora' from the same year in Norfolk.

Gilbert urged the book on John Mulso, who was less keen: he had never seen Stillingfleet's works, he said, '& indeed it is a Subject that I am not so engaged in as Yourself . . . I have no Temptation to out-door work.'

Gilbert, however, loved outdoor work. He walked the lanes and fields and woods, and when he needed a new notebook, he changed his usual heading of *Garden Kalendar* to 'A Calendar of Flora, & the Garden from August 9th 1765'. The next year, he made a separate list, his *Flora Selborniensis*, writing down the plants he found in both the wild and the garden, noting distinct stages, from 'springing' and 'shooting' to 'budding' and 'blowing' (flowering), then 'in high bloom' and fading. He gave the plants their Latin names, some taken from Linnaeus, some from the longer formulations of Ray, but he also used the lively, vigorous common names. On 12 March 1766, on a soft, mild day:

> Furze, *Genista spinosa vulgaris*, in bloom.
> Laurel, *laurocerasus*, budding for bloom.
> Dog's mercury, *cynocrambe*, blowing, the male bloom only.
> Birch, *betula*, budding.
> Wood-laurel, *laureoa*, in bloom.
> Humble-bee comes forth, *Bombylius*.
> Periwinkle, *vinca pervinca minor*, in bloom in Shrub-wood: this is a scarce plant.
> Jack in the hedge, *alliaria*, springing all the winter.
> Ragweed, *Jacobaea*, shooting.
> Hounds-tongue, *cynoglossum*, springing.
> *Malva sylvestris*, the common mallow, grows.
> Ground-ivy, *calamintha humilior folio rotundiore*, creeps about all the winter.
> Wood-ruffe, *asperula*, appears, or rather has not disappeared the winter thro'.
> Mezereon blows.
> Crocuss make a most gallant show.

'Mezereon' – the lovely purple *Daphne mezereum*, which we see as an ornamental shrub – is, in fact, a native. Gilbert found it in the Hanger, saved the seed and sowed it in his garden.

Although he compiled his *Flora* for his own interest, it was very much of its time. Ten years later, the Birmingham doctor William Withering (who introduced digitalis into British medicine, following folk usage) published a two-volume *Botanical Arrangement of All the Vegetables Naturally Growing in Great Britain*, giving details of habitat, time of flowering and use as food and drugs. Botany was fashionable, patronised by George III's mother Augusta, who developed her gardens at Kew in the 1760s, with the help of Lord Bute, in deliberate

 | A YEAR WITH GILBERT WHITE

competition with Buffon's magnificent Jardin du Roi. At the same time, the excitement generated by Linnaean taxonomy led to a boom in books, including James Lee's *Introduction to Botany* and Philip Miller's *Short Introduction* to Linnaean terms, both published in 1760 and often reprinted. In 1765, Gilbert obtained a copy of the Latin *Flora Anglica*, published in 1762 by William Hudson, which used the new terms, and on the title page of some early years of *The Naturalist's Journal*, he notes that plants and insects are named following Linnaeus, and 'the birds according to Ray'.

In his *Flora Selborniensis*, Gilbert listed 439 species, often noting precisely where they grew. What would he find if he went out today? In March 2023, the Botanical Society of Britain and Ireland published its *Plant Atlas 2020*, following twenty years of fieldwork by thousands of volunteers. They recorded over 3,400 species, finding that non-native plants, many spreading from gardens, now outnumbered native ones. Changes in farming and grazing have affected heather and harebells; the draining of meadows has blitzed the devil's-bit scabious that butterflies love; the fertilising and reseeding of old grasslands have culled many arable flowers, like the corn marigold.

Tuesday 13
44. 30 3/10. E.   *Apricot in full bloom: peaches & nectarines*
Grey, sun, sweet day,   *blowing.*
red even:

Fruit trees were another passion that Gilbert and Thomas shared. Given the frosty winters, it's impressive to see how early their apricots and peaches blossom, planted against warm south-facing walls.

Wednesday 14
35. 30 3/10. E.   *Frost, ice, deep fog, hot sun, cloudless.*

Today Gilbert's weather seems to move through entirely different seasons.

The night before, William Herschel had been looking at the constellation of Gemini through his telescope, when he saw a faint, glowing object swimming slowly across the background of stars. It was, he realised, not a comet, as he first thought, but a new planet. He called it *Georgium sidus*, in honour of the King, but fellow astronomers demanded a mythological name, in line with the rest of the planetary family. From 1783, 'George's star', the seventh planet, would become Uranus.

Thursday 15
30. 30 5/10. E.　　　　　*On this day Lord Cornwallis gained a*
Frost, ice, fog, sun, grey.　　*considerable victory over Gen. Greene at*
　　　　　　　　　　　　　　Guildford [sic] in N. Carolina.

History runs alongside the journal, which records major events bluntly, as if Gilbert thinks them important to notice, but totally unrelated to immediate life. The full dispatches giving details of the Battle of Guilford Court House, when Cornwallis's troops defeated an American force of twice their number, did not arrive for weeks, but when Gilbert read the reports in the papers, he went back and added this note. After that battle, the American war seemed to swing in favour of the British, but their casualties were great, and as Cornwallis pushed further into Virginia with his weakened forces, Greene would take control of the southern states again.

Friday 16
46. 30 4/10½. NE.　　　　*Humble bee.*
Dark & harsh, sun.

The bumblebee was often called the 'humble-bee', simply because it hums and buzzes as it flies. Even the generic Latin name, *Bombus*, meaning 'booming', has a buzz.

I learn from the Bumblebee Conservation Trust that there are twenty-four species of bumblebee in Britain. Their life cycle reads like a fantasy of power and greed. Most live in colonies with a single queen,

　　　　　　A YEAR WITH GILBERT WHITE

who wakes in the spring, feeds on what flowers she can find – hazel catkins, blackthorn, brambles or the celandine – and looks for a site to nest. Some queens choose low places – under sheds or flowerpots, in compost heaps or old mouse and vole nests, or among tangles of dried grass; others prefer trees or lofts or bird boxes. The queen lays her eggs on a compacted pile of pollen and wax, sipping nectar collected in a 'pot' of wax. Then she's on the move, gathering more nectar to feed the grubs, until they are fat enough to spin cocoons, later to emerge as the first, all-female, set of worker bees. As the summer warms, the nest grows: the males are born, as are the new queens, who will feast and grow large and mate. When the old queens die, the new ones sleep through the winter in their turn, to begin this round again in the spring.

Saturday 17
40. 30 2/10½. E.   *Dust begins to be very troublesome.*
Dark, sun, pleasant.

It is hard to walk or ride. Dust and sand and grit sting the eyes and fill the nose and mouth. Every breath is a struggle.

In the city, some roads are paved with cobbles, others with large stones covered with layers of gravel; in the 1760s, Westminster obtained an Act for paving its streets with Aberdeen granite. But most roads, even in London and its suburbs, are just compacted earth, turning to mud in the rain and dust in the heat. Tradesmen come out to water the streets in the early mornings; in South Lambeth, clouds of dust, thrown up by carts and carriages, blow across gardens and fields.

Sunday 18
44. 55. 30 1/10. E, W.   *The chif-chaf, or small uncrested wren, was*
Deep fog, sun, summer.   *heard at Selborne. The first summer-bird.*

The first call of the chiffchaff is noted in Selborne, reported, perhaps, by Thomas Hoar. Gilbert waits eagerly for this little bird every year, as birders still do. In years with a run of warm days, it might arrive in late

February, but the usual time was now, mid-March. The previous year, he heard it on the same date as today:

> The uncrested wren, the smallest species, called in this place the Chif-chaf, is very loud in the Lythe. This is the earliest summer bird of passage, & the harbinger of spring. It has only two piercing notes.

The chiffchaff gave rise to one of Gilbert's discoveries. In the journal, he gives it three names: 'willow-wren', 'small uncrested wren' and 'chif-chaf'. (The *OED* notes Gilbert's work as the first written usage of the name 'chif-chaf'.) This little bird, pale brown and buff, is almost indistinguishable from two other warblers, the willow warbler and the wood warbler; today, we group his 'willow-wrens' as 'leaf warblers'. Gilbert was the first person to identify them as three different species, distinguishing them at first by their song. 'I make no doubt,' he wrote confidently to Thomas Pennant,

> but there are three species of the willow-wrens: two I know perfectly, but have not been able yet to procure the third. No two birds can differ more in their notes, and that constantly . . . for the one has a joyous, easy, laughing note; the other a harsh loud chirp.

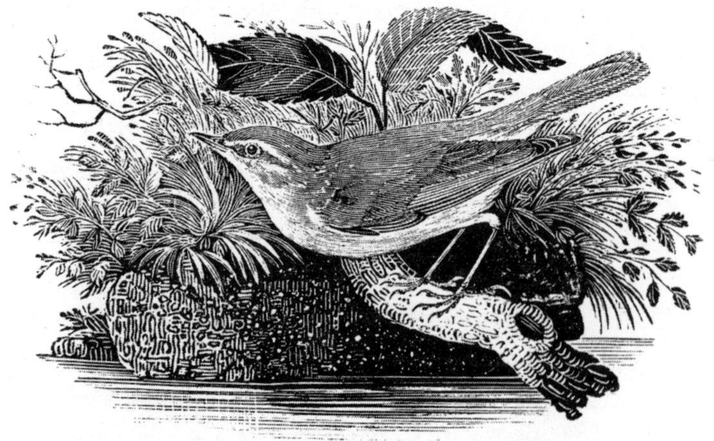

108 | 'The Willow Wren' by Thomas Bewick, in *Land Birds* (1797).

His prose effortlessly echoes the flowing, falling cadence of the willow warbler, as opposed to the chiffchaff's 'harsh loud chirp'.

Soon after writing that, he found the third species: the wood warbler, slightly larger, with brighter yellow–green colouring and feathers tipped with white. Describing his discovery, he said that he had specimens of all three 'now lying before me' and could see that the smallest, the chiffchaff, had black legs, while those of the other two were flesh-coloured. The wood warbler, he wrote, 'Haunts only the tops of trees in high beechen woods, and makes a sibilous grasshopper-like noise, now and then, at short intervals, shivering a little with its wings as it sings.' He was sure that it was the *regulus non cristatus* of Ray, 'Yet this great ornithologist never suspected there were three species.' It was a rare moment of self-congratulation.

Gilbert also noted the bird's cleverness. In one letter, he wrote: 'A further instance I once saw of notable sagacity in a willow-wren, which had built in a bank in my fields.' He and a friend had been watching the female bird on her nest,

> but were particularly careful not to disturb her, though we saw she eyed us with some degree of jealousy. Some days after as we passed that way, we were desirous of remarking how this brood went on; but no nest could be found, till I happened to take up a large bundle of long green moss, as it were, carelessly thrown over the nest in order to dodge the eye of any impertinent intruder.

'Sagacity' was a term often used in natural history for behaviour that looked as though it were governed by reason. Most writers explained this as 'instinct', a divinely inspired response to circumstance. Gilbert, however, followed Locke and Hume in seeing intelligence, as well as instinct, in birds and animals, noticing how quick they are to learn and to see what 'will turn to their own advantage'. Farmer Benham's poultry, for example, watch for wagons loaded with wheat, & running after them pick up a number of grains which are shaken from the sheaves by the agitation of the carriages. Thus when my brother used to take down his gun to shoot sparrows, his cats would run out before him to be ready to catch up the birds as they fell.

He credits animals and birds with feelings, as well as cleverness; or rather, he translates what he sees into human emotions. He mentions birds' 'tenderness' and 'complacency', as well as their anxiety and fear, and he imagines their sheer joy in singing and flying as they 'toy in the air'. They could never be 'machines' to him, as they were to Descartes.

Monday 19   *LONDON*
44. W. Wh. frost, fog, sun.

When he's in South Lambeth, Gilbert spends time in the noisy, smoky, ever-expanding city, with its new squares and mansions, its alleyways and slums, societies and clubs. He goes to Ben's bookshop in Fleet Street to talk to fellow naturalists; to the Royal Society; to the Physic Garden in Chelsea; to exhibitions like Ashton Lever's famous display of fossils, which had opened in 1775 in Leicester Square.

Tuesday 20
60. 30 2/10. W.   *Sun, sweet day.*

Wednesday 21   *SOUTH LAMBETH*
60. W. Sun, summer,
red even:

Thursday 22
60. W.   *Fair, clouds, sultry, small shower.*

In the sunny March days, Gilbert, Thomas and Ben brood together on what to do with John's natural history of Gibraltar. In the end, the project will be shelved. But they are equally concerned with the prospect of Gilbert's own book on Selborne, an idea that he had been mulling over for the past few years. His brothers played key roles in his growth as a writer. John's efforts in Gibraltar had honed him as a naturalist; Ben had introduced him to the work of Stillingfleet, and to Pennant and Barrington; Thomas had encouraged his interest in trees and gardens, and in the past.

In his desire to write about Selborne's 'few antiquities', Gilbert was following Robert Plot, whose *Natural History of Oxfordshire* (1677) had dealt with 'antiquities' in its final chapter. By the end of the 1770s, however, this interest seemed to be taking over, to the annoyance of John Mulso, who wrote bluntly: 'I fear the sweet & elegant Simplicity of your Observations will be overwhelmed by the Rubbish of the Antiquities of your Native Place.' Gilbert's antiquarian friends might admire his research, Mulso grumbled, 'but I doubt whether the Book will be the better for it in the Eye of the World'.

Gilbert was undeterred. He traced the Anglo-Saxon names and words, with Thomas and his daughter Molly providing their own definitions. (One friend, full of admiration, called Molly 'Sister Antiquary'.) While they looked up books for him in London, and a friend copied deeds in Magdalen College library, Gilbert hunted down Norman grants and medieval land holdings, consulting old deeds and manorial court rolls, and studying charters and ecclesiastical registers and documents in the Winchester diocese. A key strand was the story of Selborne's Dominican priory, established by the Bishop of Winchester in 1233, only to founder amid scandal two centuries later. In an amused letter to his nephew Sam Barker, Gilbert described the enquiry ordered in 1373 by William of Wykeham, Bishop of Winchester, which condemned the monks as 'mighty hunters', keen on 'junketings and feastings', letting '*suspectae*' (dubious women) in after dark, neglecting buildings, pawning plate and 'lying naked in bed without their breeches, for which they are much reprimanded'.

When the Priory was finally dissolved in 1484, the then bishop, William of Waynflete, took it over with all its lands in order to supplement the income of Magdalen College, Oxford, which he had founded a quarter of a century earlier. The college thus became Selborne's lord of the manor.

Friday 23
44. 30 3/10. E.　　　　　*Sun, cold air.*

When he wrote of the lax monastic rule, Gilbert quoted the fourteenth-century *Vision of Piers Plowman*, 'one of the keenest pieces of satire now perhaps subsisting in any language, ancient or modern':

> Now is religion, a rider, a romer by streate;
> A leader of love-days, and a loud beggar;
> A pricker on a palfrey from maner to maner,
> A heape of hounds at his arse, as he a lord were . . .
> . . . Of the poor they have no pity, and that is her charitie;
> And they letten hem as lords, her lands lie so broad.

Thomas was also fascinated by *Piers Plowman*. Since the mid-century, interest had grown in early writers, with the publication of books like Elizabeth Cooper's *The Muses Library: or, a Series of English Poetry, from the Saxons to the Reign of King Charles II*, which included accounts of Langland, Gower and Chaucer, and Thomas Percy's *Reliques of Ancient English Poetry* (1765). The White brothers' interest was fuelled by the first two volumes of Tom Warton's *History of English Poetry*, which appeared in 1774 and 1778. For the last decade or more, Warton had been writing this history in a wandering, back-and-forth, mistake-strewn but brilliantly pioneering fashion. No one before him had tried to organise English poetry into some form of sequence: his first volume, beginning after the Norman conquest, dealt with the Middle English authors, especially Langland and Chaucer, while the second roved broadly through the thirteenth and fourteenth centuries.

Increasingly, however, as he thought of Selborne's antiquities, Gilbert looked back to earlier eras that Warton had ignored, tracing how the life of Saxons, and the Celts before them, was inscribed in the landscape of Selborne itself; Edith – or 'Editha', as Gilbert calls her – the wife of Edward the Confessor, had at one point been lady of the manor. He made lists of local names of villages, fields and families, and of local terms, pondering their derivation: the pastures of the Lythe, from '*Hlive*'; 'ether', the wickerwork that fastens a hedge, from 'ether, an hedge'; the brushwood 'called *rise*, from *hris*, frondes'. 'When the good women call their hogs,' he wrote, 'they cry *sic*, *sic*, not knowing that *sic* is Saxon or rather Celtic, for a hog.' Selborne itself, he was sure, came from *sell*, meaning 'great', and *burn*, a brook; in his letters and journal he often calls it by one of its variant names, 'Seleburne'.

Saturday 24

35. 30 5/10. E, W.   *The dust on the roads is become a terrible*
Cold fog, sun, summer.   *nuisance. Apricots begin to set.*

The nights are still cold, with frost at times, but at midday the sun is hot, and although the apricots thrive in Lambeth gardens, many plants thirst and droop. Writing to Sam, Gilbert moans that 'the degree of dustiness is horrible, and not to be described'. As he and Thomas walked out that morning, a northerly gale had risen, filling the air with 'such a cloud from road to road' that they could hardly see ahead.

Sunday 25

30 4/10. E, S.   *Plants languish for want of rain.*
Wh. frost, hot sun.   *First radishes.*

They pick radishes, one of the easiest, earliest vegetables. Back home in Selborne, Gilbert often planted them in late January, then in successive plantings throughout the spring. Many years before, in 1752, early in their gardening careers, he and his brother Thomas had tried companion planting, not for the sake of the radishes, but for the flowers: 'Mem.

Sowed Radishes with the Stocks as Miller directs'. Stocks were favourite flowers in country gardens, with their sweet scent and jewelled colours, but in his *Gardeners Dictionary*, Philip Miller had pointed out that if they were planted in a sunny place, they were 'very subject to be eaten by a sort of fly' (presumably aphids). The remedy was to sow radishes between them, which the aphids would go to first, but they should not be sown too thickly, since that would crowd out the stocks and make them leggy and spindly.

The stocks had come from Thomas's garden in London, and the note was in his writing. That spring, he and Gilbert had worked together in The Wakes' garden. They had been busy: 'planted, shaded and watered the Laurestinus near the Bench in the Field & the Passion flower on each side the Street door', Thomas had written. They had planted cucumbers under hand-glasses (a bell-shaped glass, used like a cloche) and more in the hotbed; they had moved maize from pots into beds on Baker's Hill. Comparing batches of the seeds from the previous year, Thomas had noted their source as carefully as Gilbert would have done: 'Sow'd three Rows of French Beans in the Field gardn, first Row from the Tub in the Barn second from the paper bag in the Kitchen third from the Chaise.'

Monday 26
29 9/10. W, N.   *Sun, clouds, harsh wind.*

The transformation of the garden at The Wakes was an aesthetic as well as horticultural project. When Gilbert was proctor at Oxford, he and Thomas went round the Physic Garden (now the Oxford Botanic Garden), and Gilbert took Ben, with his future wife Anne Yalden and her brother Will, to see the gardens at Blenheim and Stowe. Both these estates demonstrated the change of taste from the formal spaces and topiary of Tudor and Stuart days to a new style, softening the boundary between tame and wild. In an influential *Spectator* essay of 1712, Joseph Addison had insisted, for example, that he would rather see a tree in its natural shape than one 'cut into a Mathematical Figure', and that he

          A YEAR WITH GILBERT WHITE

preferred an orchard in bloom to 'all the little labyrinths of the most finished parterre'. The grandest gardens were slow to change. Stowe had been a political, Whig landscape, with its classical 'Temple of Ancient Virtue' matched by a 'Temple of British Worthies', displaying statues of Elizabeth I, Drake, William III, Milton and Newton. Then, after 1741, when the young Lancelot 'Capability' Brown became head gardener, the landscape softened, with a lake, clumps of trees and wandering paths.

The Wakes' garden became a playful echo of such grandeur, mixing Virgilian groves with fashionable Gothic and 'picturesque' details. This blended style was very much in fashion in the 1750s and '60s, as the frontispiece to John Hill's *Eden: or, a Compleat Body of Gardening* suggests, with its classical goddesses, urns and obelisks, although much of the content is firmly practical. One of the first things Gilbert did in 1751, before his year as proctor in Oxford, was to plant five spruce trees in a 'quincunx' on Baker's Hill, a small copse arranged like the numbers on a domino or playing card. He linked the garden to the countryside, making gaps in the hedgerows and creating vistas. In 1752, his brother John began digging the 'Zig-Zag' path up the Hanger. Two years later, in a grand, if bizarre, gesture, Gilbert put six farm gates in perspective across the meadows, a nod to classical arches. His friend John Mulso was impressed, if baffled. After mulling this over, he wrote:

> We have not reformed our Ideas of your six Gates, which we conceive to be pretty but to sound oddly in Description: We take them to belong to Fields which thro' an Opening are seen in Perspective, One above Another, yet not so as to join; & the Image itself is not ridiculous in our Minds, but new to our Observations.

Gilbert kept adding things throughout the 1750s. To create vistas, he placed oil jars on pedestals, nine feet high, like classical urns. Then he put up a wooden, painted figure of Hercules, peering out from the trees a few yards into the Hanger. It sounds comical, but visitors would know the allusions: to Hercules' unresting labours, appropriate for a

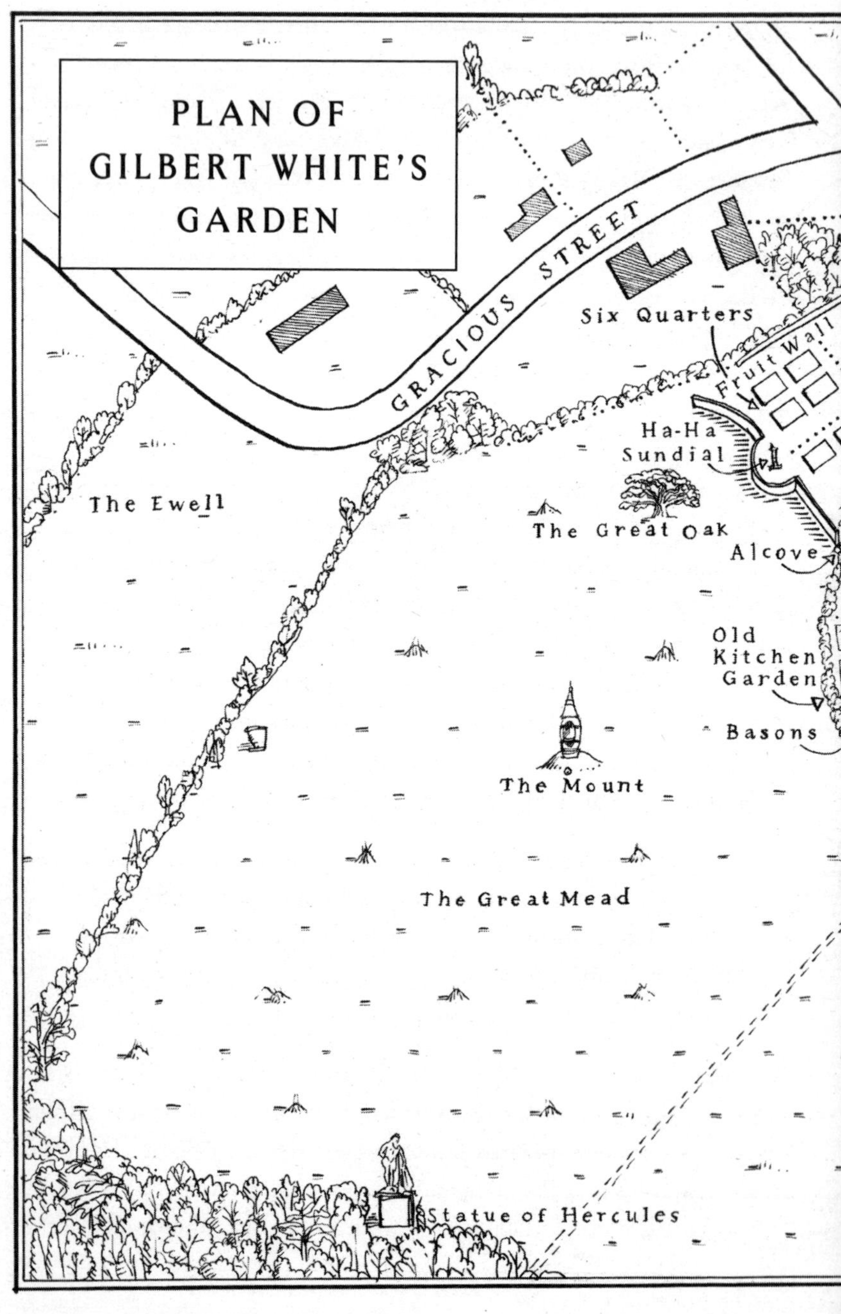

PLAN OF GILBERT WHITE'S GARDEN
GRACIOUS STREET
Six Quarters
Fruit Wall
Ha-Ha
Sundial
The Ewell
The Great Oak
Alcove
Old Kitchen Garden
Basons
The Mount
The Great Mead
Statue of Hercules

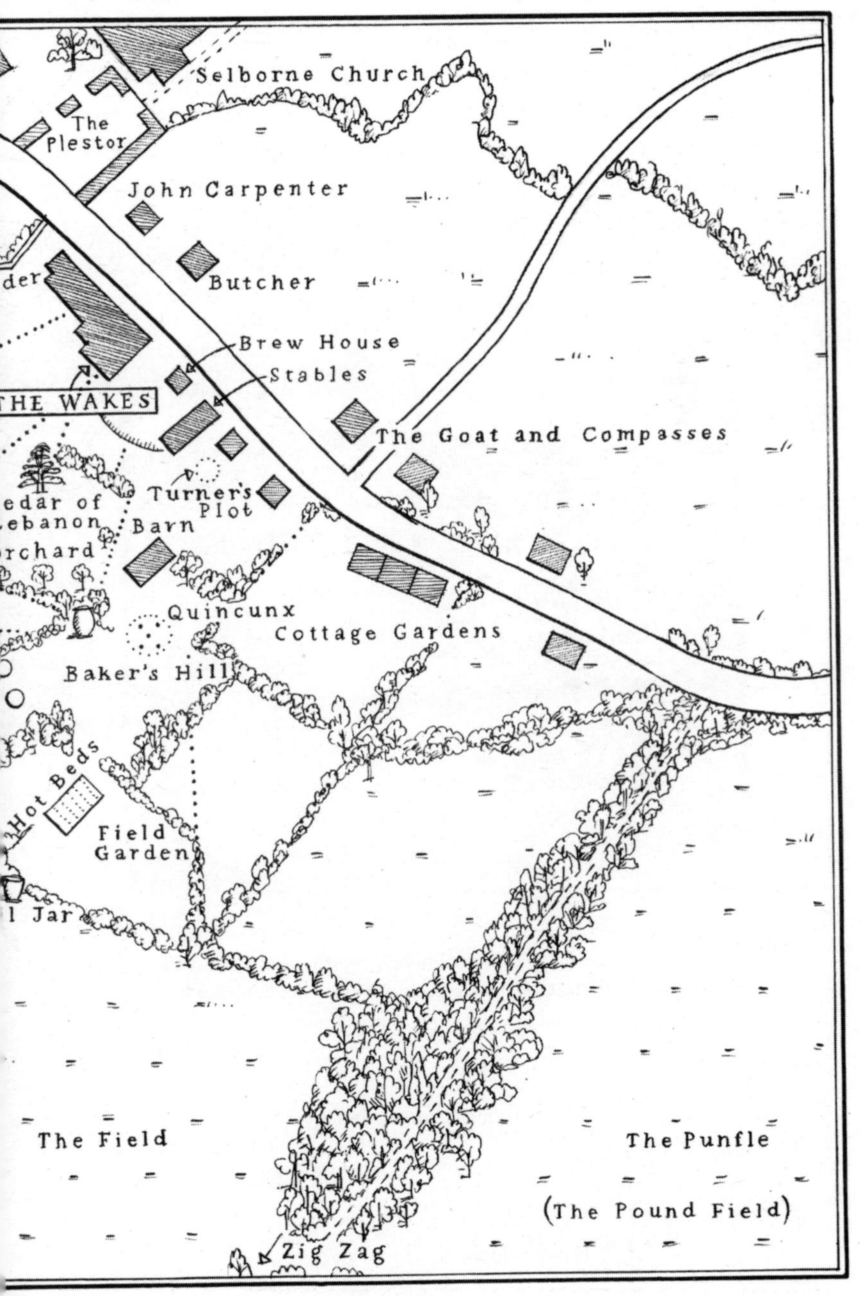

Selborne Church
The Plestor
John Carpenter
Butcher
Brew House
Stables
THE WAKES
The Goat and Compasses
Turner's Plot
Barn
Cedar of Lebanon
Orchard
Quincunx
Cottage Gardens
Baker's Hill
Hot Beds
Field Garden
Jar
The Field
The Punfle
(The Pound Field)
Zig Zag

garden; to his quest to win the golden apple of the Hesperides, a regaining of Eden; to a crossroads in life, 'the Choice of Hercules', between virtue and pleasure – a common contemporary theme.

Another feature was a low mount in the middle of the meadow, with a revolving seat on top made from an old port barrel, so you could see the garden from different perspectives. And once Hercules was in place, Gilbert set up his own obelisk and built a 'hermitage' at the top of the Zig-Zag – a place for feasts and fun.

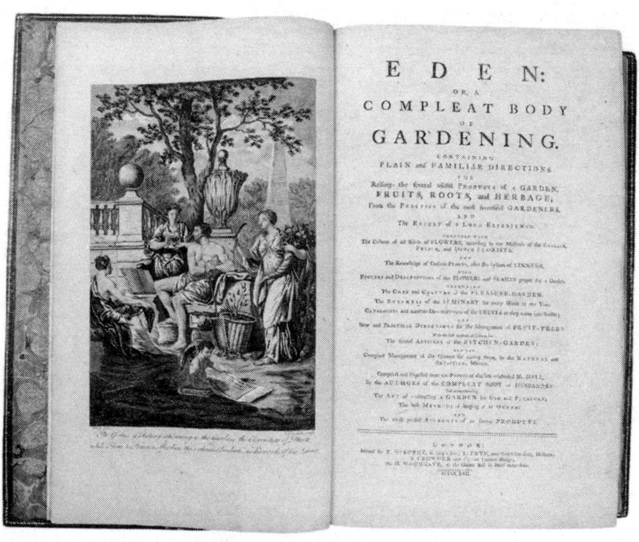

The frontispiece to John Hill's *Eden: or, a Compleat Body of Gardening* (1757). The caption runs: 'The Genius of Botany explaining to the Gardner the Characters of Plants, while Flora and Pomona offer him their choicest Products as rewards of his Labour.'

Tuesday 27

30. 34. N.　　　　　　　*Sun, & clouds, harsh.*

Wednesday 28

34. 29 9/10. NE.　　　　　*Sun, ice, harsh, sleet.*

　　　　　　　　　A YEAR WITH GILBERT WHITE

The last major garden work was the building of the ha-ha in 1761, the ditch designed to both ambush and surprise visitors – hence the cry 'ha-ha!' – which let Gilbert look across to the meadow and the woods, with no wall to break the view. When it was finished, he thought it 'an excellent fence against the mead, & so well fast'ned into the clay bank, that it looks likely to stand a long while'. The ha-ha is still there today.

Once the terrace was levelled and grassed, he put up a sundial of Portland stone, with a brass plate, and built his alcove near the ha-ha – a place to watch the birds. Finally, he moved his cauliflowers and beans, lettuces and radishes and fruit bushes from the old vegetable beds to 'six quarters', large plots on the level ground above the ha-ha, where they were easy to water and plant, and where he could wander admiringly between the beds.

Thursday 29	*ALTON*
NE. *Ice, sun & harsh*	*Young goslings.*
wind.	*Young thrushes.*
Friday 30	*SELBORNE*
29 6/10½. NE.	*Apricots, peaches, & nectarines are well blown.*
Ice, sun & harsh wind.	

With his back to the cold north-easterly wind, Gilbert makes his way home, stopping in Alton again. When he reaches Selborne, all the early-blossoming fruit trees are in full bloom, despite the frost. Some had been planted twenty years before, when he built his fruit wall. Long, the builder, had constructed this when he worked on the ha-ha, and when it was nearly finished, Gilbert rootled around the site of the old Priory to find 'stones of a sandy nature' to use as coping at each end and got Long to insert a plaque among the bricks, saying simply: 'G. W. 1761'.

Gilbert's first planting along the fruit wall, however, had had to wait: the soil, he said, 'lay in great Clods as hard as stones, being so much trod by the masons, & hardened by a hot, sunny Summer'. Once the rain had softened the ground, he enriched it with three coats of loam and dressed it with sand and ashes. He already had vines from the Snookes' garden at Ringmer, and by late autumn – the best time for bare-root planting – he was cursing with impatience. Due to the 'negligence of Murdoch Middleton', the nurseryman, his fruit trees did not arrive until late December. Finally, in the last week of 1761, he was able to finish the task. He planted the trees and vines in this order, from the ha-ha towards the house:

Breda Apricot; Sweet-water vine; Roman Nectar: Mr. Snooke's black-cluster vine: Roman Nect.: white Muscadine vine: Newington Nectar: Mur. Middleton's Sweet-water vine: Nobless peach: Mr Sn: white Muscadine; Nobless peach: John Hale's 2 Passion flowers, one at each end of the wall.

Gilbert's apricots and peaches can be seen in the plates in some early-nineteenth-century books, such as George Brookshaw's *Pomona Britannica; or a Collection of the Most Esteemed Fruits* (1804–12) or *Pomona Londinensis* (1813–18) by William Hooker, draftsman for the Horticultural Society. The Noblesse peach, an old, very popular variety, is in both books, and so is the Roman nectarine. They sound delicious. And although they may not appear in modern catalogues, survivals appear under new names: Gilbert's Breda apricot is the *Prunus armeniaca* 'Bredase', with early pale-pink flowers and dark orange fruit, while a descendant of his 'Sweet-water vine' appears as 'Buckland Sweetwater', with pale-green grapes turning yellow as they ripen.

Saturday 31

43. 29 7/10. NE.   *Cucumber-plants show fruit; but are rather*
Dark, sun, & harsh   *drawn, from the long dry season, which never*
wind, hail & rain.   *is favourable to hot-beds.*

After the cold drought, Gilbert eyes his cucumbers forlornly. Out goes March, not like a lamb, but like a roaring lion, in hail and rain and wind.

APRIL

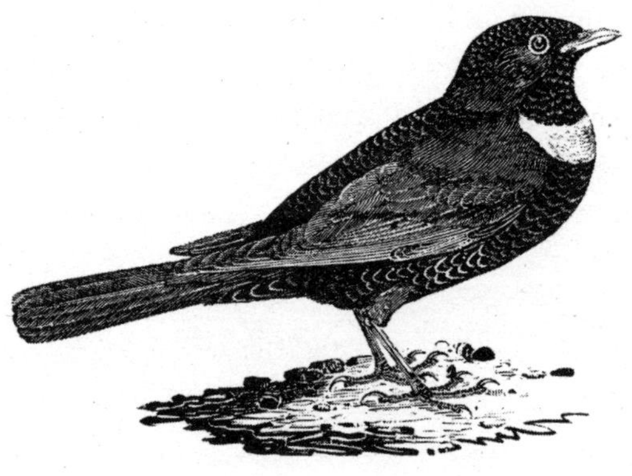

'The Ring Ouzel' by Thomas Bewick, in *Land Birds* (1797).

M IGRATION IS ONE of the great themes of *The Natural History of Selborne*, one of the subjects Gilbert felt most uncertain about, argued about and worried about. He describes all migratory birds as 'birds of passage', although now we use the term only for birds passing through, stopping on their journey from south to north, north to south. The excitement he feels when he sees the summer birds arrive is intense, as keen as his exhilaration in the late 1760s, when he made the first entries in his *Naturalist's Journal*, tingled by the thought of James Cook and Joseph Banks circling the globe, and wrote his first letters to Pennant and Barrington – early steps towards the book he might write, one day.

Sunday 1
49. 29 3/10¾. E, SE. 19.   *The tortoise came-out for two hours.*
Sun, pleasant day.   *Cucumber-fruit blows.*

Here comes Timothy, testing the air. The previous autumn, Gilbert had found the perfect place for him, or so he thought:

> 14 November 1780: Timothy lies in the border under the fruit-
> wall, in an aspect where he will enjoy the warmth of the sun, &
> where no wet can annoy him: a hen-coop over his back protects
> him from dogs, &c.

Four days later, he adds a comment:

> The severity of the weather quickened Timothy's retreat: he used
> to stay above ground 'til about the 20th. At Ringmer he used to lay
> himself up in a wet swampy border: indeed he had no choice.

While Timothy explores, the cucumbers are doing better, their yellow flowers opening. Gilbert had recorded their growth for the past twenty years. Thus, on 7 April 1762: 'The forwardest Cucumber about as big as the top of one's finger. The plants now grow away.' Two weeks later, on the 26th: 'Cut the first Cucumber. There are plenty coming on.' This year, there will be plenty, too.

Poor Timothy is weighed when he appears, and is a little fatter than when he arrived last year. Every ounce matters. On he goes, chomping at what greens he can find.

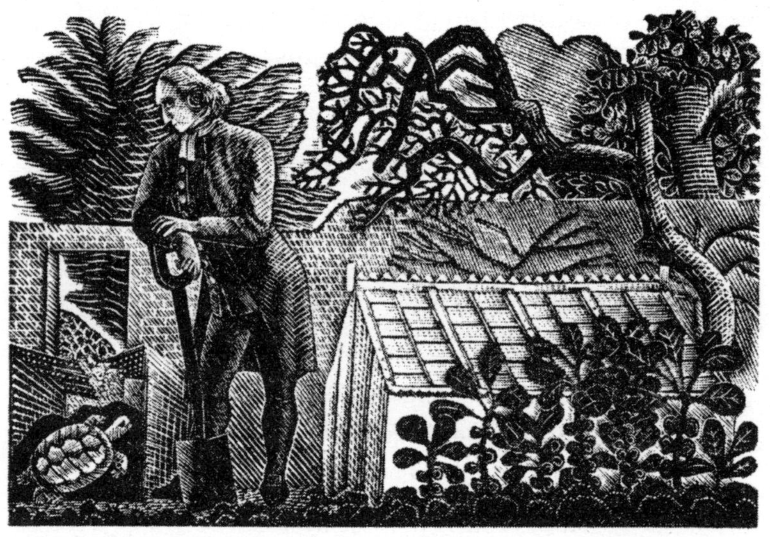

Gilbert White in his garden, with Timothy in the corner, by Eric Ravilious, who illustrated the 1938 Nonesuch Press edition of *The Writings of Gilbert White*. In January 1936, he told a friend: 'The History of Selborne is a grand book and I read it every minute I can spare from engraving and other jobs.'

 A YEAR WITH GILBERT WHITE

The sound of the wryneck cheers him. It's about the same size as a sparrow but mottled and speckled, with a dark band running back from the eyes. He watches it catch beetles, moths and flies and pick up ants with its sticky tongue, and he listens to its sharp, stuttering call. If threatened, it hisses loudly, twisting its head round so far that its beak points over its back – hence the name.

Across southern England, wrynecks often arrived at the same time as the cuckoo, so that people called them 'cuckoo's mate' or 'cuckoo's messenger'. Today, they haven't bred in the UK for the past twenty years, but they still stop here as birds of passage, heading for Scandinavia in the spring, and in the autumn, back to Africa again.

Gilbert looks up to the birds, down to the insects. When the bumble-bee appears, so does its mimic. 'The *Bombylius medius* abounds,' Gilbert had written in early April 1776.

It is an hairy insect like an humble-bee but with only two wings, & a long straight beak, with which it sucks the early flowers, always appearing in March. The female seems to lay it's eggs, as it poises on it's wings, by striking it's tail on the ground, & against the grass that stands in it's way in a quick manner for several times together.

He must have been kneeling down or lying flat on the grass to see this so closely. But he is puzzled: is the fly laying eggs or merely seeming to, 'as if in the act of'?

Wednesday 4
46. 29 2/10. NE.   *Grass lamb. Young ducks are hatched.*
Dark, harsh wind.   *Swallow appears.*

'Grass lamb' and 'house lamb' are old terms, the latter for lambs born and fed in a barn. By now, grass lamb is for sale at the butcher's across the way: roast lamb for Easter. Prices rarely appear in the journal, but on 12 April 1783, Gilbert will note: 'Grass-lamb six pence pr pound: veal 5d. Fresh butter 9½d.'

The first ducklings break through their shells and scuttle to the water in straggling lines. But today's significant note is 'Swallow appears.' He looks out for them year after year, celebrating their arrival with an explosion of exclamation marks: *Hirundo domestica!!!*

Following Ray and Willughby, and after them, Linnaeus, Gilbert grouped the swallows, house martins, sand martins and swifts together as 'hirundines'. In modern classification, the swallows and martins still appear under the umbrella of Hirundinidae, but not the swifts. Nineteenth-century ornithologists realised that swifts belong, with hummingbirds, to the order of Apodiformes, although they are different families. The name comes from the Greek word meaning 'footless', because of their short legs; in heraldry and in medieval manuscripts swifts sometimes have no feet at all.

These birds were faithful to the village, neighbourly, 'useful' as well as beautiful:

> The hirundines are a most inoffensive, harmless, entertaining, social, and useful tribe of birds; they touch no fruit in our gardens; delight, all except one species, in attaching themselves to our houses; amuse us with their migrations, songs, and marvellous agility; and clear our outlets from the annoyances of gnats and other troublesome insects.

Every year, as he welcomed them, he wondered where they had been all winter. The previous generation of naturalists, including Ray, had plumped for migration, imagining the birds seeking winter quarters in warmer lands. But because swallows remained in Britain so late, often seen in early November, opinion swung round to the idea that they stayed here, hibernating in a 'torpid state' in caves and crannies, or perhaps underground. Some writers even thought that they might spend the winter in ponds or lakes. When Gilbert was staying at Sunbury with John Mulso one autumn, he watched swallows gather in the reed beds by the Thames and pondered, briefly, if this might support the idea 'of their retiring under water'. Linnaeus had suggested this, and so had Alexander Berger, whose calendar Gilbert read in Stillingfleet's *Tracts*:

> A Swedish naturalist is so much persuaded of that fact, that he talks, in his calendar of *Flora*, as familiarly of the swallows going under water in the beginning of September, as he would of his poultry going to roost a little before sunset.

Gilbert never accepted this particular idea. 'We must not, I think, deny migration in general,' he urged Barrington, 'because migration certainly does subsist in some places, as my brother in Andalusia has fully informed me.' One of Barrington's objections was the need to cross great oceans, but John White had told Gilbert of vast migrations of different birds, sweeping across to Africa. Flying over the Channel, across France and Spain, and then over the Straits of Gibraltar, 'a bird may travel from England to the equator', Gilbert wrote, 'without launching out and exposing itself to boundless seas'.

All the same, he dithered over whether his hirundines migrated or stayed in some secret place over winter. One Michaelmas Day, he told Pennant, he came closest to seeing 'anything like actual migration'. In early-morning fog, on a high common near the coast, he saw swallows roosting on the stunted bushes, but as soon as the mist lifted, 'they were all on the wing at once; and, by a placid and easy flight, proceeded on southward towards the sea'. This led him to express his own uncertainty. Seeing swallows and martins on cottage roofs, he said,

> I could not help being touched with a secret delight, mixed with some degree of mortification: with delight, to observe with how much ardour and punctuality those poor little birds obeyed the strong impulse towards migration, or hiding, imprinted on their minds by their great Creator; and with some degree of mortification, when I reflected that, after all our pains and inquiries, we are yet not

quite certain to what regions they do migrate; and are still further embarrassed to find that some do not actually migrate at all.

Thursday 5
28 9/10¾. E, SE.   *Searched the S.E. end of the hanger for house-*
Dark & still, clouds,   *martins, but without any success, tho' many*
small rain.   *young men assisted. They examined the beechen-*
      shrubs, & holes in the steep hanger.

In this spring of 1781, the village turns out to help him in his quest for 'torpid' birds; he wants to prove things, one way or the other. The previous October, he had watched a large flock of about 150 martins, who spent days 'in the sheltered district between me and the Hanger, sailing about in a placid, easy manner, and feasting on those insects which love to haunt a spot so secure from ruffling winds'. Hoping, if possible, to find their winter roosting place, he noticed that 'for several evenings together, just at a quarter past five in the afternoon, they all scudded away in great haste towards the south-east, and darted down among the low shrubs above the cottages at the end of the hill'. This seemed a perfect spot to hibernate, the ground being steep as a roof and free from floods, and covered in beech scrub so thick that not even the smallest spaniel could get in.

Now spring has come, and although that scrubby land does not belong to him, he sets about his search for the birds' 'secret dormitories' at the end of the hill, 'where I imagined they might slumber out the uncomfortable months of winter'. The hunt will take a week.

Friday 6
29 2/10. SW, W. 15.   *Swallow at Newton*
Dark, showers, hail,   *Wheat looks well on the strong land.*
bright & chill.

Until the mid-1760s, Gilbert had seen himself as a solitary researcher, eager to exchange ideas but lacking vital contacts. This was solved in

 A YEAR WITH GILBERT WHITE

1767, when his brother Ben took over the publishing of Thomas Pennant's *British Zoology*. The first edition, a large, expensively illustrated folio published the previous year, was well received but did not sell as well as Pennant hoped, so Ben persuaded him to produce an expanded second edition, which could be published in three volumes in a smaller format, making it cheaper and more appealing. Preparing to revise his book, Pennant sent out questionnaires, collecting information wherever he could. Ben told him of Gilbert's work – perhaps they even met in the bookshop – and when Gilbert wrote to him tentatively, Pennant snapped up the offer of help.

Six years Gilbert's junior, smooth-faced, bumptious, tetchy and determined, Pennant came from old Flintshire gentry and had been a dedicated naturalist, so he said, ever since he was given Willughby's *Ornithology* when he was twelve. From 1750 onwards, he published articles in the Royal Society's *Transactions* on earthquakes in Wales, tortoises, penguins and corals, went fossil hunting and mineral collecting, toured Europe and corresponded with experts, including Linnaeus and Buffon. In 1767, he was elected a fellow of the Royal Society. But while he was skilled at compiling information, he had none of Gilbert's experience in the field and welcomed his insights. Gilbert was delighted, explaining how isolated he had felt:

> It has been my misfortune never to have had any neighbours whose
> studies have led them towards the pursuit of natural knowledge:
> so that, for want of a companion to quicken my industry and
> sharpen my attention, I have made but slender progress in a kind of
> information to which I have been attached from my childhood.

Over the next few years, from their first exchange in early August 1767, Gilbert's letters dashed from subject to subject, rich with detail, spiky with queries, and all immensely useful to Pennant. In 1773, Gilbert wrote with some amusement to his brother John:

I have received a most violent complimenting letter from Mr.
Pennant lately. He is going to publish a second edition of 'Brit Zool.'
and is to do wonders with the information extracted from my letters.
I shall take the opportunity of laying before him the more glaring
faults in the first edition.

He didn't hold back, sending corrections, anecdotes and suggestions,
apologising if these had 'a quaint and magisterial air'.

It was hard to keep up while Pennant brought out new editions,
with extra material on reptiles, fishes and molluscs. At the same time,
with unstoppable energy, he began an extremely successful series, *Tours*
of Scotland, England and Wales, and the Continent, while also moving on to Indian and Arctic zoology. Ben White found him hard going:
he and Pennant, Gilbert told John, 'always quarrel and squabble by
letter, but accord well when they meet'. It's not surprising Ben made
up with Pennant: he was a prolific book-buyer as well as a profitable
author. Indeed, Ben's son Benjamin would still be working with him
in the 1790s.

Gilbert hoped that Pennant might visit him in Selborne, but this
didn't happen. And when Pennant invited Gilbert to Flintshire, he had
declined, pleading lack of time and coach-sickness. He could manage
trips to Ringmer, Oxford and London, but not 200 miles to North
Wales. The very thought of the young Joseph Banks (whom he met in
London in 1767, and to whom he wrote personally) setting off with
James Cook on his voyage to the South Pacific in 1768 filled him
with alarm. Two years before, aged twenty-three, Banks had joined
an expedition to Newfoundland and Labrador, publishing the first
Linnaean description of the region's plants and animals. Elected to
the Royal Society, he was then invited to join Cook on the *Endeavour*.
Writing to Pennant, Gilbert admitted how odd he felt when he read
of Banks 'bound for the South Seas'. He was full of admiration for his
contempt for danger, but also concerned:

If he survives, with what delight shall we peruse his Journals, his Fauna, his Flora! If he falls by the way, I shall revere his fortitude, and contempt of pleasures, and indulgences: but shall always regret him, though my knowledge of his worth was of late date, and my acquaintanceship with him but slender.

Saturday 7
47½. 29 1/10. S. 15.   *Dark & moist, rain, rain.*

Gilbert found his second major correspondent, Daines Barrington, through Pennant, and also through his brother Ben, who had taken over the publishing of Barrington's *Naturalist's Journal*. In his Preface to the *Journal*, Barrington suggested that under 'Miscellaneous Observations', the user might note the effect of the weather on the flowering of plants and the behaviour of animals, relating these to measurements from instruments. If people across the country kept this up over time, 'perhaps the very best and accurate materials for a General Natural History of Britain may in time be expected, as well as many profitable improvements and discoveries in agriculture'. This was an aim that Gilbert – even though he thought it unrealistic – thoroughly approved of.

Gilbert met Barrington in London in May 1768, and again the following summer. If Pennant could be seen as a professional, making a career out of natural history and travel writing, Barrington was an amateur. A viscount's son, he was a judge, a naturalist and an antiquary, writing articles of rather dubious accuracy on topics from card-playing to Caesar's alleged crossing of the Thames and the history of archery. He could be awarded 'the leaden mace of the Antiquarian Society', thought Horace Walpole. 'He is not one of our plodders; rather the other extreme. His corporal spirits (for I cannot call them animal) do not allow him time to digest any thing. He gave a round jump from ornithology to antiquity; and, as if they had any relation, thought he understood every thing between them.'

Barrington loved playing with theories, determined, he said, to replace superstition with 'facts' based on rational enquiry, although quick to damn any arguments that disagreed with his own. He sprayed ideas around like fireworks, many of them, as has been pointed out, extravagantly ludicrous, like his conviction that Greek and Roman information on natural history was lacking because their dress 'prevented them being so much in the field as we are', or that fossils were produced accidentally by burrowing insects. Yet he was also energetic and thought-provoking. In early summer 1769, Gilbert responded eagerly to his requests for information on the arrival and departure of birds of passage, and on the times at which birds sang. Barrington was particularly interested in birds' songs, puzzling whether these were inherited or learned through imitation, something that he tried to investigate in his own collection of caged birds. Bizarrely, he claimed that Londoners who kept birds were likely to know more about birdsong than country people, who heard them 'only two months a year', when they were mating. Gilbert disputed this, sending lists of the birds that sang until midsummer and others that continued all year.

In Pennant and Barrington, Gilbert had two correspondents eager to hear about his observations and ideas. He had to be careful, though, to tailor his account to their personalities, interests and views. They disagreed, for example, about migration. While Pennant largely accepted the idea, Barrington vehemently opposed it. Even when pressed by Gilbert, he stuck to his belief that at least some stragglers stayed behind, and published a long essay arguing the point in the Royal Society's *Transactions* in 1772.

Sunday 8
50. 29 3/10. W, S. 46.   *Ivy berries are black & full ripe.*
Sun, brisk air, rain,   *Full moon.*
rain.

Before ivy berries split and fall, they look as rich as blackcurrants. The birds pounce on them: a blackbird can strip a wall in minutes. On this

        A YEAR WITH GILBERT WHITE

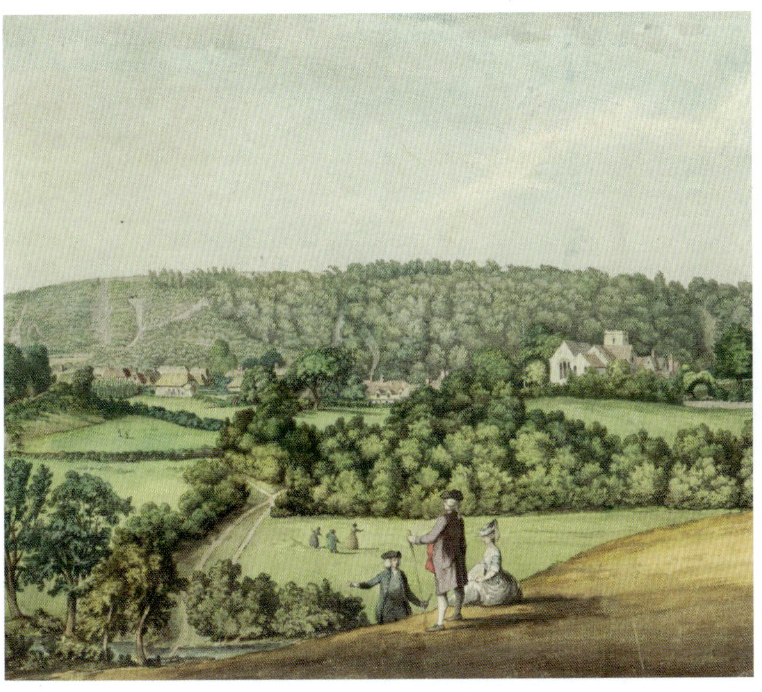

Detail from *Selborne from the Short Lythe*, one of the series of watercolours that Gilbert commissioned from the artist Hieronymus Grimm in 1776, hoping to have them engraved in his book. Looking across Dorton valley to The Wakes – Gilbert's house – and the Hanger behind.

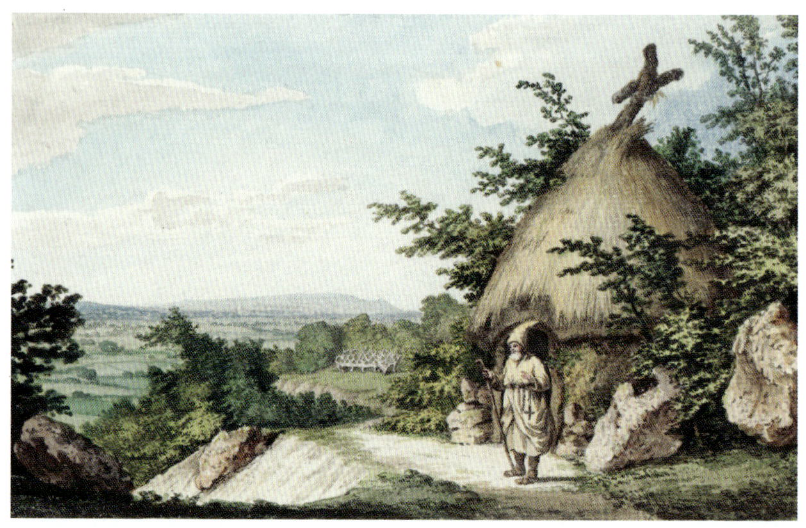

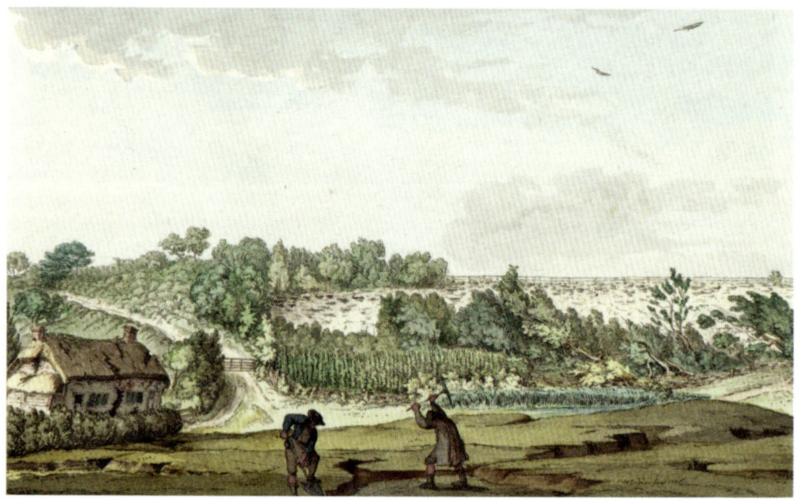

Four more watercolours by Hieronymus Grimm, painted in 1776.

ABOVE *The Hermitage*. The hermit is Gilbert's brother Harry, dressed up for the show.

BELOW *Hawkley After the Earthquake*, showing a tumble-down cottage, fallen trees and the great cracks left in the ground.

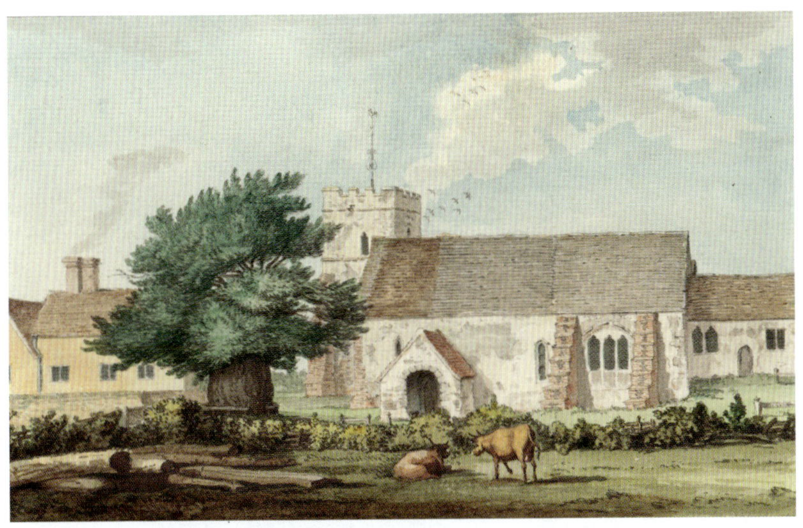

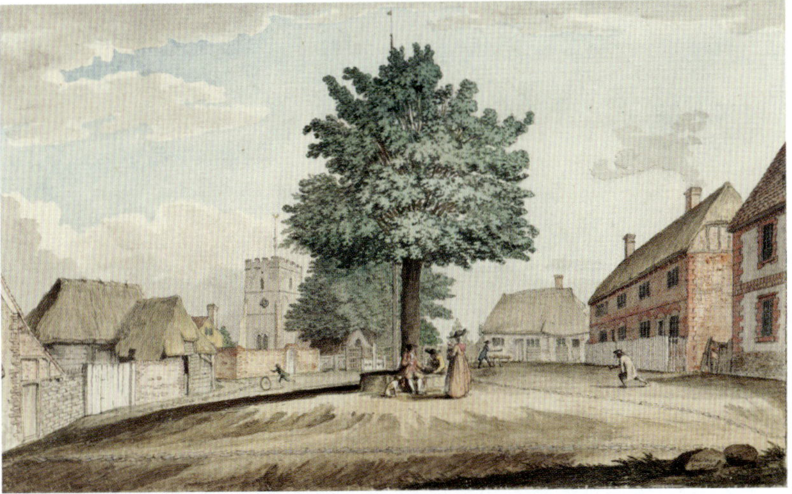

ABOVE Selborne church, seen from the south with the yew tree and the bench for churchgoers. Behind, on the left, is the Tudor vicarage where Gilbert was born.

BELOW In Grimm's scene of the Plestor, neighbours gossip under the sycamore, while children play in the open space. The top of the maypole, with its wind vane, appears above the tree.

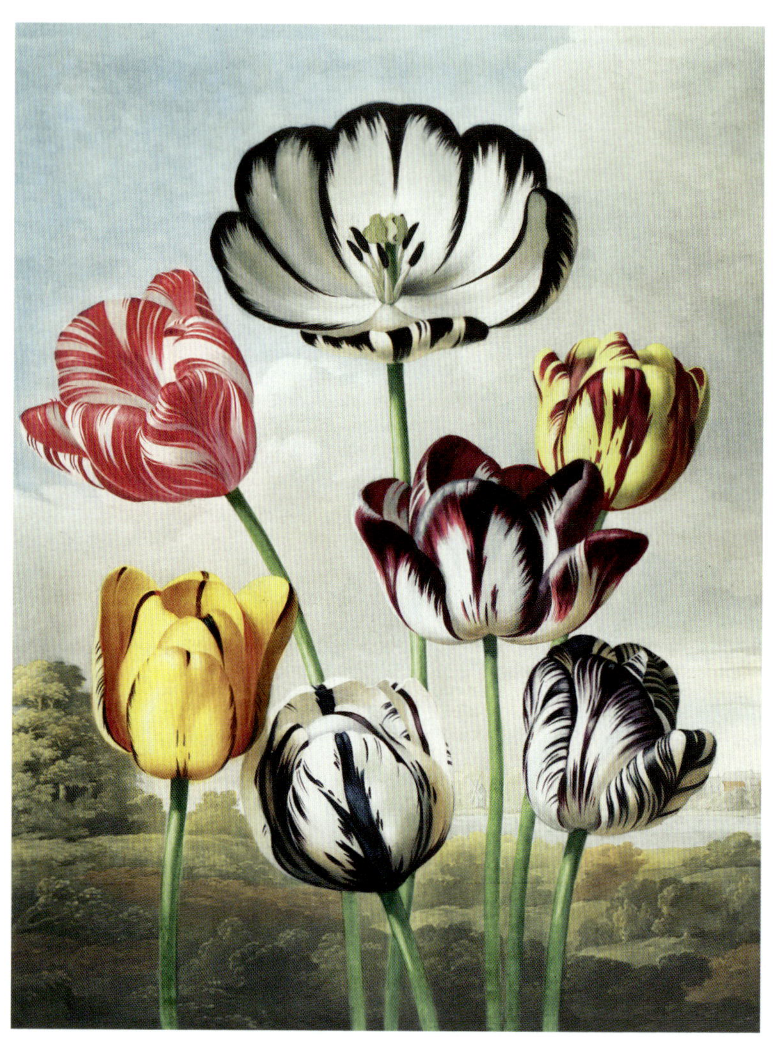

'Tulips' by Philip Reinagle, from John Thornton's *The Temple of Flora* (1797).

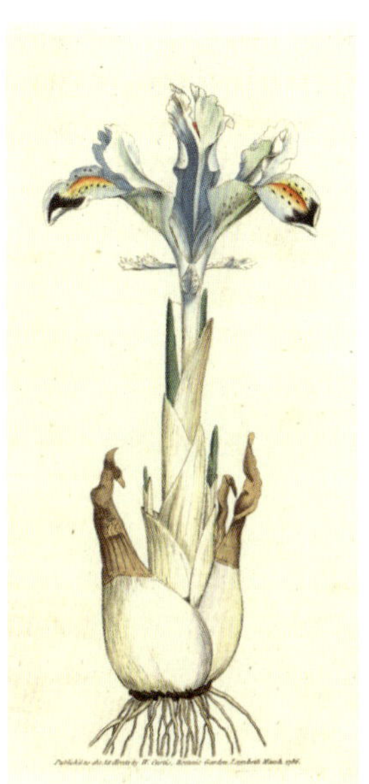

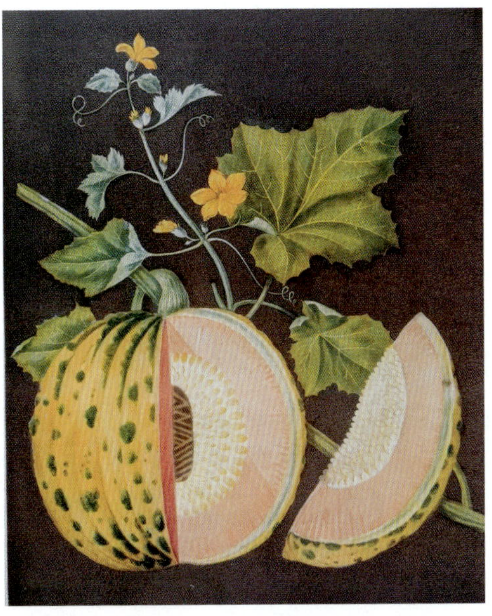

'Persian Iris' by James Sowerby, from Curtis's *Botanical Magazine, or the Flower Garden Displayed* (1787).

'Canteloupe' by George Brookshaw, from his book *Pomona Britannica* (1812).

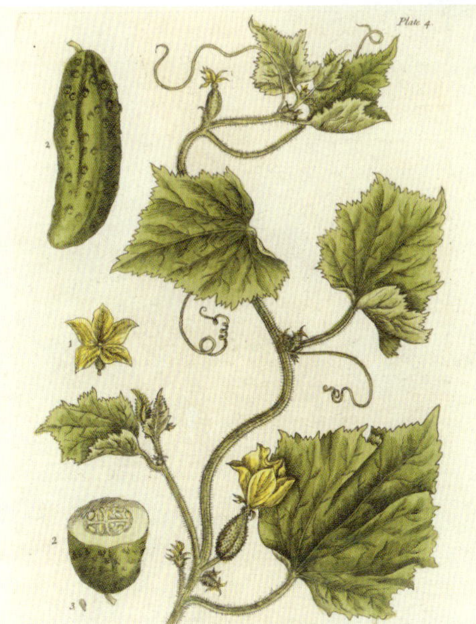

'Garden Cucumber', from Elizabeth Blackwell's *A Curious Herbal*, issued in weekly parts from 1837 to 1839.

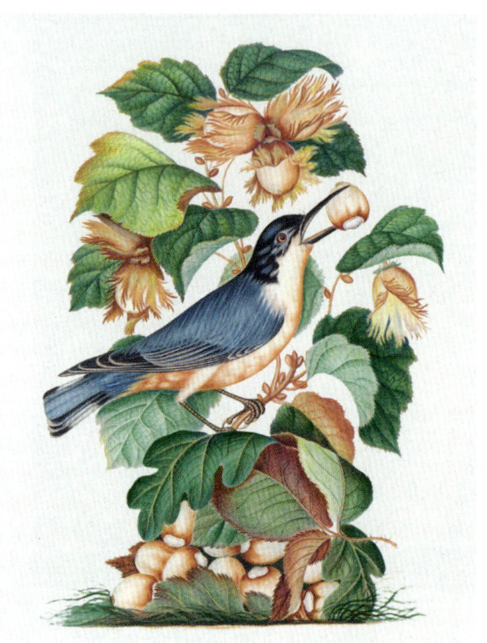

'Nuthatch with Hazelnuts and Oak and Bramble Leaves' from James Bolton's *Harmonia Ruralis* (1794–6).

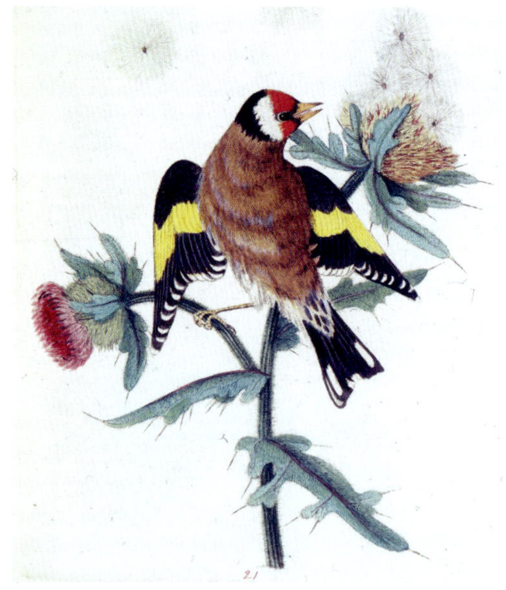

'Goldfinch on a Thistle' from James Bolton's *Harmonia Ruralis*. This decorative field guide was dedicated to 'The British Ladies, to naturalists, and to all such as admire the Beauty or Melody of the Feathered Warblers'.

ABOVE

A page from Gilbert's first copy of *The Naturalist's Journal*, May–June 1768. His detailed barometer readings would begin the following year.

BELOW

Gilbert's *Naturalist's Journal* for the last week of June 1781, with his long note about the honey buzzard.

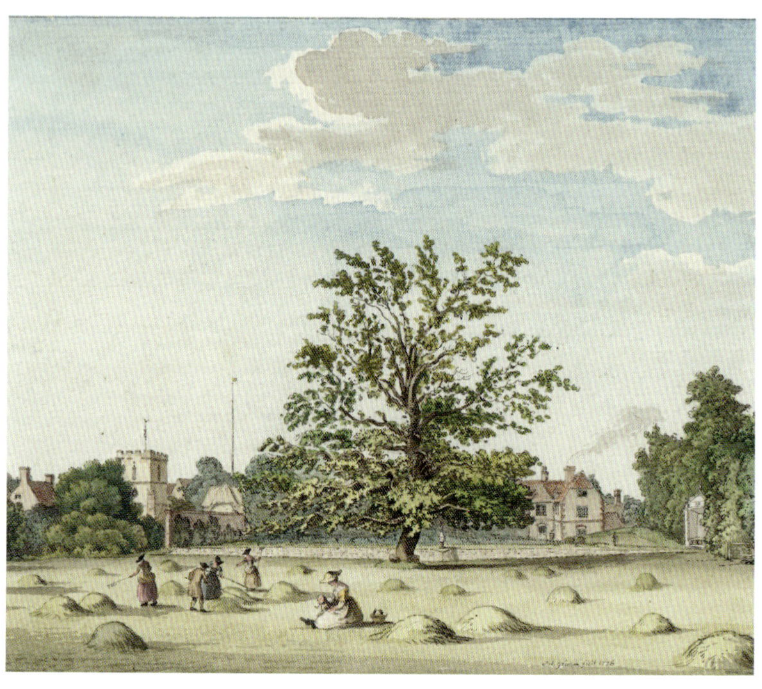

Detail from *Haymaking*, Hieronymus Grimm (1776). Behind the haymakers and the great oak tree, the ha-ha stretches across the garden, from the fruit wall on the left to the 'alcove' on the right, where Gilbert sat to watch the birds.

weekend seven years before, Gilbert had watched a ring ouzel, on its spring migration, also devouring these ripe berries.

Over the years, he has seen ring ouzels arrive on Noar Hill, looking like blackbirds but with curving white chest bands. They would stay for a few days in the spring and for nearly a fortnight in the autumn, feeding 'on haws, yew berries, &c: also on worms'. He assumed that in the autumn they were heading from breeding grounds in the north to wintering places overseas. Then an observation from Pennant, who saw ring ouzels in the Welsh mountains in late autumn, shook his confidence. He had to confess, 'not without some degree of shame, that I only reasoned in that case from analogy' – understandably, since before birds were ringed, it was impossible to track their routes.

He tussled long with this issue, deciding eventually that as ring ouzels were seen all winter, from Scotland to Sussex, 'we may conclude that their migrations are only internal, and not extended to the continent southward'. In fact, they do migrate to southern Spain and North Africa, returning in spring to breed in the uplands of Wales, Scotland and Ireland (and, as Gilbert's correspondent Sampson Newberry told him, 'on sides of small brooks on Dartmoor'). In spring and autumn, they pause on their way, building up their fat reserves and immune systems, lowering the risk of infection and disease.

Monday 9
53. 29. W, S. 41.   *Four swallows seen near the Priory.*
Rain, rain, dark.   *Some cucumbers seem to set: the plants*
                             are weak.

On his walks, he counts the swallows as they come, and neighbours tell him when they spot them, in barns, by ponds, by the ruined Priory.

In his garden, the cucumbers are setting in his cold frames. He has tips to help them on:

If bees, who are much the best setters of cucumbers, do not happen to take kindly to the frames, the best way is to tempt them by a little honey put on the male & female bloom. When they are once induced to haunt the frames, they set all the fruit, & will hover with impatience round the lights in the morning, 'til the glasses are opened. *Probatum est.*

Today, in a flustered letter to Molly, he laments a serious problem. To deter highway robberies, Post Office officials recommended cutting a banknote in half and sending the two pieces by different posts. They even printed an advertisement showing where to cut the note. Gilbert had sent half a £10 banknote to his brother Henry at Fyfield, or so he thought. Goody Hampton, his trustworthy 'weeding woman', had taken it to the post office, but now Henry's son Sampson had turned up at The Wakes, saying that though the letter was opened 'safe and unruffled', no banknote was there. Gilbert hunted everywhere. Had he put it in a letter to Mrs Bentham, his old tutor's wife, in Oxford? ('If it should prove so, it will also prove that my memory is very bad.') What should he do with the remaining half? Should he send it to London?

Having turned the whole dilemma over to Thomas and Molly, he ended his letter by returning to cheerier things. Sampson had brought him a new dog, Rover, of indeterminate breed, 'whom, if he behaves quietly, I shall approve of, because he is both large, and good for nothing: I mean has no sporting blood in him.' As for the banknote, Molly and Thomas wrote with advice but heard no more. Used to her uncle's absent-mindedness, Molly thought that perhaps he had found it, though 'probably he put it into Mrs Bentham's frank I think'.

Tuesday 10
60½. 29 4/10½. S. 13.　　　*Shell-snails come-out in shoals.*
Rain, sun, summer-like.　　　*Grass grows.*

The snails slide out after the rain. They are less hardy than the shell-less snails, 'called slugs, which silently and imperceptibly make amazing havoc in the field and garden'. At the same time four years ago, Gilbert had noted that 'slugs, which are covered with slime, as whales with blubber, are moving all the winter in mild weather'. By contrast, snails hibernate in clusters, sticking to each other's shell under flowerpots and stones. In April, he writes, they emerge 'in shoals' or, more threateningly, in 'troops'.

He reminds himself that they provide food for the thrushes, judging by the snail shells scattered along his paths. But, to a gardener, they are still pests. In the *Garden Kalendar* for April 1756, he had noted briskly: 'No snail ever comes near a place well-sprinkled with quick-lime, especially in a frame where the wet is kept-off. And what is very strange, quick-lime, tho' plentifully shaken upon them, will not injure the youngest, or tenderest plant.'

Wednesday 11
53. 29 1/10. N, NE. *Nightingale, Cuckow, House-martin, & Middle*
Dark & mild,   *yellow wren, appear.*
rain, rain.

This is the last day of the hunt for hibernating martins. Accepting that they can find no trace of them, Gilbert adds a note and a final, hopeful, query:

> While two labourers were examining the shrubs & cavities at the S.E. end of the hanger, a house-martin came down the street & flew into a nest under Benham's Eaves. This appearance is rather early for that bird. Quae: whether it was disturbed by the two men on the hill.

Other birds arrive, including the cuckoo, which comes from the rainforests of the Congo. The cuckoo, however, bothers him. In February 1770, Barrington had suggested that a cuckoo did not simply find the nearest convenient nest, but sought out 'a nurse in some degree congenerous, with whom to entrust its young'. This idea, Gilbert responded, was perfectly new to him and struck him strongly. He talked to neighbours and discovered that around the village, cuckoos were seen only in the nests of wagtails, sparrows, pipits, warblers and robins, 'all soft-billed insectivorous birds'. Whatever the choice,

> This proceeding of the cuckoo, of dropping its eggs as it were by chance, is such a monstrous outrage on maternal affection, one of the first great dictates of nature; and such a violence on instinct; that, had it only been related of a bird in the Brasils, or Peru, it would never have merited our belief.

If it turned out that the cuckoo was indeed capable of seeing which species were the best mothers and left their eggs only with these, this would be a marvel, he felt, another example of the astonishing ingenuity of natural design. The traditional religious explanation was that instinct – complex, apparently inbuilt animal behaviour – was 'designed' by God for the welfare of the species, operating in a quite different way to human reason. 'Philosophers have defined instinct,' Gilbert writes,

> to be that secret influence by which every species is impelled naturally to pursue, at all times, the same way or track, without any teaching or example; whereas reason, without instruction, would often vary and do that by many methods which instinct effects by one alone.

This description sounds like theories relating to 'innate reflexes': the way babies chew, swallow, stand and step, or caterpillars weave cocoons. But in terms of modern evolutionary psychology, it also resembles the idea that the minds of all living creatures have a range of in-built structures and capacities, inherited from ancient ancestors and adapted over time. 'Instinct' is still a matter of argument, as it was for Gilbert.

As far as he could see, far from always operating on 'the same way or track', instinctual behaviour was variable and limited. And although instinct might be a blind drive towards 'self-preservation or propagation of the species', the surrender to habit could be dangerous. One pair of martins, for example, built their nest in the same place every year, although it was always washed down in heavy rain: 'Thus is instinct a most wonderful unequal faculty; in some instances so much above reason, in other respects so far below it!'

Thursday 12
50. 29 4/10. NW. 43.   *Planted four rows of potatoes.*
Sun, soft air, showers.   *Vines show shoots three inches long.*

Planting potatoes is a standard spring task: first earlies, second earlies, main crop. As a child, I was told you should plant them on Good Friday, which feels odd, given that Easter is a moveable feast. But sure enough, in 1781 tomorrow is Good Friday.

Gilbert had begun growing potatoes in mid-March 1756. Each year, he planted more. In 1759, he cut fourteen large potatoes into pieces before planting them and got a huge crop: 'several single ones weigh'd about a pound. Put-by about 30 of the finest as a supply for a crop next year.' In later years, he moved them to new patches to avoid blight, and was, apparently, the first person in Britain to experiment with different composts, trying dung with and without thatch or putting 'old-thatch in four of the trenches, & peat-dust in one for experiment sake', as he did in April 1765. The latter was a success: next year, the peat dust went into every trench.

He was proud of the way his experiments helped local people. In 1778, he reported that potatoes 'have prevailed in this little district, by means of premiums, within these twenty years only; and are much esteemed here now by the poor, who would scarcely have ventured to taste them in the last reign'. The 'last reign', that of George II, had ended in 1760. Potatoes, brought to Europe from the Americas in the mid-sixteenth century, took a long time to be accepted in southern England. While people in Ireland and the north grew them enthusiastically, southerners thought them fit only for cattle or the poor and sick. Their link to deadly nightshade, another plant of the Solanaceae family, tainted them as 'evil', used by witches and suspected of causing leprosy, scrofula and fevers. And because they were popular on the Continent, they were also linked with Catholicism and the banished Stuart dynasty. (At a 1765 election in Lewes, in Sussex, not far from Ringmer, the cry was: 'No Popery, no potatoes.') Yet by the late eighteenth century, they were on the tables of both rich and poor. In 1787, Gilbert would write confidently:

> The quantity of potatoes planted in this parish was very great, & the produce, on ground unused to that root, prodigious. David Long had two hundred bushels on half an acre. Red or hog-potatoes are sold for six pence per bushel.

A bushel is a measure of volume rather than weight, then equal to the volume of eight gallons of water, so this is a substantial – even 'prodigious' – amount of potatoes.

This is one instance of Gilbert's 'useful' application of knowledge. Another is his insistence that with regard to botany, it was not enough to be a technical phytologist, concerned with plant science and taxonomy. Instead, the botanist should 'investigate the laws of vegetation, should examine the powers and virtues of efficacious herbs, should promote their cultivation; and graft the gardener, the planter, and the husbandman, on the phytologist'. You needed order – 'without system the field of Nature would be a pathless wilderness' – but the ultimate aim should be to help agriculture and thus the health of the nation.

When he thought about gardening or farming, Gilbert liked to imagine progress fostering improved health. Writing about leprosy, in a letter to Barrington dated 8 January 1778, he suggested that the eradication of the disease in England was largely due to a better diet. Three or four centuries ago, 'before there were any enclosures, sown-grasses, field-turnips, or field-carrots, or hay', the cattle that grew fat in summer were simply turned out in the autumn 'to shift as they could'. All meat eaten in winter or spring was salted. 'But agriculture is now arrived at such a pitch of perfection, that our best and fattest meats are killed in the winter.' Furthermore:

     A YEAR WITH GILBERT WHITE

The plenty of good wheaten bread that now is found among all ranks of people in the south, instead of that miserable sort which used in old days to be made of barley or beans, may contribute not a little to the sweetening their blood and correcting their juices.

People ate more vegetables, as 'every middle-aged person of observation may perceive, within his own memory'. Labourers had their gardens, and the farmers grew beans, peas and greens. This change, he thought (suiting his tone to flatter Barrington's belief in 'improvement'), was thanks to people of rank promoting horticulture, pursuing 'the elegant science of ornamenting without despising the superintendence of the kitchen quarters and fruit walls'. As he was doing, in a small way, at The Wakes.

Gilbert's local vision has been held to anticipate the modern idea of a 'bioregion', an area that contains one or more self-sustaining ecosystems, or can be defined by the particular culture of a people who have lived there for generations. But Selborne was far from self-sufficient. Its inhabitants depended on grain merchants for seed, on nurserymen for trees, on markets, auctions and fairs to sell hops and livestock. Burbey's shop – where Timothy sprawled on the scales when he was weighed, 'to the great diversion of the shop-keeper's children' – sold books, newspapers, patent medicines, Madeira wine and sheet music. The local was always part of a bigger picture. Arguing against the idea that botany was a frivolous pursuit, Gilbert wrote:

The productions of vegetation have had a vast influence on the commerce of nations, and have been the great promoters of navigation, as may be seen in the articles of sugar, tea, tobacco, opium, ginseng, betel, paper, &c. As every climate has its peculiar produce, our natural wants bring on a mutual intercourse; so that by means of trade each distant part is supplied with the growth of every latitude. But, without the knowledge of plants and their culture, we must have been content with our hips and haws, without enjoying the delicate fruits of India and the salutiferous drugs of Peru.

A footnote adds: 'See the late Voyages to the south-seas.'

This sanguine approach to trade is jarring to us now. Opium, ginseng, and quinine from Peru, certainly brought medical benefits, though the dangers of opium addiction were becoming clear. But what of the dark side of that 'mutual intercourse', of colonial occupation and slavery? Even a family like the Whites was collusive. In the early 1760s, Thomas White's firm of ironmongers, White, Yalden and Smith, was in a lengthy dispute over payments with John Thomas, an ironmonger in Barbados. What was the company supplying? Leg irons? Its agents in Barbados, the Irish firm of Anthony Lynch, organised slave auctions in Bridgetown. A decade later, Henry White's pupil, Francis Halliday, was the son of a sugar plantation owner from Antigua.

The Whites knew what was going on. The intellectuals they admired – Burke, Johnson, Adam Smith, Rousseau – opposed the slave trade, and from the 1760s, the Quakers and campaigners like Granville Sharp had been mobilising against it with increasing passion. In 1772, the ruling in the case of James Somersett had seen the virtual end of slavery within England itself. But the fight was barely beginning. In November 1781, on the orders of the captain, 133 Africans were thrown overboard from the slave ship *Zong* and drowned. The owners claimed for the value of their 'cargo', and when the case reached court in 1783, it was presented not as a trial for murder, but merely an insurance dispute.

Public outrage intensified. In May 1789, just after *The Natural History* was published, William Wilberforce made a passionate speech in Parliament, calling for the slave trade to be outlawed. One of his points was that slavery, which caused such misery, ran against the 'natural' law of a divinely created universe: 'I could not believe that the same Being who forbids rapine and bloodshed, had made rapine and bloodshed necessary to the well-being of any part of his universe.' What did a parson and naturalist like Gilbert White think of this? He left no comment.

Morning frost, then soft air. The snails are a weird sight – so clever, the way they seal their shells if the air is too dry, and shelter during the day, coming out in the cool night. It's hard to miss seeing their copulation. As they are hermaphrodites, with both male and female organs, snails can carry both sperm and eggs. In courtship, they wave their tentacles in the air and along the ground, smelling and tasting the slime before they approach a mate, then tasting and smelling again, sometimes for hours, before one snail shoots a tiny dart into the other, releasing hormones to prevent the sperm being killed. Then they each push out a penis from the side of their head, joining together. Soon dozens of small white eggs are laid, in a damp nest underground.

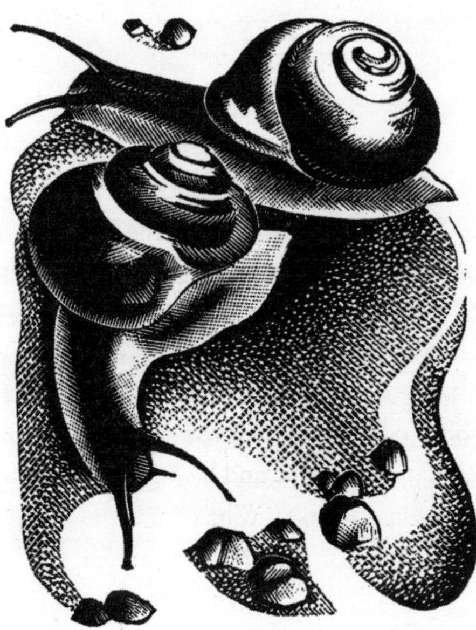

'Snails' by Agnes Miller Parker (1936).

After writing this, I saw a snail by our shed. Feeling a queasy respect, I vowed to leave it rather than fling it over the hedge. Then I turned round, took a step – and heard a crunch.

Thinking of snails, here is John Clare again, in April 1825, watching as carefully as Gilbert, whose *Natural History of Selborne* he so admired: 'I observed a snail on his journey at full speed and I marked by my watch that he went 13 inches in 3 minutes, which was the utmost he could do without stopping to wind or rest.'

Saturday 14
47. 29 4/10½. W, S.   *Frost, ice, sun, fine day.*

Looking at his fruit trees, two days before, he had cheered the green vine shoots; yesterday, he saw apricots swelling. It's exhilarating when things shoot ahead.

In his early gardening fever, in the 1750s, Gilbert's passion had been for growing melons, an obsession of many ambitious gardeners. Mid-April was a key time. Experimenting with different varieties from nurserymen or friends, Gilbert planted the seeds in pots, and in mid-April he moved them to his huge melon frames, the largest over 40 feet long, some covered with glass lights, others with paper. He filled these with cartloads of fresh dung, and as the steam rose from the manure, he earthed it over or bored holes in the back wall to keep the heat down. Every April, the *Garden Kalendar* reported his struggles: the bed was too hot; rain flooded the frame; frost turned the steam into wavy icicles.

In 1755, his brother John had been helping and writing the *Kalendar*'s notes. On 31 March, John wrote, they sowed 'one pot of Mr Garnier's Cantalupe 1753, one pot of Ld. Lincolns Green Cantalupe 1751, one pot of Mr Hunter's Yellow Cantalupe 1752 and one pot of Miller's very fine old seed'. Then Gilbert took over:

April 2. Cast 20 cart-loads of Dung in the melon ground.

14: 15 Made a large melon bed with 20 loads of dung for six lights in the field-garden. The weather wet, & unfavourable. The melon-seeds in the pots came-up weak, & poor, the season not favouring.

16 Sowed a pot of Romania-Melon seed 1753: & a pot of Zatta 1751.

19 Turn'd out two pots of Cantaleupe, & two pots of Andalusian-melons into the two great frames. The plants in thriving condition, but the bed hardly shews signs of Heat . . .

20 The Romania, & Zatta-melons appeared out of the ground.

21 Turn'd out two pots of Cantaleupe-melons in to the two single lights, the one Glass, the other paper.

And so it goes on . . .

Mid-April was also the time to start planting out annuals: 'purple double stocks' and Brampton stocks, 'Love lies a Bleeding, Painted Lady Peas, Larkspurs, Lupines, & Double Poppies'. Most of these seedlings were from Thomas's London garden, but the Brampton stocks came from the Snookes at Ringmer. These were the most valued, according to Miller's *Gardeners Dictionary*, thanks to 'the largeness of their flower and the brightness of the Colour'.

Sunday 15
47. 29 5/10. W.   *Wh. frost, sun, soft & grey.*

Today is Easter Sunday. Villagers across the country celebrate Easter in the old way, baking bread and hot cross buns on Good Friday to give luck all year, rushing to the village field to join in races and wrestling and skipping matches. When Gilbert preaches at Farringdon, the church is fuller than usual, with the gentry making a special appearance.

One of his favourite Easter sermons, which he preached thirty-one times in his forty-six years as a curate, was based on a text from Acts 26:8: 'Why should it be thought a thing incredible with you, that God should raise the Dead?' I don't share his faith, but I can see how he could preach this amid the bursting new life of spring. Elsewhere, he makes delight in the world and sheer sensual pleasure – with caveats – into a natural part of worship, an amazed gratitude:

If we do but consider the works of God, both without us, and within us; what a beautiful, and glorious World he hath made for us to inhabit; and what a multitude of delightful Beings he hath filled it with, and how many capacities and Powers of enjoying and making use of every one of these he hath created in us, such as all our outward and inward Senses, whereby *he* communicates to us, and *we* receive the pleasure of all his works . . .

As a curate, Gilbert was a pivotal local figure. He had a clear, traditional, practical view of his parish duties. He read out the banns, married the couples, baptised their babies and buried their dead, registering the details in his clear, firm hand. He looked out for the poor, listened to people's woes and cheered their successes, worried over the sick, shared gardening and farming chat. Like his grandfather, he was keen on practical improvements and diligently kept up the payments for the dame school, the small village school for younger children, run by women of the parish. There was nothing solemn about his interest in parish lives. When he wrote to his brothers, to Sam Barker or to Molly, news of garden, weather and birds flowed in and out of local gossip. To Sam, on 17 April 1786:

All my apricots were cut off by that violent weather in the beginning of March! So deep was the snow, and so starved the birds, that the poor ring-doves came into our gardens to crop the leaves and sprouts of the cabbages! Hay is become very scarce and dear indeed! My rick is now almost as slender as the waste of a virgin; and it would have been much for the reputation of the last two brides that I have married, had their wastes been as slender . . . The first swallow that I heard of was on April 6th, the first nightingale April 13th.

          A YEAR WITH GILBERT WHITE

Monday 16
SE. *Sun, summer-like.*

WORTING

Two house-martins in the village.

He's off on a brief trip to Oxford – as a fellow he has to be there from time to time. But he travels in stages, stopping first at the village of Worting, just west of Basingstoke. This is home to a young squire, John Edwards, who has been improving the old manor house of Worton Hall, adding new wings, a ha-ha and a walled vegetable garden – the kind of place that a keen gardener like Gilbert always likes to see.

On his way, he looks out for house martins. They are easy to spot, smaller and plumper than a swallow, with shiny blue–black back, wings and forked tail, a white front and white feathers round their feet, and always 'more backward than swallows', sometimes not arriving until May. This year, they are early, flying high, hunting insects. For some time after they arrive, he notices, they pay no attention to nest-building, 'but play and sport about, either to recruit from the fatigue of their journey, if they do migrate at all, or else that their blood may recover its true tone and texture after it has been so long benumbed by the severities of winter'.

Tuesday 17
62. S.
Sun, sultry, sweet even:

CAVERSHAM, READING

Gilbert's next stop is Caversham, three miles outside Reading, where he crosses the bridge over the Thames. Here, he stays with John Loveday, a scholar and antiquary, known for his intrepid travels on horseback, but now living in calm retirement at Caversham Court with his third wife, Penelope, and their daughters.

Famously hospitable and kind, Loveday helped Gilbert when he was puzzled by documents relating to Selborne Priory that he had found in the Magdalen College archives and also lent him a history of the

Templars. He had heard that Gilbert went to Oxford twice a year: 'So it will be time enough to return ye book in one of those excursions; when I hope you will make ye experiment whether a warm bed, & hearty welcome will not be much at your service under my roof.' Gilbert called on him almost every April, becoming very fond of him; a further bond was that he owned two tortoises, fussing over them as much as Gilbert did over Timothy.

<table>
<tr><td>Wednesday 18</td><td>OXFORD</td></tr>
<tr><td>Sun, clouds.</td><td>Some bank-martins at Wallingford-bridge.</td></tr>
<tr><td></td><td>Cut the first cucumber.</td></tr>
</table>

From Caversham, the road takes him over the Chilterns, coming down to the Thames again at Wallingford and then following the river up to Oxford. It's the beginning of Trinity, the summer term, and the city is full of blossom. He has people to see and work to do. But his mind is on the 'bank-martins', the sand martins he has seen at Wallingford. These are the smallest of the swallow family and, at first sight, the least glamorous, with their dark-brown back and pale front, 'what is usually called a mouse-colour', Gilbert wrote dismissively. They don't sing but are 'rather mute, making only a little harsh noise when a person approaches their nests'; they don't swoop like the swallow or glide like the swift, but 'have a peculiar manner of flying; flitting about with odd jerks, and vacillations, not unlike the motions of a butterfly'. (In Valencia, he notes, referring to John's letters, they are called '*Papilion de Montagna*'.) Most disconcerting of all, they avoid people:

> There are few towns or large villages but what abound with house-martins; few churches, towers, or steeples, but what are haunted by some swifts; scarce a hamlet or single cottage-chimney that has not its swallow; while the bank-martins, scattered here and there, live a sequestered life among some abrupt sand-hills, and in the banks of some few rivers.

Although there were colonies near Selborne, in the sandpits of Woolmer Common and by the stream at Oakhanger, the birds never came near the houses. Indeed, he thought, they only gathered near open waters, 'and in particular it has been remarked that they swarm in the banks of the Thames in some places below London Bridge'. One year, after staying in South Lambeth he jotted down a note:

> Some few bank-martins haunt round the skirts of London, & frequent the dirty pools in St George's fields, & near White-chappel: they build perhaps in the scaffold-holes of some deserted house; for steep banks there are none.

In the early 1770s, he described how they nest in riverbanks or cliffs, tunnelling in for about two feet (sometimes as much as four) and lining the nest with feathers and straw. Again, he seems not exactly to disapprove – he rarely moralises about birds or animals – but to shiver a bit, noting, as ornithologists do today, how prone the deep nests are to fleas and lice: 'we have seen fleas, bed-fleas (*pulex irritans*), swarming at the mouths of these holes, like bees on the stools of their hives'. But as he watches the birds, he begins to admire them:

> Perseverance will accomplish any thing: though at first one would be disinclined to believe that this weak bird, with her soft and tender bill and claws, should ever be able to bore the stubborn sand-bank without entirely disabling herself: yet with these feeble instruments have I seen a pair of them make great dispatch: and could remark how much they had scooped that day by the fresh sand which ran down the bank, and was of a different colour from that which lay loose and bleached in the sun.

This leads him to questions: How long does it take them to dig the tunnels? Why are some left unfinished? Do the birds give up on reaching harder strata or meeting loose soil, 'liable to flounder, and threatening to overwhelm them'? One thing is clear: they don't hibernate in them, since people who have dug out their burrows in winter have found nothing but empty nests. They were off, flying to the warm south.

As one question leads to another, I think of Gilbert's own 'perseverance': he never gives up looking, thinking, trying to work things out.

Thursday 19
Shower, dark.

Friday 20
NW.   *Clouds, sun.*

In 1773 and 1774, Gilbert wrote two papers on the martins, swifts and swallows, which were published in the Royal Society's *Transactions*. He was delighted to see them in print, although he wrote a hair-tearing letter to Sam Barker, furious at a slack copy-editor who 'makes me say that "swallows eat *grass*"', had put 'caves' instead of 'eaves', and had included 'many more inaccuracies too numerous to mention'.

The papers stemmed from a suggestion by Daines Barrington, who read them at Royal Society meetings. He was impressed by Gilbert's observations, and Gilbert lent him some of his completed journals, which Barrington marked and annotated. But when he suggested they collaborate further, Gilbert wisely kept him at arm's length. 'Mr Barrington wants me to join with him in a Natural History publication,' he told Sam Barker in 1776, 'but if I publish at all, I shall come forth by myself.'

By that point, he had been thinking of a book for several years. One early idea, in 1769, had been that he and John might write something jointly, compiling parallel journals of a single year, one from Selborne and one from Gibraltar. Then he thought he might write a special, expanded journal of his own. At the start of 1771, he told John: 'As matter flows in upon me I begin to think of comprising a nat: Hist: of Selborne in the form of a journal for 1769.' That July, he explained to Thomas Pennant that he felt diffident about embarking on any publication, but if he did try something, 'it should be somewhat of a Nat.

          A YEAR WITH GILBERT WHITE

History of my native parish, an *annus historico-naturalis* comprising a journal for one whole year, and illustrated with large notes and observations'. This might, he hoped, encourage 'more able naturalists' to write of other areas, slowly building a full picture. Then, three years later, in April 1774, he told John:

> Out of all my journals I think I might collect matter enough, and such a series of incidents as might pretty well comprehend the Natural History of this district, especially as to the ornithological part; and I have moreover half a century of letters on the same subject, most of them very long, all which together (were they thought worthy to be seen) might make up a moderate volume.

His letters, he said, 'lie in my cupboard very snug'.

It was a brilliant decision to compile a book based on those letters. Letters were, first of all, the established way of exchanging information in the sciences, pushing knowledge forward as part of a communal enquiry: papers in the Royal Society's *Transactions* often appeared as letters addressed to a fellow. Gilbert knew William Derham's 1718 selection of John Ray's *Philosophical Letters* to 'his ingenious correspondents, natives and foreigners', which included letters from the ornithologist Francis Willughby. Linnaeus and Buffon wrote copious letters, and the correspondence of Joseph Banks, as president of the Royal Society, would stretch to thousands of pages. But Gilbert's own decision was more personal. Letters were dynamic, an active exchange. They invited a response; they could jump, stray, recap and reconsider. They were vehicles of 'candour and openness', in which one could admit mistakes or leave a subject and come back to it with new information or opinions. Furthermore, when they included anecdotes, as his personal letters always did, they could appeal to the imagination and the feelings. In that respect, their power had been vividly shown by Samuel Richardson's epistolary novels *Pamela* and *Clarissa*. Not that Gilbert mentions Richardson — both he and Mulso, who diligently ploughed through *The History of Sir*

Charles Grandison, were far keener on Laurence Sterne – but the novels' popularity showed, nonetheless, how letters could bring a world to life.

Saturday 21   *ALTON*
Sun, brisk air.   *White-throat on the road.*

He is nearly home again, his journey from Oxford brightened by the sight of the whitethroat, another little warbler arriving from Africa. In icy winters, whitethroats might not appear until mid-May, but this month the weather is kind, and a hedge beside a dusty road is a likely place to spot one. The males, with their white throats and pale-buff chests, are building the nests, while the females hop about, judging them and deciding which nest is best. Gilbert watched them closely, at Selborne and at Ringmer, but he did have preferences, and this was not his favourite bird:

> The note of the white-throat, which is continually repeated, and often attended with odd gesticulations on the wing, is harsh and displeasing. These birds seem of a pugnacious disposition; for they sing with an erected crest and attitudes of rivalry and defiance; are shy and wild in breeding time, avoiding neighbourhoods, and haunting lonely lanes and commons, nay even the very tops of the Sussex-downs, where there are bushes and covert; but in July and August they bring their broods into gardens and orchards, and make great havock among the summer-fruits.

He puzzled over how the small, soft-billed birds – the warblers, pipits and flycatchers – could survive migration. It was upsetting, as well as incredible, to imagine these tiny birds flying so far across the sea. 'I am at a loss even what to suspect about them,' he wrote.

> Subsist they cannot openly among us, and yet elude the eyes of the inquisitive: and, as to their hiding, no man pretends to have found any of them in a torpid state in the winter. But with regard to their

A YEAR WITH GILBERT WHITE

migration, what difficulties attend that supposition! that such feeble bad fliers (who the summer long never flit but from hedge to hedge) should be able to traverse vast seas and continents in order to enjoy milder seasons amidst the regions of Africa!

Sunday 22
59. 29 7/10. W.
Sun, brisk air, showers
about.

SELBORNE
Few swallows & house-martins yet.

The swallows and house martins are late. And when the martins arrive, they will not come from the scrub near the village, whatever Gilbert hopes, but from far away, from the damp, broad-leaf regions of West Africa, from Senegal to Gambia, and from the savannah and tropical forests of Cameroon, Gabon and the Congo.

Monday 23
52½. 29 7/10¾. NW, N.
Sun, sun & clouds,
dark.

Cucumbers set, & swell. Early tulips blow. Sowed large white cucumbers. Many beeches in the hanger are come into leaf; the wild cherries blow, & make a beautiful appearance; pears blow well; & vines show much promise of fruit; the crop of apricots is great; & peaches & nectarines are set. Apple-trees blow.

Gilbert admires his cucumbers. He looks beyond the vegetable plots to the greening Hanger and the wild cherries, then turns back to his orchard and fruit wall, his grapevines, apricots and peaches and pears, and the new apple blossom. In his flower beds, the first tulips begin to bloom, standing proud, in succession, for the next month or so.

Gilbert's journal makes me wonder how many other men and women kept notes like this? How many recorded the weather or followed Benjamin Stillingfleet's suggestion of noting the growth of wildflowers and the 'coincidences' of birds arriving, singing and nesting? Here is the poet Thomas Gray, writing to Tom Warton on 22 April 1760 about the journals that they both kept: 'I have left no room for weather: yet I have observed the birth of the spring, wch (tho' backward) is very beautiful at present. Mind, from this day the Therm:r goes to its old place below in the yard, & so pray let its Sister do. Mr Stillingfleet (with whom I am grown acquainted) has convinced me, it ought to do so.' In a gossipy letter a couple of months later, Gray added brief notes from his recent journal. On 20 April, an unusually warm day:

Therm: at 60. Wind S:W. Sky-Lark, Chaffinch, Thrush, Wren, & Robin singing. Horse-Chesnut, Wild-Bryar, Bramble, & Sallow had spread their leaves. Haw-thorn & Lilac had form'd their blossoms. Black-thorn, double-flower'd Peach, & Pears in full bloom. Double-Jonquils, Hyacinths, Anemones, single-Wallflowers & Auriculas in flower. In the fields Dog-Violets, Daisies, Dandelion, Buttercups, Red-Archangel, & Shepherd's Purse.

Gray kept records from 1753 onwards. Like Gilbert, he read Ray and Derham, and in Cambridge libraries he unabashedly annotated many books, including early herbals. In his copy of Linnaeus's *Systema Naturae*, he scribbled on almost every page, translating Linnaean terms into different languages, making poetic versions in Latin, drawing shells, insects and birds. Like Gilbert, he snapped up *The Naturalist's Journal*, filling the columns with notes, keeping it up each year until just before his death in 1771.

In 1766, Gray and Gilbert had been writing in parallel. If I look up Gilbert's 'Flora' for 20 April that year, the day of the notes that Gray sends to Warton, I find that the same birds sing, the same plants flower. They were both caught up in the new, engrossing habit of watching and recording the natural world around them.

Tuesday 24
52½. 29 8/10½. N.   *Laurels blow.*
No dew, dark, sun, sweet even:

Now, the laurels bloom. I'm not fond of them – too shadowy and solemn.
They grow so tall and bulky, blocking out the light. Yet every year I am
astonished when they erupt in a cloud of white, with long, upright spikes
covered in blossom. In 1755, Gilbert had created a walk down Baker's
Hill, planting it with seventy-four laurels, with two hollies between each
pair. He also planted a separate Portuguese laurel, a more delicate variety
that flowers later, in early summer. He saunters up his laurel walk today,
admiring the heavy flowers.

Wednesday 25
55. 29 9/10½. N.   *Rain seems to be wanting.*
No dew, sun & clouds,   Lathraea squammaria *[tooth wort] going*
fine even: *out of bloom.*

In Selborne, it's dry and warm, despite the northerly wind. The peculiar
flowers of the toothwort are beginning to fade. Toothwort is a parasitic
plant that draws its nutrients from the host and produces no chloro-
phyll at all; its bald, leafless stalks rise out of the ground around the
roots and suckers of trees, including hazel, beech and walnut, and its
double-lipped flowers appear on only one side of the stalk. It's hard to
find, but it still grows, apparently – though I have never seen it – deep
in Selborne lanes. By summer, it has completely disappeared.

Thursday 26
50½. 29 9/10. N.   Antyrrhinum Cym. *[toadflax] in beautiful*
Dark & harsh, sun,   *bloom. A pair of Nightingales haunt my fields:*
dark & moist.   *the cock sings nightly in the Portugal-laurel,*
                                             & balm of Gilead fir.

The walls are covered with the tiny toadflax flowers. In the meadow beyond, the nightingales are like spirits of spring. Even the trees in to-day's journal entry sound exotic: the laurel from Portugal; the fir from Canada and North America, its resin, so Miller's *Gardeners Dictionary* says, used to salve wounds. The nightingale's song fills the air like the perfume of the biblical balm. Putting it first in a list for Barrington of birds that sing in the night, Gilbert quotes Book III of Milton's *Paradise Lost*, where:

> . . . the wakeful Bird
> Sings darkling, and in shadiest Covert hid
> Tunes her nocturnal Note.

Friday 27
29 8/10. N.   *Dark & harsh.*

Saturday 28
49. 29 6/10. N.   *Flesh-flies appear.*
Sun, hot sun, & cold   *Chafer comes out.*
air, sweet even:

He wakes to a shining morning after the dark day before. The warmth brings out the flesh flies (of the grimly named family Sarcophagidae), with their bulbous red eyes and black-and-grey-striped and chequered back, which settle on manure, carrion, rubbish and old meat. There are sixty-five species of these flies in the UK, and they are hard for a lay person to tell apart. The eggs hatch inside the female, who lays the maggots straight into a suitable site, where they burrow in until the light and warmth are right – then out they fly.

At the same time, the chafer beetle staggers out. There are even more species of chafers – eighty in the UK alone – all looking rather fine with their shield-like backs, some black, some rose, some, like the scarab, a bright iridescent green. Laid underground, their eggs turn into grubs (a curse to fine lawns), which can live and grow in the soil, amazingly, for as long as five years. Then they pupate, and sometime in April or May, they crack their hard shells. Out the beetles come, nearly all within a week; sometimes, on a fine day, all together in a sudden rush.

Gilbert found it hard to distinguish between the innumerable species of insects. But he had help from friends. When Thomas Pennant and Joseph Banks could not visit him in the spring of 1768, he had written resignedly to Banks, wishing him a good voyage and adding that unless Richard Skinner, a fellow of Corpus Christi, Oxford, 'should happen to come (as he has partly promised) I must plod on by myself, with few books and no soul to communicate my doubts or discoveries to'. Skinner – whom Gilbert described later as 'the same chatty, communicative, intelligent, gouty, indolent mortal as he used to be' – did come the next summer, with another Oxford friend, William Sheffield. They were, Gilbert said happily, 'the only naturalists that I ever yet had the pleasure of seeing at my house. They are both excellent botanists, and the latter makes very good progress in Entomology. There was great satisfaction in walking out with these men, because no bird, plant or insect came before them unascertained.'

Both men were good friends. Sheffield helped Gilbert with the specimens that John had sent from Gibraltar, while Skinner was warmly encouraging, suggesting in 1771 that Gilbert should write an account of the local migratory birds: not a bad idea, Gilbert thought. Through Skinner, he also came to know the botanist John Lightfoot, who toured Scotland with Pennant, and whose *Flora Scotica* would appear in 1778. From Scotland, he told Gilbert of his journey 'from venison down to barley Bannocks, and from claret down to whisky, and from a good feather bed to one of heath with a plaid for a covering'.

Sunday 29
52. 29 6/10. N.   *Hanger almost in full leaf.*
Sun, sun & clouds,   *Swallows now in plenty; few house-martins.*
red even:

Sun shines through the beeches, a haze of limpid green. The swallows are here, and some martins. When he returns in his mind to their arrival, and the whole issue of migration, Gilbert's attention embraces both the local and the distant.

In his quest to identify a different species of swallow that John had found in Gibraltar, which sounded like a sand martin, Gilbert dissected local martins and ploughed through his books. 'After an ineffectual search in Linnaeus, Brisson, &c.,' he told Pennant, 'I begin to suspect that I discern my brother's *hirundo hyberna* in Scopoli's new discovered *hirundo rupestris*' – a crag martin. Not that he always agreed with the accounts he found: turning to Michel Adanson's *Voyage au Sénégal* (1759), he hotly disputes Adanson's claim to have seen European swallows there in winter: 'he does not talk at all like an ornithologist; and probably saw only the swallows of that country, which I know build within Governor O'Hara's hall against the roof'. Books carried Gilbert across the globe, from the Arctic to the Antipodes. He mentions the migrating birds hitching a lift on ships, as described in Frederik Hasselquist's *Voyages and Travels in the Levant*, but his interests go beyond this topic: he cites Peter Kalm's *Travels in North America* on deforestation; he notes the roving Romany bands 'on the confines of Tartary' in John Bell's *Travels from St Petersburg in Russia, to Diverse Parts of Asia*; the clouds of venomous insects in Ecuador in Antonio de Ulloa's *A Voyage to South America* (1758); the prick-eared dogs drawing the Tartars' sledges in Evert Ysbrants Ides' *Three Years Travels from Moscow Overland to China* (1706).

He was moved by the prospect of global expeditions finding new species. In 1772, he sent Sam Barker a long extract from William Sheffield's description of the wonders brought back from the *Endeavour* expedition, displayed in Joseph Banks's house in Burlington Street – 'an immense magazine of curiosities'. These ranged from weapons to cloth to insects to three thousand dried plants, '110 of which are new genera and 1300 new species', as well as 'an almost numberless collection of

animals: quadrupeds, birds, fish, amphibia, reptiles, insects and ver-
mes, preserved in spirit, most of them new and nondescript'.

Monday 30
51. 29 5/10½. N.   *Men pole their hops.*
White frost, hot sun,   *Dragon-fly &* musca meridiana.
clouds, red even: *Ponds begin to be dry.*

We are back from boundless seas to Hampshire hop fields. The hop
growers put up their tall chestnut poles, stored since last autumn, and
the women tie thick string to pegs in the ground, running it up to
hooks at the top of the poles. Tamed hedgerow climbers, the hops
grow each spring from rootstock left in the ground over winter, twin-
ing up with astonishing speed, sending out curling side shoots, their
greeny-yellow flowers hanging down in garlands.

This has been a warm week in Selborne, despite early frost. Around
the shrinking ponds dragonflies hover and flash. In the meadows, the
noonday fly, with its fat black body and tawny wings, lights greedily on
moist cow pats. The morning mist gives way to a sky of dizzy blue, as if
it just remembered its true colour. May is nearly here.

MAY

Gilbert White's account of the field crickets, from the manuscript
of *The Natural History of Selborne*.

Selborne in mid-May. Bluebells and buttercups. Ragged-robin and cranesbill, tall nettles, brambles rustling with birds. It's no idyll – the Alton to Petersfield bus lumbers past, and you have to be quick to dodge the commuter traffic – but when I walk through the churchyard, past the lines of sloping headstones to the gate, where the path dives down and the valley of Dorton waves with silky grass, it's like stepping back in time.

'All nature is so full,' Gilbert wrote to Thomas Pennant, when Cook and Banks set sail, 'that that district produces the greatest variety which is the most examined.' If he looked globally, he imagined more species than one could comprehend, an infinite wealth. But the near was also infinite: the soil at his feet, the fly on the cow pat, the beech leaf unfurling would take a lifetime to explore. From the late 1760s, his belief in local observation intensified. In September 1770, he told Pennant that studies like Giovanni Scopoli's new *Annus Primus Historico-Naturalis*, identifying the birds of Tyrol and Carniola, should be encouraged:

> For, as no man can alone investigate all the works of nature, these partial writers may, each in their department, be more accurate in their discoveries, and freer from errors, than more general writers; and so by degrees may pave the way to an universal correct natural history.

A month later, he repeated this to Daines Barrington, saying that 'every kingdom, every province, should have its own monographer'.

In looking at his parish, Gilbert knew, too, that he must include the part that people played in creating landscapes and habitats. He saw that how these varied depended partly on human intervention: on planting and coppicing, making ponds and ploughing fields, on stubble and furrows, on barns, where owls roosted, and cottages, where martins built under the eaves. Farmers and cottagers were also creatures, and creators, of his natural history.

Gilbert liked to be involved in the farming year. He spoke the farmers' language and could talk easily of crops and markets, of the weight of pigs and the tying of hops. He knew their wives, who ran the dairies, dug the vegetables, baked the bread and fed the families. He had particular friends, including John Hale, who lived opposite him, and the Knights, at whose ponds at Gracious Street he saw a kingfisher flash by, and the Berrimans, whose erratic family life provides many tales. Many others appear in his journal, like Farmer Spencer, who builds a noble wheat rick and has trouble with his hops; Farmer Parsons, who sows his wheat in furrows that have been drowned in winter; and Farmer Turner, who, in Gilbert's opinion, harvests his hay too early. Some evade all praise or blame, like the idiosyncratic Farmer Canning of Fyfield, who 'plows with two teams of asses, one in the morning, & one in the afternoon'.

Tuesday 1
52. 29 6/10½. N.   *Glow-worms shine.*
Cold & dark, hot sun,
red even:

At night, the glow-worms flicker. Selborne is a good place to find them, as they like chalky soils. It's the females who shine. They look dull: little beetles, with no wings. Their segmented bodies appear almost like larvae, but from those segments they produce a constant, bright, greeny-yellow light. The light is bioluminescent, produced in a way I find hard to put into words, but according to the Natural History Museum: 'a molecule called luciferin is combined with oxygen to create oxyluciferin. A chemical reaction with the light-emitting enzyme luciferase produces their illuminations.' Climbing to the top of a stalk of grass, the female glow-worm turns upside down and shines her light upwards, tempting the males that are flying above and scanning with their large, photosensitive eyes. From May to September, she shimmers and shines. Then her light dies, and so does she.

          A YEAR WITH GILBERT WHITE

'Crink' is a great word. In 1761, when Thomas White was helping in The Wakes' garden, the two brothers had gone out to find the cause of that 'chearfull shrill cry'. Gilbert described their expedition in his *Garden Kalendar* in an unusually long note, later adapted in his *Natural History*. We see him in action: looking, analysing, thinking, drawing conclusions from comparisons with insects he knew. Yet his description also shows his amused astonishment and his profound imaginative sympathy.

The brothers found the field crickets in the Short Lythe, a steep, rocky meadow across the stream from the church, dotted with gorse. With their wings and ornamented shell cases, they looked like familiar house crickets. They had 'large brawny thighs, like Grasshoppers, for leaping', but when dug out, they simply crawled along 'in a very shift-less manner', and could be easily caught. From one cricket, bruised by their digging, Gilbert took a batch of eggs, which he said were long and yellow, with a very tough skin. This made it easy to identify the fe-male, who had a long 'terebra' at her tail (in *The Natural History* he calls this 'a long, sword-shaped weapon'), which, he assumed, was useful for pushing the eggs into crannies. She was duller than the male, with his black body and yellow stripe, 'like a Humble bee'. Gilbert assumed, again, that only the male made the shrilling sound, 'out of rivalry, & emulation at breeding time, as is the Case with many animals'.

Field crickets are solitary creatures, and Gilbert found that when he put them into a hole in a dry wall, they fought fiercely, and 'the first that had got possession of the chink seized an other with a vast pair of serrated fangs so as to make it cry-out'. They must use these fangs, he thought, to dig 'their curious regular Holes; as they have no feet suited for digging, like the Mole crickets'. Shy insects, they stopped singing when he and Thomas approached, darting into hiding, from which he deduced that they were tasty food for several kinds of birds. The problem was getting them out of their holes: 'We found it difficult not to squeese them to death in breaking the Ground.' To avoid crushing them, they found that 'a pliant stalk of grass, gently insinuated into their caverns, will probe their windings to the bottom, and quickly bring out the inhabitant; and thus the human inquirer may gratify his curiosity without injuring the object of it'.

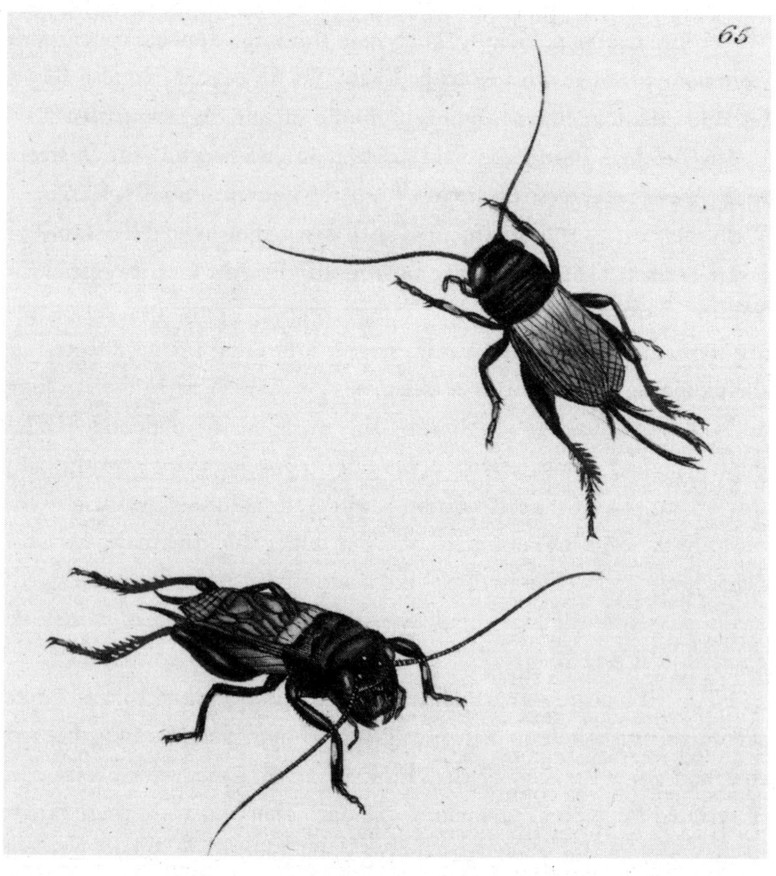

 'The Field-Cricket', *Gryllus campestris*, by James Sowerby, from *The British Miscellany* (1806).

There was a darker sequel. Gilbert remembered that in his youth, the hills had echoed with the chirping of innumerable crickets, but when he looked for them in the Lythe years later, they had vanished; he thought that local boys, using his trick with the grass, had caught them all. Over time, with the loss of grassy heaths to forestry, field crickets nearly disappeared altogether: by the 1980s, there were only around a hundred left, on a single site in west Sussex. In an extraordinary venture, volunteers moved some of the insects to restored heathland, to start new populations. And the technique they used to catch them? It was Gilbert's 'tickling', pushing a blade of grass into their burrows.

Thursday 3

52½. 29 5/10½. E, SE, E.
Small shower, sun, dark,
small shower, sweet even:

Three pairs of swifts. House-martins begin to come: they frequent their nests. Cucumber-beds are now in high-order, & the plants are full of fruit.

The swifts shoot through the air, their curved wings black against the sky. They fly so fast, reaching up to 70 miles per hour, that only a swooping peregrine falcon can match them.

'Swift appears,' he had jotted down the day before: this was the sight he had been waiting for, a moment of unmixed joy. He counts the pairs as they come. Ten years before, towards the end of May, he had written: 'We have round this church usually about 8 pairs of swifts: they do not come all together, but in a straggling manner, a few at a time: perhaps a pair many days before the rest.' Another year, he counted fifteen pairs. Today's three are the first arrivals.

Our swift, *Apus apus*, is one of a hundred different species. Many are confined to small regions, usually in tropical climates in the southern hemisphere, but the common swift appears across the whole great northern land mass, from Ireland to China, and all of these birds, in their millions, fly thousands of miles, from their breeding grounds to southern

Africa in the autumn and back again in the spring. Gilbert has no sense of those extraordinary flights, but he breathes in awe at the swifts' circling, soaring flight, the way they cut through the air. Despite his amazement, he is still coolly interested in them as specimens, and nesting gives him a chance to look more closely. On 6 May 1780, he wrote:

> I opened a hen swift, which a cat had caught, & found she was in high condition, very plump & fat: in her body were the rudiments of several eggs, two of which were larger than the rest, & would probably have been produced this season. Cats often catch Swifts as they stoop down to go under the eaves of low houses.

Although swifts like to nest high up, in cracks in the walls of castles, towers and steeples and under church roofs, in Selborne (despite the cats) they often built their nests on the lowest cottages, 'raising their young under those thatched roofs'. Otherwise, they were always in the air, able to fly continually and range far, Gilbert realised, because of the power created by the size of their wings, longer in proportion to their small bodies than those of any other bird. He saw how they rested as they flew, raising their wings to curve above their heads. He noted how they fed high in the air, proving that insects could exist at high altitudes, but he also watched them sweeping low over ponds, catching caddis flies and dragonflies.

In his paper for the Royal Society in 1774 (published the following year), he put forward something quite new, based on 'many years exact observation'. He was the first person to see that swifts mated on the wing:

> If any person would watch these birds on a fine morning in May, as they are sailing round at a great height from the ground, he would see, every now and then, one drop on the back of another, and both of them sink down together for many fathoms with a loud piercing cry. This I take to be the juncture when the business of generation is carrying on.

It took two centuries for ornithologists to accept this finding. He was also the first person to see swifts drinking, and to record their behaviour in the nest and in fledging – things that few people have seen, even today. He worked out that they had only a single brood, and he countered the idea that they could not take off from the ground. In his journal, in 1776 he wrote: 'I saw two swifts, entangled with each other, fall out of their nest to the ground, from when they soon rose & flew away. This accident was probably due to amorous dalliance. Hence it appears that swifts when down can rise again.' He was right: despite their short legs, adult swifts can take off if they push hard with their wings and have a clear space in front of them.

He never stopped watching them, in sun and rain, seeing, in 1789, that when it was pouring, 'swifts skim with their wings inclining, to shoot off the wet'.

Friday 4
53. 29 6/10. N, N.   *Cut some cucumbers, fine fruit.*
Shower, dark & cold,
showers.

It's turning out to be a cold, dry May, the temperature hovering at just over 50°F (10°C). But in the hotbeds, the cucumbers thrive under their glass lights. He monitored them assiduously and worked out early on how the fermentation process in manure and compost produced gases that could harm the plants. Following Stephen Hales's thinking about ventilation, in 1758 he had worked like a chemist, much as Joseph Priestley, thirteen years later, would use a candle to test the purity of air. Here is Gilbert's report:

Tryed an experiment late in ye evening with a Candle on the two Cucumber-frames after they had been close covered-up some Hours. On putting the Candle down a few Inches into that frame that has leaded lights & no Chimney, the flame was extinguished at once three several times by the foul vapour: while the frame with the tiled lights, & Chimney was so free from vapour that it had no sensible effect on the flame. I then applyed the candle to the top of the Chimney, from whence issued so much steam as to affect the flame, tho' not put it out. Hence it is apparent that this Invention must be a benefit to plants in Hot-beds by preventing them from being stewed in the night time in the exhalations that arise from the dung, & yir own leaves.

Saturday 5
48. N, N.   *Not enough rain to measure.*
Dark & harsh, sun
& clouds, very cold air.

He worries again about the lack of rain. But an equal danger is the late frost that kills the tips of shoots on the walnut, ash and laurel, and nips the new growth on hops, potatoes and beans. Even Gilbert's annuals in his cold frames could be burned by the ice where they touched the glass.

There's no frost today, but the temperature is down to 48°F (just under 9°C). The chill does not stop the birds coming. In early May, Gilbert can usually hear a host of late migrants: the redstart whistling, wood warblers chirping and the blackcap with its tuneful chattering. People questioned whether blackcaps migrated at all, but Gilbert was sure: 'I think there is no doubt of it: for, in April, in the first fine weather, they come trooping all at once, into these parts, but are never seen in the winter.' In cold springs like this one, they arrived later, in May.

The spotted flycatcher, clicking and twittering, was often the last to arrive. Gilbert was the first naturalist to notice how the flycatcher poses, alert, on a chosen perch, then dashes out to snatch insects, moths and butterflies. When he described this, the rise and fall of his prose echoed the bird's own balletic leap, flight and return:

There is one circumstance characteristic of this bird, which seems to have escaped observation, and that is, it takes its stand on the top of some stake or post, from whence it springs forth on its prey, catching a fly in the air, and hardly ever touching the ground, but returning still to the same stand for many times together.

Sunday 6

48. 29 7/10¾. N, N.   *Dark & cutting wind, still.*

Not all birds are greeted warmly. He looks sternly at the willow wrens, 'horrid pests in a garden, destroying the pease, cherries, currants, &c.; and are so tame that a gun will not scare them'. And on 6 May 1784, he would write: 'The polyanths blow finely, especially the young seedlings from Bramshot-place, many of which will be curious. Shot three green-finches which pull-off the blossoms of the polyanths.'

Some wild birds, uninterested in the garden, do not stay nearby for long. The lapwings, with their tumbling flight and peewit call, nest in the tussocky grass or stubble, but gather in flocks as soon as the young are fledged and fly off to the high downs and sheep walks. The bird's old name is 'green plover', from the Latin *pluvia*, 'rain', apparently from their flocking in autumn, when the rains come. The Latin name *vanellus*, 'little fan', refers to its wavering, noisy, 'lapping' flight. In Selborne, Gilbert had watched them in late April 1766: 'The lap-wing, or bastard plover, *capella, sive vanellus*, is paired, & flies around with a querulous note.' But they were under threat as their eggs were a delicacy. One note in the journal from spring 1769, written when he was staying in London, reads: 'Green gooseberries. Lapwings eggs in the poulterers.'

Other visitors are almost invisible, identified only by their call. In May 1786, he will write a note on an interleaved page: 'Those that are much abroad on evenings after it is dark in the spring & summer, frequently hear a nocturnal bird passing by on the wing, & repeating often a short, quick note.' He had noticed this for years, but only recently worked out which bird it was:

I find now that it is the Stone-curlew. Some of them pass over or near my house almost every evening after it is dark from the uplands of the common & N: field away down towards Dorton: where among the meadows & streams they may find a greater plenty of food. Birds that fly by night are obliged to be noisy: their notes are signals or watch-words to keep them together, that they may not stray, & lose each other in the dark.

Birds of the same species, he concluded, look after each other, keeping their fellows safe. But amid the varied flocks, some birds are predators and some are prey, and the smaller ones must defend their nests fierce-ly. Last year, in May, he had written: 'The missel-thrush drives the mag-pies, & Jays from the garden.' But the battle was unequal. A few days later: 'Magpies beat the missel-thrushes' nest to pieces, & swallow the eggs.' Like the lapwings, the mistle thrushes left when their young fledged and flew to the sheep walks and wild commons.

Monday 7
48. 29 7/10. NE.   *Vast bloom among the apples: the crop but*
White frost, dark &   *small. No rain to measure since April 12.*
sharp air, sun, sharp.   *Full moon.*

Tuesday 8
48. 29 4/10½. NE.   *Timothy lies very close this cold weather.*
Dark & harsh, sun,   *No house-martins appear.*
cold wind, dark & still.

No tortoise about, no martins. A dark, dull day: good weather for working on his book or writing letters. He sends one to Ralph Churton, a young cleric and writer from Brasenose College, Oxford, who had stayed with him the previous December. This time, he invites him to stay over Whitsun, at the start of June. 'As you have seen Selborne, and the nakedness of the land at Xmas,' he writes, 'you will not do it

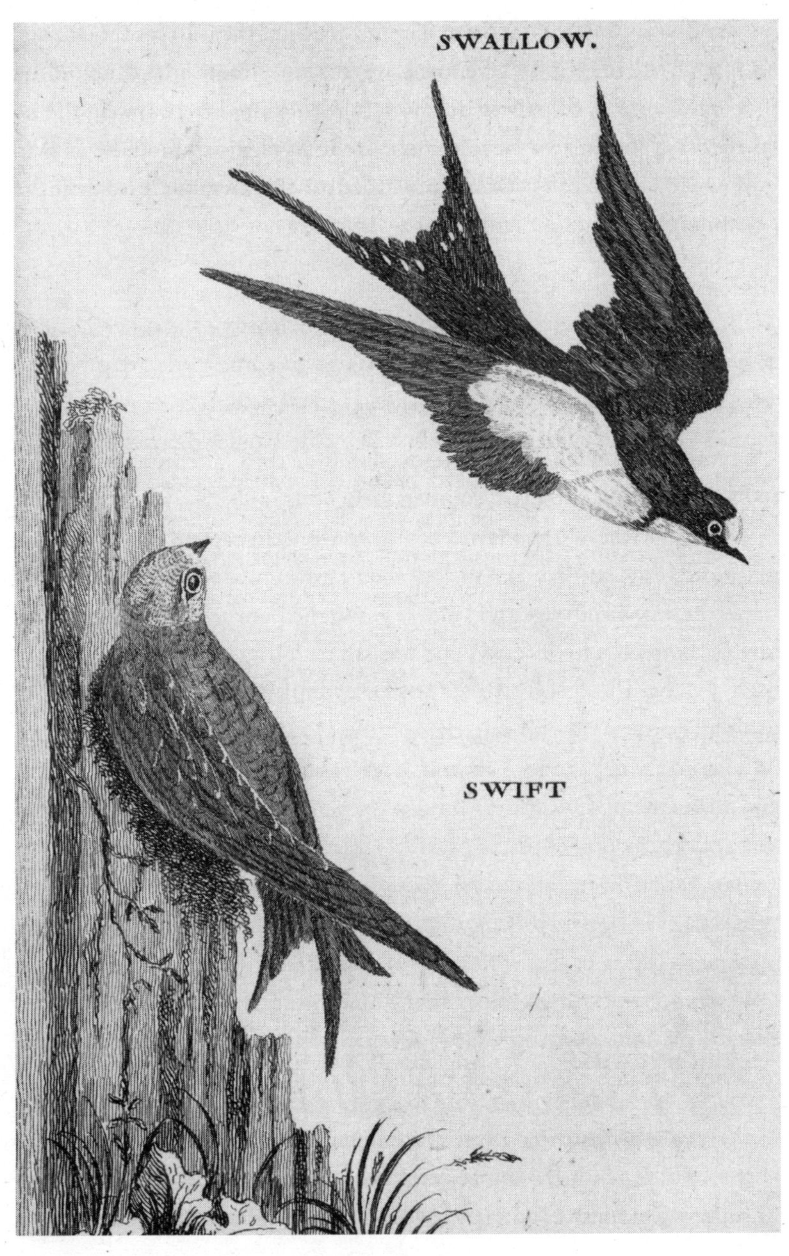

'Swallow' and 'Swift', from Thomas Pennant, *British Zoology*, Vol. I, Part 2: 'Birds' (1776).

justice if you do not come and visit it in all its glory, in its full foliage and verdure.' If Ralph came via Caversham, Gilbert added, could he pick up a bundle of papers he had left with John Loveday? And if he labelled his luggage to be left at the Belle Savage, on Ludgate Hill (a famous coaching inn), 'to be forwarded to the Swan at Alton by the Southampton coach, it will I trust, come safe'.

Wednesday 9

47. 29 3/10. NE.   *Many swifts: house-martins encrease & come*
Very white frost, sun,   *to their respective nests.*
& cold air, mild even: *Large well-grown cucumbers.*

This time the previous year, walking alongside the Oakhanger stream up to Priory Farm, Gilbert had counted forty nests under the farm's eaves. In mid-May, he knew, 'the martin begins to think in earnest of providing a mansion for its family'. The shell of the nest was made of mud and earth, strengthened with twigs and straw. He watched one martin build, seeing how it clung on with its claws and pressed its tail against the wall to keep itself steady. They worked slowly, like careful builders who raise mud walls a layer at a time to stop the soft mud collapsing, and let it harden, building only in the morning and 'dedicating the rest of the day to food and amusement'. Outside, the nest was knobbly and rough; inside, it was soft and warm, with a lining of straw, grass, feathers and moss.

After such hard labour, he thought – 'as Nature seldom works in vain' – it was not surprising that martins bred for several years in the same nest. Three to five white eggs are laid and hatched. To begin with, to protect the nestlings, the parent birds carefully remove their caustic excrement, but soon the young ones do it themselves, thrusting their tails out through the opening of their nest. Once grown,

> they soon become impatient of confinement, and sit all day with
> their heads out at the orifice, where the dams, by clinging to the nest,
> supply them with food from morning to night. For a time the young

are fed on the wing by their parents; but the feat is done by so quick and almost imperceptible a slight, that a person must have attended very exactly to their motions before he would be able to perceive it.

Gilbert is that exact observer, watching until all the young birds can fly – then it's time for a second brood.

If anything, he makes the birds almost too human. The martin is not only a 'provident architect', but shows 'prudence and forbearance' and 'tender assiduity' – good Protestant virtues. It takes about ten days, he reckons, for martins to finish their nest, often only for eager house sparrows to bustle in and force them out. This really annoys him, to judge from one letter. 'When the house-sparrows deprive my martins of their nests,' he writes, 'as soon as I cause one to be shot, the other, be it cock or hen, presently procures a mate, and so for several times following.' 'Several times' suggests a ruthless devotion to 'my' martins.

Unlike the martins, the swifts are not careful builders, their nests in crannies and holes being 'very rudely and inartificially put together' with dry grass and feathers. He never saw them collecting material (though John told him they did collect feathers in Andalusia), and he thought they might take over sparrows' nests, 'well remembering that I have seen them squabbling together at the entrance of their holes; and the sparrows up in arms, and much-disconcerted at these intruders'.

Thursday 10
49. 29 2/10. NE. *All sorts of hirundines now abound.*
Very wh. frost, hot sun, *A small sort of caterpillar annoys the goose-*
still, red at sun-set. *berry trees.*

There are nests everywhere. Swifts shriek, swallows swoop, martins build. In the vegetable garden, caterpillars munch away. Picking the bugs off the gooseberries was one of the many jobs done by Thomas Hoar. His patience showed in every season: in the way he gently shook the snow off the branches of the evergreens and covered up the lettuces in winter, or spent hours over the fruit bushes and trees in spring. In eleven years' time, on 12 May 1792, when Thomas is well into his seventies, Gilbert will write: 'an army of caterpillars infest my young goose-berry trees, which were planted this spring . . . Thomas picked the trees carefully, & gave them a good watering.'

Friday 11
54½. 29 5/10½. 63.　　　　*Fern-owl chatters. When this bird is heard,*
NE, S, SW, S.　　　　　　*summer is usually established.*
Misty rain, dark,
hot sun, red even:

Gilbert thought the fern-owl – also known as the nightjar or churn-owl, or 'goatsucker' – another summer visitor from sub-Saharan Africa, was 'a wonderful and curious creature'. The bird had its own sense of time, he thought, being 'most punctual' in starting its song at dusk: 'so exactly that I have known it strike up more than once or twice just at the report of the Portsmouth evening gun, which we can hear when the weather is still'. There was no bird, he said, that he had studied more; at the end of his life he will be planning a monograph. He was sure that it chattered while it flew (although modern ornithologists disagree), but more often when perched on a bough, 'and I have for many an half hour watched it as it sat with its under mandible quivering'. He thought the bubbling sound came from vibrations in the windpipe, like a cat purring. Once, when his neighbours came to tea in the hermitage, a churn-owl settled on the cross above the thatched roof, chattering for many minutes, 'and we were all struck with wonder to find that the organs of that little animal, when put in motion, gave a sensible vibration to the whole building!'

This kind of observation, so close and domestic, allowed him to correct Pennant's statement in the second edition of *British Zoology* in 1768, that the nightjar chatters '*only* in its flight', and to counteract his deduction that the sound was produced by air resistance as the bird flew with its mouth open to catch insects. Gilbert, who watched narrowly, knew better.

Saturday 12

59, 66. 29 5/10. SE, S. 40.	*My well sinks very fast: indeed much water*
Sun, sultry, strong gale,	*has been drawn lately for watering.*
dark, thunder, & showers.	*Mr Yalden's tank is almost dry.*

A dry May was dangerous, depleting precious water supplies just when everything was bursting into growth. Gilbert's father John had dug a new well at The Wakes, which rarely ran out, but higher up at Newton Valence, the Yaldens worried constantly about the water level.

For farmers, the anxiety was intense, and Gilbert felt for them. His grandmother Rebecca came from a farming family, and in a small way he was a farmer himself. As well as The Wakes, where neighbouring farmers ploughed his land for him and harvested his barley and hay, he owned Sparrow's Hanger, a patch of farmland behind the cottages across the street, and another small farm nearby. Both were rented to tenants. In 1780, his aunt Rebecca Snooke had left him Iping Farm, in Sussex, and although the income went to his siblings, he kept an eye on what was going on.

Gilbert's small-scale farming was like that of the minor gentry who mowed the hay from their estates and the parsons who farmed their glebe land. John Mulso was one of those parsons. He had left his first living in Sunbury in 1760, and for seven years was the rector of Thornhill, near Wakefield, in Yorkshire, a place he came to hold dear, despite the winds and cold. It had a well-stocked garden and orchard, and, Mulso reported, 'I have above twenty Acres of good Pasture in Hand & *at* Hand: above twenty Load of good Hay in my Stables', and even more pleasingly, 'two Cows, by name *Nancy & Halifax*', as well as pigs, ducks, chickens and pigeons.

Mulso loved his domestic life in Yorkshire, although he was rather bluff about his wife Jenny's pregnancies and labour ('in ye groaning way' again), and about his own evident devotion to his children. 'My family encreases apace, if my Income would keep pace with it,' he wrote in 1763. 'It will be a new Scene to you to see me so busy in keeping my Brats in Order; I make most Noise, but Mrs Mulso speaks more to ye purpose.' But these were hard years. Jenny was often pregnant and ill. In 1764, within the space of a month, their young son George died and their daughter Hester was born. They battled on companionably, raising their family and reaching for their spectacles to read aloud to each other in the freezing winters.

Sunday 13
62, 68. 29 6/10. NW, NW.   *The rain last night broke the stems of several*
Sun, sultry, dark, showers.   *of the tulips, which are in full bloom.*
The rain from the s.

A garden, as Mulso found in Yorkshire, can be hard work, even in a promising spring. The stems of my own tulips are broken, not by rain, as Gilbert's were, but by two stray sheep who have eaten them all – flowers and buds and leaves. They have left the daffodils, in disdain. And this morning, field mice have devoured the bean shoots. The irritation is shared: on 14 May 1789, Gilbert wrote, 'Mice infest the hot beds, & spoil the plants.' The next day, he caught one, with grim glee.

Monday 14
63, 69. 29 5/10½   *The hops wanted rain, & began to be annoyed*
NE, S, SW. 32, 34.   *by aphides. The ground finely refreshed.*
Thunder showers, sun,   *Vast rocklike, distant clouds.*
sultry, sweet afternoon.

In the journal, even plants gain a personality, like these hops wincing under the aphid attack. Hop growers still dread damson-hop aphids, which feed on the sap, damaging the leaves and ruining the crop. Later, they get inside the cones, making them brown and frail, and bringing mould and viruses. Before pesticides, there was no way to deal with them, and an aphid storm was alarming in an area where hops were a staple of the local economy.

Hops were also vital for home-brewed beer. Gilbert built his own brewhouse next to The Wakes, opening it in 1765. The following spring, he noted in his *Garden Kalendar*, he brewed half a hogshead (about 30 gallons) of strong beer, using six bushels of malt from Farmer Knight's barley, plus a couple of pounds of good hops, and water from his well. At a time when beer was thought safer to drink than water, brewing was a shared concern, and Gilbert often took his home-brewed ale across the road to 'discuss' it with John Carpenter. His brother Henry was also brewing at Fyfield, using naked barley, a variety where the grain falls from the husk without complicated 'hulling'. Gilbert wrote in his journal, with some envy:

> Bror Harry's strong beer, which was brewed last Easter monday with the *hordeum nudum* [naked barley], is now tapped, & incomparably good: it is some what deeper-coloured than beer usually is in this country, not from the malt's being higher dryed; but perhaps from the natural colour of the grain. The barrel was by no means new, but old & seasoned. Wheat, it seems, makes also high-coloured beer.

Gilbert's brewhouse is now a micro-brewery, whose beers include a strong 'Zig-Zag' and milder 'Bostal'. One bitter, called 'Garden Kalendar', uses hops grown in the garden: drinkers on the website Untapped judge it to be sweet and fruity, 'Very quaffable' and 'Tasty, but very lively to pour'.

Tuesday 15
62. 29 5/10½. NE.   *Killed some hundreds of shell-snails about the*
Dark & moist.   *garden. The boys every day kill some wasps, that*
                                      feed on the sycamore-bloom on the Plestor.

He stomps round the garden, crushing snails underfoot. There's a murderous tone to this entry, as he kills the snails, and the boys from the village kill the wasps buzzing round the sycamore. This was the tree that his brother Thomas had planted to replace a huge oak tree that fell in the great storm of 1703, which his grandfather had tried vainly to prop up.

Every year, hoping to protect his late-summer fruit, Gilbert paid boys to bring him wasps and wasps' nests. I admire their disdain for stings, but how did they kill them? With beer traps? To me, a wasp is a wasp, but apparently there are seven thousand species in the UK. The Natural History Museum is adamant about their importance, as they catch millions of insects each year to feed their larvae: 'without wasps, the world could be overrun by spiders and insects'. The adults live on sugar, from nectar and aphid honeydew (the sweet secretion of the larvae), and – as we know – from jam and beer and ripe fruit and cake. They find the nectar-rich sycamore flowers delicious, and so do the bees, as Gilbert noted:

> The sycamore or great maple is in bloom, & at this season makes a beautiful appearance, & affords much *pabulum* for bees, smelling strongly like honey. The foliage of this tree is very fine, & very ornamental to outlets. All ye maples have saccharine juices.

Wednesday 16
60. 29 6/10½. NE.   *Several small wasps appear, as well as large*
Dark & moist, &   *breeders. Most growing weather.*
warm.

The 'large breeders' he mentions today are the queen wasps, who emerge from hibernation in spring and start to build their paper nests. Their first eggs hatch (like those of bees) into sterile female workers, who take over the building of the nest, collecting nectar and insects for the larvae. These are Gilbert's 'small wasps'. At the end of summer, fertile males and females – next year's queens – will appear and swarm and mate. When winter comes, the old queens die, and the workers, too. Then the new queens hibernate, and the cycle begins again. It seems very wasteful.

The early honeysuckles are on the verge of flowering. One of the first things Gilbert had done when he began gardening in the 1750s was to plant honeysuckles in the old orchard and near the house. He kept adding more: in March 1755, he planted two Dutch honeysuckles (*Lonicera periclymenum Belgica*), with red and cream flowers, against a trellis,. with strawberries nearby. He trained some honeysuckles as standards, running them up a pole so that they billowed in a mass of entwined stems. He greeted the Dutch honeysuckle first: 'Dutch honeysuckle in fine bloom,' he had written on 23 May 1775. It smells heavenly, but it is so vigorous and pliant that it's very hard to train. Gilbert thought so, too, noting that it was a 'most lovely shrub; the only objection is that having a limber stem, & branches, it does not make a good standard'.

The hawthorn is in flower now, too, buzzing with bees, its honey-sweet scent masking all other smells. A decade on, Gilbert would write: 'My white thorn, which hangs over the earth-house, is now one sheet of bloom, & has pendulous boughs down to the ground.'

Friday 18
56½. 29 6/10. NE, N. 28.   *Filled all the hand-glasses with white*
Shower, dark & still, grey.   *cucumber-plants.*

White cucumbers are less common than the familiar green ones, but several varieties exist, crisp and sweet, especially when small. In the mid-eighteenth century, gardeners preferred them because they were less watery and had fewer seeds. Gilbert raised his in hand-glasses, or bell-glasses, an early, if heavy, kind of cloche. This was even more la-bour-intensive than the hotbed, as you had to turn the bells upside down every day to let them dry out and stop condensation falling on the plants,

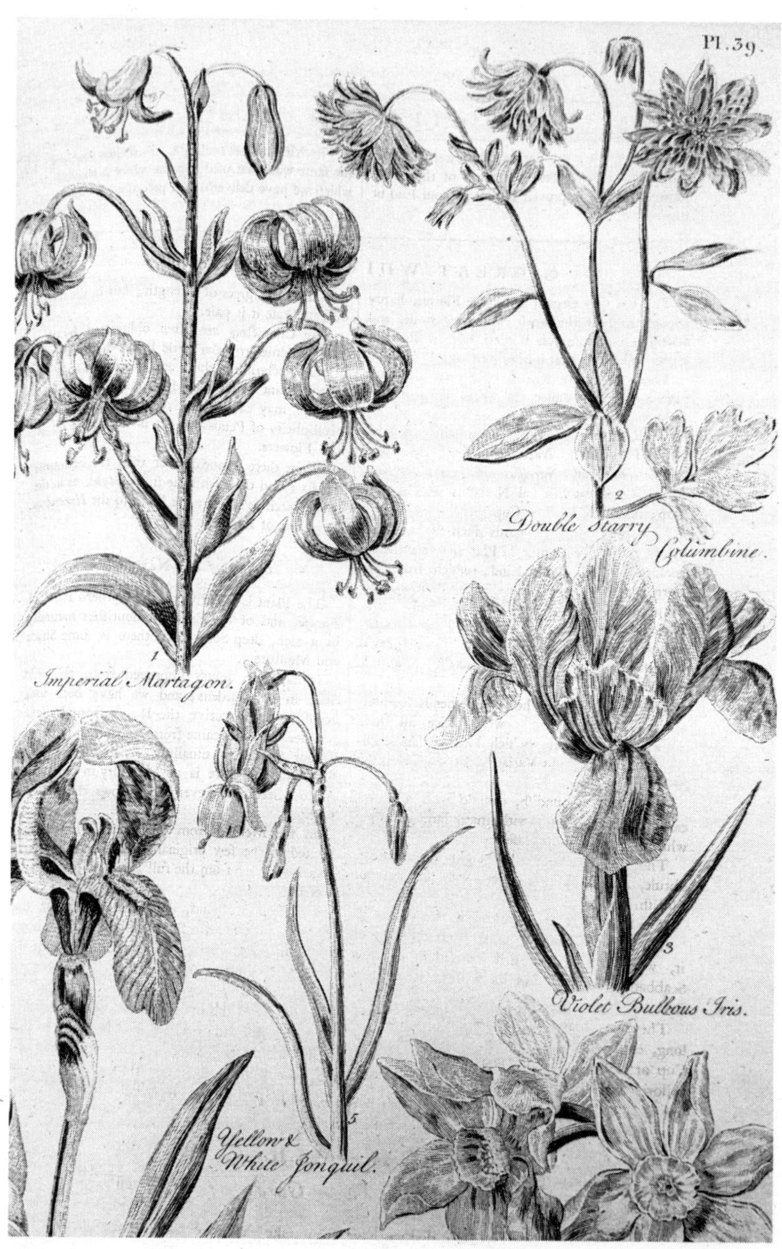

 The imperial martagon and other late-spring flowers, in John Hill's *Eden: or, a Compleat Body of Gardening*, one of many books Gilbert turned to for advice.

and also cover them with matting on cold nights. When the young plants filled them, the bells were raised on bricks to let the air in, and in June they were removed completely. More work for Thomas Hoar.

Saturday 19
62. 29 5/10. NE.   *Orange-lily begins to blow.*
Fog, dark & warm, wet.   *St foin begins to blow. Growing weather.*

Lilies are another sign of coming summer, especially the orange lily, *Lilium bulbiferum*, Gilbert's 'fiery lily', as he describes it on 26 May. Within days, if he is lucky, this will be followed by the martagon, with its pink-purple Turk's cap flowers. Both are European natives, the orange lily from the Alpes-Maritimes, the martagon from high Swiss meadows. They are easy to grow, favourites both then and now. Over many years, Gilbert watched the buds unfurl in mid-May.

In 1781, it is, for once, good growing weather, and his meadows are full of flowering sainfoin. A legume, like clover and lucerne, sainfoin (from the French for 'healthy hay') provides an easy, nutritious summer feed for horses and cattle, while also replenishing the soil after arable crops, fixing three times more nitrogen in the soil than the old custom of leaving a field fallow for a year. It had been grown on the Continent for centuries, and in southern England for over a hundred years, and it thrives on Selborne's chalky soil. With its deep roots, it seems unbothered by drought, its spikes of pink flowers waving above tall stems, attracting clouds of insects and bees.

Sunday 20
60½. 29 6/10. NE. 33.   *Wheat very gross in some fields.*
Showers, dark & moist,
gleams & clouds, red even:

Today, five weeks after Easter, is Rogation Sunday (from the Latin *rogare*, 'to beseech'), when the congregation asked for a blessing on the crops and the livestock and the whole farming year. It was also, traditionally, the day for 'beating the bounds', when the men of the village walked the boundaries of their parish, marking it with sticks, ensuring that no one was encroaching on their common land. In medieval times, this long walk was accompanied by village processions, games and feasts, but after the Reformation, it was cannily transformed into a way to define the parish, cementing the community.

Selborne villagers hung fiercely on to their customary rights: to let their hogs forage for beech mast; to graze sheep and cattle on the common and Dorton field; to dig peat from the forest and take fallen timber from the woods. In May 1703, Gilbert's grandfather had led the beating of the bounds, a long three days of walking: 'The Company are to meet at Temple Farm to Breakfast', as was carefully recorded in the parish register in beautiful copperplate. The village's common rights were confirmed in Chancery sixteen years later, when Magdalen College, as landlord, had tried to claim all rights to the woods and common. In the mid-eighteenth century, beating the bounds had become ever more important, as many villages faced the threat of enclosure, with local landlords enclosing commons and wastes, and larger farms swallowing smaller ones. After 1760, the pace of enclosure increased furiously; this was the era of Oliver Goldsmith's 'The Deserted Village', published in 1770, with its lament for the 'bold peasantry', dispossessed and driven out:

> Amidst thy bowers the tyrant's hand is seen,
> And desolation saddens all thy green:
> One only master grasps the whole domain,
> And half a tillage stints thy smiling plain . . .

Selborne was lucky, as Magdalen, apart from its claim in 1719, was an indifferent rather than interfering landlord. The college archives contain only a small handful of Enclosure Acts, and it engaged in just a few confrontations. But it was important to keep up the tradition every few years, and in Selborne, the trek around the parish was repeated

  A YEAR WITH GILBERT WHITE

in the 1740s, and again in 1765 and 1775, led by the vicar, Gilbert's friend Andrew Etty. In the 1770s, Sir Simeon Stuart, the landowner at Hartley, above the Lythe, had blocked off old paths, removed hedges and tried to manage land at Dorton, within the Selborne boundary. In defiance, on 5 May 1780, under Revd Etty's leadership, two dozen men and boys from the village had got together – among them, Gilbert's friends Robert Berriman, John Burbey, Thomas Carpenter, Thomas Spencer, Richard Lasham and John Hale – to mark the boundaries again, walking up hill and down, banging in yew stakes where hedges were missing, following a route 'Taken from the oldest records as they were constantly perambulated in ancient Times'.

Gilbert keeps an eye on these matters. In 1789, he will write a firm note on rights of way 'from time immemorial' in the church register, signing it: 'Gilbert White, an ancient inhabitant and native of Selborne'. He will still be on the alert in the last year of his life, when Ben's son James tells him of a speculator's plans – unknown to Magdalen – to buy and enclose local land.

Monday 21
59½. 29 8/10. NE, E. 5.   *Tulips make a gaudy show.*
Sun, clouds, & showers,   *Horse-chest-nut blows finely.*
sweet even: *Grass & corn grow wonderfully.*

The showers are welcome. The tulips flaunt their colours, the horse chestnut holds up its flowers like great candles, the cereal crops, lumped together as 'corn', are doing well. This year, as Gilbert had noted the day before, the wheat looks heavy, 'gross' – thick, fat, strong.

Wheat, the first crop grown on newly ploughed land, is the most valuable cereal. With a growing population and increasing demand for bread, its price is constantly rising. In July 1773, Gilbert recorded the price at Farnham market as £17 12s 6d per load, '& very little left in the kingdom'. There were profits to be made. In *The Farmer's Letters to the People of England* (1767), the agriculturalist Arthur Young had advocated turning sheep walks and wastes over to arable, and everywhere the yield was rising. This was largely due to the adoption of the new four-stage 'Norfolk' rotation, promoted by the Norfolk politician Lord Charles Townshend ('Turnip Townshend') in the 1730s. In this system, four different crops were grown in succession over four years: wheat, turnips, barley, then clover or sainfoin, undersown with ryegrass. Turnips were the revolutionary element, acting as a winter cover crop for cattle.

Under this system, over the past decade the Selborne crops have not always flourished as they were supposed to. 'Delicate harvest weather. Many loads of wheat housed,' Gilbert had written in August 1770. But then came winter floods, followed by frost. In March 1771: 'Turneps are all rotten, & the wheat-fields look quite bare, & destitute of all verdure.' The only option was to start again. 'Farmer parsons sows wheat in his fallow behind Beacher's shop, which was drowned in the winter. Mem: to observe what crop he gets from this spring-sowing.' Local farmers tried different varieties of wheat, to Gilbert's intense interest. In July 1773: 'Several fields of cone, or bearded wheat growing this year round the village: the bloom of this wheat is of a brimstone colour. The bloom of some beardless wheat is purple. Qu: what sort? The bloom of wheat in general is whitish.'

Some Selborne experiments ran contrary to the prevailing wisdom. In November 1777: 'Men stack their turneps, a new fashion that prevails all at once; & sow the ground with wheat. They dung the fields in summer as for wheat.' As if by common agreement, the farmers were upturning the Norfolk cycle, planting turnips first, digging them out before winter (perhaps remembering how they rotted in previous winters), then sowing their wheat. It seemed to work. On 13 August 1778, seven months after he mentioned the 'new fashion', Gilbert wrote: 'There is in this year the greatest crop of wheat in the North-field that ever was remembered.'

Gilbert took care of his own crops. He ploughed three times before sowing his barley, and in May, after the barley was over, he undersowed it with white clover, ryegrass and 'a quarter of meadow-grass-seeds from a farmer's hay-loft'.

Arguments continued about the 'new' husbandry. In the past decade, in the wake of Arthur Young's *Farmer's Letters and his Rural Oeconomy* of 1770, a flurry of books had appeared, from David Henry's weighty *Complete English Farmer* (1771) to specialist works like G. Robinson's *The Improved Culture of Three Principal Grasses, Lucerne, Sainfoin, and Burnet* (1775). Gilbert and his brother Thomas were both convinced of the importance of differentiating between grasses. Writing to Sam Barker in 1776, Gilbert insisted:

> A knowledge of the grasses is the most desireable part of botany, because the most useful; but it is the most neglected, for graziers and farmers do not seem to distinguish any one sort of *Gramen* from the other; the annual from the perennial, the succulent from the dry, or the aquatic from the upland. Whereas by attention their meadows and pastures might be much improved; and it is an old maxim, that he is an useful member of society, and a good common-wealths-man, 'who can procure two blades of grass where only one grew before'.

Thomas agreed. One section of William Curtis's botanical garden at South Lambeth was devoted to grasses, and Thomas sent him specimens of turf from Hampshire and Sussex. In 1790, Curtis would write his *Practical Observations on the British Grasses, Especially Such as are Best Adapted to the Laying Down or Improving of Meadows and Pastures.*

Tuesday 22
57. 29 9/10. NE.   *The wind breaks-off the leaves of the beeches.*
No dew, strong,
cold wind.

As the wind tears the trees, birds' nests rattle and sway. Some birds have found shelter, like the blackcap, now sitting on its eggs in the cup-shaped nest in Gilbert's shrubbery. He had described its trilling, fluting song in May 1770. 'Black-cap sings sweetly, but rather inwardly: it is a songster of the first rate. It's notes are deep & sweet. Called in Norfolk the mock-nightingale.' The real nightingales have finished their nests of grass stalks and dead leaves. Two years ago, on 22 May 1779, Gilbert had written: 'A boy took my nest with five eggs, but the cock continues to sing: so probably they will build again.' Next day, it was still singing.

In May, boys (and surely some girls?) are out bird-nesting all over the country, and in Selborne, they bring nests and eggs to Gilbert.

Wednesday 23
53. 29 9/10. NE.   *The wind injures the foliage.*
Cold wind, strong
gale all day, cloudless,
red even:

The fresh leaves are so vulnerable. Opposite our house in Borrowdale, a great beech is glowing with new, pale leaves, opening from the lower branches upwards. Behind it, a rowan is almost ready to flower, a huge ash is hanging out fronds of leaves, as well as 'keys' – the dangling bunches of seeds that have stayed on the tree all winter – and a horse chestnut is holding up emerald fans.

'The hanger is bursting into leaf every hour,' Gilbert wrote one year. 'A progress in the foliage may be discerned every morning, & again every evening.' I think of this as I look from my kitchen window over the beck, to the wood climbing the fellside to the skyline. This is not a beech wood like the Hanger, but one of tawny oaks, scattered with birch, ash and bird-cherry, but it makes me realise that I, too, like Gilbert, am looking at a whole hillside that is greening day by day.

Thursday 24
53. 29 9/10. NE, E.   *Cold air, cloudless, strong gale, red even:, still.*

Friday 25
52. 29 8/10. E.   *Tacked the vine-shoots: there is a*
White frost, cloudless,   *promise for a good crop.*
sharp wind, red even:

In the brisk wind, Gilbert and Thomas Hoar work on the vines. Left to themselves, the plants would scramble and climb, producing side shoots and leaves instead of fruit, so they trim the new shoots on the trunk and tie the long canes onto horizontal wires. The buds will form a canopy of leaves and tendrils, carrying the fruit, making the bunches easier to pick.

Saturday 26
52. 29 7/10½. NE, E, SE, NW.   *Fiery lily begins to blow.*
Very white frost,   *Finished the vines.*
cloudless, red even:

Frost in May! But the lilies blaze in defiance, and the vines are neatly tied. Thomas seemed to enjoy work that involved spending long, patient hours on a fiddly task. On 28 May 1785, Gilbert will notice that the vine near the scullery is infested with cocci, Linnaeus's *Coccus vitis vinifera* (now *Pulvinaria vitis*). He finds the insects skulking under the loose bark, throwing out 'a cotton-like web, among which they have laid innumerable eggs. Thomas has been employed in killing them for many hours.' At the end of that month, he writes: 'Thomas persists in picking the *cocci* off the vine, & has destroyed hundreds.'

For the past four years, Gilbert has seen the damage the cocci made, without seeing the insects themselves. He assumed they had originally come from southern Europe and was surprised they had survived a harsh winter. One badly infected vine was right under the window of his study, where he kept his specimens, and he wondered if they had arrived in the boxes that his brother John had sent to him from Gibraltar:

True it is that I have received nothing from thence for above 12 years: but as insects, we know, are conveyed from one country to an other in a wonderful manner: & as this insect from it's sluggish nature can extend it's depredations but slowly, it may possibly have escaped our notice 'till lately, tho' brought long ago.

Then Gilbert quotes a long passage on the coccus, from John's book, 'which I have before me in M:S'. So the *Fauna* was not lingering on the shelves in Ben's bookshop; it was in Gilbert's study all the time.

Sunday 27
55, 66. 29 8/10. NE, SE.   *White frost, cloudless, sweet even:, red.*

It's late May, and in Selborne the lanes are edged with cow parsley, nodding and waving, brimming with white. Gilbert swishes his way past it, watching for birds. He watches in the farmyards, too, with equal fascination. In a late letter in *The Natural History* about bird songs and calls, he turns to the yard. 'Take a chicken of four or five days old,' he writes, 'and hold it up to a window where there are flies, and it will immediately seize its prey, with little twitterings of complacency; but if you tender it a wasp or a bee, at once its note becomes harsh, and expressive of disapprobation and a sense of danger.' How can this be?

In the farmyards, where he notes the chickens' sense of danger, the hens – such docile, domesticated birds – turn out to have a darker side. Cruelty is here, human and avian. A neighbour, Gilbert writes, furious at a sparrowhawk attacking his poultry, had trapped it in a net, clipped its wings, cut off its claws, stuck a cork on its bill and thrown it to the hens:

Imagination cannot paint the scene that ensued: the expressions that fear, rage, and revenge inspired were new, or at least such as had been unnoticed before: the exasperated matrons upbraided, they execrated, they insulted, they triumphed. In a word, they never desisted from buffeting their adversary till they had torn him in an hundred pieces.

The air crackles with fear and rage. Farmyard birds and animals have their own inner beings, hatreds and desires. He picks out, for example, one particular pig. It's hard to know the natural lifespan of a hog, he writes, because it isn't profitable for a farmer to keep that 'turbulent animal' for its full time. But one neighbour, who could afford to, kept his old Bantam sow – 'as thick as she was long' – until a grand old age. For ten years or so, she produced two litters a year, about ten piglets at a time; once, over twenty, but as that was double the number of her teats, several died. She knew what she wanted and how to get it:

> From long experience in the world, this female was grown very sagacious and artful: – when she found occasion to converse with a boar she used to open all the intervening gates, and march, by herself, up to a distant farm where one was kept; and when her purpose was served would return by the same means.

They estimated that she had, in her time, borne over three hundred piglets. Marvellous as she was, she was not an object of sentiment. Fattened up after her last, much smaller, litter, she proved 'good bacon, juicy, and tender; the rind or sward, was remarkably thin'.

Farmyard life demonstrates, too, Gilbert's view that 'there is a wonderful spirit of sociality in the brute creation, independent of sexual attachment'. Bonds can even grow between different species. One friend, he reports, who had a single horse, also had only one solitary hen:

> These two incongruous animals spent much of their time together in a lonely orchard, where they saw no creature but each other. By degrees an apparent regard began to take place between these two sequestered individuals. The fowl would approach the quadruped with notes of complacency, rubbing herself gently against his legs: while the horse would look down with satisfaction, and move with the greatest caution and circumspection, lest he should trample on his diminutive companion. Thus, by mutual good offices, each seemed to console the vacant hours of the other.

Why is this so moving? Loneliness, companionship, care, affection – all these are here.

Monday 28
59. 29 8/10½. E, SE, NW.　　　　　*White frost, cloudless, fine, gale, sweet even:, red.*

Tuesday 29
59, 70. 29 7/10. E, SE, S.　　　　　*The limes begin to show bracteal*
Dew, cloudless, sweet even:　　　　*leaves. St foin blows out.*

Across the road from The Wakes, the pollarded limes that hide the blood and the guts of the butcher's shop are ready to flower. Between the heart-shaped leaves, which the moth caterpillars and aphids devour, pale-green bracts appear. Each has a thin stalk dangling down, with a bud at the end like a small berry. Soon these will burst into clusters of greeny-yellow flowers, dripping nectar, sending yet another scent floating on the breeze, pulling in the bees.

Wednesday 30
63, 73½. 29 6/10. SE, S, SE. Tulips begin to go-off.
Sun, sultry, grey, sweet even:

Thursday 31
63½, 72. 29 6/10½. NE, SE.
Sun, cloudless, sweet even:

The last two days in Selborne are really warm. The tulips are turning blowsy, beautiful in death.

JUNE

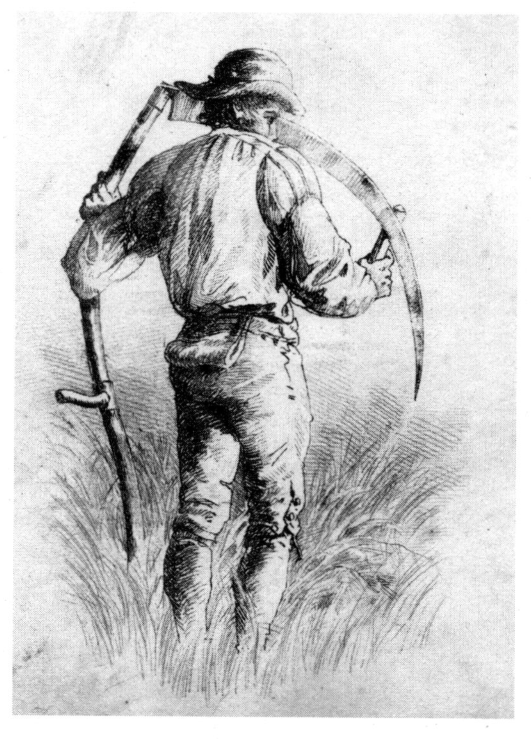

'Sharpening the Scythe' by W. H. Pyne, from his book *Rustic Figures in Imitation of Chalk* (1817). The pouch on the mower's belt is so he can carry his whetstone.

T HE DAYS ARE LONG, with mist in the morning and blue twilight. The earth bakes and the soil crumbles, grass turns brown
and plants wilt, but in the dappled shade of the Hanger it feels
cool. Five years from now, as May slips into June, Gilbert will write in
his journal:

> The grass-hopper lark whispers in my hedges. That bird, the fern-owl,
> & the nightingale, of an evening may be heard at the same time: &
> often the wood-lark, hovering & taking circuits round in the air at a
> vast distance from the ground.

> While high in air, & pois'd upon it's wings,
> Unseen the soft, enamour'd wood-lark sings.

'Wood-larks in summer,' he adds, 'sing all night in the air.'

The couplet is from his poem, 'The Naturalist's Summer-Evening
Walk', the only one of his poems included in the first edition of *The
Natural History*, which he was working on from time to time during this
summer of 1781. There is no clear timeline to the writing of his book, although one can identify key stages: his correspondence with his brother
John in Gibraltar; Daines Barrington's suggestion that he might write
a book; Gilbert's assertion in 1774 that he had plenty of material in his
letters and journals. His 'writing' was a process of gradual accretion, as
he cut and revised his letters to Thomas Pennant and Barrington and
added material from his journals. The book seemed to grow organically,
like a garden that has a basic structure but changes all the time as one
adds new plants, removes others, adjusts the balance or colour.

By 1781, he was working on the *Antiquities* and beginning to see
how he could give shape to the first part of his book, *The Natural History*,
by framing it with invented introductory and concluding letters. He
may, at times, have thought of adding more poems – we cannot know.

In writing poetry, Gilbert cloaked his engagement with nature in formal dress. While he saw himself as a scientist – a 'natural philosopher'

– his response was also conditioned by the pastoral verse that he had embraced in his youth. His student years were in his mind this year, when Samuel Johnson's essay on William Collins, who had died in 1759, was published in his *Lives of the Poets*. Johnson's account – an extended version of a sketch attached to an edition of Collins's poetry in 1763 – recognised his friend's striving for 'the grandeur of wildness and the novelty of extravagance', and was tenderly sympathetic to his agonised mental struggles. This year, too, a letter appeared in the *Gentleman's Magazine* from a fellow student, describing Collins as 'warm in his friendships, and visionary in his pursuits', and vividly describing how he was rescued in a fit of despair in Merton Lane in Oxford by two friends (one of them was Jo Warton). The handwriting, it was said, was that of Gilbert White.

Gilbert's own poetry was sedate rather than wild and visionary. But beneath his easy-going surface was a man of deep feeling. 'You are a Man, as I have long known, so very much Master of your Passions,' wrote his old friend John Mulso, '& so guarded in your Behaviour & even in your Expressions, that when I see a little Ebullition I guess there is a considerable Fire beneath.'

Friday 1
65, 79. 29 6/10½. SE, S, SW. Grass-walks burn very much.
Hot sun, sultry,   *Ground chops.*
cloudless, red even: *Roses begin to blow. Wheat spindles for ear.*

I'm writing this at the end of a late-spring heatwave, and I'm thinking of Gilbert's grass walks 'burning' at The Wakes. On the first day of June 1781, he notes that the temperature is already 65°F at eight in the morning, rising to 79°F (26°C) at midday. The earth is hard and cracked, like a choppy sea. The old roses are coming into their own – damasks and Bourbons – making rivers and pools of scent. In the fields, the plaited spikes of wheat are forming above their long stems, like spindles, twisting the yarn.

Saturday 2
68½, 76. 29 5/10. SE, S, SW.   *Tulips are gone.*
Sun, cloudless, sultry,   *The heat injures the flowers in bloom.*
broken clouds, sweet even: red.   *Stfoin in full bloom. Fly catcher has*
                                                             five eggs.

The flycatchers, whose arrival he watched in May, like to nest in climbers, in thick ivy or rambling honeysuckles. At The Wakes, one pair often chose the vine over the parlour window, so that Gilbert could peer in and see the brown-and-red-speckled eggs in a woven nest of straw and moss, lined with feathers. In early June 1785, four years from now, he will watch the male feed the hen in her nest and see their five fledglings fly at the end of the month. A year later, he notes that in the garden of his neighbour, Richard Butler, a spotted flycatcher has built its nest on a shelf in an outhouse, behind the head of an old rake. It was only five feet from the ground – a foolish choice: 'On the same spot a pair of the same birds built last year: but as soon as there were young the nest was torn down by a cat.'

The Wakes' flycatchers, however, survived, one pair nesting over the window, and another in the Virginia creeper over the garden door.

Sunday 3
66, 73. 29 4/10½. SW, W.   *Wheat-ears begin to burst-out.*
Clouds, sprinklings,   *Boys bring hornets.*
sun & brisk gale, dark.

Whit Sunday, and a warm day again. Gilbert has his well-thumbed Whitsun sermon ready. His theme is the blessing of unasked-for gifts – of the Holy Spirit, love, the reward of good works.

Hornets were hardly the gifts he preached about, but he was undoubtedly pleased to receive them from the boys at his door. With their brown and yellow stripes and reddish wings, they look daunting because they are so huge and their humming is so deep and loud. Like social wasps, hornets build large, wave-like, papery nests from chewed-up wood and dry grass, often in trees, but unlike wasps, they are attracted to the light and gather round lamps or lighted windows in the dusk, buzzing ferociously. They seem threatening, but only the females sting, and this hurts less than a honeybee sting, or so the Sussex Wildlife Trust tells me, adding: 'the simple fact is that the European hornet is a docile creature, avoiding conflict and rarely displaying any form of aggression unless the nest is approached or the colony is threatened. It suffers from an undeserved reputation.' Are they really, then, gentle creatures?

The hornets we fear today are the darker Asian hornets, with their orange faces and yellow legs, which arrived in France in 2004 and have been found across the south of England since 2016. They lurk outside the hives of honeybees, ambushing workers as they go in and out, chopping them up to feed their larvae – specialist predators, murderous beasts.

Monday 4
63, 65. 29 5/10. W, NW.   *Clouds, strong gale, sun, cool air, chill.*

June was a time for visits, paid and returned. This June, John and Jenny Mulso come to stay, with their children. Gilbert's friendship with Mulso has not faded since their student days. Fourteen years before, in 1767, Mulso had moved from his windy Yorkshire parish to Witney, where Gilbert could ride over to see him when he was in Oxford. He was always delighted to see 'my good friend Mr: John Mulso Rector of Witney', but equally excited one year to find the rare base hoarhound, or downy woundwort, 'the *Stachys Fuchsii* of Ray', growing in a corner of Witney Park, and again near Burford. It was still flowering, he wrote in his journal, '& abounded with seed: a good parcel of which I brought away with me to sow in the dry banks round the village of Selborne'. Mulso would have been amused. He knew Gilbert so well, and had imagined him the year before, out walking, 'wth your Eyes fixed on ye Ground most Part of the Summer. You will pass wth the Country Folks as a Man always making of Sermons, while you are only considering a weed'.

A YEAR WITH GILBERT WHITE

Mulso was right: sermons had indeed given way to weeds, and birds, and insects, and weather. Gilbert stopped writing his sermons when he became interested in botany: he wrote his last, on charity (Corinthians 13:1–3), at the start of June 1765, and preached it at Farringdon on the 9th of that month. Now here's a curious thing: his sermons, with their fervent language, had adopted the conventional Anglican theology of divine reward and punishment, sin and redemption, mercy and grace, faith and good works. Yet there is no hint of these doctrines in the journals or *The Natural History of Selborne*. His writings on nature suggest a different kind of faith, closer to the deism of writers like Erasmus Darwin.

As a physico-theologist, Gilbert looked for the divine in the physical world, not in the Bible and the Gospels. The word 'God' appears only a handful of times in *The Natural History*, and 'Creator' only once. When baffled, he appeals to 'Providence', where provision always comes with a hint of chance, accident or surprise. Worship gives way to 'wonder': at the limbs of a frog, the longevity of a tortoise or the possibility that the cuckoo might choose the nest of a particular species to leave its egg:

> this would be adding wonder to wonder, and instancing in a fresh manner that the methods of Providence are not subject to any mode or rule, but astonish us in new and variable appearances.

'Wonder' implies mystery, beyond human understanding. His use of the word reminds me of William Cowper, writing his famous hymn 'God Moves in a Mysterious Way' in 1773, at the same time as Gilbert was slowly planning his book. Cowper was seeking consolation in the face of despair and depression – 'The bud may have a bitter taste, / But sweet will be the flow'r' – while Gilbert was marvelling at the intricacy of the world. But the faith in 'design' is the same:

> God moves in a mysterious way,
> His wonders to perform;

> He plants His footsteps in the sea,
> And rides upon the storm.
>
> Deep in unfathomable mines
> Of never failing skill;
> He treasures up His bright designs,
> And works His sovereign will.

Tuesday 5
60, 63. 29 3/10½. W, S.   *Grey, no dew, sun & clouds,*
                            dark, rain, rain.

Rain, rain, rain. Ditches gurgle with water, field springs bubble through the grass, meadowsweet drinks in the damp. Sometimes, June heat ends in still wilder storms. Three years from now, on 5 June 1784, Gilbert will record a huge hailstorm: 'Much damage done to the corn, grass & hops by the hail; & many windows broken! Vast flood at Gracious street! . . . Hail near Norton two feet deep.' Next day, after excited talk in the village, he would add a long note, describing how the downpour caused a flash flood in the Oakhanger stream,

> doing great damage to the meadows, & fallows by deluging the one, & washing away the soil of the other. The hollow lane by Norton was so torn & disordered as not to be passable 'till mended: rocks being removed that weighed 200 weight. The flood at Gracious street ran over the goose-hatch, & mounted above the fourth bar of Grange-yard gate. Those that saw the effect that the great hail had on ponds & pools say, that the dashing of the water made an extraordinary appearance, the froth & spray standing-up in the air three feet above the surface! . . . The rushing & roaring of the hail as it approached was truely tremendous.

Wednesday 6
61, 63. 29 2/10. W, S. 27.   *The garden is somewhat refreshed.*
Rain, sun & clouds,   *Elders begin to blow.*
sweet even: *Full moon.*

A good day – the flowering of the elder is Gilbert's symbol of high summer, and the rain has helped the dusty garden. But the year before, this month was disturbed not by deluges, but by political storms. On 6 June, Gilbert wrote: 'Terrible riots in London: & unpresidented burnings & devastations by the mob!' Across the river in South Lambeth, his family were safe, but the yelp of horror was a measure of his fear.

There was industrial conflict in the north, trouble in Ireland and unrest prompted by disastrous news of the American war. In April 1780, John Cartwright and others had founded the Society for Constitutional Information, campaigning for reform, and in June, the Duke of Richmond had introduced a bill into the Lords to 'restore' universal male suffrage and annual parliaments. Just as these were being debated, Lord George Gordon marched on Parliament, heading a mob carrying the Protestant Association's petition against the Roman Catholic Relief Act of 1778, which allowed Catholics to hold landed property. This had been a liberal measure, an apparently uncontroversial correction of anti-Catholic statutes, and the violent reaction of Gordon's crew took almost everyone by surprise. The riots, which lasted from 2 to 9 June, were as much an anti-establishment protest as a sectarian demonstration. Catholic chapels were burned and homes attacked, prisoners were freed from Newgate, the Bank of England was besieged. About three hundred people were killed.

Writing to her brother Tom, Gilbert's niece Molly was as much amazed as afraid:

> Last night there were seen fires in seven different places tho in
> general they have the precaution not to burn houses but to bring the
> furniture into the street and burn it in several heaps. There is a guard

at Lambeth palace and at other places where they have threatened to come but the soldiers seem to be of little service in quelling the riot, as many of the Guards declare they would be of the same side if they dare . . . at present things are in a very bad situation.

The archbishop had left Lambeth Palace, and many people had fled. 'I think if my Uncle White hears of these riots he will very likely not come to Town, as a little matter intimidates him, and I think this is much more frightful than a French invasion, at least I am more alarmed at it.'

The Gordon riots overcame Gilbert's practice of excluding politics from his journal. This was partly because he was worried for his brothers and their families; partly because he himself, as Molly suggested, loved a quiet life and was fearful of any mob. It was Protestant violence, not Catholic faith, that appalled him.

Molly's comment about the French invasion suggests how anxious he could be. A recent invasion scare was still in people's minds. In the summer of 1779, a combined French and Spanish fleet had been spotted off Plymouth. All the counties on the south coast had been thrown into panic and confusion. The danger passed – the enemy fleet hovered off Cornwall, and then a violent easterly gale drove them away, out into the Atlantic. But the threat was real enough. It turned out that an army of 40,000 men had gathered in Normandy, with 400 transport ships; the plan had been to seize the Isle of Wight and then take Portsmouth, only 25 miles from Selborne.

Thursday 7
60½, 63. 29 2/10. W, NW, SW.   *Much distant thunder.*
Dark, moist, sun & clouds, thunder,   *Great showers to the NE. & NW.*
showers, great showers about.

The last week has been cooler, and now Gilbert hears the rumbling of far-off thunder, bringing more rain in its train. After the showers, dragonflies and damselflies glitter over streams and ponds, and mayflies rise in dancing clouds.

Gilbert watched the mayflies on the pools by Gracious Street, where the swallows and martins swooped to catch them. Ten years ago, in 1771, when he was riding over to see his brother Harry at Fyfield, he had been stunned by the number of mayflies on the watercress streams at Alresford: 'The air was crouded with them, & the surface of the water covered. Large trouts sucked them in as they lay struggling on the surface of the stream, unable to rise til their wings were dryed.'

Gilbert put the mayflies into his summer-evening poem, among the cast of birds and animals:

> When day declining sheds a milder gleam,
> What time the may-fly haunts the pool or stream;
> When the still owl skims round the grassy mead,
> What time the timorous hare limps forth to feed;
> Then be the time to steal adown the vale,
> And listen to the vagrant cuckoo's tale;
> To hear the clamorous curlew call his mate,
> Or the soft quail his tender pain relate;
> To see the swallow sweep the dark'ning plain
> Belated, to support her infant train;
> To mark the swift in rapid giddy ring
> Dash round the steeple, unsubdu'd of wing . . .

The poet's tone alters as the light fades. He talks of 'melancholy joy', of 'a pleasing kind of pain'. The dew, when it falls, feels cold. 'Away, retire,' he writes,

> For see, the glow-worm lights her amorous fire!
> Thus, ere night's veil had half obscur'd the sky,
> Th'impatient damsel hung her lamp on high:
> True to the signal, by love's meteor led,
> Leander hasten'd to his Hero's bed.

I can see Gilbert's pleasure in the conceit of the lamp as glow-worm attracting her mate, but it's a startling leap from a pastoral evening to the tragedy of Hero, lighting her lantern to call Leander across the stormy Hellespont. Even if it is merely a standard trope, there's something disquieting here.

The Virgilian pastoral is often disturbed by erotic yearning or by change and transience, and so are Gilbert's poems about Selborne. Single as he was, he seems rather to have relished the 'pleasing pain' of longing.

Friday 8
57. 29 2/10. NW, SW, SE.   *Begin to put out the annuals.*
Dark, showers, showers,
showers.

Saturday 9
58. 29 4/10. E, NE, N.   *Put out more annuals: they were pricked*
Dark & moist, showers,   *out in a second bed, & are stocky.*
thunder, showers.   *A pair of swallows hawk for flies 'til within*
    a quarter of nine o' clock: they probably
    have young hatched.

Practically, rather than poetically, Gilbert plants out the annuals, as he has done every June for the last thirty years. He grew these from seed, raising the seedlings in a cold frame or a nursery bed filled with compost. How close he feels to us, employing terms we still use today, like 'pricking out'. He plants his annuals near the house, in specially made banks, where the plants could rise in tiers, as well as in the twenty round 'basons' on Baker's Hill. It will be a grand, gaudy show: sweet williams, pinks, African and French marigolds, marvel of Peru, China asters and sunflowers – red and pink, yellow, orange and bronze.

Indoors, creatures are stirring, including the cricket on the hearth, the star of folk stories. On 9 June 1782, he will write: 'When the servants have gone to bed some time, & the kitchen left dark, the hearth swarms with young crickets about the size of ants: there is another set among them of larger growth: so that it appears that two broods have hatched this spring.' In 1785, he will ponder them again: 'Crickets sing much on the hearth this evening: they feel the influence of moist air, & sing against rain.' They feel the need for a mate even more, the lovesick males scraping and chirping for hours in a frenzy of hope.

Sunday 10
58. 29 4/10. E, SE. 87.   Heavy showers about. Wheat out in ear,
Showers, showers, dark   & not lodged in this district.
& still.

The wheat spikes have emerged from the flag leaf, the last leaf of the plant. Once fertilised, the kernels will begin their slow stages of ripening, changing from soft blue–green to dusty gold. This year, at least at the moment, the wheat stands high, not flattened and 'lodged' by rain.

On his evening walk, Gilbert looks up to see Venus, which, he writes in a note, 'is just become an evening star'. In the spring, with a night sky undimmed by light pollution, the planet was so bright that it cast shadows of the window bars on the floors and walls. Now, it is paler, but he watches it until it sets in the south-west, over the end of the Hanger, in 'strong twilight'. I look up, too. It is indeed extraordinary to see Venus shine so clearly, all on its own in the pale evening sky, while a ghostly moon swims up.

Monday 11
58½. 29 5/10. E, S, West.   Bees swarm much.
Sun & clouds, sweet even: Sheep are shorn. Planted-out annuals.

When the hive is full, a new queen bee appears and the old queen flees with her followers, searching for somewhere to live. The hives at The Wakes were really 'Thomas's bees', despite Gilbert's possessive tone:

My bees when swarming settle every year on the boughs of the Balm
of Gilead Fir.

Yesterday they settled at first in two swarms, which soon coalesced
into one. To a thinking mind few phenomena are more striking than
the clustering of bees on some bough, where they remain in order, as
it were, to be ready for hiving . . .

He quotes Book IV of Virgil's *Georgics* – '*arbore summa Confluere,
& lentis uvam demittere ramis . . .*' – where the bees, bursting out of the
oxen's guts, 'trail in unending clouds, and now surge / To a treetop and
dangle in clusters from the limber boughs'.

The shorn sheep he sees today also appear in the *Georgics*, grazing
in the shade of great oaks in Book III, and treated with olive oil and
hellebore and bitumen after shearing. They are there, too, in the poets
Gilbert read who look back to Virgil: in James Thomson's 'Summer' and
James Dyer's didactic *The Fleece* (1757), of which Johnson said, sternly:
'The subject, Sir, cannot be made poetical.' In Selborne, shearing always took place in the second week in June, beginning without fail on
a Monday. Shepherds and villagers moved from farm to farm, flock to
flock, gathering the sheep on the downs, herding them in pens, washing them, grabbing and holding them, clipping them with their shears,
folding the fleeces, stamping the owner's brand on the sheared sheep
with melted tar – a raucous, smelly, sweaty, song-filled, communal task.

Tuesday 12
60½. 29 4/10. N. NE. 22, 87. Vines begin to blow: the bloom is early.
Dark, heavy showers.   Thinned the apricots, peaches, & nectarines.

It's a miserable day, but Gilbert and Thomas Hoar are still busy outside, in the orchard and along the fruit wall. The steady temperature
of the past two weeks has been just what the grapes needed for flowering. Grapes are hermaphroditic plants; they need no bees or wind to
pollinate them. The buds form a cluster; to be technical, the five petals

in the bud form a shell, a calyptra, enclosing the male stamens, which have two pollen sacs each and surround the female parts. When they flower, as Gilbert's are doing now, the petals curve outwards as tiny white flowers; when these dry and fall off, the sacs burst, spilling a mass of pollen onto the female stigma. Soon, with good weather and good luck, the grapes will begin to form.

All is calm and busy, but three years from today, 12 June will be a day of drama and relief. In late May 1784, Timothy the tortoise would vanish, leaving Thomas disconsolate and Gilbert dismayed. He told Molly: 'We have lost poor Timothy, who, being always in a great bustle in such hot weather, got out, we suppose, at the wicket, last Thursday, and is wandered we know not whither.' It is not until 12 June that he can report Timothy's rescue from a nearby field. Timothy, too, Gilbert imagined fancifully, was subject to heartache and longing, and had conceived an idea that something special was to be found 'in the range of the meadow, and Baker's hill',

> and that beautiful females might inhabit those vast spaces, which appeared boundless in his eye. But having wandered 'til he was tired, and having met with nothing but weeds, and coarse grass, and solitude, he was glad to return to the poppies, and lettuces, and the other luxuries of the garden.

After the Mulsos come to stay that summer, their daughter Hester (always called 'Hecky', like her aunt Hester Chapone) sends Gilbert some verses on the tortoise. In return, he writes a long letter in Timothy's voice, recounting his history, his move to Selborne and his escape and hunt for love. For Timothy, Arcadia proves empty:

> Know then, tender-hearted lady, that my greatest misfortune, and what I have never divulged to anyone before is — the want of society of my own kind. This reflection is always uppermost in my own mind, but comes upon me with irresistible force every spring.

Wednesday 13
61. 29 3/10½. S, SW.   *The house-martins, which build in old nests*
Dark, sun & clouds,   *begin to hatch, as may be seen by their*
sweet even: *throwing-out the egg-shells.*
    Some wheat lodged. Wheat begins to blow.

Today, Gilbert counts the eggshells on the ground and waits for the young house martins to appear. Over the years, he has made many similar entries, noting how the thrown-out shells marked the hatching of an early brood, implying that the parents used a nest built the previous year. They started at crack of dawn: 'Martins begin building at half-hour after three in the morning.' If he watched them then, he must have been an early riser, like the birds.

In South Lambeth, Thomas was equally entranced by the martins, although in 1782, his enthusiasm would leave Gilbert with one criticism:

> My Bro.r Thomas White nailed-up several large scallop-shells under the eaves of his house at South Lambeth to see if the house martins would build in them. These conveniences had not been fixed half an hour, before several pairs settled upon them; & expressing great complacency, began to build immediately. The shells were nailed on horizontally, with the hollow side upward; & should, I think, have had a hole drilled in their bottoms to let-off moisture from driving rains.

In London and in Selborne, Gilbert watches the birds defend their nests. As soon as a hawk appears, he writes, one bird 'calls all the swallows and martins about him, who pursue in a body, whilst they buffet and strike their enemy until they have driven him from the village, darting down from above on his back, and rising in a perpendicular line in perfect security'. A brilliant piece of writing, as well as observation.

Thursday 14
61. 29 4/10. SE, SW. 22.   *We have planted-out a vast show of*
Rain, rain, dark, red even: *annuals, which will want no watering.*

Rain on Tuesday, and again last night, has softened the ground. The soil is now dark and moist, so his seedlings won't shrivel.

Friday 15
60. 29 3/10. S, SE.   *Grey, cloudy, small scuds.*

Saturday 16
59½. 29 4/10¼. S, SE.   *My garden in nice order, & full of flower*
Sun & clouds, rainbow,   *in bloom. Lilies, roses, fraxinellas, red*
showers about, fine   *valerians, Iris's, &c &c. now make a gaudy*
afternoon.   *show.*

Sunday 17
61. 29 5/10. S, SE.   *Wheat blows finely, & promises for a great*
Shower, sun & clouds.   *crop.*

Monday 18
62. 29 5/10½. S, SE. 22.   *The St foin is in a bad way about the*
Early showers, clouds,   *neighbourhood.*
heavy showers, thunder,
vast showers about.

While he checks the state of the annuals, wheat and sainfoin, he notices the insects, too. One of these is a wild bee, which he watches boring holes for its nest in his grass walks, when the morning sun shines on the grass. Giving this its Linnaean name, *Apis longicornis*, he used its appearance as a regular marker for high summer. Long-horned bees, Britain's largest solitary bees (modern name *Eucera longicornis*), like a habitat rich in legumes such as sainfoin and clover. It was the adult female that Gilbert watched making her burrow, which she smooths and fills with a pollen-and-honey paste for the larvae to feed on.

Other June insects catch his eye. He sees a 'Dragon-fly with blue upright wings, *Libellula virgo, sive puella*', one of the chaser, darter and skimmer dragonflies. He delights in a hummingbird hawk-moth: 'A vast insect: appears after it is dusk, flying with an humming noise, & inserting its tongue into the bloom of the honeysuckle: it scarcely settles on the plants but feeds on the wing in the manner of humming birds.' Hovering over the flowers, it probes for nectar with its long, thin tongue, bending back its orange–brown wings – its wingspan can reach nearly 6 centimetres. There are butterflies, too, some less welcome than others: 'White butter-flies innumerable: woe to the cabbages!'

Tuesday 19
64, 70. 29 5/10. S, SE, 11.   *A strange swarm of bees came & settled on*
Shower, sun, sultry,   *my balm of Gilead Fir.*
soft hot even: *Much thunder, & heavy rains to the N:E.*
    Vast hail storm at Farnham.

This swarm from a stranger's hive – did someone come and collect it?

Wednesday 20
67. 29 5/10. SE, E.   *Much thunder, & vast showers to the*
Sun, sultry, clouds, fog.   *westward. Vast storm, & rain at Winton.*
    Young pheasants. These storms were very
    terrible at Sarum, & in the vale of white-
    horse; &c.

Thursday 21
66½. 29 3/10¾. N, NE.   *Finished cutting the St foin, which has*
Fog, sun, sultry,   *stood full long. The 14th crop. Sold it to*
sweet even: red.   *John Hale. In some parts a good burden.*

Mid-June has been mild, with the temperature in the low-to-mid-sixties Fahrenheit (15–18°C), and Selborne has escaped the storms. In foggy, heavy weather, Gilbert's men cut the sainfoin – about ten days later than usual – and he sells it to his farmer friend across the road.

Midsummer is a season of haymaking and harvest, but it's also a time for flirtation and romance. It may be a jolt to turn from cutting sainfoin to songs and dalliance, but looking back at Gilbert's life, I can see that almost twenty years before, he had been diverted from his farming and his nature notes by a round of festivities full of pastoral romance.

It was a summer of celebration. After the death of his uncle Charles White, vicar of Bradley, Gilbert now owned The Wakes outright and was happily acting as host to a large, enjoyable gathering. The setting was poetic, with the thatched hermitage near the top of the Zig-Zag poised like an eyrie above the woods and meadows. Gilbert described its charm in his poem 'An Invitation to Selborne':

> Oft on some evening, sunny, soft and still,
> The Muse shall lead thee to the beech-grown hill,
> To spend in tea the cool, refreshing hour,
> Where nods in air the pensile, nest-like bower . . .
> . . . Romantic spot! from whence in prospect lies
> Whate'er of landscape charms our feasting eyes;
> The pointed spire, the hall, the pasture-plain,
> The russet fallow, or the golden grain,
> The breezy lake that sheds a gleaming light,
> Till all the fading picture fail the sight.

John Mulso could imagine how much he enjoyed taking his visitors up the hill and pointing out the view. 'Yes, I see you upon ye Area of ye Hermitage,' he wrote,

the arm extended & the Finger pointing out ye happier Lights & Shades of ye Prospect! I see You under ye Beeches of the Lythe, You are in more soft & mild attitudes, a Sort of Pastoral Spirit possesses You; You hardly want to look over ye blue Forest, so contented are You in your green Recess . . .

The little hermitage might have appealed to solitary meditation –
like 'the Mossy Cell' of Milton's 'Il Penseroso' – but in June 1763, it was
also a perfect place for parties. The group who gathered there included
several of Gilbert's relations, as well as Mulso's brothers, Thomas and
Ned, who were staying at The Wakes along with Thomas's wife Mary
and a young friend, Harriot Baker. To add to the crowd, haring forty
miles across country to visit them came two young vicars: Gilbert's
brother Harry, from Fyfield, and his cousin Basil Cane, whose parish
lay just over the border with Wiltshire.

The lure for Harry, Basil and Ned Mulso, all in their early thirties,
lay across the road at the vicarage, where three of Mrs Etty's cousins had
come to stay: Anna, Kitty and Philadelphia, daughters of the wealthy
doctor William Battie. Anna was twenty-one, Kitty nineteen and Del-
phy a couple of years younger than Kitty. While they were there, Kitty
scribbled down her impressions of all their excursions, walks and jol-
lities in a packed, helter-skelter diary, which she titled 'A little Journal
of some of the Happiest days I have had in the happy Valley in the year
1763'. Writing about the 22 and 23 June (the Ettys' wedding anniversary), she bubbled breathlessly away, without a thought of punctuation,
describing how they 'sang and played' until late in the evening:

> . . . Went to bed between twelve & one o Clock was very merry after
> supper the next day being Mr. & Mrs. Etty's wedding-day we kept it
> with mirth & jollity. The morn was spent at the Harpsichord a Ball at
> night began minuets at half an hour after seven then danced country
> dances till near eleven went to supper after supper sat some time sung
> laugh't talk'd & then went to dancing again danced till 3 in the morn:
> at half an hour after four the company all went away we danced 30,
> danced, never had I such a dance in my life before nor ever shall I have
> such a one again I believe.

In her list of those there, she placed Gilbert, a sedate forty-two-year-
old, not with the dancers, but with the matrons, among 'Spectators'.

(Telling him of a ball at his house the following year, Mulso wrote: 'How you would have stared! & what Music Book must I have got for You to have studied in a Corner?')

The next day, at tea, Harry White appeared in full fancy dress as the 'Old Hermit' and read their fortunes. To Kitty, the hermitage was the most romantic place she had ever seen, especially in the evening. 'To see it by Lamp light,' she wrote, 'it look'd sweetly indeed. Never shall I forget the happiness of this day which exceeded any I ever had in all my Life, sweet Hermitage agreeable Company fine day good spirits.'

Friday 22
64. 29 3/10¾. NE, SE.   *Began to stop down the vines, which are in full*
Grey, blue mist, sun,   *bloom.*
brisk air, dark, wet.

As he prunes the lush growth on the vines, I wonder if Gilbert ever stopped to remember that long-ago June of 1763? Amid the fun there had been spots of seriousness. One morning, for example, Thomas Mulso gave 'a discourse upon Natural Phylosophy & Astronomy' and read passages from James Thomson's *Seasons*. 'I hope I edify'd by his sensible discourse,' wrote Kitty, solemnly.

I warm to Kitty. She liked mock haymaking more than discourses: 'went into the Hay field toss'd the hay about a little', she writes casually. She loved music and dancing. One Sunday, Ned Mulso 'sung us a song made upon the 3 sorceresses set to the Pastorrella', and the sisters decided they must all be shepherdesses. Kitty became 'Daphne', while Harry White, Basil Cane and Ned Mulso ('the Poor bewitched men') took the names of Strephon, Corrydon and Collin. In the Turkish tent set up in the meadow, 'we Shepherdesses danced; at nine the lamp was lighted, enchanting scene oh never did I see anything like it 'tis 'tis Arcadia Happy Happy Vale when shall I see thee again'.

At these dances, Gilbert was once again in the wings, supervising costumes. Kitty kept a wry verse, in his handwriting:

> Gilbert, a meddling, luckless swain
> Must alter Ladies dresses
> To dapper hats, & tucked-up train,
> And flow'r-enwoven tresses.
>
> But now the Lout with loss of heart
> Must for his rashness pay:
> He rues for tamp'ring with a dart
> Too prompt before to slay!

Was he slain? Harry White and Ned Mulso certainly were. When the girls left, as John Mulso put it, his brother and Harry were 're-duc'd, by ye departure of the *Sorceresses*, to the Elegiac Strain; and must at least hang Verses on the Beeches of the Hanger & ye Noar, if they do not serve themselves in ye same way'. Harry wrote a maudlin poem called 'Daphne's Departure', while Ned, Mulso reported, was still smarting months later: 'no great Matter, especially as it purges off in Poetry: when Passion is fancifull it is not dangerous'. With Gilbert, he feared it might be, 'for we, my Friend, begin to grow into a more serious Age, & to mean a little more what we profess'. When Gilbert went, uncharacteristically, to London, hoping to see the Batties, Mulso warned him to take care.

He may, fleetingly, have thought of marriage. Among the poems that he revised from time to time was 'Selborne Hanger. A Winter Piece. To the Miss Batties', written in November 1763. Although self-mockingly theatrical, it does suggest that something was lost. The Hanger mourns: 'When spouting rains descend in torrent tides, / See the torn zig-zag weeps its channelled sides':

> Amidst this savage landscape, bleak and bare,
> Hangs the chill hermitage in idle air;
> Its haunts forsaken, and its feasts forgot,
> A leaf-strown, lonely, desolated cot!

The poem ends with a plea for the girls' return. But they never spent another summer here. All three made good marriages, with appropriately well-off husbands. But Kitty kept her journal, with its youthful, ecstatic farewell:

> Adieu, happy Vale, enchanting Hermitage, much-loved stump, beauteous Hanger, sweet Lythe: to all I bid adieu with grateful thanks: may the Woods flourish; may no mischievous Boy hurt the little Nest; may all the good inhabitants have as many happy days there as I have had 'tis the sincere wish of Daphne

And so Gilbert returns to solitude again.

Saturday 23
62. 29 5/10. NE, N. 24.
Rain, dark & moist.

We pick the caterpillars, which again annoy the goose-berry-bushes. The wheat is in full bloom, & is not lodged. The large white cucumbers begin to set. Finished the stopping down the vines: the grapes begin to set.

It's a rainy Saturday, but everything in the garden and the fields is looking good. The sawfly caterpillars, which eat the gooseberry leaves from the ground up, leaving every branch bare, are being painstakingly removed. The wheat is flowering, the cucumbers are swelling, the vines have been thinned. Vines put on a lot of growth in the warm weather and need a seasonal pruning to avoid a great tangle of leaves, so now Gilbert and Thomas Hoar cut back vigorous shoots and stop any new flowers. That done, they can look forward to healthy bunches of big grapes rather than tiny new ones. A satisfying task.

Sunday 24
60. 29 4/10. NE.
Grey, & mild, dark
& still.

There are this summer about this church 11, or 12 pairs of swifts.

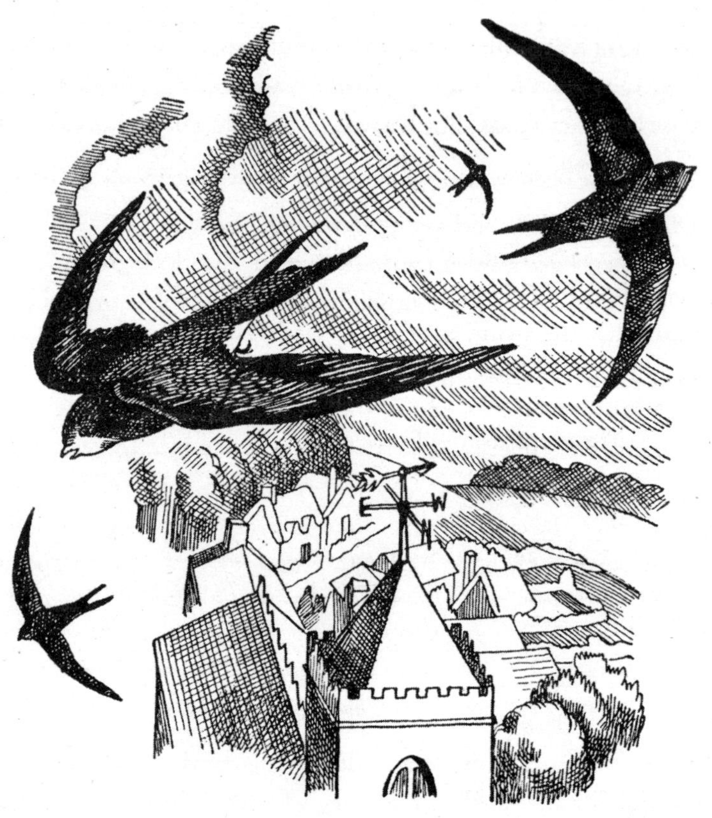

'Swifts Round the Church' by John Nash (1951). Nash was one of the leaders in the revival of landscape art from the 1930s to the 1950s, and his illustrations for *The Natural History of Selborne* are full of joyous spirit, energy and wit.

Midsummer's Day. Today, craning his neck, Gilbert watches the swifts scream in circles round the church. 'Just before they retire they squeak & dash & shoot about with wonderful rapidity. They are stirring at least seventeen hours when the days are longest.' He had made a note on this at his brother Harry's house in Fyfield on 25 June 1774, adding a touch of sentiment:

The swifts that dash round churches, & towers in little parties, squeaking as they go, seem to me to be the cock-birds: they never

     A YEAR WITH GILBERT WHITE

squeak 'til they come close to the walls or eaves, & possibly are then serenading their females, who are close in their nests attending the business of incubation.

I, too, have been watching swifts today, hurtling round the barn opposite, circling over our roof, whooshing past the chimney pots. They are still there when the last light is glimmering. Experts remain unsure of the purpose of these 'screaming parties', though they do seem to indicate that the swifts are nesting nearby. They are not confined to males, though, as Gilbert thought. The early groups are probably made up of older pairs meeting again; in June, they include young birds pairing for the first time; later, they will be swelled by this year's young. They start with one or two, then more join, then a whole crowd. As the light goes, the circles scatter, some birds going to their nests, others flying unimaginably high, to sleep on the wing in the clear upper air.

Monday 25

60. 29 4/10, 5/10. S, SE.   *Our fields of pease are in a sad lousy state.*
Dark & moist, grey,   *Took-off the frames from the cucumber-beds,*
fine even: *which have not born now for many weeks.*

A glum, grey day and lousy peas. Gilbert could mean that the peas are infested, not with lice, but with caterpillars, but it's more likely he sees them as lousy in the modern sense, already used in his day, meaning poor, shoddy and pathetic, thirsting for rain. He turns to the garden, braced for action. The first batch of cucumbers are yellowing and limp under the frames. Time to lift the glass off at last.

Tuesday 26

60. 29 6/10. NE, N, NW.   *My grapes are very forward, & out of bloom.*
Grey, threatning, sun,   *Fly-catchers have young.*
red even: vast dew.   *Young redstarts come abroad.*

This is more cheering: the grapes are promising, and young birds are fledging. The spotted flycatchers have four or five chicks, and might well have a second brood. The redstarts have six or seven, emerging from shiny blue eggs. Wrens, warblers and treecreepers all bring out their broods. When Gilbert began his journal in the late 1760s, he had noted the appearance of young birds throughout the month. Thus, in 1769:

1st Young redbreasts
13th Young titmice
14th Young *reguli non cristate*
19th Young sparrows
21st Young white-throats
23rd Young nightingales

The sweet-singing nightingales, Gilbert noticed, are 'very jealous of their young & make a jarring harsh noise if you approach them'.

Wednesday 27
60. 29 7/10. NW, W.   *The honey-buzzard sits hard.*
Sun, sun, heavy clouds,   *Young martins peep out of their nests.*
sweet even:

This summer, a pair of honey buzzards is nesting in a tall, slender beech tree in the Hanger. This week, he adds a long note describing their shallow, twiggy nest, lined with dead leaves. 'A boy climbed this tree,' he writes, 'tho standing on so steep & dizzy a situation, & brought down one egg, the only one in the nest, which had been sat-on for some time, & contained the embrio of a young bird.' The egg was smaller than the common buzzard's, not so round, with small red spots at each end, 'surrounded in the middle with a broad red zone'.

The hen bird is shot, and when Gilbert examines it, noting its black upper beak, short, stubby legs and long tail, he finds that it fits perfectly with the description in Willughby's *Ornithology* in 1676. He watches it fly. On the wing, he says, you can easily distinguish the honey buzzard from the common buzzard wheeling in high circles 'by it's hawk-like appearance, small head, wings not so blunt, & longer tail'. When the hen lies eviscerated on his bench, he finds its craw is full of frogs' limbs and 'snails without shells' – or slugs. Yet even in this state it keeps a touch of glamour, its irises remaining 'of a beautiful yellow colour'. Honey buzzards do have piercing eyes, fiercely yellow against their grey plumage. Summer visitors, they breed across southern England, from Devon to Norfolk, camouflaging their nests in the woods with a cover of leaves and bringing more branches from time to time to keep them green.

Writing his account, Gilbert deals crisply with the raid on the nest and the shooting of the hen. But he ends on a more melancholy note. 'The male honey-buzzard,' he writes, 'still haunts about the hanger; & on sunny mornings soars above the hill to inhale the coolness of the upper air.'

Thursday 28
64. 29 9/10. W, NW.   *Begin to cut my meadow-hay.*
Sun, sun & clouds,   *The early cucumbers, which have not born for*
sweet even: red.   *many weeks, now begin to show fruit.*

Now his own haymaking is starting. Fellow villagers come in to help, the men mowing, the women raking and tossing, and building the stooks. They start early, when the dew makes the grass easier to cut. First comes the swish of the long scythes. These are designed for right-handers, cutting from right to left, so that mowers can work in a team, moving together as if in a ballet, carefully spaced so that no blades touch, no ankles are cut. Every mower carries a whetstone to sharpen his blade. This, too, found a place in pastoral poetry, and Gilbert looked back to his favourites, Thomson and Milton, for examples. In 'Summer', he noted that Thomson

> mentions the whetting of a scythe as a pleasing circumstance, not
> from the real sound, which is harsh, grating, & unmusical; but from
> the train of summer ideas, which it raises in the imagination. No one

who loves his garden & lawn but rejoices to hear the sound of the mower on an early, dewy morning.

'Echo no more returns the chearful sound
Of sharpening scythe' . . .

Milton also, as a pleasing summer-morning occurrence, says [in 'L'Allegro'], 'The mower whets his scythe.'

When I visit Selborne, Keith Oakley, the head gardener at The Wakes, shows me how to hold a scythe, how to sweep it low and cut a swathe. I can see how the shaft is made to fit the height of a man, with handles, or 'grips', at chest and hip height. To cut, you twist to the right and swing the scythe close to the ground, so that the curving blade cuts deeper, arcing round your feet. After each swing, a heap of hay lies by your left boot. Then comes another step, another swing, leaving the heaps in a windrow, marking the edge of each swathe. In Gilbert's day, from these windrows the sweet-smelling hay was raked out to dry, then gathered into small heaps, or footcocks, which were tossed and raked into larger stooks, and finally piled onto a cart and carried off to build the rick.

In June, everyone is busy in the gardens and fields, including Gilbert's brothers Harry, in Fyfield, and Thomas and Ben, on the fringes of London. In the 1780s, Ben will gradually turn his business over to his sons Benjamin and John and become a 'gentleman farmer' on his Vauxhall estate. Seven years from now, in June 1788, watching the haymaking around Clapham and Battersea, Gilbert notes with some awe that Ben has already cut 87 acres of hay. Instead of sainfoin he sows lucerne (or alfalfa), and Gilbert counts '77 rows of Lucerne, each 48 yards long', which supplies Ben's horses with 'green meat' all summer long. His garden was impressive, too, with fifteen frames for melons, sixteen for cucumbers and '40 hand-glasses for ridge Cucumbers & other purposes'. Feeling slightly rivalrous, Gilbert is pleased when he comes home to find his own double-scarlet pomegranate and his passion flower blooming.

Friday 29
63. 30/10. W.   *Wheat begins to turn colour.*
Vast dew, sun, brisk   *Jasmine blows. China hollyhock blows.*
gale, fine even: *Rasps begin to ripen. Currans turn colour.*

Among the fruit bushes and raspberry canes, the currants show hints of red and black. Wheat glints pale, its kernels forming. Jasmine scents the air, and hollyhocks flower. These are now so far from 'exotic' that I quite forget the hollyhock came from China, its sturdiness a symbol of endurance. Seeds carried along trading routes reached the Middle East by the time of the Crusades, and, so the story goes, Eleanor of Castile brought some home from Palestine in 1272. Hollyhocks flower in illuminated books of hours and early herbals. Although Linnaeus changed the genus name from 'Mallow' to *Alcea* (which we still use), an irritated Philip Miller at the Chelsea Physic Garden wrote firmly that he would continue with 'Rose Mallow'. In his *Gardeners Dictionary*, Miller listed eleven varieties: single and double, white and yellow, scarlet and purplish black. They stood tall in the garden of The Wakes.

On this date, seven years before, Gilbert saw the first swallow fledglings, down by the stream: 'Some swallows this day bring out their broods, which are perchers, they place them on rails that go across a stream, & so take their food up & down the river, feeding their young in exact rotation.' This surprised him, as the young normally appeared in the first week of July. Sometimes, however, he saw them in the third week of June, and once, in 1776, on the 15th: 'very early indeed: probably the dame bred in an old nest, & so lost no time in building'. He particularly enjoys watching the swallows that fledge from nests in chimneys:

The progressive method by which the young are introduced into
life is very amusing. First they emerge from the shaft with difficulty

enough, and often fall through into the rooms below. For a day or so they are fed on the chimney top, and then they are conducted to the dead leafless branch of some tree, where, sitting in a row, they may be called *perchers*. In a day or two more they become *flyers*, but are still unable to take their own food; therefore they play about near the place where the dams are hawking for flies; when a mouthful is collected, at a certain signal given, the dam and the nestling advance, rising towards each other at an angle, and the young one all the while uttering such a quick little note of gratitude and complacency that a person must have paid very little regard to the wonders of nature that has not often remarked this feat.

One year, a cat went down a neighbour's chimney in search of those nests. Gilbert doesn't say if it caught its prey or fell down to the hearth, covered in soot, like the owls when they tried the same stunt.

Saturday 30
65. 29 8/10. SW, S.   *Green cucumbers bear. White cucumbers swell.*
Fog, sun, summer day, *Wheat is out of bloom, & the grain forming in*
mackarel sky, sweet even: *the husk. Sweet day. Lime-trees begin to blow.*
creeping mists.   *Some of the forwardest of those broods of young*
          martins that were hatched in old nests are out.

About nine in the evening a large shining meteor appeared falling from the s; towards the E: in an inclination of about 45 degrees, & parting in two before I lost sight of it. I was in Baker's hill in the shrubbery, having a very bad horizon; & therefore could not see how & where it fell.

Under mackerel skies and drifting mists, Gilbert breathes the honey-rich scent of the limes. On his evening walk, a falling star shoots across the sky. But where he is standing, he has to twist round to watch, as it disappears behind the cottages and trees. However accurate he is about the angle, his view, he knows, is partial.

       A YEAR WITH GILBERT WHITE

JULY

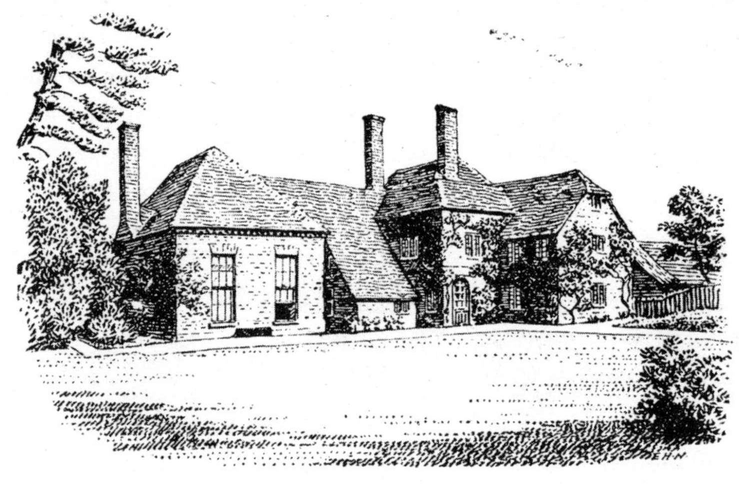

The Wakes, with Gilbert's new room on the left. Copied by E. H. New in 1900 from the 1802 edition of *The Natural History of Selborne*.

WHEN I VISIT SELBORNE in July, the village is almost hidden, cloaked, embraced, smothered in green. The trees have the heavy, dark fullness of high summer. Hedges are pushing across paths and straggling into meadows. Along the track towards the Priory, the tall, waving grass on the slopes looks dusty and bleached and dry. Yet despite our worry about the lack of insects, I find the meadows alive with bees and butterflies and moths, alighting for a moment, flickering and sailing off in every direction. On the other side of the valley, the beeches seem to touch the sky, their smooth grey trunks like leaning columns.

Sunday 1
64, 73. 29 4/10. SE, S.   *Wheel round the sun.*
Dew, sun, sultry with flisky *Some few young swallows are out.*
clouds, dark heavy horizon.

It is a soft, hot day, fanned by a southerly breeze. Beneath the 'flisky clouds', swallows circle high. Dogs pant and slumber in the heat, and cattle and sheep gather in the shade of the trees. On days like this, Gilbert notices how the cattle wade belly-deep into ponds to keep cool and 'ruminate and solace themselves from about ten in the morning to four in the afternoon':

> During this great proportion of the day they drop much dung, in which insects nestle; and so supply food for the fish, which would be poorly subsisted but from this contingency. Thus Nature, who is a great economist, converts the recreation of one animal to the support of another!

Monday 2
69. 3/10½, 4/10. SW, W.   *Made my rick of meadow-hay, which contains*
Sun, fog, dark &   *six jobbs, without one drop of rain. Some part*
threat'ning.   *of it would have been better, I think, had there*
    been some sun on the day of making.

Black clouds and a hint of rain. But the rick is made, even if the hay could have done with a bit more drying in the sun. Haymaking, which has been going on now for a couple of weeks, is long, hot work. In July 1783, when Gilbert's thermometer will reach 74°F by eight o'clock in the morning and 80°F at noon, he will write: 'The heat overcomes the grass-mowers, & makes them sick.'

Building his hayrick had made Gilbert happy for over twenty years now, and he could look back to his *Garden Kalendar* and his journal to check the dates on which the ricks were made. On 7 July 1759, for example, when Farmer Kelsey's labourers were helping him:

> Finished my Hay-rick in most excellent order. The weather has been so perfectly hot, & bright for these five days past that my Hay was all cut, & made in that time. The Crop was so great that Kelsey's people made 8 carryings of it: & the burden in the great mead was supposed to be greater than ever was known. To my own stock I added two tons from Farmer Lassam, which in all made a considerable rick.

Tuesday 3
64½. 4/10½, 29 5/10. SW, SW. *Rasps ripen. All fruits are forward.*
Sun, strong gales, sun *Cucumbers bear well.*
& dark clouds.

In between inspecting the garden and admiring the fruit, Gilbert goes to his study, where he is still adding to and shaping his book. It's ten years since he first thought of it, six years since his papers on the hirundines were published. He had shown part of an early draft to Mulso soon after that, in July 1775, provoking a rush of enthusiasm:

> You have a double Felicity in your Manner of Entertainment; You can gratify your Visitors both with beautiful Originals, & high Descriptions; Representations studiously copied from Nature & finished with a Masterly Hand. As you intend your Works for ye Public, I would not say so much in a Strain of Flattery; for tho' I would not tell

an Author how much I disliked his Productions, yet I might slubber them over with a hasty careless Compliment, or lose them in Silence . . .

Mulso was not one for silence, and he grew more and more impatient. In March 1776: 'The lateness of the Season now makes me suspect that your work will not come forth this Spring . . .'.

June 1777: 'As I do not see any Advertisement in the Papers, I conclude by ye Time of Year that You have deferred your Publication 'till next Winter. I wish you had not: Your Brother Ben is a timid man, & You yourself are too modest & nice . . .'

October 1777: 'I am angry that You speak so faintly about your own Work'. He expects it, he says, '*next Winter*'.

September 1780: 'Pray does your Book come out this Winter? I really cannot hold out any longer.'

I bet Gilbert groaned. It was now 1781. Mulso would have to hold out for eight more years until he held *The Natural History of Selborne* in his hands.

Wednesday 4
63. 29 8/10½. SW, SW.   *The bloom of the lime hangs in beautiful*
Sun, small showers, sun,   *golden tassels. The late orange, & white*
brisk gales, fine even: *lily make a fine contrast.*

Gilbert loves this moment, with the flush of the first lilies and the lime tassels swaying. A few years from now, he would discover that the limes that screened the butcher's shop had another use, too. In July 1790, his friend Richard Chandler, who had been travelling with his family in the south of France, will tell him that, there, an infusion of lime-tree blossoms is greatly valued 'as a remedy for coughs, hoarseness, fevers, &c', and that at Nîmes, he had seen

an avenue of limes that was quite ravaged & torn to pieces by people greedily gathering the bloom, which they dried & kept for their purposes.

Upon the strength of this information we made some tea of lime-blossoms, & found it very soft, well-flavoured, pleasant saccharine julep, in taste much resembling the juice of liquorice.

Gilbert does not say if he tried these infusions again, or if they helped his coughs.

Thursday 5
61. 29 7/10¾. SW, E.   *Men begin to mow their meadows.*
Sun, summer's day,   *Gardens suffer for want of rain.*
sweet even: red.   *Full moon.*

So far, this has been a dry month, good for hay, hard for gardeners. Swallows skim low over the meadow, and young perchers settle on Gilbert's walnut tree.

People from the village tell Gilbert of their findings and bring him gifts. One July, five young kestrels are found in an old magpie's nest. In July 1789, a woman will bring nightjar's eggs, uncovered near her home on the edge of the Hanger, and a peat cutter will give him eggs that he found in a bog on the moor; these were not snipe's eggs, as the man thought, but also nightjar's eggs, which look much the same. Perfectly camouflaged by their mottled plumage, like the bark of a tree, nightjars lay two eggs, directly on the ground; when they sit on the nest, they look like little logs. Gilbert loved these strange birds, which could only be seen for two hours a day, '& then in a dubious twilight, an hour after sun-set, & an hour before sun-rise'. In the last summer of his life, on 27 August 1792, he would watch one hurtle across the garden at dusk, showing off, he said, chasing moths, 'hawking round, & round the circumference of my great spreading oak for twenty times following, keeping mostly close to the grass; but occasionally glancing up amidst the boughs of the tree'. In its swooping flight it almost outmatched the swallow.

Other unusual birds come his way. In July 1792, Farmer Hoare's son will shoot 'a hen Wood-chat, or small Butcher-bird' that was washing, with her mate, at the Well Head spring. This was a small shrike, *Lanius senator*, only the size of a sparrow but easily spotted with its bright red–brown head. He had seen another variety of this family, with a tawny back, grey–blue head and black streak around the eyes, five years before, in South Lambeth: 'A pair of red-backed Butcher-birds, *lanius collurio*, have got a nest in Bro: Tho: outlet,' he wrote. 'They have built in a quickset-hedge. We took one of the eggs out of the nest: it was white; but surrounded at the big end by a circle of brown spots, *coronae instar.*' A month later, he found another nest nearer home, in Alton.

The name 'Butcher-bird' is apt (*Lanius*, its Linnaean name, comes from the Greek for 'butcher'). It's a hoarder, dashing from a high perch to catch its prey – beetles, flies, wasps, ants, grasshoppers – then carrying its victims to a 'larder', impaling them on thorns or even barbed wire (but this is rare), or pushing them into cracks. This graceful, if violent, red-backed visitor is now glimpsed only rarely on Britain's east coast on its passage to northern Europe in May and June, and again in early autumn, when it flies back south to Africa.

Friday 6
64, 71. 29 4/10¾. S, S.   *Brisk gale.*
Sun, sun, dark clouds,   *The wheat, in large fields, undulates before*
shower, showers.   *the gale in a most amusing manner.*

A strong southerly rushes through the Hanger, loud as a river. Saplings lean, leaves twirl and in the fields the wheat ripples like a sea.

In the evening, the rain comes. Gilbert often noticed that as soon as there were July showers, 'myriads of frogs, a second brood,' began to migrate from James Knight's ponds below Gracious Street, filling the lanes again. 'Some of the little frogs from the ponds,' he wrote in July 1776, 'stroll quite up the hill; they seem to spread in all directions.'

He comes in from the wind, perhaps a bit disheartened by the way it flattens his annuals and topples his hollyhocks. This week, the main event has been weighing Timothy, who has gained half a pound since emerging in April and is now 'seven pounds, & one ounce'.

He writes another note, a miniature story:

A pair of sparrow-hawks bred in a crows nest in the hanger. A boy climbed the tree, & found the young so fledge that they all escaped: but he brought down a young blackbird, a young h: martin & jay, clean picked & half devoured, which the dams had carryed to their brood. The old ones have made havock for some days among the young swallows & martins, which being but just out have no powers or command of wing. They carried-off also from a farm-yard a young duck larger than themselves.

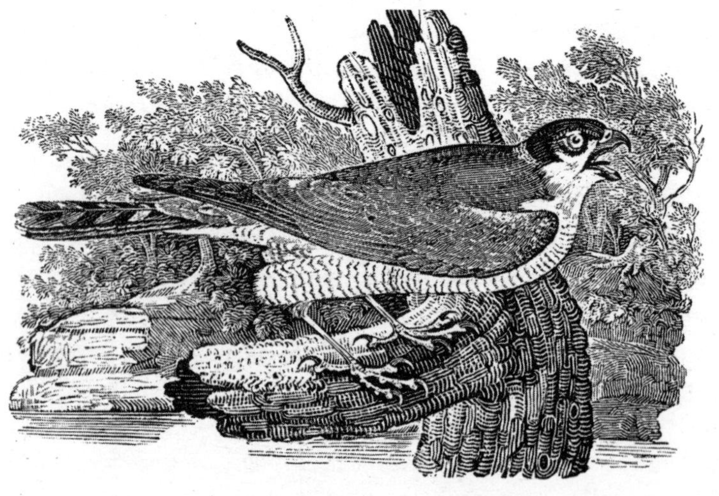

 'The Sparrowhawk' by Thomas Bewick, in *Land Birds* (1797).

This was too good to leave out of his book. He looked again at the two correspondences that formed the body of the work and inserted this story in 'Letter 43', addressed to Thomas Pennant, a concocted letter that he probably never sent. In it, he turns the brisk report of the journal into smoother prose, adding drama, cajoling the readers, animating the birds. The sparrowhawk's brood become 'so daring and ravenous' that they are 'a terror to all the dames in the village that had chickens or ducklings under their care'; when the boy climbs the tree, he discovers 'that a good house had been kept: the larder was well-stored'; the feeble young martins will eventually have the strength and skill 'to set such enemies at defiance'. But the fat duck disappears. Perhaps it wasn't true?

Late next July, a sparrowhawk will create more chaos, but this time it is doomed: 'Will: Tanner shot a sparrow-hawk, which had infested the village for some time.'

As if summoned, a sparrowhawk shot across my own back door yesterday, hurtling up to raid the sparrows' and martins' nests under the gutters. It had no luck and perched angrily on the fence. Every small bird vanished. The whole garden was silent.

Sunday 8
63. 29 3/10, 5/10. SW, W. 115.   *The cart-way runs.*
Showers, strong gales,   *H: martins feed their young on the*
vast showers, thunder,   *wing.*
showers, clouds.

In the pouring rain, the street becomes a stream. In a note against today's entry, Gilbert mentions the house martins who lost their nest under the stable eaves, 'in part by a drip, just as most of the young were flown. They are now repairing their habitation in order to rear a second brood.'

Every time he saw something striking, like the martins rebuilding or feeding their young on the wing, he wanted to add it to his book, as he did with the honey buzzard and sparrowhawk. This is one reason that he kept putting off its publication. He would confess, in 1792, that he had

> suffered all my life long by that evil power, call her the *Daemon* of *Procrastination*; & wish that Fuseli, the grotesque painter in London, who excells in drawing witches, daemons, incubus's & incantations, was employed in delineating this ugly hag, which fascinates in some measure the most determined & resolute of Men.

Many distractions caused delay. One was his decision to add the further part on the history of the village, the *Antiquities*. Another was his conviction, in the spring of 1776, that he needed illustrations. John Mulso, who had hoped to see the book that spring, feared, rightly, that 'the want of that Ornament, which You seemed to have set your Heart upon, will make it impossible. I feel an Impatience, & the more for your Sake, as the Tast of ye Town in reading is capricious, & natural Observations have had a Run, & at a high Price.'

Gilbert was not to be swayed. On 8 July that year, he wrote: 'Mr Grimm, my artist, came from London to take some of our finest views.' After consultation with family and friends, he had approached the Swiss artist Hieronymus Grimm, who was known for his topographical drawings. Grimm had worked in the Alps and studied in Paris, before moving to England in 1768 and making his name with the illustrations for Francis Grose's *The Antiquities of England and Wales* in 1773. After that, he gained commissions across the country, including recording 'everything curious' for his chief patron, Sir Richard Kaye (the British Library has over three thousand of his drawings for Kaye).

Gilbert knew that Grimm's work would be expensive. It cost him 2½ guineas for each week that Grimm stayed in Selborne, but he felt it was worth it. He thought that Grimm's style seemed right, although he worried that his trees were not so good and 'he has a vein of humour, but I shall not allow him to call it forth, as all my plates must be serious'. But it is those touches of humour that bring his scenes alive:

Harry as the hermit; the small girl looking down at The Wakes from the hermitage; neighbours gossiping on the Plestor; the woman dandling her baby on her knee among the hay-cocks.

Grimm's twelve scenes showed Selborne from all sides. A view from the Hanger, gazing down across the village, was balanced by one from the Short Lythe, looking past the church to the woods behind. Another view, down Hucker's Lane, past a pigsty, cottage and a couple with a pony, conjured the depth of the sheltered Dorton valley. Beyond the village, Grimm, hunting for the wild and irregular aspects that were considered the essence of the picturesque, drew the split earth and toppled trees of Hawkley after the earthquake, and made 'a grotesque and romantic drawing' of a waterfall in a deep stream bed, with tangled tree roots like those of the hollow lanes.

Grimm stayed for a month, before going to the Yaldens to sketch at Newton Valence for a week. His stay gave Gilbert immense pleasure. 'You are enjoying Yourself, like an Italian magnifico, with your designer at your Elbow,' Mulso teased. And so he was. Grimm was a clever, witty man who produced biting satirical sketches of high-society London politicians, but he was also fascinated by landscapes and ancient buildings, as Gilbert and his brother Thomas were. In the late 1770s, he made watercolours for the Society of Antiquaries' *Vetusta Monumenta*, a record of historical monuments the Society felt were at risk. Gilbert was fascinated by Grimm's whole artistic process, recording each stage. 'He first of all sketches his scapes with a lead-pencil,' he told his brother John, 'then he *pens* them all over, as he calls it, with indian-ink, rubbing out the superfluous brush-strokes; then he gives a charming shading with the brush dipped in indian-ink; and last he throws a light tinge of watercolours over the whole.'

But Grimm's seductive pastoral sketches – showing the leisured family gazing down from their 'oriental tent' or mock hermitage, while villagers sweat in the cornfields below – employ a very different 'language' to that of Gilbert's journals, where delight in the natural world is juxtaposed with drought and blighted wheat, parasitic fleas and epidemics that slay children. He inhabited both worlds at once.

Monday 9

62. 29 7/10. W, W.	*Young swallows come out; & young fly-catchers.*
Gales, clouds, showers,	*The solstitial flowers begin to fade.*
grey even:	*Trenched out celeri. Sowed endive.*

Everything moves on. Fledglings leave their nests, June flowers fade. Celery needs planting in trenches, and endives must be sown for salads. Beyond the garden, some wildflowers are already shedding seed: cinquefoil and meadow saxifrage, purple orchids, tufted vetch and wild carrot, ragwort and scabious, corn marigold and burdock.

One year, John Mulso, who was staying with Gilbert, found on the Zig-Zag path a clump of three or four plants of rare *Hypopitys lutea*, or 'yellow bird's nest' (now *Monotropa hypopitys*), a parasitic plant dependent on nearby fungi. Now, in July, it was in flower. The hedges are a tangle of wild roses and honeysuckle, but not all the scents are sweet. Wild camomile – 'stinking May-weed' – smelled vile, and 'Stinkhorns, or stinking morel, fungus *phalloides*, appear in the Lyth, & smell abominably. Lin[naeus] for a certain reason, calls it *phallus impudicus*. It is not uncommon.' When Gilbert described this to Mulso, he replied jokingly, 'I thank you for your learned dissertation on the Canker or Stink pot. I knew in general that all Flesh was Grass, but I did not know that Grass was Flesh before.'

Tuesday 10

61. 29 5/10¾. SW, W. 24.	*The forward broods of the h: martins are out.*
Rain, rain, cloudy,	*Much hay damaged.*
gales, grey.	

He watches young martins leave their nests, but indoors, out of the rain that is soaking the hay, he can admire the work he has done on the house, completed just the previous year. In the mid-1770s, he had felt the need of more room, especially when his family came to stay. He enjoyed having young people around him and felt they needed a space in which to play music, to dance, to play games and charades. He was impressed by Thomas's and Ben's houses in South Lambeth, and by Henry's extension at Fyfield, and by the work he saw around Selborne. 'The spirit of building prevails much in this district,' he told his brother John in May 1777. 'Richd Butler, the thatcher, is going to enlarge his house; John Bridger of Oakhanger builds a new one next spring; and Mr P.[owlett] of Rotherfield began pulling down yesterday.'

That summer, on 6 June, he had written in his journal, 'Began to build the walls of my parlor which is 23 feet & half by 18 feet; & 12 feet high & 3 inch:.' The 'great parlour' was a single-storey room at the end of the house, with two long windows looking out over the garden. Its building was beset by problems, beginning with wet 'drowning weather'. But, he wrote stoically to Thomas, 'the walls, I trust, will be the stronger; since the mortar is the better blended into the chinks and crevices during so sloppy a season'. Within a month, the roof was up but he had to wait until the following spring for the walls to dry out. At last, on 3 July 1778, comes the journal entry: 'Began to inhabit my new parlour.' To begin with, it was empty and echoing, but gradually it was painted, papered and furnished. On 11 July 1780, he could write: 'Finished my great parlor, by hanging curtains and fixing the looking glass.'

Gilbert's account books show how he splashed out, paying George Kemp, the foreman bricklayer, 2s a day and his assistant 1s 6d, while the bricks cost 16s 10½d per thousand and the iron nails 1s 8d a pound. The 'flock sattin' wallpaper was expensive, at £9 15s, and the room was beautified with a marble fireplace, a looking glass from London and 'a fine stout Turkey carpet' from Mr Luck of Cheapside, at eleven guineas. Gilbert's niece Molly told her brother Tom, who was at school at Fyfield, that the room 'looks very handsome indeed: The paper, a sort of light brown, with a coloured border, is extremely elegant, and the glass and other furniture are very neat and handsome; in short the *tout en semble* has a very pleasing effect, and it is, I think one of the pleasantest rooms I ever was in'.

Wednesday 11
67. 29 6/10¾. W.   *Trenched-out some celeriac, & some of the new*
Dark & moist, grey,   *advertized large celeri. Planted out some endive.*
brisk gale, sun, grey.   *Jasmine now blows finely.*
                            No swifts appear.

Now, a year after Molly's admiring letter, the room is in full use, and he is thinking not of furniture and wallpaper, but of the garden. As well as the new variety of celery, he and Thomas Hoar are sowing long rows of greens: broccoli, savoys, winter spinach and turnips 'for spring-Greens'. Jasmine now outdoes the scent of roses. One warm July, when it was in full flower, he had found the heady fragrance wafting up the wall at night overwhelming. 'The jasmine is so sweet,' he wrote, 'that I am obliged to quit my chamber.'

In his first decade in the garden, in the 1750s, his main preoccupation had been not with the vegetables or flowers, but with his melons. This became an obsession. Each July, he watched anxiously, writing detailed bulletins almost daily as they swelled and ripened in his hotbeds. In 1758, he found 'about thirteen brace of Canteulupes set; some very large. Plants in vast vigour with leaves near a foot in Diameter. More fruit setting every day . . . Two plants in new frame have 8 brace of fruit between ym.' And so he went on, year after year, pride mixed with worry: 'cut a brace of melons'; 'More melons'; 'Melons come in heaps.'

Thursday 12
64, 69½. 29 8/10. SW.   *Only one swift.*
Dark, sun, gales, hot,   *The lapwings continue on the upland-fallows.*
grey.   *Several swifts came to roost in the evening.*

The weather is freakish: the sun strong, the wind blowing hard, the evening dull. Lapwings are still nesting on the bare fields on the downs, and in a note this week he writes that three or four pairs have hatched their broods on the bare sheep pastures of the high common.

But where are the swifts? None yesterday, and only one this morning, although to his relief, he sees them circling in the dusk. He had worked out long ago that swifts generally lay only two eggs, sometimes three, and that they began to sit about the middle of June '& have squab young before the month is out'. The adults protected their nests, once chasing and driving off a hawk while 'squeaking a little', though they did not strike as fiercely as swallows.

At the start of July 1774, a note in his journal described how at Fyfield, where Henry was enlarging his house to make more space for his school, Gilbert had got a bricklayer 'to open the tiles in several places round the eaves of my Bror's brewhouse', so that he could examine the swifts' nests, confirming his suspicion that they never laid more than two eggs. This must make a difference, he thought, to the way the nestlings were fed. While martins and swallows dashed back and forth continually to feed their young, swifts 'seem much at their leisure, & do not attend on their nests for hours together, nor appear at all in blowing wet days. Swifts retire to their nests in very heavy showers.' He was wrong here: it's now known that instead of 'retiring', swifts fly to the south coast and even across to Europe to avoid a patch of rough weather, while the young survive, not because there are so few of them, but because they sink into a torpid state and need less food.

The next July, Gilbert removed another tile. The dam refused to move, so strong, he thought, were her feelings for her young. Having lifted her out, he and Henry brought down the two young squabs and put them on the grass,

> where they tumbled about, and were as helpless as a new-born
> child. While we contemplated their naked bodies, their unwieldy
> disproportioned abdomina, and their heads, too heavy for their necks
> to support, we could not but wonder when we reflected that these

shiftless beings in a little more than a fortnight would be able to dash through the air almost with the inconceivable swiftness of a meteor; and perhaps, in their emigration must traverse vast continents and oceans as distant as the equator.

Suddenly, the swiftlets fly. Unlike swallows, swifts are not perchers. From the moment they barrel out of their dark, cramped nests into the bright day they are in the air. They will stay aloft, not touching the ground for two years, until they themselves nest. But Gilbert found that this did not always hold true. Some young swifts, he noticed touchingly, do not fly straight away; instead, 'they settle on, & cling to the walls of houses, & seem to be at a loss where to go: are perhaps looking for their nest'. He wondered often if their skill in flying was learned as well as instinctive: 'swifts dash & frolick about, & seem to be teaching their young the use of their wings'. This year, in a long note opposite the week ending on 7 July, he rejoices in the number of young joining the circling parties:

> About eight in the evening they get together in a large party, & course round the environs of the church, as if teaching their broods the art of flying. As yet they do not retire 'til three quarters after 8 o' the clock; & before they withdraw the bats come forth: so that day & night-animals take each others places in a curious succession!

Friday 13
66. 29 7/10½. SW.   *Hay does not make. Two swifts about all*
Grey, dark, sprinklings,   *day; they probably have young not flown.*
sprinklings, grey & mild. *Men hoe their turnips.*

Saturday 14
64½. 29 6/10¾. SW, NW. 23. *The hay that is down is now entirely spoiled.*
Dark & moist, soft showers *These soft rains sop & drench every thing.*
all day, grey.   *Many swifts in the evening.*

A young man brought me a live specimen of a Papilio Machaon, taken below Temple. The first specimen that I ever saw of that species in these parts was in my own garden last Augt 2nd.

He sloshes through the puddles, looking glumly at the sodden hay. The trees drip, the garden flowers bend and break. One bright spot is the gift of a butterfly, caught on the slopes below Temple farm. He recognises it from the description in Linnaeus as the beautiful Old World swallowtail, or yellow swallowtail, the largest British butterfly, with wide, pale-yellow wings (up to 6 cm in width) that are striped with black veins and bordered with black. In his *Systema Naturae* of 1758, Linnaeus called it '*Papilio machaon*', taking the name from Machaon, a healer like his father Asclepius, placing it at number 27 in a list of swallowtail species named after figures in the *Iliad* – Aeneas, Helen, Hector, Ulysses, Agamemnon, Patroclus, Ajax . . .

In 1784, Gilbert would see another swallowtail in the Ettys' vicarage garden, 'very rare in these parts'. Today, the native subspecies, *Papilio machaon britannicus*, is mostly confined to the fens of East Anglia, where the larvae feed on the milk parsley of the Broads. But another subspecies, *gorganus*, flies over from the Continent, sometimes in clouds, their larvae feeding on plants like wild carrot in Sussex, Kent – and in Gilbert's Hampshire.

Sunday 15
60½. 29 8/10½. N, NW.   *The farmers complain of smut in their wheat.*
White dew, sun, shower,   *Red martagons blow.*
bright.   *Many swifts.*

Church bells ring out, but there's no sense of celebration. As the wheat grows taller, worrying signs appear. Some spikes look broad and flat and are turning a dull, smoky green: these are signs of smut, a disease that can ravage a crop. Inside the seed heads, the fungus *Ustilago tritici* is turning the kernels that should become the grain into a mess of black spores. Hence the name 'smut', from the German for 'dirty'. And it stinks: in 1793, Arthur Young, in his *Annals of Agriculture*, will describe it as smelling like salted Newfoundland codfish. The yield is badly affected, and there is no way of saving the whole crop, only of treating next year's seed. Young looks at farmers' methods across England: some steep it in brine for a day or soak it overnight in a creamy mass of lime mixed with water; some wash it in arsenic; some manure the fields with sheep dung before sowing.

Gilbert can offer no advice. Abruptly, he turns to martagon lilies and swifts.

Monday 16
60. 29 9/10. N, NW.   *Wheat-harvest begins at Headley.*
Sun, cold dew, summer   *Wheat turns colour.*
weather, red even: *Martins frequent their nests for a second*
    brood. Numbers of swifts.

Up in Borrowdale, in the fells, we don't have a wheat harvest – no amber rustling fields. But the swifts are circling, and through our open window, I can also hear a cuckoo and a woodpecker (both of which sometimes make me want to cry, 'Stop!'), as well as the squabbling sparrows, who have taken over old house martins' nests, to the annoyance of the latter, who had to rebuild. Behind the birdsong is the sound of the sheep, the bark of a dog, the rustle of trees and the chatter of the river – and the drumming of motorbikes storming up Honister Pass.

Tuesday 17
60½. 29 8/10½. N, NW.   *Rasps, currans, & goose-berries all ripe:*
Cold dew, sun,   *apricots turn colour.*
sweet weather, red even: *The sparrow hawks continue their*
    depredations.

Gilbert writes of 'summer weather', 'sweet weather' and 'red even:[ing]'. The temperatures he has recorded over the past week range between

60° and 70°F (around 16–21°C). The warmth, he often notes in his journals, brings out the snakes. He finds the harmless blindworm, '*anguis fragilis*, so called because it snaps in sunder with a small blow', and uncovers clusters of grass snake eggs in his hotbeds.

Wednesday 18	*BRAMSHOT PLACE*
62. 29 8/10½. NE.	*Lapwings haunt the uplands still.*
Vast dew, sun, sun,	*Farmers complain their wheat is blited.*
sweet even: red.	*Swifts abound.*

Today is his birthday, but he chooses not to recognise it. It comes and goes without fuss, and he sets off to visit his friend, Mr Richardson, at Bramshott Place, on the Hampshire–Surrey border. As he rides over the hills and past the heaths of Woolmer Forest, he sees lapwings on the downs. Next year, coming back from another visit to Bramshott, he finds them again: 'A great flock of lap-wings passes over us from the uplands to the forest.' The lapwings, with their high, whistling 'peewit', accompany his summer journeys.

Thursday 19	
30. N.	*House martins abound at Lipock.*
Sun, air, dark horizon.	*Barley large & fine; wheat mildewed.*

Friday 20	
30. NE.	*Pease are hacking.*
Dark, sun, glorious day.	*Very ripening weather.*

Saturday 21	*SELBORNE*
30. 65. NE.	*Wheat-harvest at Bramshot. Wheat much*
Grey, sun, glorious season,	*discoloured.*
red.	

Bramshott Place was a Tudor manor house in Liphook, or 'Lipock', as Gilbert writes it, presumably echoing the local pronunciation. The house was pulled down in 1850, but the rose-coloured brick gatehouse still stands. Gilbert enjoys going there, comparing the harvests and exploring the garden and surrounding countryside, admiring the rowan and alders growing in wild areas near the stream, and noticing how Richardson's sandy soil is unexpectedly fertile. His garden, Gilbert writes in a note on the blank page opposite this week,

> abounds in fruit, & in all manner of good & forward kitchen-crops. Many China asters this spring seeded themselves there, & were very forward: some cucumber plants also grew-up of themselves from the seeds of a rejected cucumber thrown aside last autumn.

You can see them walking together, Gilbert asking questions and Richardson, or his gardener, describing the thrown-out cucumber that has seeded so well. One day, they ride a mile to the north to Dowlands (now Downlands), 'the seat, lately of Mr Kent'. Nicholas Kent had bought the place in 1742, building a square Georgian mansion in front of the fifteenth-century farm and creating a landscape with avenues, walled gardens, orchards and lakes. In particular, Gilbert notices 'a large *Liriodendrum tulipifera*, or tulip-tree, which was in flower. The soil is poor sand; but produces beautiful pendulous Larches.' He had planned to compare the wells here to those at home, learning that the one at Dowlands was 130 feet deep. But he loses his note of the Bramshott well's depth and leaves a gap, never filled in. He ends, perhaps with a touch of envy: 'Mr R's garden is at an average a fortnight before mine.'

Back home, the flycatchers that nested above his door 'have quite forsaken my house & garden: they never breed twice'. At night, among the stars, 'The planet Mars figures every evening, & makes a golden & splendid shew.'

On 22 July 1770, Gilbert had seen young martins treading in their nests, so keen to leave that they 'flie-out one on the back of the other'. Their numbers amazed him. Last year, in late July 1780, he had walked on a bright, sunny day through Dorton meadow and past the ponds below Comb Wood, where coots and moorhens skittered on the chalky, silvery-green water among the bulrushes. Not much further on was Priory farm, with forty martins' nests round its eaves. Gilbert did his sums: 'At 4 young to a nest only, the first brood will produce 160; & the second the same, which together make 320; add to these 40 pairs of old ones, which make in all 400; a vast flight for one house!!'

He's fascinated by the annual variation in some plants. Hollyhocks are biennials, and when the seed is shed, genetic differences appear: the seedlings of a flower that was red last year may turn out pink; a double becomes a single, and vice versa; plain flowers may bear stripes or develop contrasting centres. In late July 1783, Gilbert will note again: 'My China hollyhocks, after standing a year or two, lose all their fine variegated appearance, & turn to good common sorts, being double, & deeply coloured.'

Tuesday 24
66, 73. 29 6/10. w, sw, s.   *Gardens much burnt-up. Several begin*
Sun, sultry, mackerel sky,   *wheat-harvest.*
grey, hot.   *Ponds fail. My well is very low.*

Part of Barrington's aim for his *Naturalist's Journal* was that records of temperature and rainfall might be used to build an annual calendar to help with sowing, planting and harvesting. If anything, though, Gilbert's journals showed how hard it was to define 'July weather' precisely enough ever to forecast or generalise – beyond the fact that the mean temperature was warm. July 1781 has alternated between dry spells, showers and storms. In other years, the month saw nothing but rain. On 29 July 1777, Gilbert's daily notes ran: 'Dark, rain, rain, vast rain.' A flood at Gracious Street damaged mills and soaked the fields. A few miles to the east, the rain tore holes in the turnpikes, covered meadows with sand and silt, swept away part of a bridge and sent hay tumbling downriver. Two post boys drowned, one near Haslemere and another on the road from Alton to Farnham, where the 'Gent in the chaise saved himself by swimming'.

In other dramatic Julys, drought replaced floods, leaving soil baked hard as stone, 'as rough as the sea in an hard Gale: the Clods stand an end as high as ones knees'. In 1778, his brother Thomas's thermometer in South Lambeth, in the shadiest part of the garden, had reached 88°F, and in Selborne, that heatwave had ended in thunder and gales: 'Some people in the village were struck down by the storm, but not hurt. The stroke seemed to them like a violent push or shove.' Weather was a powerful, unpredictable force, always beyond their control.

Wednesday 25
65. 29 5/10. sw, w.   *The crop on my largest Apricot-tree is still*
Sun, sultry, dark,   *prodigious, tho' in May I pulled off 30, or 40*
small shower.   *dozen. Swifts still.*
                              Watered the annuals.

Two years from now, weirder weather will come. Towards the end of June 1783, people across the country, from Cornwall to Ireland, Yorkshire to Kent, noted great falls of honeydew and continual, creeping mist. 'The sun, "shorn of his beams" appears thro' the haze like the full moon,' wrote Gilbert. The red glare scared the country people, he said, who 'look with a kind of superstitious awe at the red louring aspect of the sun thro' the fog'. This continued for weeks.

Later, turning his journal entries into a letter that he would insert at the end of his *Natural History*, Gilbert called that summer 'an amazing and portentous one, and full of horrible phaenomena'. The sun at noon was 'as blank as a clouded moon', and even more lurid as it rose and set. Leaves fell from the trees, meat turned bad in a day, and flies swarmed, making horses frantic. There was good reason to fear, Gilbert admitted, as news came of earthquakes in Calabria and Sicily, and of a volcano apparently springing up off the coast of Norway. No one realised yet that the cause of the haze cloaking Europe was a violent volcanic eruption in Iceland, the 'Skafka fires', which had covered the country with poisonous gas and toxic ash. Earthquakes followed, livestock died, crops failed and famine spread. In Iceland, ten thousand people died, a fifth of the population.

Gilbert's brother-in-law Thomas Barker described these weeks as 'very like Virgil's description of the summer after J. Caesar's death', with a sun like rusty iron. Gilbert himself turned to Milton, quoting Book I of *Paradise Lost*, where Satan appears like an 'Arch Angel ruined', with his 'excess / Of Glory obscured':

> As when the sun, new risen,
> Looks through the horizontal, misty air,
> Shorn of his beams; or from behind the moon,
> In dim eclipse, disastrous twilight sheds,
> On half the nations, and with fear of change
> Perplexes monarchs . . .

The blackbirds & thrushes, that have devoured all the wild cherries in the meadow, now begin to plunder the garden. Watered the garden.

It's hard to imagine blackbirds and thrushes descending in such great numbers. But in July, while he fumes at these robbers, Gilbert keeps a lookout for other birds, nesting and fledging. On 25 July 1770, he had found a baby cuckoo on the ground in a lark's nest. It had grown far too big for the nest and, he wrote, it was very pugnacious '& would pursue a person's hand to some distance from the nest. The dupe of a dam was attending at a distance in a solicitous manner with food in her mouth.' You can see him bending down, stretching out his hand,

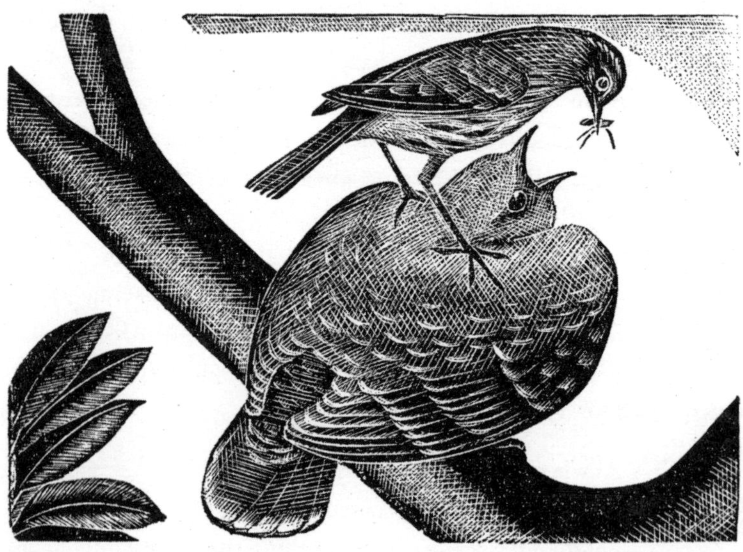

'Cuckoo and Meadow Pipit' by Claire Oldham (1947). Oldham is one of the least known of the wood engravers for *The Natural History of Selborne*. The niece of Arthur Conan Doyle, she was a self-taught artist who lived in the South Downs. Her work always has great boldness and spirit.

dodging the sharp beak. He's still fascinated by the adult cuckoo's clever choices: a robin's nest in a hole in a rock, a water wagtail's nest among the boulders of the hollow lane. On 4 July 1784, he will share the amazement of his godson Littleton Etty, when he finds a cuckoo in a yew hedge in the vicarage garden. The nest could hardly hold the fat, aggressive bundle:

> By watching in a morning we found that the owners of the nest were hedge sparrows, who were much busied in feeding their great booby. The nest is in so secret a place that it is to be wondered how the parent Cuckow could discover it. Tho' the bird is very young, it is very fierce, gaping & striking at peoples fingers, & heaving up by way of menace, & striving to intimidate those that approach it.

> When the cuckoo was put in a cage, the sparrow still came to feed it.

Friday 27
63. 29 7/10. W, SW. W. *Wheat-harvest begins to be general.*
Grey, sun, dark   *Cran-berries ripen.*
horizon.   *Some wheat housed.*
          Watered kidney-beans.

In the last week of July, as the wheat harvest gets under way, you feel the season turning. Gilbert is watering his beans, swelling in their pods, and admiring his cranberries. In the dusk, beetles hum and rooks fly to roost in the woods. As the sun sets, an owl glides down from the Hanger, hunting mice for her young. She'll also take nestlings, and the swifts pursue her, but 'not with any vehemence'.

Saturday 28
63. 29 6/10½. SW.   *Gathered apricots.*
Grey & mild, clouds, *Gleaners bring home bundles of corn.*
moist, grey.   *Swifts.*

The black-birds, & thrushes come from the woods in troops to plunder my garden. The white throats are bold thieves: nor are the red breasts at all honest with respect to currans. Birds are guided by colour, & do not touch any white fruits 'til they have cleared all the red: they eat the red rasps, currans, & goose berries first.

The men are reaping slowly, cutting with a curved sickle, as people have done since the Bronze Age, gathering a sheaf of wheat in their left hand and cutting with the right, sweeping the blade through the held bundle. In early morning and late evening, women and children move among the stubble, bending to collect the stray stalks and ears left by the reapers – a cottagers' ancient right. Next will come the drying, threshing and winnowing.

Meanwhile, the thieving birds again rouse Gilbert's fury, though he is touched with amusement at the whitethroats' daring and the robins' cheek. Blackcaps, too, he notes, are great thieves of the cherries, but his favourite, the flycatcher, 'is a very harmless, & honest bird, medling with nothing but insects'. Watching the birds gobble the berries, Gilbert is convinced they go for red fruit first. When he first noted this, a comment in another hand read: 'May they not like the more pleasant acid of the red?' This is doubtful, but studies have shown that birds are indeed attracted to certain colours, particularly red; other than ripeness, no one knows why.

Whatever the reason, Gilbert is not putting up with the plunder. A separate note reads: 'We shot 30 black-birds, & thrushes.' And he adds: 'Timothy comes-out but little, while the weather is so hot: he skulks among the carrots, & cabbages.'

Sunday 29
65, 69½. 29 7/10½. W, NW.
Small rain, sun, sultry,
grey, distant sea fog, bright.

Hops blossom.
Red-breasts eat the berries of the honey-
suckle.

When the hops flower, Selborne's growers cut down the male plants and keep the female ones, whose yellowy-green flowers hang down like soft pine cones, ripening and giving off their wafting, yeasty smell.

Honeysuckles are ripening, too, Gilbert notices. As each petal drops, it leaves a small round seed, forming a tight cluster. I'm watching now, to see if the robins eat the berries of the honeysuckle that climbs over our woodshed. They seem entirely uninterested.

And perhaps *today* is, in fact, Gilbert's birthday? Precisely a year ago, Molly had written to her brother Tom: 'This day my Uncle White is sixty years old, he told me, when we came here, that he had made a mistake when he said it was the 29th of June.' Getting it wrong by a month is certainly a 'mistake', but is he wrong again? Well, he's both wrong and right. In September 1752, the Calendar (New Style) Act had brought Britain's Julian calendar into line with the Gregorian calendar, used on the Continent since 1582, and the adjustment meant the 'loss' of eleven days. Many found the shift upsetting: it affected saints' days and feast days – for decades, people in Britain still talked of 'old Michaelmas' and 'old Christmas Day' – and, of course, birthdays. So the 29th is the 'old' 18th. Sometimes, Gilbert can be stubbornly old-fashioned. But whichever date he chooses, he is now sixty-one, sometimes out of breath, and complaining of gout in his fingers and ringing in his ears.

Monday 30
65, 75½. 29 7/10½. SW, S.   *Swifts.*
Wet mist, sun, cloudless,   *The ants, male & female, & workers, come*
sultry, red even: *forth from under my stairs by thousands.*
Wheat housed.

Gilbert had written about these ants three years before. A colony of black ants, he said,

> comes forth every midsummer from under my stair-case, which
> stands in the middle of the house; & as soon as the males & females

(which fill all the windows & rooms) are flown away, the workers retire under the stairs & are seen no more. It does not appear how this nest can have any communication with the garden or yard; & if not, how can these ants subsist in perpetual darkness & retirement!

Every year, in calm, hot, humid weather, the ants fly. Suddenly, the ground is covered with winged ants, alates, emerging from cracks in the pavements or the edges of paths. In 2023, a mile-long swarm floated in the wind off the south coast of England. These are the large, sexually mature queens and the males (drones) leaving the nest to mate, while the wingless female workers remain. The males soon die, their life's work complete. The young queens, laden with sperm for a lifetime of egg-laying, chew off their wings and found new colonies, digging their underground chambers.

Gilbert was no expert entomologist, but he had learned from the *Historia insectorum* of John Ray (the first person to isolate formic acid, by boiling a bucket full of crushed wood ants), and from Réaumur, Buffon and Linnaeus. When he first mentioned flying ants in 1768, he referred to the Revd William Gould's concise *Account of English Ants* of 1747. Pulling together existing knowledge, Gould identified five different kinds – hill ants, jet ants, red ants, common yellow ants and small black ants (in fact, there are over fifty species in Britain) – concluding with a chapter entitled 'Reflections on the Final Cause, and Use of Ants', their chief use being, it seemed, to 'Provide Sustenance for Many Species of Animals'.

The ants Gilbert sees are the *Lasius niger*, black garden ants. They like warm, open areas but also nest in walls and beneath floors. His dismay at the thought of them living in perpetual darkness is like a cry against the grave, but they usually find a way outside. When they flew, did he open all the windows and doors, flap wildly with his hands, clear them off the tables and chairs, brush them from the floor? Or did he just sit still and watch?

 A YEAR WITH GILBERT WHITE

No cloud in the sky. A heavenly day of ripening apricots, grapes and corn. From his new parlour, Gilbert can look down the length of the fruit wall to the meadow and the Hanger beyond. His notes for the last two days include the single word 'Swifts'. To his joy, in this fine harvest weather the swifts are still here. Any day now, they will go.

AUGUST

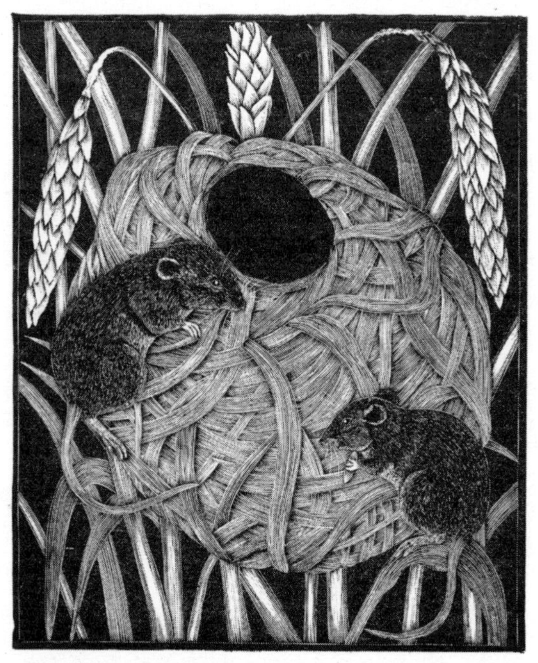

'Harvest Mice' by Eric Fitch Daglish, from *The Natural History of Selborne* (1929).

AUGUST WAS USUALLY a busy month. Sometimes Gilbert was away, staying with the Mulsos or visiting Thomas and Ben in South Lambeth or Henry in Fyfield. Before his aunt Rebecca Snooke died, he might have been riding along the downs above Ringmer, in Sussex, feeling the breeze from the sea, talking to shepherds about wheatears and watching the thumping bustards treading the grass. The summer of 1781, however, is quiet, with no flurry of people or trips. By late middle age, his restlessness has abated – or has it? Sometimes, beneath his love of Selborne, I feel a faint longing to be elsewhere, a touch of the melancholy that haunts his poetry. Did he miss the lost opportunities – the chance of an academic life, the possibility of travel? He reads travel books avidly and is fascinated by his friends' accounts of life abroad, whether it be Ralph Churton in France or Charles Etty in China. Yet he himself never visits foreign lands, nor expresses any desire to do so. It's another area where the blinkers come down, another underground current.

The absence of summer travels, however, was amply offset by the descent on Selborne of his ever-expanding family. He looked forward to their visits, if sometimes feeling rather overwhelmed. 'You know my uncle objects to having a very large party in his house at once,' his niece Molly wrote, postponing her twin brothers' visit from their school in Fyfield. It was, after all, quite a small house, even with the new room. And when they did come, she said, the boys should arrive by half past one, as 'your uncle dines *punctual* at *two*'. They should bring a stout pair of boots for walking, and Tom must get his hair cut.

Wednesday 1
70, 72½. 29 7/10. NW.   *Wheat housed.*
Shower, sun, brisk gale,   *The honey-bees suck the goose-berries,*
red even: *where the birds have broke the skin.*

Entries in his journal follow the rhythm of August's slow days: harvesting and gleaning, bees on the gooseberries, the first autumn crocus, snakes basking, insects humming, bats flying high. The wheat crackles and rustles; much of it has already been piled onto wagons and stacked in the barns or ricks, and in the fields, sharp stubble scratches the gleaners' legs.

Writing to Molly today, Gilbert tells her that they are in the middle of harvesting, in glorious weather. The wheat 'has much straw, but proves light and blasted', although it is apparently much better than in other regions. And although the gardens are burned dry, he reports that his nephew John – Gibraltar Jack of old – has told him that Selborne is far greener than South Lambeth. Molly and her father Thomas are planning to come and stay, and Gilbert thanks her for sending some tea and a chest, which Thomas Hoar will fetch from Alton. 'We shall be very glad to see you and your father whenever it is convenient,' he writes, 'and hope we shall meet happily together.'

The Saturday before, the Forts and the Hounsoms, from Sussex, who were staying with the Yaldens, had come over to dinner. Mr Hounsom had been a linen draper in Fleet Street, near Horace's Head bookshop. Ben's son Edmund had been briefly apprenticed to him, and a decade from now Gilbert's niece Anne Woods would marry the Hounsoms' son John. So they were close to the family. But not above passing on gossip. On the coach, meeting a woman going to Selborne, Mrs Hounsom had asked her if she knew Mr White. 'Yes, replies the woman, by character; that is the gentleman that *starved his niece*.' When challenged, she insisted this was true, as she stayed with relations in Selborne every year. (Was this a village memory of little Nanny White, pale from consumption?) 'Thus, you see,' Gilbert warned Molly,

> you have been looked upon as one of the *Children in the wood*, and
> I as the *Unnatural Uncle*. I must desire you therefore to come down
> as plump and cheerful as possible; and to eat and drink plentifully
> all the time you stay, that I may no longer labour under the atrocious
> imputation of starving my relations!

Although it was a joke, there's a touch of hurt here.

Thursday 2
63½, 66½. 29 8/10. NW.   *Delightful harvest weather.*
Chill air, sun, sweet   *Swallows, & h: martins congregate:*
moon-light, red even: *the old ones sit on the second eggs.*

The day before Gilbert wrote that letter to Molly, Gibraltar Jack and his widowed mother Barbara came to dinner. A big change was on hand, as during this month Barbara would come to live permanently at The Wakes. Gilbert had always liked her and had written to her sympathetically when she was worried about John's health or Jack's career. He may have felt some apprehension about the change to his old routines, but once she arrived, they fell into an easy companionship, although he never called her anything but 'Mrs White' or 'Mrs J. White' in his journal and letters.

From now on, his journal entries often mention the fruit from his garden appearing in the kitchen in jellies and jams and preserves, sticky with juice and full of sugary sweetness: 'Mrs J. White made Rasp, & strawberry jam & redcurran jelly, & preserved some cherries.'

Friday 3
60. 29 9/10. NE, SE, SW.   *One swift.*
Chill air, sun, sultry,   *Now the ants under the staircase have*
red even: *sent-out their males, & females, they no*
                              longer appear. Much wheat in shock.

The parlour is clear of ants, which must be a relief. In the fields, the cut wheat is bound into heavy bundles and stacked in 'shocks', or stooks, with five or six shocks leaning together and two on top, like a roof, keeping the heads of the grain dry and off the ground.

Dust rises, and the breeze, veering round all day, sends the first thistledown blowing. On 3 August 1783, Gilbert will note: 'Thistledown flies.' As the purple thistles fade and the seeds ripen, the wind carries away the fine, silky filaments; a single plant can send out over a hundred thousand seeds as far as a mile away, covering fields and hedges. At one point, Gilbert complains that James Thomson, whose poem 'Summer' ends before the harvest is in, was wrong to make this-tledown fly so early. But he clearly loves Thomson's image, which he quotes more than once:

> Wide o'er the thistly lawn, as swells the breeze,
> A whitening shower of vegetable down
> Amusive floats. The kind impartial care
> Of Nature nought disdains; thoughtful to feed
> Her lowest sons, & clothe the coming year,
> From field to field the feather'd seeds she wings.

Saturday 4
60½. 29 9/10½. NE, SE, SW, W.   *Pair of swifts. Several wheat-ricks*
Sun, sultry, sweet even: red.   *The house-martins begin to hatch, &*
Full moon.   *to throw-out their egg-shells.*
     Pair of swifts only.

Poppies flower in the corn and wheat ricks rise in the farmyards, long square stacks, sometimes as big as a cottage. In the rick-yards, the thatchers – or sometimes simply the farm labourers – move in with their long ladders in order to roof the stack over before the weather changes, holding the straw down with spars of wood and long rows of tarred rope. It makes me think of Gabriel Oak in Hardy's *Far from the Madding Crowd*, desperately trying to protect Bathsheba's wheat ricks and barley – 'these heaps of treasure in grain' – from the storm by dragging large waterproof coverings across the yard to cover the grain.

Working on the ricks, though thirsty and dusty, was well paid, and far faster than thatching the roof of a house. If properly watertight, the cereal stayed dry in the rick, to be threshed over the winter when needed – cut in slices at a time, like a vast cake. But not all ricks held up well. They could spontaneously combust, burning from the inside if the hay was wet; they could slip and slide down; they could be invaded by

      A YEAR WITH GILBERT WHITE

rats. On 4 August 1789, at Grange Farm, Farmer Spencer's rick 'slipped down as it was building'. The following year, Spencer would try again, building a huge rick near his house. 'Five wagons were going all day,' said Gilbert, bringing wheat from a mile away. This rick, too, meets with disaster: 'Farmer Spencer's wheat-rick, when it was near finished parted & fell down.' At the same time, John Hale was trying a different technique, building a 'large wheat-rick on a staddle' – a raised platform on toadstool-shaped stones, to stop the rats getting in – but the following year, his rick fell, too. (A small wooden barn on staddle stones still stands at Manor Farm, in Farringdon.)

Rick building was still more difficult later in the year. One November, Gilbert noted that it looked like fine weather for the barley, which hadn't been sown until the rains had come in June. Farmer Canning, who had 48 acres, was ricking one field, but the grain was lank, and it was too cold and damp for the crop to dry before being stacked. Within two days, Gilbert wrote, his new ricks 'smoke & ferment like hotbeds already'.

Sunday 5
62, 67. 29 8/10. NE.   *Small scuds of rain.*
Sun, dark clouds, strong gust,   *No rain to measure since July 14.*
red even:

This week, he fills the blank page with more notes. One of these, a rare intrusion, was inserted later, when the papers brought the news. 'Aug 5th,' it runs. 'On this day a bloody & obstinate engagement happened between Admiral Hyde Parker, & the Dutch fleet off the Dogger bank' – so near home, just off the Kent coast.

Gilbert was alert to naval news: the Ettys' son Charles sailed with the East India fleet, and John Mulso's youngest son Billy had joined the navy, sailing with his uncle, Admiral Young. The previous December, Britain had declared war on the Dutch Republic, whose ships were continuing to trade and to carry French goods to America. Since then, the British navy had blockaded Dutch ports and sent warships to escort trading convoys to the Baltic. At the start of August 1781, Admiral Parker, returning from the Baltic, spotted the Dutch fleet escorting its merchant ships, and the battle began. Gilbert's 'bloody & obstinate' is an accurate description: casualties were high, before the Dutch fleet retreated to safety, and while the British press claimed victory, so did the Dutch.

Two other notes filled the blank page. One recorded the vine leaves turning purple and the grapes being very forward. The other returned to flying ants, this time looking at those outside: the black ants emerging from under stones and covering the borders; the wood ants swarming over their heaped-up nests. He wrote this note in a very different style to his usual curt entries:

> Every ant-hill is now in a strange hurry & confusion, & all the winged ants, agitated by some violent impulse, are leaving their homes; & bent upon emigration, swarm by myriads in the air, to the great emolument of the hirundines, who live luxuriously. Those that escape the swallows, return no more to their nests; but looking-out for new retreats, lay a foundation for future colonies. All the females at these times are pregnant.

The language is more elaborate, and a word like 'emolument' weighs down the sentence. It feels as if he was playing with modes of description, turning the moment into a story of flight, alarm, instinct and colonisation. The empire of the ants.

Monday 6
64. 29 7/10. NE. 9. *The fern-owl appears in the evening about the zigzag.*
Shower, clouds, *Fly-catchers.*
sun, sweet even: *The first brood of swallows, & martins congregate*
in great flocks: the second broods are now hatching.

The fern-owl, or nightjar, continues to fascinate him. With its cleverly adapted night vision, it catches moths and insects, seeing their

A YEAR WITH GILBERT WHITE

silhouettes against lighter sky. In the warm summer dusk, Gilbert watches the birds skim over the trees. With their long tails, flat heads and pointed wings, they look rather like kestrels or cuckoos; in 1770, when a countryman told him he had seen a young fern-owl in a smaller bird's nest being fed by the little bird, it turned out to be a cuckoo in a meadow pipit's nest. Five years later, in a discussion with Daines Barrington about the position of a cuckoo's stomach (finding, when he dissected one, that it was not below the neck, but lower, behind the sternum and over the bowels), Gilbert told him that he had also dissected a nightjar, 'which, from its habits and shape, we suspected might resemble the cuckoo in its internal construction'. Which it did. When he opened the crop, 'It was bulky, and stuffed hard with large *phalaenae*, moths of several sorts, and their eggs, which no doubt had been forced out of these insects by the action of swallowing.'

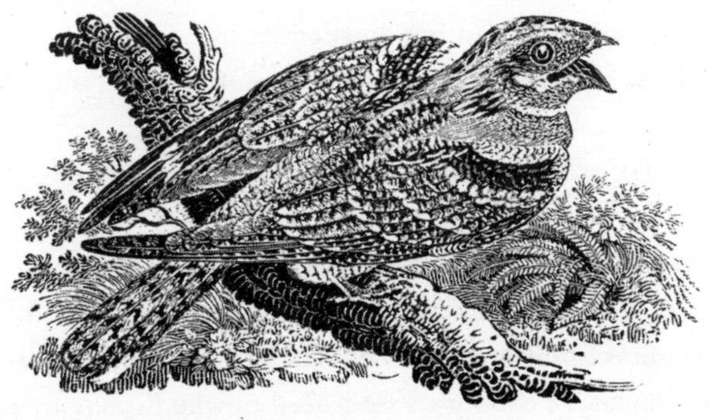

'The Nightjar, Fern-Owl or Goatsucker' by Thomas Bewick, in *Land Birds* (1797).

'We kept a young fern-owl for some days in a cage, & fed it with bread, & milk,' he would write on 23 August 1786, but neither he, nor the bird, liked its lack of freedom: 'It was moping, & mute by day; but, being a night bird, began to be alert as soon as it was dusk, often repeating a little piping note. Sent it back to the brakes among which it was first found.' A few years later, in 1790, a year after his *Natural*

History of Selborne was published, he thought of writing an essay on the nightjar for the Royal Society. He wanted to dispel the old superstition that gave them the name 'goatsucker'. The smallest attention, he wrote indignantly, would show that 'these poor birds neither injure the goatherd nor the grazier'. With their diet of moths and beetles, they were harmless and could not make cattle sick, 'unless they possess the powers of animal magnetism, & can affect them by fluttering over them'.

Tuesday 7
62, 67. 29 6/10¾. NE, SE, SW.   *Much wheat housed.*
Cold white dew, sun, sultry,   *Heavy showers to the N:E.*
dark & mild, red even: *One swift only.*

As my eye scans the columns of Gilbert's journal, I absorb the weather notes almost without thinking. The formulaic terms are a handy shorthand. I can see how they let him check back to see how drought and rain, heat and cold affected planting and harvesting, nesting and fledging and migration. Every now and then, I imagine him walking across the grass to the ha-ha, looking up at the wind vane, feeling the breeze on his face or the back of his neck as it swings round, and watching for those showers far away.

The dew glistens, then the sun comes and the air thickens, before a cloudy, soft afternoon and a ruddy sunset, promising another fine day tomorrow. He is often out in the garden late on these August nights: 'The night-moths, & earwigs, I find, feed on the flowers by night, as the bees & butterflies do by day: this I found by going-out with a candle.' The moths were food for bats, which always intrigued him. In his first packed letter to Thomas Pennant, he had written of a tame bat that took flies from the hand, neatly shearing off the flies' wings, bringing its ears round to hide its head, like birds of prey when they feed. But it would also eat meat, making the story of bats going down chimneys and gnawing bacon 'not improbable'. Watching it fly easily from the floor, he could contradict the idea that bats can't rise from a flat surface

    A YEAR WITH GILBERT WHITE

– although this is very unusual, and they really do struggle to fly from that position – and he noticed that it ran, too, though 'in a most ridiculous and grotesque manner'. He had seen bats drink on the wing, like swallows, he told Pennant, looking back to one warm summer evening when he was staying with John Mulso, and they had taken a boat from Richmond to Sunbury: 'I think I saw myriads of bats between the two places: the air swarmed with them all along the Thames, so that hundreds were in sight at a time.' It's more likely, perhaps, that they were not drinking but catching insects from the surface, but it was still an extraordinary spectacle that he could not forget.

His journal records a bat flittering on a 'sweet afternoon' in April, and even earlier, in a freezing February, at the Gracious Street pond, 'dipping down, & sipping the water, like swallows, as it flew: all the while the wind was very sharp, & the boys were standing on the ice!' These were common bats, pipistrelles, but his real discovery was the large noctule bat, *Nyctalus noctula*, which he was the first to describe in English. He called it '*vespertilio altivolans*', as it flew so high, like the swifts. These bats roost in cavities in trees and old woodpecker holes. On successive nights, 7 and 8 August 1771, he had managed to get hold of two. Both were male, rather to his disappointment. He described their large wingspan of fourteen inches or more, their big heads and muscular shoulders, their packed stomachs and fat-covered inner organs. They had a certain beauty, he thought, with their sleek, chestnut-coloured fur, but their smell was vile, 'very rancid and offensive'. He was quite right about this: when irritated or alarmed they emit a really unpleasant musk. This is also produced to attract females to a 'harem', which is why it may have been so pungent in the males Gilbert was looking at. Holding his nose as he dissected them, he mentioned a peculiar structure in their ear. This was the flap of skin known as the tragus – the central ear lobe, in front of the ear canal – while the strong, musky smell of the males came from a white, fatty substance produced by large glands at the corners of their mouths. Gilbert thought that this bat had not been identified yet in Britain, but knew this could be decided only by further examination. He was proud, but cautious.

Wednesday 8
66. 29 7/10. NE, SE.　　*Some titlarks, as usual at this season, frequent*
Dark & moist, small　　*the grass-plots. Fly-catchers.*
showers, dark &　　*Much wheat housed.*
moist, dark.　　*We have shot 31 black-birds, & saved our*
　　goose-berries.

Gilbert's titlarks included both the meadow pipit, *Anthus pratensis*, and the tree pipit, *Anthus trivialis*. Both are small birds, with brown feathers streaked with creamy white, their high-pitched call – 'pip-it' – giving them their name. The one that he saw around his lawns was the little meadow pipit, which nests on the ground, but the bird that he sometimes heard carolling above the wood was the tree pipit. 'Titlarks,' he wrote, 'not only sing sweetly as they sit on trees, but also when they play and toy about on the wing; and particularly as they are descending, and sometimes as they stand on the ground.'

Today, he also spots flycatchers and applauds the good wheat, now safely stacked in ricks and barns. But the triumphant note comes with the shooting of the blackbirds. Getting out a shotgun was a common response to raiding birds at the time, but still, I'm challenged by the contrast between Gilbert's ferocity and his eager collecting and dissecting, and his tenderness and empathy with so many creatures. He seems to switch roles, as if choosing between two people within him: gardener trumps naturalist; 'scientist' downs patient watcher. It is as if – despite his deep sense of the interconnectedness of all life – he hasn't entirely banished the classical and religious idea of the Great Chain of Being, as embodied in the passage from Genesis that he knew well:

And God said, Let us make man in our image, after our likeness: and let them have dominion over the fish of the sea, and over the fowl of the air, and over the cattle, and over all the earth, and over every creeping thing that creepeth upon the earth.

Gilbert does, however, speak out against gratuitous cruelty: against the boys who torment squirrels or the men who attack swifts, which are beaten down with poles as they try to go under the eaves, or 'wantonly and cruelly shot while they have young'.

Thursday 9
66. 29 6/10. SW, S.   *Watered the fruit-wall border.*
Dew, sun, sun & brisk   *One swift, perhaps a pair, going in & out at the*
gale, soft showers,   *eaves of the church. Why do these linger behind*
showers.   *the rest, which have withdrawn some days? have*
     they a backward brood delayed by some accident?
     Swallows & h: martins hatch.

The swifts under the eaves of the church, staying on after the others have left, will puzzle him for most of the month. They can wait for a week or so.

In one August letter to Barrington, Gilbert wrote that every ornithologist ought to be able to identify a bird both in the air and on the ground. Then he had fun, letting himself go, leaping into one of his most exuberant passages, where all his poetic gifts, as well as his humour, come into play, his language and rhythms inhabiting the flight of the birds. Wonderful to read, too long to quote in full:

Rooks sometimes dive and tumble in a frolicksome manner; crows and daws swagger in their walk; wood-peckers fly *volatu undoso*, opening and closing their wings at every stroke, and so are always rising or falling in curves. All of this genus use their tails, which incline downward, as a support while they run up trees. Parrots, like all other hook-clawed birds, walk aukwardly, and make use of their bill as a third foot, climbing and descending with ridiculous caution . . .

Then come the magpies and jays, the heavy-footed herons, the pigeons clashing their wings – and the birds that 'have movements peculiar to the season of love'. The greenfinch, in particular,

> exhibits such languishing and faltering gestures as to appear like a wounded and dying bird; the king-fisher darts along like an arrow; fern-owls, or goat-suckers, glance in the dusk over the tops of trees like a meteor; starlings as it were swim along, while missel-thrushes use a wild and desultory flight; swallows sweep over the surface of the ground and water, and distinguish themselves by rapid turns and quick evolutions . . . Skylarks rise and fall perpendicularly as they sing; woodlarks hang poised in the air.

Friday 10

69. 29 6/10½. SW, S.   *Sun, sultry, sweet even: red, lightening to the E.*

In the warmth, the snakes slide out again. Journal entries over the years record the finding of grass snakes' eggs, but adders – 'vipers' to Gilbert – were, he knew, viviparous, 'hatching their young within their bellies, and then bringing them forth'. On 2 August 1775, in Ringmer, he and Sam Barker had found a large adder, 'heavy and bloated, as it lay in the grass basking in the sun'. They killed it without compunction, took it home, cut it up and peered inside. Its abdomen, Gilbert wrote in *The Natural History of Selborne*, was 'crowded with young', fifteen in all, the shortest seven inches long:

> This little fry issued into the world with true viper-spirit about them, shewing great alertness as soon as disengaged from the belly of the dam: they twisted and wriggled about, and set themselves up, and gaped very wide when touched with a stick, shewing manifest tokens of menace and defiance, though as yet they had no manner of fangs that we could find, even with the help of our glasses.

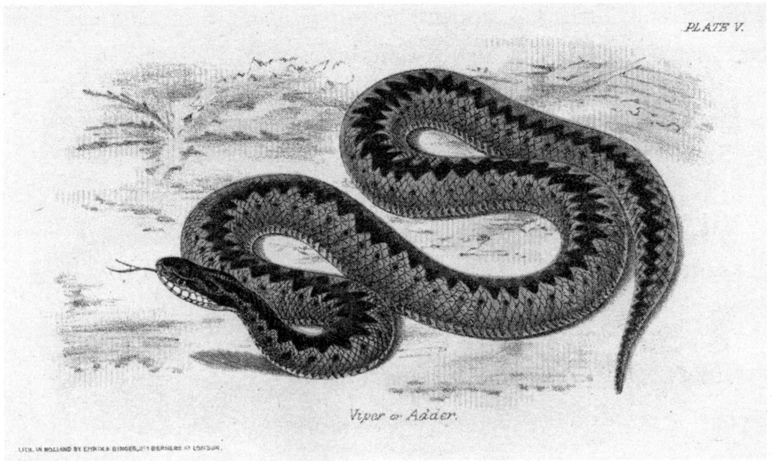

'Viper or Adder' by M. C. Cooke, from his book *Our Reptiles and Batrachians* (1888).

The dam, though, had formidable fangs, 'which we lifted up (for they fold down when not used) and cut them off with the point of our scissars'. Gilbert rejected the country belief that when an adder dam sensed danger, she would open her mouth, and the young would rush back in to safety. If that was so, he pointed out, they would probably be found somewhere in the neck, not the stomach. And anyway, he added, in a letter to his brother John, her windpipe was far too thin to hold them. If they really wanted to get back inside, they'd be better off heading for her anus.

Years later, quoting *A Midsummer Night's Dream* – 'there the Snake throws her enamel'd skin' – Gilbert would give a startling description of finding a newly cast slough. He imagined the snake 'changing his coat', entangled in the grass. It looked, he said, as if it had been turned inside out, '& as drawn off backward, like a stocking, or a woman's glove. Not only the skin, but scales from the very eyes are peeled off, & appear in the head of the slough like a pair of spectacles.' Picking up the skin, he peered through those 'spectacles', with a sudden sense of fellow feeling. The eye scales loosen as the new skin is forming, he wrote, and while this is happening, 'the creature, in appearance, must be blind, & feel itself in an awkward, uneasy situation'.

A swift, or rather a pair, still frequent the church-eaves, with great assiduity; & have perhaps a brood of backward young.

Note: The reapers were never interrupted by rain one hour the harvest thro'.

Staying with the harvest, we can leap back across the years to one of Gilbert's most significant discoveries: the harvest mouse. At the time, no one had identified this as a distinct species, but although Gilbert was the first to do so, the German naturalist Peter Pallas discovered one around the same time in the Volga region of Russia. Because Gilbert's book took so long, Pallas was the first to name it in print, in 1771, as *Micromys minutus* – the smallest, tiniest mouse.

Nests of these tiny golden mice were often found when the sheaves of wheat and barley were carried to the rick yards. When Gilbert mentioned this in the late spring of 1767, Thomas Pennant asked if he could get him a specimen. In early August, Gilbert explained that so far, he hadn't had a chance, but 'The person who brought me the last says there are plenty in harvest, at which time I will take care to get more; and will endeavour to put the matter out of doubt, whether it be a non-descript species or not.' That autumn, he got hold of a juvenile mouse and a pregnant female, 'both of which I have preserved in brandy'. Their colour was like that of a red squirrel or a dormouse, though their bellies were white, and they were much smaller than a house mouse.

They never enter into houses; are carried into ricks and barns with the sheaves; abound in harvest; and build their nests amidst the straws of the corn above the ground, and sometimes in thistles. They breed as many as eight at a litter, in a little round nest composed of the blades of grass or wheat.

Harvest mice are among Britain's smallest mammals, the only ones with a prehensile tail, and the only ones to build a nest of living grass above the ground. Attached to the tall stalks of wheat, or to long grass at the field edges, the nests are made of leaves split into thin strips but still attached to the plant, so that the nest is firmly anchored on the swaying stalks. The one Gilbert saw – 'This wonderful procreant cradle, an elegant instance of the efforts of instinct' – was found in a wheat field, 'suspended in the head of a thistle'. He described how the strips were woven together into a tight ball, 'perfectly round and about the size of a cricket ball'. The nest was so ingeniously made that it was hard to find where the entrance could be (if you can see a hole, it shows the nest is empty), and so tightly packed that it would roll across the table without suffering any damage, even though it contained eight naked, blind baby mice. How, in that cramped ball, could the dam manage to give a teat to each? How did she herself squeeze in, when the nest was stuffed to the brim with babies that were getting bigger every day?

And what did the mice do in the winter? A couple of months later, in the freezing January of 1768, Gilbert had the answer. Although in summer their nests hung high on the standing corn, he found that in winter, some 'burrow deep into the earth, and make warm beds of grass', while many stayed in the corn ricks in the farmyards. One of his neighbours, moving an oat rick under cover for winter, found almost a hundred mice under the thatch. Most were caught, and Gilbert measured some, finding that from nose to tail, 'they were just two inches and a quarter, and their tails just two inches long. Two of them, in a scale, weighed down just one copper halfpenny, which is about a third of an ounce avoirdupois; so that I suppose they are the smallest quadrupeds in this island.' A full-grown house mouse, he reckoned, weighed six times as much.

Harvest mice are so secretive, and their hearing is so acute, that they dash away at the slightest rustle. No one knows exactly how many there are in Britain today, although thanks to a survey by local farmers, we do know that there are still plenty in Selborne.

Sunday 12

70½.76. 29 6/10½. W.   *One swift only still seen haunting the eaves of the*
Wet fog, sun, sultry,   *church.*
brisk gale, dark clouds   *Barley & oats cut.*
to NW, red.   *Hops begin to be full formed.*

The crops come in succession: barley, oats, wheat, hops and field beans. The fields are a patchwork of colour, as John Clare wrote:

> The wheat tans brown and barley bleaches grey;
> In yellow garb the oat-land intervenes
> And tawny glooms the valley thronged with beans.

By mid-August, most of the barley and oats have already been cut, but sometimes they were left until much later. In some years, up the hill at Newton Valence, Gilbert's friend Richard Yalden was stacking his barley well into the autumn days.

Monday 13

70. 29 6/10. W. 18.   *The pond on Selborne down has still some good*
Rain, dark, sun,   *water in it; Newton pond is all mud.*
brisk gale, showers   *Fly-catchers. Many annuals are shriveled-up for*
about, red even: *want of moisture. The drought is very great.*
     Hops are injured for want of rain.

The showers are welcome, but although a little rain has come, it's not enough. The sunflowers and asters droop, their leaves crinkling and turning brown, and people worry about the hops. But Gilbert had noticed for years that when the large ponds in the valleys became dry, the small ones higher up were often hardly affected. 'To a thinking mind,' he wrote, 'few phenomena are more strange than the state of little ponds on the summits of chalk-hills, many of which are never dry in the most trying droughts of summer.'

There were many of these little round ponds on the nearby downs, including one on the down above the Hanger. No more than three feet deep in the middle, it was never 'known to fail, though it affords drink for three hundred or four hundred sheep, and for at least twenty head of cattle beside'. This saucer-shaped basin was one of the many artificial 'dew-ponds' found in chalky landscapes like those in Hampshire, Sussex, Derbyshire and part of Yorkshire; there were once over a thousand in the grasslands of the South Downs. Some may have been old marl or chalk pits, but most were deliberately dug to provide water for livestock. The majority are very old: Wood Pond, on Selborne Common, is thought to be Saxon, while deeds from the thirteenth century record the drinking rights of villagers with livestock on the common. The ponds were made in the same way for centuries: the base was lined with a layer of chalk or clay, then puddled (like the canals) by tramping it down, until not a single air bubble remained, so that it would set, silky, smooth and hard as concrete, and cattle could drink easily without breaking it. Sometimes the chalk base was layered with straw for insulation, so that when the water level fell, moist air gathered over it, reducing evaporation.

Gilbert puzzled over how the ponds retained their water, and why they seemed deeper in the morning than in the evening. Could it be, as Hales had written in his *Vegetable Staticks*, that more dew fell on moist earth and water? But dew rises from the earth, rather than falling on it, so that was no explanation. He was nearer an answer when he noted that the hill air was 'loaded with fogs and vapours . . . a considerable and never failing resource'. Trees helped, too: two beeches dripped moisture over the Selborne pond when cloud or mist gathered. Once again, Gilbert looked for local knowledge, talking to early risers like fishermen and shepherds, who knew 'what prodigious fogs prevail in the night on elevated downs, even in the hottest parts of summer, and how much the surfaces of things are drenched by those swimming vapours, though, to the senses, all the while, little moisture seems to fall'. The exact mechanism of the replenishment of dew ponds (also called 'mist ponds' or 'cloud ponds') is, however, still debated.

Tuesday 14
65. 29 5/10½. W. 30. *Apricots are over: the crop was prodigious.*
Grey, sun, strong gale, *Tyed up endive.*
rain, rain, rain-bow, *China asters begin to blow. Peaches & nect:*
yellow even: *begin to blush, & swell.*
 Watered the fruit-wall border.

The bank-martins at the sand-pit on Short-heath are now busy about their second brood, & have thrown out their egg-shells from their holes. The dams & first broods make a large flight. When we approached their caverns they seemed anxious, & uttered a little wailing note.

Wednesday 15
63. 29 2/10½. SW. 20. *Missle-thrushes in small flocks.*
Dark & windy, rain, *White-throat.*
rain, sun. *China-asters begin to blow.*

Even on a wet and windy day, the birds gather. He sees mistle thrushes, with their black spotted bellies and flashes of white under their wings, alert and upright as they feed on the ground. I think of them in pairs, or as solitary birds, aggressively defending their own bramble patch, but after breeding, mistle thrush families sometimes join up together, and in late summer, when the berries are ripening, they can appear in bands of up to thirty birds. By the end of autumn, they will have separated again.

Little whitethroats are also around, light-brown warblers with pale chests, bringing out their young in the scrubby bushes and staying until they leave for Africa in late September. In mid-August, many other birds appear in Gilbert's journals, too. Yellowhammers feed their young with crane flies; stone curlews flock on Selborne Down on moonlit nights; lapwings gather; young blackcaps descend on the raspberries. Wagtails flock round the cattle, as Gilbert had described in a long note on 26 August 1776:

> While the cows are feeding in moist low pastures, broods of wagtails, white & grey, run picking round them close up to their noses, & under their very bellies, availing themselves of the insect flies that settle on their legs; & probably finding worms & *larvae* that are roused by the trampling of their feet. Nature is such an oeconomist that the most incongruous animals can avail themselves of each other! Interest makes strange friendships.

Despite all these birds, the trees and bushes are quiet. Up until this month, the dawn chorus has been loud, as birds sing first to attract a mate and then to warn others off their territory until their first brood has hatched. Then the birdsong falls away. August is the most silent month, Gilbert admits, but not completely so. In the list he had sent to Barrington at the start of their correspondence, Gilbert noted that the blackcap sings from the middle of April to 13 July, the titlark until 16 July, the whitethroat to 23 July (although he had earlier noted that it sang on, with a 'mean note', until September) and the yellowhammer until 21 August. The dates seemed suspiciously precise, and he felt an explanation was needed. 'For many months,' he wrote,

> I carried a list in my pocket of the birds that were to be remarked, and, as I rode or walked about my business, I noted each day the continuance or omission of each bird's song; so that I am as sure of the certainty of my facts as a man can be of any transaction whatsoever.

As he listened to the birds, however, the dates in that list kept slipping. In August, the robin keeps trilling, while the nuthatch 'is very loquacious at this time of year', and the woodlark – its Linnaean name, *Lullula arborea,* echoing its gentle trilling – sings, 'suspended; in hot summer nights all night long'.

Barrington had requested the list as part of his research into whether song was innate or learned, a subject, he felt, 'that hath never before been scientifically treated' – he did not know of previous research in Germany. His experiments were odd but original: he 'educated' nestling linnets with different larks and found that they copied them; he heard a goldfinch, hung in a cage in a garden, sing like a wren. He was on to something. Extensive research has shown that birds learn to sing in two phases, using two different neural pathways. Baby birds go through a 'sensory phase', when their brains take in the basic shape of their parents' song, but then, like babies, they babble in a way of their own, before a second, longer 'sensorimotor phase', when they listen more carefully and adapt and refine their song to match the parental (or proxy's) template. And while a whole species shares a basic song, individuals and regions can develop their own variations, like human dialects.

Barrington had also asked an experienced harpsichord tuner to estimate what keys different birds sang in, and in order to work out the mechanics, he had persuaded the surgeon John Hunter to examine their vocal cords. Hunter found that the best singer, the nightingale, had the strongest and most developed larynx, and, unsurprisingly, that it was far stronger in the male. In all birds, the males sing more; the part of their brains responsible for song, the 'higher vocal centre', is four times larger than that of the females. This makes sense, as males sing to attract a mate and warn off rivals.

Thursday 16
63. 29 3/10. S, W.   *Sowed a plot of winter-spinage, & pressed the*
Sun, clouds & brisk   *ground close with the garden-roller.*
gale, cool.   *The ground turned up very dry, & harsh.*

Planning for winter, today Gilbert and Thomas Hoar sow spinach in the newly rolled beds, despite the dry soil. In some years, the ground is almost impossible, but they find a way round it: 'Spinach – ground hard & cloddy, would not rake – levelled it down as well as we could with a garden roller, & sprinkled it over with fine dusty mould to cover the seeds.'

The garden is also his larder in a different way. Proud of his ingenuity, on 5 August 1780 he had noted: 'My pendent pantry, made of deal, & fine fly-wire, & suspended in the great wall-nut tree, proves an incomparable preservative for meat against flesh-flies. The flesh by hanging in a brisk current of air becomes dry on the surface, & keeps tender without tainting.' He hangs it out this year, too.

Friday 17
62. 29 5/10. SW, S. 22. *The small pond in Newton great farm field,*
Sun, showers,   *near the verge of the common is full nearly of*
showers, bright.   *good clear water! while ponds in vales are*
          empty.

My well is low in water; but a constant spring bubbles up from the bottom. Some neighbouring wells are dry. My well is 63 feet deep. One swift!

Gilbert's capacity for delight rarely fails – an exclamation mark here for the clear water of the dew pond, another for the solitary swift – and he also takes pleasure from his well, which is outdoing those of his neighbours. He is still fascinated by that single swift, so late, after others have gone. He writes a note: 'The crevice thro' which the swift goes up under the eaves of the church is so narrow as not to admit a person's hand.' But who climbed the ladder to reach into that narrow slit? Did he try himself? Or was it one of the village boys?

The spotted flycatchers nesting in the vine above the parlour window and in the climbers by the garden door were a part of the summer household. They were among the birds that kept singing after nesting, and Gilbert could hear their 'sibilous, shivering noise' until August. The pair in the vine offered one of his most vivid examples of the concern of animals and birds for their young. One year, he said, perhaps in a spell of grey weather, they built their nest on a bare bough. But when hot sun shone down before the young were fledged,

> the reflection of the wall became insupportable, and must inevitably have destroyed the tender young, had not affection suggested an expedient, and prompted the parent-birds to hover over the nest all the hotter hours, while with wings expanded and mouths gaping for breath, they screened off the heat from their suffering offspring.

Bird behaviour does prompt astonishment. Today, I read a superb essay on the goldcrest, the smallest European bird. This tiny bird lays up to twelve eggs in a mossy, feather-lined nest. But the hen is too small to cover all the eggs, so how – as Gilbert might ask – does she keep them evenly warm? One researcher noticed that when the female emerged, her legs and feet were bright red rather than the usual brown. This led to the discovery that within the nest, she pumps blood into her legs, moving them round like 'thermal rods', maintaining the constant 39°C that the eggs need.

Mr Pink's turnips are infested with black caterpillars; he turned 80 ducks into the field, hoping they would have destroyed them; but they did not seem much to relish the sort of food.

I have known whole broods of ducks destroyed by their eating too freely of hairy caterpillars.

It's Sunday, but he's less concerned with the church service than with Farmer Pink's ducks. The caterpillars ravaging the turnips were the larvae of turnip sawflies, *Athalia rosae*, black with a pale strip down their sides. These were a real pest in the chemical-free eighteenth and early nineteenth centuries. In late spring, the little orange–brown sawflies laid hundreds of eggs on the undersides of the turnip leaves, and the emerging larvae then chomped their way through them, turning the leaves into skeletons. When mature, the larvae dropped into the soil to pupate, and between May and September, three more generations of egg-laying adults appeared. Plovers and larks ate these caterpillars avidly, so Farmer Pink's eighty ducks would not have suffered. But Gilbert was right in his concern about other caterpillars: the brightly coloured hairy ones can be toxic, and most birds sensibly ignore them.

In summer, the turnips were also under attack from the black or metallic-green flea beetles, which make round holes in the leaves, using their long back legs to hop away when approached. But Gilbert can make even these pests sound strange and grand. On 22 August 1772, he had seen them swarm in the fields, 'invigorated by this burning season', when

> they destroy every turnep as fast as it springs: they abound also in gardens, & devour not only the tender plants but the tough outer leaves of cabbages. When disturbed on the cabbages they leap in such multitudes as to make a pattering noise on the leaves like a shower of rain.

61. 29 6/10. NW.   *The young swallows & h: martins cluster on*
Grey, cool, sun,   *roofs in the sun, now the mornings are chilly.*
sweet autumnal day.   *Autumnal crocus's blow.*

There's a nip in the morning. Gilbert watches for signs of the changing season, like the first autumn crocus, pale lilac above its slender stalk. Its folk names include 'meadow saffron', but also 'naked boy' or 'naked lady', because it is unclothed by leaves; these will appear much later, in the spring. Its flowers, too, appear barren, as the ovaries of these odd, hermaphroditic plants are deep below the ground. They look like normal crocuses but are really members of the lily family, and beautiful as they are, they are deadly poisonous. In Greek mythology, the alkaloid from their roots was used by Medea of Colchis to kill her enemies and grant youth to her followers, hence their Latin name, *Colchicum autumnale.*

Another sign of coming autumn is the renewed singing of the birds. Around the middle of the month, 'several birds begin to reassume their spring notes', including the wren, the chiffchaff and other small warblers.

Tuesday 21

59½. 29 8/10½. NE, SW.   *No wasps, but several hornets, which devour the*
Sun, cool, sweet   *nectarines. The wasps are probably kept down*
autumnal day, red   *by the numbers of breeders that the boys*
even: *destroyed for me in the spring.*
     Gathered the first plate of peaches & Nectarines.
     Vivid N: Aurora.

He is on the alert from now on, watching out for the wasps and hornets that attack his ripening fruit. In September 1780, he had watched the hornets pounce on the bees in the orchard: 'Hornets settle on mellow fruit among the honey-bees & carry them off,' he wrote, adding a quote from the *Georgics*: '*Aut asper Crabro imparibus se immis armis*' – the vicious hornet has attacked their unequal arms.

This year, there are plenty of hornets, but far fewer wasps. In the past, they had been 'very troublesome at the melon-bed, gnawing great holes in ye fruit. Set bottles of treacle & beer.' The farmers had destroyed many nests, ploughing them up every day, and the village boys continued their hunt; one year, they even 'broke up the arch of a bricked grave' in the churchyard to get at a nest, which Gilbert duly paid for. He keeps count – fifteen, sixteen nests. They are curiosities, though, as well as dangers. In August 1776, he had investigated one nest 'consisting of many combs', containing wasps in all stages, from freshly laid eggs to the young emerging from their pupae. He was intrigued by the contrasting constructions. Wasps, he wrote, built 'with the raspings of sound timber; hornets with what they gnaw from decayed. These particles of wood are neaded-up with a mixture of saliva from their bodies, & moulded into combs.'

Other insects abound. The females of the wool-carder (or hoop-shaver) bee are using their strong jaws to shave off long silvery plant fibres to make nests. Horseflies lay their eggs on the flanks of the horses. Little black weevils bore holes in unripe peaches. Pond-skaters skim the surface of pools and streams. In this last instance, Gilbert's weakness as an entomologist sends him off in the wrong direction. In August, for example, he watches the pond-skaters skittering, indulging in gripping sex – 'high copulation', as he puts it:

The females, who vastly exceed the males in bulk, dart & shoot along on the surface of the water with the males on their backs. When a female chuses to be disengaged she rears & jumps & plunges like an unruly horse; the lover thus dismounted soon finds a new mate.

The females as fast as their curiosities are satisfyed retire to another part of the lake, perhaps to deposit their foetus in quiet; hence the sexes are found separate except where generation is going-on.

From the multitudes of minute young of all gradations of sizes these insects seem without doubt to be viviparous.

He was right about their size, as females are twice as large as the males, and right, too, about the females 'retiring', but not about the reason. Males apparently want to mate as often as they can; the females resist with a kind of genital shield, but they 'retire' simply to find calm water where they can lay their eggs, attaching them to stones or water plants. These then hatch and go through five larval stages as nymphs, before emerging as adults. The reason Gilbert saw so many young was that mating and hatching continue over such a long period.

Wednesday 22
60. 29 7/10¾. NW, SW. *Hop-picking begins in the neighbourhood.*
Sun, sweet autumnal *One swift still!*
day. *Grapes just begin to turn colour.*

The chilly feel that occasions the young martins to cluster on sunny roofs, probably induces the swifts to withdraw. Many bunches of grapes quite black!

Hop-picking usually begins in Selborne in early or mid-September, so it's early this year. The hop bines have curled to the tops of the poles, and the cones have ripened in the mild, dry weather.

Villagers who grow only a few hops turn out as a family: the men pull down the poles and carry them into the yard, where the women and children settle on the ground to strip off the cones, throwing them into large woven baskets to take to market or sell to a local hop-drier. By contrast, in the big, south-facing hop gardens beyond Gracious Street and around Farringdon, the work is more organised. Here, the poles are left standing on their hills, soaring like a green jungle until the bines are stripped off. Groups of labourers gather before dawn. Men and women work side by side, and children run between the poles, the long, twisting bines slapping their faces and the cones tickling their heads. All day, the pickers throw the cones into long cribs of sacking tied to wooden

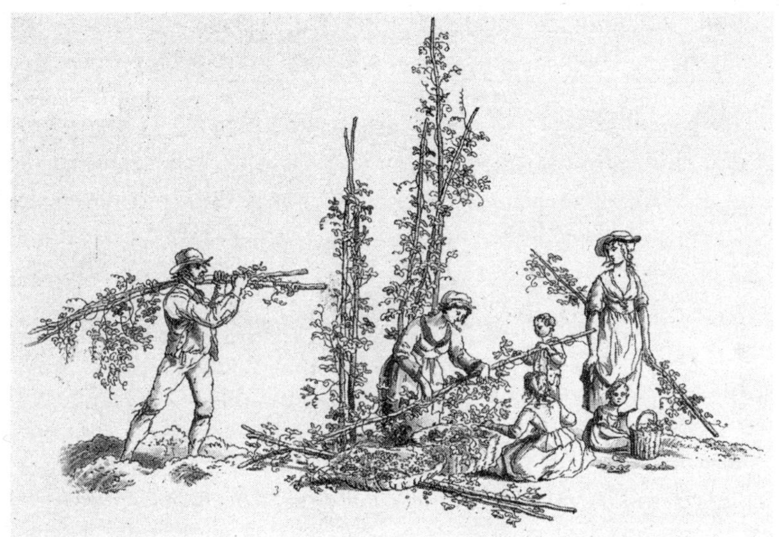

Detail from 'Hop-Picking, September 1804' by W. H. Pyne, from his book *Microcosm, or a Picturesque Delineation of the Arts, Agriculture, Manufactures etc., of Great Britain* (1808).

frames, and from time to time the 'busheller' comes to empty the cribs into baskets, a bushel in each, to be carted to the kiln.

Thursday 23
64, 69. 29 5/10. S, S.   *Second broods of swallows begin to come forth.*
Vast dew, sun, sultry,   *Caught 8 hornets with a twig tipped with bird-*
Sweet even: red,   *lime. No wasps in my garden, nor at the grocer's,*
clear in the S.   *or butcher's shop.*

Five or 6 hornets will carry off a whole nectarine in the space of a day.

The wasps have vanished. He checks across the street with Burbey, the grocer, and John Hale, the butcher. The fruit is safe. And a note on the opposite page comments that 'Tho' white butterflies abound, & lay many eggs on the cabbages; yet thro' over-heat & want of moisture they do not hatch, & turn to palmers [hairy caterpillars]; but dry & shrivel to nothing.'

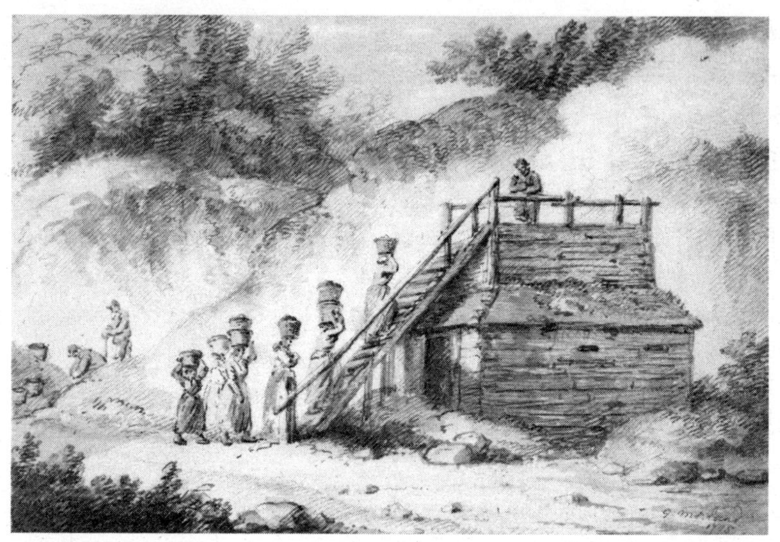

A Hop Kiln, George Morland, *c.*1790. Morland (1763–1804) enjoyed huge popularity for his acutely observed scenes of rural life, and equal notoriety for his bohemian lifestyle, drinking and debts.

The hornets are the main foe now. Quicklime mixed with water can be an effective insecticide, rapidly drying out the insects' bodies, though Gilbert's killing them individually with a birdlimed stick seems both fiddly and brave. The following year, the wasps and hornets will be defeated by heavy rain: 'Not one wasp or hornet to be seen: nor if there were, is there any fruit to support them. On such a summer, it seems quite a wonder that the whole race is not extinct.'

Friday 24
64½, 71. 29 2/10½. SE, S, SE.
Grey, sun, sun, sultry,
dark & threat'ning,
still & close, rain.

Hop-picking. The hops are small,
& injured by the heat.
No wasps.

One swift still frequents the eaves of the church & moreover has, I discover,
two young nearly fledged, which show their white chins at the mouth of

the crevice. This incident of so late a brood of swifts is an exception to the whole of my observations ever since I have bestowed any attention on that species of hirundines!

The fledgling swifts, so late in the summer, baffle him even after long years of watching birds. In these dark, showery, heavy, late-summer days, he keeps an eye on them every day as they peep out of their nest.

The smell of drying hops is strong and sweet; in the evenings, Gilbert writes, it fills 'the whole air of the village'. In Hampshire, the hops were not dried in round oast houses, as they were in Kent, but in square barn-like buildings, with a furnace on the ground sending heat up through a low floor of latticed planks, covered with horsehair matting. Carried up the stairs in their baskets, the hops were spread on this mat, and the heat rose through them for a day or more. Once they were brittle, crumbling in the hand, they were shovelled into bags, which were trodden down to compact them, before they were sewn and sent to the brewery.

Saturday 25
65. 29 4/10½.
W, W. 50.
Great showers in the
night, sun, showers,
gales, dark & warm.

The two young swifts put-out their heads, &
look very brisk. Fly-catchers.
No wasps.

Sunday 26
65. 29 5/10½. SW. 12.
Sun, warm, small
rain, dark & close.

Young swifts as before.
Young martins, second brood, put-out their
heads.

All his thoughts are on those swifts, although as usual he is over at Farringdon, giving his sermon, chosen from the many that he had written so long ago.

Monday 27
65, 73. 29 4/10. SW.   *Young swifts as before.*
Sun, sultry, grey   *Harvest is over. No wasp. Fly-catchers.*
& mild.   *Hop-picking becomes general.*

Swifts again, and flycatchers, which he is watching rather sadly, knowing they, too, will leave soon. 'A fly-catcher brings out a brood of young,' he will write on 26 August 1792, '& yet they will all withdraw & leave us by the 10th of next month.'

'Harvest is over': the church harvest festival was a Victorian invention, usually held at the end of September, on the Sunday nearest to the equinox. The festival of Gilbert's time was a rowdier, secular 'harvest home', when people carried boughs and sheaves of corn in a procession and celebrated at a great meal in a barn, with drinking and singing, shouting and reciting. On 26 August 1783, John Mulso writes: 'We held our *Harvest home* last Night: but tho' I had some *Rithmers* about me we had no Poetry stirring . . . So we shall have Hymns for *Heroic Poems*; & your *Dermot* and *Sheelah* Pastorals.' Mulso and Gilbert both seem to have enjoyed Swift's 'Pastoral Dialogue' of 1729, with its debunking of rural idylls and pastoral images of nymphs and swains:

> *Sheelah*: Thy breeches torn behind, stand gaping wide;
> This petticoat shall save thy dear backside;
> Nor need I blush, although you feel it wet;
> Dermot, I vow, 'tis nothing else but sweat.
>
> *Dermot*: At an old stubborn root I chanced to tug,
> When the Dean threw me this tobacco plug:
> A longer ha'porth never did I see;
> This, dearest Sheelah, thou shalt share with me.

          A YEAR WITH GILBERT WHITE

Tuesday 28
68½. 29 2/10½. SW. 30, 12.   *Young swifts could not be seen all day.*
Showers, showers,   *Peaches & nectarines come very fast, & are*
showers, thunder.   *well flavoured.*

Now the wheat is cut, 'hop-picking becomes general'. Gilbert always
followed the fortunes of the hop fields. When hail tore off the tips of
the tender shoots in a thunderstorm, he noticed that the hops had soon
thrown out fresh runners, and suggested that growers nip out the tops
regularly, as they did with melons and cucumbers. He also proposed
that some male plants, which were usually discarded, should be left to
help pollination. Both ideas, in time, were followed successfully.

Wednesday 29
63. 29 5/10¾. SW, W.   *Young swifts not seen.*
Strong wind, sun &   *The hornets, tho' few in number, make havock*
clouds, still & mild.   *among the nectarines. Peaches & Nect: very*
                             finely flavoured.

Thursday 30
63½. 29 5/10. SE. 12.   *No young swifts to be seen.*
Grey, sun, dark &   *Not one wasp. We have destroyed the greatest*
moist, soft even: *part of the hornets.*
                             Thunder much.

Sowed a plot with brown Dutch lettuce, for plants to stand the winter.
Between nine & ten at night a thunder-storm with much vivid lightening
began to grow up from the N:W & W: but it took a circuit round to the S:
& E. & so missed us. We had only the skirts of the tempest, & a little heavy
rain for a short time. Ten miles off to the southward there were vast rains.

The storm, with its longed-for rain, marks the end of the heat of high
summer.

66½. 29 5/10¾. SW, S.   *Much distant thunder again to the S.*
Grey, sun, sun, sweet   *Began to use endive, which is large & dry,*
cool & pleasant.   *well-blanched.*

No swifts. We searched the eaves to no purpose. In searching the eaves for the young swifts, we found in a nest two callow dead swifts, on which had been formed a second nest. These nests were full of the black shining cases of the hippoboscae hirundinis.

As the storm retreats, Gilbert accepts that the late swifts have gone. The second brood had hatched in a new nest, built over one with dead chicks inside. It's a grim sight, the nests peppered with the black shells of the pupae of parasitic louse flies. He will watch the nests again, next August. 'A fledg'd young swift,' he will write, 'was found alive on the ground in the church-yard: it was full of *hippoboscae*. We gave it two or three flies, & tossed it up on the church.' I hope it survived and flew to Africa.

SEPTEMBER

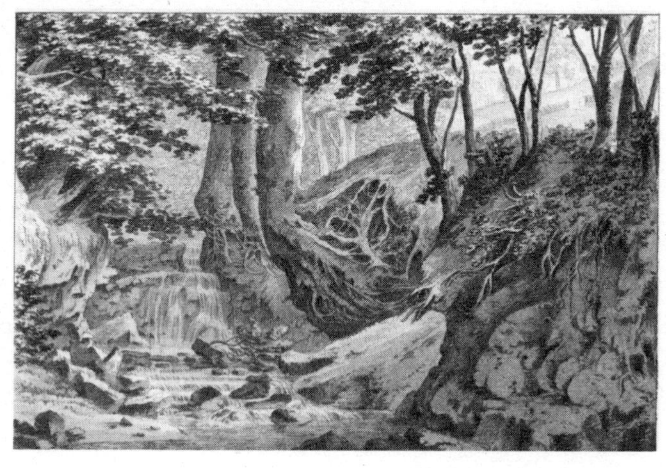

Hieronymus Grimm, *Waterfall in the Hollow Stream Bed in Silkwood Vale* (1776).

A T THE START OF the month, it's still hot, and wells run out across the country. In Rutland, Tom Barker noted, 'From the latter part of July to the beginning of September it was very dry, hot, and burning; much scorching sun, the ground very much burnt up, and great want of water.' But the showers come, and within a fortnight the burned grass is green again and new shoots of wheat appear under the hedges, where stray ears escaped the gleaners. Windfalls soften and rot, buzzing with wasps. Spiders' webs float. Under the harvest moon, mist creeps across the valley.

Gilbert feels the days shortening. The arcs intersect: the rising and setting of the moon, the cycle of the seasons, the times of sowing and harvest, flowering and seed, the movements of the planets as the Earth rolls. Gilbert's journal acknowledges that the idea of 'time' is endlessly mutable; everything has a different time span – the creation of mountains, the age of a yew tree, the passing of empires, the life of a fly or a man. We talk of 'declining days', 'sunset years'. Gilbert has gout in his hands, his joints are stiff and his hearing is getting worse. As the month goes by, he buttons up his coat and thinks of lighting fires in the parlour.

Saturday 1
65, 70½. 29 6/10½. SW.   *Peaches & Nect: now delicate.*
Grey, sun, sweet day,   *No wasps. Some hornets.*
yellow even: shower.   *Grapes grow black.*
                              We have caught about 20 hornets with a twig
                              tipped with bird-lime.

Gilbert picks the first peaches and nectarines and ties the best bunches of grapes inside crepe bags to protect them. The hornets, however, still cluster round them. As well as his limed twigs, he sometimes hangs up bottles of treacle and beer to attract them, but he can never win completely.

But at least the wasps have been conquered. In a murderous mood in 1775, he had watched them attack his grapes, even though, he wrote:

'We have, I should think, destroyed 50000.' (Really?) Yet, as a naturalist, he was intrigued to see how wasps and bees worked in tandem, but were also at war. On 5 September 1776, he had noted: 'Some wasps on the wall-fruit. Where the wasps gnaw an hole, the honey-bees come and suck the pulp.' But a week later, he recorded how the wasps plundered hives and killed the bees, especially in a wet month, when the bees were feeble. Another year, he watched the wasp queens 'come in a door & seem as if they were going to hide, & lay themselves up for the winter'. And what, he added, did wasps live on in the wild? 'Wasps abound in woody, wild districts far from neighbourhoods: how are they supported there without orchards, or butchers shambles, or grocers shops?' Later, he went back to this entry and added a footnote, as if rebuking his own stupidity: 'Wasps nesting far from neighbourhoods feed on flowers, & catch flies, & caterpillars to carry to their young.'

Sunday 2

65½, 70. 29 5½. NE, S.   *Dark, sun & clouds, hot, showers about.*
                            Full moon.

It's a hot day, and a showery, moonlit evening. He's amused by the way that all the insects, including butterflies and moths, share the flowers so neatly. 'The day & night insects,' he noted in September 1775, 'occupy the annuals alternately: the *papilios, muscae & apes* are succeeded at the close of day by the *phalenae*, earwigs, woodlice, &c.'

Monday 3

66½, 70½. 29 6/10.   *Wall-fruit dead-ripe.*
SW, S, SW.   *Fallows in delicate order.*
Grey, sun, sweet day,   *Turnips grow.*
soft even:

In these warm days with southerly winds, he admires the fallows, the harvested fields that will be left unsown for a season, which are looking trim with their good, rich soil. The fruit is for now, the turnips are for winter.

        A YEAR WITH GILBERT WHITE

66. 29 4/10½. SW, NW. W. Sun, sun, dark & moist, rain all night.

Second broods of swallows, & h: martins come out very fast. Vast flocks of hirundines. Some hornets. No wasps. Gathered one bunch of black grapes, which was ripe & well-flavoured. It grew close to the wall, pressed down by a bough. Wall-fruit is over.

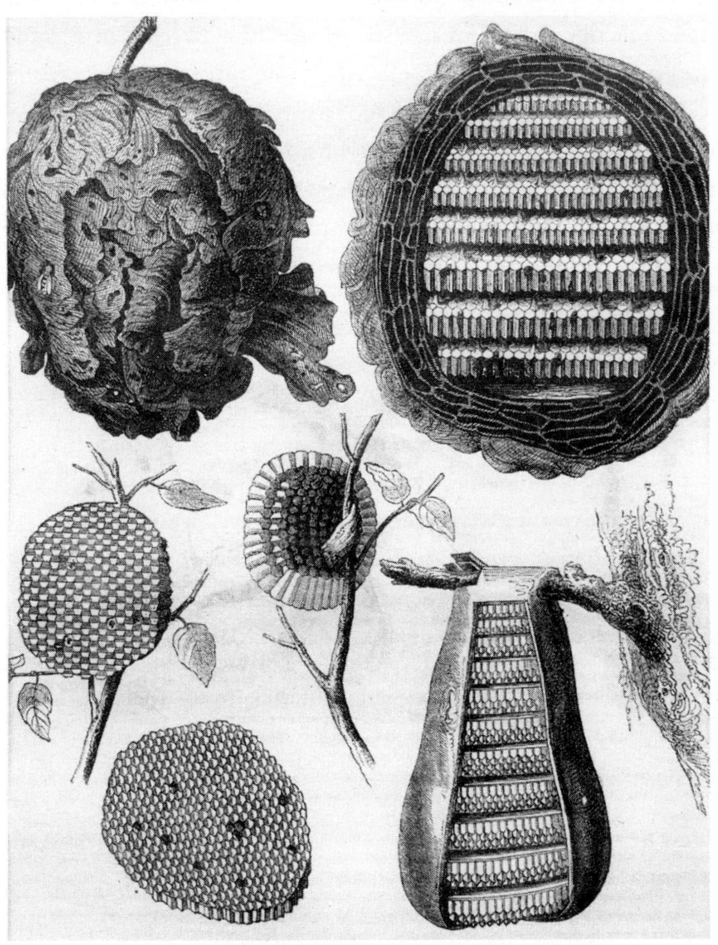

'Wasps' Nests', from *Cassell's Natural History* (1880).

Those second broods entertain him. 'The young martins of the first flight,' he had written in September, three years ago, 'are often very troublesome by attempting to get into the nest among the second callow broods; while their dams are as earnest to keep them out, & drive them away.' Next year, in 1782, he will see them clustering on the church tower in their hundreds. 'Vast flock of martins & swallows,' he says. 'The air is full of flying ants, & the hirundines live luxuriously.'

Insects fly and buzz and crawl. Once the flying ants have left, sometimes cockroaches arrive. An invasive species that arrived in Britain in the seventeenth century, they moved slowly, very slowly, across the land. Gilbert found them first in 1790, when a neighbour reported 'a kind of *black-bob*' in her kitchen at daybreak. In 1792, his sister-in-law Barbara White will still be fighting them. One can almost hear her fury, and Gilbert's amusement:

Mrs J. White, after a long & severe campaign carried on against the *Blattae molendinariae* which have of late invaded my house, & of which she has destroyed many thousands, finds that at intervals a fresh detachment of old ones arrives; & particularly during this hot season: for the windows being left open in the evenings, the males come flying in at the casements from the neighbouring houses, wch swarm with them. How the females, that seem to have no perfect wings that they can use, can contrive to get from house to house, does not so readily appear. These, like many insects, when they find their present abodes over-stocked, have powers of migrating to fresh quarters.

As quickly as Barbara defeats them, another insect appears: 'Since the *Blattae* have been so much kept under, the Crickets have greatly encreased in number.' She can't win.

Wednesday 5
63. 29 4/10. W. 82, 22.   Rain, rain, rain, dark & blowing.

          A YEAR WITH GILBERT WHITE

In these dark days, lapwings roam the stubble and ravens play in pairs in the air. They will still be there next month: 'A vast flock of ravens over the hanger: more than sixty!'

Smaller birds gather in flocks. In the generation after Gilbert's death, riding through Wiltshire in the late summer of 1826, William Cobbett – radical journalist, politician and farmer – noticed that the field thistles, loved by the goldfinches, had been cut down in the harvest. 'But they grow alongside the roads,' he added, 'and in this place in great quantities. So that the goldfinches were got here in flocks, and as they continued to fly along before me for nearly half a mile, and still sticking to the road and the banks, I do believe I had, at last, a flock of ten thousand flying before me.' An astonishing thought.

Thursday 6
59. 29 5/10. NW.   *Fallows are in delicate order.*
Sun, sun & air, sweet even:

Gilbert writes to Molly: 'The great heats are now abated, and the dust is layed; but the lovely weather continues.' He had been hoping that she and her father would turn up and surprise him, and was waiting for her letter – perhaps lost in the post? ('I just saved my credit,' Molly joked to her brother Tom, 'for I imagine he received my letter as soon as I did his.') The peaches and nectarines were nearly over, Gilbert said, but he promised her grapes, and no wasps. Knowing they would want to walk over to the Yaldens', he added: 'Your father's hazel-stick is looked out, and wiped; and the Bostal is in good order.'

The Bostal was a new route up to Newton through the Hanger. Older guests like John Mulso had complained good-temperedly of puffing up the steep Zig-Zag, and perhaps Gilbert was not finding it so easy himself: he complained to Barbara White of 'shootings in my back and bowel', acknowledging that this 'pulled me down very much'. In the summer of 1780, he had decided to make an easier path, a gentler slope through the trees. His brother Thomas put up the money, and Gilbert arranged the work. When the digging turned out to be too much for old Larby, who did occasional jobs for him, he hired 'a whole band of myrmidons', who redid Larby's path, which was 'so narrow, hollow and clayey' that the rain would have made it impassable, and finished the whole route. An added bonus for Gilbert was that in their digging, they found pyrites as round as balls in the clay, and large ammonites in the chalk. It didn't seem to worry him that he was not actually the owner of the Hanger, but Magdalen, as landlord, appeared unconcerned – if indeed the college was ever consulted.

Gilbert was pleased. The Bostal, he thought, was 'a fine romantic path, shady and beautiful'. When it was finished, he told Molly: 'All people agree, where party does not interpose, that it is a noble walk: but there is a junto against it, called *Zigzaggians*, of which Mrs Etty is the head; but Mr. E. and Mr. Yalden would be *Bostalians* – if they dared.' Later, he wrote to Sam Barker:

> To say the truth, the lower parts of the Bostal began to be dirty so that the Zigzaggians (who have horns and hoofs) began to triumph. Many of them, in the shape of horses and heifers, ran up and down it, doing it great damage with their feet: but to silence all clamour I had the bad part well-bedded with a quantity of fern. Since this amendment Mrs. Etty and her sister Stebbing, and Mrs. Yalden have been up and down it by night and by day: so that party feuds are like to be at an end.

Friday 7
58. 29 7/10. W, S.   Dined at Bramshot-place.
Sun, hot & bright,
sweet even:

The partridge-shooting season had begun on the first of this month. The birds reared on the sandy heaths near Woolmer, which Gilbert crosses while riding to his friends the Richardsons at Bramshott, remind him of his youth, when he would grab his gun in the early morning and head out to the fields with his dog. In his last summer, in 1792, he will tell Robert Marsham:

> Though I have long ceased to be a sportsman, yet I still love a dog; and am attended daily by a beautiful spaniel with long ears, and a spotted nose and legs, who amuses me in my walks by sometimes springing a pheasant or partridge, and seldom by flushing a woodcock, of late become with us a very rare bird.

The partridge season lasted until 1 February, and sportsmen (nearly always men) enjoyed it as a test of skill, since the birds were small and nimble and easily scared by a footstep or cracking twig, making them hard to hit. Looking back to the dry summers of 1740 and '41, Gilbert remembered that partridges 'swarmed to such a degree that parties of unreasonable sportsmen killed twenty and sometimes thirty brace in a day'. He remembers several of these 'unreasonable sportsmen'. One took pride in shooting the cock-bird of every couple after the partridges paired in early spring, knowing that a hen could be 'widowed' ten times but would always find new mates and thus keep producing eggs. Another man, who loved setting – hunting with a dog that showed where the birds lay, pointing with its nose – often shot whole coveys of partridges at once. These were all cock-birds (many hens are killed on the nest, usually by foxes), and 'these he pleasantly used to call old-bachelors'.

Each September, Gilbert follows the sporting chat: 'Shooting season but few partridges,' he writes. Or, more joyfully, at Fyfield: 'Partridges innumerable.' He also notes small oddities of timing: 'In the dusk of evening when beetles begin to buzz, partridges immediately begin to call: these two circumstances are exactly coincident.' These were the old grey partridges of the English countryside, *Perdix perdix*. The red-legged partridge, which became the dominant species, was introduced from France as a game bird only in the late eighteenth century (though

Charles II had had a go in 1673, bringing birds to Windsor Great Park from the Loire). Today, the grey partridge – which nests on the ground, and which Gilbert once watched tumbling away to distract a horseman from finding her chicks – is on the international Red List of species threatened by extinction.

Saturday 8
63½. 29 7/10 ½. SW.   *Hop-picking ends: a poor crop at Selborne.*
Dark & mild, shower,
sun, dark & hot.

In one exceptional hop season, in 1786, Gilbert will write: 'The hop-planters of this parish returned from Wey-hill fair with cheerful faces, & full purses.' But those good prices were due only to the Kentish hops being blasted by storms, after the Selborne crop was safely gathered in. Otherwise, hops were always difficult.

'No other growth, cultivated by man,' Gilbert decided, 'has such frequent & general failures.' If the summer was too cold, the cones did not ripen; if it was too hot, they shrivelled and browned. In some years, aphids destroyed them; in others, strong winds made them 'blow into flyers'. In a glut, the price collapsed; in a dearth, there weren't enough to sell. Good Selborne crops would fill four or five wagons, but in 1782, only two wagons were needed to carry all the hops of the parish to Weyhill market. The following year would be even worse: hopping lasted only two days, and in many gardens nothing was picked at all. Four years later: 'Hops so small that a notable woman & her girl can pick but nine bushels in a day, where last year they could pick 20.'

Picking was hard, and even dangerous, as Gilbert noted: 'Several women & children have eruptions on their hands, &c: is this owing to the lowness of the water in the wells, &c? It seems this often befalls after they have been employed in hop-picking.' Not many people made this connection: the first description of hop dermatitis wasn't published until 1832, and significant research was not done on it until the 1950s.

      A YEAR WITH GILBERT WHITE

Gilbert's guess was right: the rash, splotchy skin and tiny blisters can cause pain and intense itching.

A few miles away, over the Surrey border, hop gardens spread for miles. Looking out from the terrace of Farnham Castle, they spread to the horizon. Standing there in 1770, Gilbert had noted: 'About 8000 people besides natives are employed. A vast crop.' Seasonal workers poured in, many coming from the nearby port towns of Portsmouth and Southampton. Romany families also turned up, year after year. Gilbert shares the prejudice of his time towards these travellers, lacking John Clare's sympathy towards the 'quiet, pilfering, unprotected race' – though even Clare mentions their 'squalid camp' and 'stinking mutton'. Gilbert's tone is harsher: he writes of 'gangs or hordes', and of their 'cant and corrupted dialect'. (It makes me think of Harriet Smith fainting when a group surround her in the lane, demanding money, in Jane Austen's *Emma*. Austen lived at Chawton, only four miles from Selborne.)

Gilbert is curious about them, as well as uneasy. Two families, he had told Barrington in 1775, came round two or three times a year: the Stanleys and the Curleoples. The latter name intrigued him, as it seemed to have a Greek-derived ending. Did their language, he wondered, contain traces of Greek, 'brought with them from the Levant?' He was bewildered by the fact that while other tramps lodged in barns or byres, 'these sturdy savages' braved the harshest winters and were determined to live outside all year long. 'Last September,' he writes,

> was as wet a month as ever was known; and yet during those deluges did a young gypsy-girl lie-in in the midst of one of our hop-gardens, on the cold ground, with nothing over her but a piece of blanket extended on a few hazel rods bent hoop fashion, and stuck into the earth at each end, in circumstances too trying for a cow in the same condition.

Yet in this garden there was a large hop kiln, where she could have taken shelter.

There is something disturbing in this conjunction of the cow and the woman, reducing her to an animal. The scene clearly shocked him; he couldn't fathom her behaviour. He sets the whole race aside as if they were a mysterious foreign species, and pins them down by naming them as he might an unusual bird: 'Gypsies are called in French, *Bohemiens*; in Italian and modern Greek, *Zingani*.'

Sunday 9

65, 71. 29 8/¾. E, SE.   *Red-breasts whistle agreeably on the tops of*
Deep fog, sun, sultry,   *hop-poles,&c: but are prognostic of autumn.*
sweet even: *Young fern-owl.*

In the muggy warmth, as he hears the robins sing, Gilbert shivers. Yet there is beauty in this slow change of season: 'The creeping fogs in the pastures are very picturesque & amusing,' he writes, '& represent arms of the sea, rivers, & lakes.'

Monday 10

65, 68. 29 9/10. NE.   *Red-breasts feed on elder-berries, enter rooms,*
Deep fog, sun,   *& spoil the furniture.*
dark & louring.   *Bror T: & M: come to Selborne.*

Timothy, whose appetite is now on the decline, weighs only 7 pounds & ¾ of an ounce: at Midsumr he weighed 7pd:1 oun:

Gilbert doesn't usually worry about the furniture – think of the flying ants – but the invading robins might well bother the house-proud Barbara White, forced to clean up bird shit dyed elderberry-purple.

There would be a bustle today anyway, as Thomas and Molly, whom Gilbert has been hoping to see all the past week, finally appear. To mark their arrival, they troop across to Jack Burbey's store to weigh the tortoise, who has lost only a fraction of his summer weight. Last year, Gilbert had watched him slow down. On 9 September 1780: 'The motions of Timothy the tortoise are much circumscribed: he has taken

     A YEAR WITH GILBERT WHITE

to the border under the fruit-wall, & makes very short excursions: he sleeps under a Marvel of Peru.' Under this scented plant, with its brilliant flowers, Timothy dozed, coming out occasionally to eat.

Tuesday 11
65. 29 8/10. NE.   *Bean-harvest, & vetch-harvest.*
Dark, still, warm   *Grapes fine flavoured.*
& louring.

Molly brought Gilbert news of the city. She enjoyed her London life. That summer, she had been to the comic opera *La Fraschetana* at the King's Theatre in the Haymarket – a full house, as the Prince of Wales was there – and to the exhibition at the Royal Academy, admiring Reynolds's portrait of the three Ladies Waldegrave and Gainsborough's *Shepherd Boy*. But much as she liked the capital, she was jubilant to be back in Selborne, unpacking her side-saddle, longing to walk and ride.

It was almost a family reunion. While Thomas and Molly were at The Wakes, Gilbert's other brother Ben came down from London to stay at Newton Valence with the Yaldens, and Ben's daughter Jane Clements came over from Alton with her small children. Gilbert took pride in his swelling clan. The following year, on 8 September 1782, his note will read:

> On this day Mrs Brown of Uppingham in the County of Rutland, eldest daughter of my Sister Barker; was brought to bed of a daughter, her third child.
>
> My nephews & nieces living are now 17 nephews: 15 nieces: 2 grand nephews: 2 grand nieces: 2 nephews by marriage. total 38. One Niece since, 39.
>
> 8 nephews & nieces dead.

A family tea would be quite something.

Wednesday 12
29 7/10. NE, NW. 12. *Endives are large & finely blanched.*
Dark & still, rain, *Distant thunder.*
dark & still. *Fine crop of spinage.*

The vegetables are worth admiring, and the fruit is delicious, but nothing matches the melons that had been Gilbert's star achievement twenty-odd years ago. On 12 September 1758, another sociable, fine-weather time, he had written: 'Held a Canteleupe-feast at ye Hermitage: cut up a brace & and an half of fruit among 14 people.'

Thursday 13
65. 29 7/10½. NW, W. *Beans heavy.*
Dark, moist & mild.

A different harvest is ready. Farmers planted peas, beans and vetch – the wild pea that scrambles everywhere, with its pink flowers – as part of the crop rotation, the legumes fixing nitrogen in the soil after the arable crops. Beans, especially 'the common little horsebean', a kind of broad bean with large, thick, soft-lined pods, were a sure source of profit, according to the agriculturalist Arthur Young. The whole plant could make good animal feed when the frosts came: 'Bean straw, if well harvested, forms a very hearty and nutritious diet for the winter-time.'

Friday 14
63. 29 7/10. SW, S. *Bean, & vetch-harvest ends.*
Sun, grey, sun, sweet *Timothy the tortoise dull & torpid.*
even: bright & chill.

Timothy is sluggish. He brushes off all indignities, as they had noticed on the 16th of September a year ago, during yet another experiment – though one that was perhaps less alarming than the water tub. 'When we call loudly thro' the speaking trumpet to Timothy,' wrote Gilbert, 'he does not seem to regard the noise.'

Saturday 15
62. 29 2/10¾. E, SE.   *Grapes delicate.*
Grey & hot, dark to   *Thunder & lightening in all quarters round.*
the SE, thunder &
some rain, rain.

Note: The spring called Well-head sends forth now, after a severe hot dry summer, & dry spring & winter preceding, nine gallons of water in a minute; which is 540 in a hour; & 12960, or 216 hogsh: in 24 hours, or one natural day. At this time the wells are very low, & all the ponds in the vales dry.

Gilbert does like numbers, and so does his brother Thomas. I can see them together, conferring, measuring, writing down the data, adding up gallons and hogsheads, pleased that the Well Head spring burbles on, while the village wells and valley ponds are dry.

Sunday 16
65. 29 1/10½. S, S. 77.   *The boys destroyed a hornets nest: it was but*
Dark, showers, showers,   *small. Ophrys spiralis, ladies traces, seed.*
dark & mild.

Another hornets' nest gone. The meadows and the verges crackle with dry stalks and bursting seed pods, while wasps, bees and butterflies hover round the late wildflowers. Each September, Gilbert hunts for the autumn ladies' tresses (*Spiranthes spiralis*), the last British orchid to flower. From its woolly, soft stem the flowers curl upwards in a spiral, clockwise, as if following the sun, smelling faintly of almond or vanilla. In December 1778, he had written to his niece Anne Barker, who had become a budding botanist after staying with him in Selborne. He teased her that he missed his 'young housekeeper' making him syllabubs, then adds that Molly and her father have just left, although he is unsure if they had 'carried off any ladies tresses'. The plants are rare, he tells Anne, and deeply satisfying to see.

Dear Niece Anne; After I had experienced the advantages of two agreeable young house-keepers, I was much at a loss when they left me & have no body to make whipp'd syllabubs, & grace the upper end of my table. Molly & her father came again, & stayed near a month, during which we made much use of my great room: but they also have left me some times. Whether they carryed off any _Ladies Traces_ I cannot recollect: but it is easy to distinguish them at this season: for soon after they are out of bloom they throw out _radical leaves_, which abide all the winter. The plant is rare; but happens to abound in the _Long Lithe_, & will be enumerated in the list of more rare plants about Selborne. I wish we could say we had of _Parnassia_: I have sowed seeds in our bogs several times, but to no purpose. Please to let me know how many inches of rain fell in the late wet fit, which lasted about 5 weeks. The springs from being very low mounted up at a vast rate; & our _laverts_ at Faringdon began to appear last week. My Bar: is this evening at 30-3-10, the air thick, & warm, & still. Hepaticas, & winter-aconites blossom; & _Helleborus fœtidus_ in the _High-wood_, an oth rare plant. The clouds are all gone; & we may expect frost.

A botanical letter from Gilbert to his niece Anne, enclosed in one to her mother, Anne Barker, December 1778.

Monday 17

63. 29 4/10. SW, W.   *My well is very low.*
Grey, sun, brisk gale,   *Grapes delicate.*
bright, chill.   *Endives of vast size.*

Today, a sharp wind whistles and clouds scud across the sky. As usual, Gilbert's weather terms are crisp, but sometimes he looks up at the sky rather differently, with an artist's appreciation, a habit that developed after Hieronymus Grimm's stay. On 17 September 1777, for example, he gives vent to an uncharacteristic rapture: 'The sky this evening being what they call a mackerel sky was most beautiful, & much admired in many parts of the country. Italian skies!' Then he turns back into his scientific self, adding that since this unusual effect was admired at Ringmer, London and Selborne at the same time, 'It is plain proof that those fleecy clouds were very high in the atmosphere!' His interest in clouds was roused. A couple of weeks later, he asked: 'What becomes of those massy clouds that often incumber the atmosphere in the day, & yet disappear in the evening. Do they melt down into dew?' But he attempted no answer, not realising that the lower clouds appear during the day as the surface of the ground warms, and vanish when it cools.

Gilbert used only the traditional terms for clouds, such as 'mackerel skies', or his own images, like the 'vast, swagging, rock-like clouds' of autumn. It would be almost twenty years before the Quaker Luke Howard published his *Essay on the Modifications of Clouds* (1802), giving names to the three main types – cumulus, stratus and cirrus, using the Latin for 'heap', 'layer' and 'curl of hair' – and exploring the transitional forms in between.

Tuesday 18
55. 29 7/10. W, NW. 10. *Celeri very large.*
Rain & wind, grey, sun, *Fly-catchers seem to be gone: they breed but*
clear & chill. *once. Ivy begins to bloom.*
  Vast dew on windows.

The nests in the climbers above his window and over the stable door are empty now. The flycatchers have left, flying across the Sahara to the west of Africa, and the ring ouzels have arrived, stopping to graze on their way from their northern breeding grounds to their winter quarters in North Africa. Condensation mists the windows. Yet there are clouds of insects and butterflies on the ivy flowers. 'On sunny days quite on to Novr. they swarm on the trees covered with this plant,' he had written in 1772, '& when they disappear probably retire under the shelter of it's leaves, concealing themselves between it's fibres, & the tree that it entwines.'

I am watching butterflies today, 18 September 2024. In a week of glorious weather, they are darting everywhere, as if to disprove the surveys showing their decline. They are mostly red admirals and peacocks, with some whites and small fritillaries, and they fly and settle in the back gardens of our row of cottages, not in clouds, but certainly in their dozens.

The departure of the flycatcher, the coming of the ring ouzels and the flowering of the ivy are three seasonal markers. In previous years, Gilbert had seen flycatchers leave in the first week of September, around the 6th or 7th, though some were still around for a week or so more. The ring ouzels turned up a little later, around the 11th, but again it varied – sometimes he spotted them on the 14th or the 22nd, and once or twice at the very end of the month. He would take out his earlier journals and run his finger down the 'Observations' column to see when they had appeared, and then make a note, as on 15 September 1774: 'Ring ouzels appear on their autumn migration. Were first seen last year on the 30th: the year before on the 11th.'

The variations, though slight, pointed to the difficulty in making any 'natural calendar' for planting and sowing, especially as the harvests depended on the weather; the hop harvest, for example, swung between August and late September. Gilbert did not try to correlate the dates of the flowering of plants or migration of birds with his notes of weather patterns, although he sometimes hazarded a guess as to the effects of cold, storms or heat. But researchers still refer back to his journals as part of their historic data. The winters of late-eighteenth-century Hampshire were colder, and the summers cooler, than today, and as one would expect, spring-flowering plants like snowdrops and colts-foot flowered later. Comparisons are skewed, however, by the global warming that has taken place over the past seventy years. One study, which has collected data for the last fifty years, shows that twenty bird species are now laying their eggs between a week and a fortnight earlier than they did in 1971. Since insects such as aphids, flies, butterflies and moths respond most of all to climate change, this, too, affects the natural balance. If an oak, for example, which supports more insect species than any other tree, comes into leaf earlier, then the caterpillars need to be there early to feed on the young leaves, before the tannin content gets too high; and so the birds, too, have to be on the spot earlier to catch the caterpillars for their young, before they disappear. The economy of nature, as Gilbert said so often, is intricate and complex.

Wednesday 19
54. 29 6/10¾. SW.   *Many hirundines.*
Grey & cold, grey &
chilly.

Thursday 20   *MEONSTOKE*
60. 29 6/10¼. NW. 42. *[TW] The Well is now so low, that Thomas*
Rain, sun, mild,   *found some difficulty in getting water*
bright even: *sufficient to Brew with.*

Today, Gilbert sets off to call on the Mulsos. He and John Mulso had always kept lovingly in touch, and their visits grew more frequent when, after harassed years as a canon to his uncle the Bishop of Winchester, Mulso took the living of Meonstoke, only seventeen miles from Alton. On this trip, Gilbert takes Gibraltar Jack with him – now Dr John White – who has come down to see his mother in Selborne.

While Gilbert is away, his brother Thomas takes over the journal, initialling the entries 'TW'. He makes a note of the low well, which will cause problems in the brewhouse. Now that the barley is housed and the hops dried, all the home brewers are busy, and Thomas Hoar is getting started on the autumn's beer. Brewing was done in spring and autumn, when the mild, even temperatures helped fermentation. Thomas didn't ferment the barley himself to make the malt, but bought it dried and ground from a local maltster. But he would need a lot of water. First, hot water – 'liquor' – to soak the malt, mashing it to turn the starch into a sweet porridge of fermentable sugar and proteins. Then cold, to run through the soaked grain; he might do this three times, the beer decreasing in strength as less sugar was washed from the grain at each rinsing. The first run produced an ale (to which no hops were added), the second a strong beer, and the last the weaker 'small beer', which was drunk throughout the day, like water. Next, Thomas would boil the liquid for an hour or two, adding hops for bitterness. Like many home brewers, Gilbert had two coppers – one for strong beer, the other for small – and the smell would fill the house. When the beer was cooled, yeast was added, and fermentation began. Finally, after about four days, when it was alcoholic enough and the foam had been scooped off the top, they poured it into barrels to keep. Gilbert made about fifty gallons of strong beer a year. Like barley wine, it was as potent as its name suggests, with between 5 and 11 per cent alcohol; small beer was weaker, mild and nutritious, the standard drink of labourers and families.

'I only know that my strong beer is much admired by those that love pale beer,' said Gilbert proudly. 'My method,' he explained to Thomas Barker, 'is to make it very *strong*, and to hop very *moderately* at *first*; and then to put in it, at two or three times, half a pound at a time of *scalded* hops, before I tap it . . . I tap my half-hogsheads at about 12 months old; and always brew with rain water, when I can.' Lack of rain, then, was a real problem.

Friday 21

58. 29 5/10. NW.	*[TW] Hooker's hill mended by Tom Prior the*
Bright, showers, fair,	*ditch below which was made about fifty years*
chill even:	*ago, is now open'd and cleaned.*

Three generations of family life in the same spot can concertina time, as happens here, when Thomas looks at a ditch that was dug when he was six and Gilbert ten. Other memories often surface. About ten years after the ditch was made, for example, on 21 September 1741, Gilbert had gone out before dawn, taking his gun. He never forgot that day, writing about it at the time and later sending the description to his brother John in Gibraltar as an example of the kind of anecdote John might use in his book. Finally, he repeated it in a letter to Barrington, which he would edit for *The Natural History of Selborne.*

'I found the stubbles and clover-grounds matted all over with a thick coat of cobweb,' he wrote, 'in the meshes of which a copious and heavy dew hung so plentifully that the whole face of the country seemed, as it were, covered with two or three setting-nets drawn one over another.' The cobwebs were so thick that his dogs had to lie down and scrape them from their eyes. Unable to hunt with them, Gilbert turned for home: the day would turn out to be 'one of those most lovely ones which no season but the autumn produces; cloudless, calm, serene, and worthy of the south of France itself'. But at about nine o'clock:

> an appearance very unusual began to demand our attention, a shower of cobwebs falling from very elevated regions, without any interruption, till the close of the day. The webs were not single filmy threads, floating in the air in all directions, but perfect flakes or rags; some near an inch broad, and five or six long, which fell with a degree of velocity that showed they were considerably heavier than the atmosphere.

On every side they fell, over twenty square miles of the chalk downs, hanging in the trees and hedges, 'so thick, that a diligent person sent out might have gathered baskets full'. Gilbert's father, appearing in this story as 'a gentleman for whose veracity and intelligent turn we have the greatest veneration', had thought that if he rode up the Hanger, he would have got above them, as one climbs above a valley mist, but there they still were, falling constantly, twinkling in the sun.

In earlier days, Gilbert wrote, these cobweb clouds of gossamer roused many superstitions. But by the time he was writing, nobody doubted that the effect was produced by small spiders, 'which swarm in the fields in autumn, and have a power of shooting out webs from their tails so as to render themselves buoyant, and lighter than air'. Why they should have done so that day, in such numbers, remained a mystery to him, but the webs of money spiders do tend to fly as the day warms, then fall back to earth, lying across the ground.

Every fine autumn day, he watched these spiders 'shooting out their webs' and floating off, trailing a line of silk. They would take off from your finger if you picked them up, he noticed, and one, which landed on his book as he was reading in the parlour, simply ran to the top of the page and launched itself from there. But how could it float, 'when no air was stirring, and I am sure that I did not assist it with my breath'? As they shot off, 'these little crawlers', he thought, seemed to have 'some loco-motive power without the use of wings, and to move in the air faster than the air itself'.

<table>
<tr><td>Saturday 22</td><td>SELBORNE</td></tr>
<tr><td>29 4/10. SW, W.</td><td>The well at Filmer-hill is 60 yards deep: at Privet,</td></tr>
<tr><td>Bright, grey & still,</td><td>on the top of the hill, they have no wells, & have</td></tr>
<tr><td>moist & dark.</td><td>been greatly distressed for water the summer thro'.</td></tr>
</table>

The Warnford, & Meon-stoke stream as full, & bright, as if there had been no drought. Swallows, & martins.

As Gilbert walked by the River Meon when he stayed with the Mulsos, it seemed astonishing that this chalk stream should be so high, compared to the dried-up wells at home, thirteen miles away.

Mulso was delighted to see him, and his son John came back with Gilbert to Selborne, adding to the crowd of young people. He was 'prodigiously fond of music', playing the flute and violin and making everyone sing catches. He took back to Meonstoke a print of Grimm's view of the hermitage, of which Mulso approved, in a lukewarm fashion, still thinking Grimm had 'a heavy Hand at a *distant* view' and gave no real sense of the hill's height.

<table>
<tr><td>Sunday 23</td><td></td></tr>
<tr><td>29 2/10½. NW.</td><td>Few hirundines.</td></tr>
<tr><td>Sun, & clouds,</td><td>Began to light fires in the parlor.</td></tr>
<tr><td>harsh wind, showers</td><td>Aurora.</td></tr>
<tr><td>about, sharp air.</td><td></td></tr>
</table>

To the same.
Letter 23.

Dear Sir,   M[r] B[arrington]   Selborne: June 8:th 1775.

On Septem:r 21: 1741: being then on a visit, &
intent on field-diversions, I rose before day-break. When I came
into the enclosures I found the stubbles & clover-grounds matted
all over with a thick coat of cobweb, in the meshes of which a
copious & heavy dew hung so plentifully, that the whole face of
the country seemed, as it were, covered with two or three setting-
nets drawn one over an other. When the dogs attempted to hunt,
their eyes were so blinded & hoodwinked, that they could not proceed,
but were obliged to lie down & scrape the incumbrances from their
faces with their fore-feet: so that finding my sport interrupted
I returned home musing in my mind on the oddness of the occur:
rence.

As the morning advanced the sun became bright & warm;
& the day turned out one of those most lovely ones, which no sea:
son but the autumn produces, cloudless, calm, & serene, & worthy
of the South of France itself.

About nine an appearance, very unusual, began to demand
our attention, a shower of cobwebs falling from very elevated
regions, & continuing without any interruption 'til the close
of the day.   These webs were not single filmy threads floating
in the air in all directions; but perfect flakes, or rags, some near an
inch broad, & five or six long, which fell with a degree of velocity
that shewed they were considerably heavier than the atmosphere.

On every side as the observer turned his eyes might he
behold a continual succession of fresh flakes falling into his
sight, & twinkling like stars as they turned their sides towards
the sun.

How far this wonderful shower extended would be dif:
ficult to say: but we know that it reached Bradley, Selborne,
& Alresford, three places which lie in a sort of a triangle, the
shortest of whose sides is about eight miles in extent.

Gilbert's memory of the gossamer fall of 1741, in his *Natural History of Selborne*,
in a letter to Daines Barrington dated 8 June 1775.

There's no record of the temperature for two days – perhaps Gilbert's thermometer has broken again. Almost every night this week, the aurora flickers and flares. Inside, they light a fire. At dusk, the tawny owls hoot.

Gilbert loved owls. 'Owls move in a buoyant manner, as if lighter than the air,' he wrote, 'they seem to want ballast.' Barn owl nestlings, he told Thomas Pennant, were hard to raise as they needed a constant supply of fresh mice; brown owls, by contrast, would eat anything – 'snails, rats, kittens, puppies, magpies, and any kind of carrion or offal'. He watched Jack Burney's tame brown owl, seeing how it hid any food it couldn't eat at the time, and how it regurgitated the fur of mice and the feathers of birds in pellets, like a hawk. A friend in Wiltshire, he recorded, found bushels of pellets in a hollow pollarded ash, 'the mansion of owls for centuries'. In *The Natural History of Selborne*, his description of the barn owls – his 'white owls' – shows just how carefully he watched them:

> About an hour before sunset (for then the mice begin to run) they sally forth in quest of prey, and hunt all round the hedges of meadows and small enclosures for them, which seem to be their only food. In this irregular country we can stand on an eminence and see them beat the fields over like a setting-dog, and often drop down in the grass or corn.

They would carry the mouse in their claws and then, since they needed to use their feet to climb under the tiles, they perched on the chancel roof and moved the mouse from their claws to their bill, so 'that the feet may be at liberty to take hold of the plate on the wall as they are rising under the eaves'.

Barn owls, Gilbert thought ('but in this I am not positive'), did not hoot at all. Instead, all the 'clamorous noise' came from the 'wood owls', the tawny owls. But the barn owls could hiss tremendously, with a truly intimidating effect, 'for I have known a whole village up in arms on such an occasion, imagining the church-yard to be full of

   A YEAR WITH GILBERT WHITE

goblins and spectres'. They screamed, too, as they flew along, giving rise to the 'imaginary species of screech-owl, which they superstitiously think attends the windows of dying persons'.

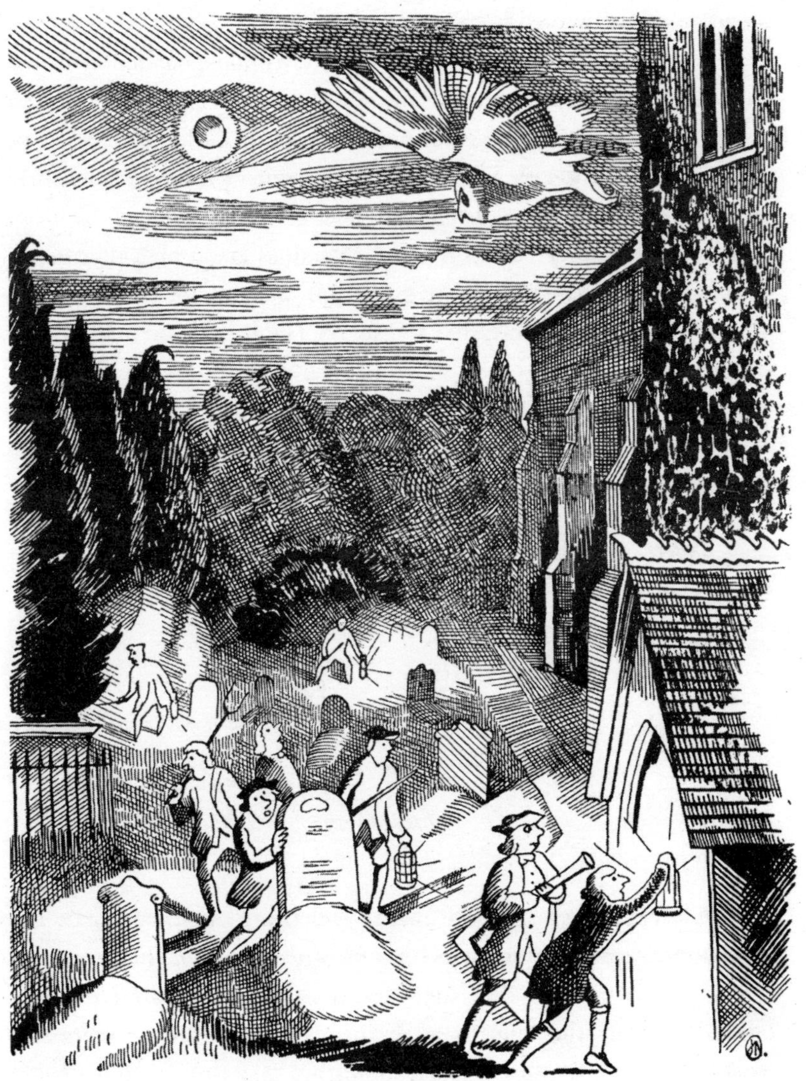

John Nash, 'I Have Known a Whole Village Up in Arms' (1951).

It's always tempting to imitate an owl, yet they hoot so differently. Responding to Barrington's interest in what keys birds sang in, Gilbert told him that one 'musical friend' (in fact, his brother Henry) 'has tried all the owls that are his near neighbours with a pitch-pipe set at concert pitch, and find they all hoot in B flat'. Back in Selborne, however, an acquaintance noted that at least one owl 'went almost half a note below A', while another neighbour, who was said to have a good ear, asserted that the local owls hoot 'in three different keys, in G flat, or F sharp, in B flat and A flat. *Query*: Do these different notes proceed from different species, or only from various individuals?'

Yet owls, however beautiful and fascinating, could be a pest, to be dealt with ruthlessly. When a pair of them raided a dovecote, one was shot as quickly as possible, 'but the survivor readily found a mate, and the mischief went on'. Then both were killed, 'and the annoyance ceased'.

Monday 24
51. 29 3/10. NW.   *Hirundines haunt sheltered vales.*
Sun & clouds, strong   *The wind blows down apples & pears.*
gales, showers & hail,   *Vivid Aurora.*
bright & cold.

Tuesday 25
48½. 29 4/10½. N.   *Wild honey-suckles blow.*
Wh: frost, sharp wind,   *Gathered swan's egg pears, a large crop.*
sun, vast lights.   *Surprising Auroras, very red in the w!!*

Note: The young swarms of bees of this summer are light; the old stocks are heavy.

At The Wakes, they are busy in the orchard. First, they rescue the apples and pears that the wind has blown down, which have to be eaten and cooked now. Then they pick more to store, holding the pears up and twisting the stem to see if they come off easily: they're still hard but 'ready', as they ripen from within and can't be left longer.

The Swan's Egg pear, squat and fat, almost as round as an apple, was crisp and sweet and was said to be good for your health. It had been a favourite since the seventeenth century; John Evelyn, who had grown it in his garden at Sayes Court, wrote that 'its flesh is melting and full of a pleasant juice'.

Gilbert's timing was in tune with tradition. In 1729, in his *Pomona: or, The Fruit Garden Illustrated*, the garden designer Batty Langley had said that Swan's Egg pears should be gathered on 20 September and eaten soon after. Like all winter pears, these have to be brought in before any danger of frost. And now the first frosts are coming, white on the grass in the mornings, shrivelling the leaves of the cucumbers, making the annuals droop.

Wednesday 26

47. 29 3/10½. NW.   *Few hirundines. Dug up potatoes: Earthed up*
Frost, sun, sharp air,   *celeri. Swallows seem distressed by the cold.*
dark & harsh, rain.   *Gathered knobbed-russetings, a large crop.*

Frost and sun, a brisk feel. The knobbed russets that they pick today look disconcertingly like the newly dug potatoes, bumpy in shape, with lumpy, rough skin. Said to be the oldest of all apples, these greeny-yellow russets may look grotesque, but they are crisp, sweet and nutty. Gilbert picked them with pleasure every year, till the end of his life.

Today, he adds a note against the day's entry: 'Our building-sand from Wolmer forest,' he writes, 'seems pure from dirt: but examined thro' a microscope proves not to be sharp, & angular, but smooth as from collision. It is of a yellow colour.' We don't often see Gilbert with a microscope, yet he had one at hand when he was dissecting birds and other animals and examining the contents of their stomachs. The most popular microscope in his day was the model developed by the instrument maker John Cuff, which was easy to use and focus, with a concave mirror at the base to concentrate the light rays onto a sample that was placed on a 'stage' and with another 'condensing lens' above.

Today, peering at the sand, Gilbert turns into a geologist, if on a small scale. His concern is practical, too: perhaps he is worried that his builders aren't using the best stuff, as angular sand, which contains more quartz – the so-called 'sharp sand' – would be better for building than the rounded type that is smoothed by wind and water. The Woolmer heaths were formed on the sandstones of the Folkestone Beds, a marine shallow-water deposit. Did he wonder, on seeing that the Woolmer sand was so smooth, if it had been under water at some point? He takes his enquiry no further, but it's moving to think of him, for a moment, seeing the world in a grain of sand. As Blake said: 'Hold Infinity in the palm of your hand / And Eternity in an hour.'

Thursday 27

50. 29 4/10. NW.　　　　*Many swallows at Oakhanger.*
Grey & windy, sun,　　　*Gathered Cadilliac-pears, dearlings, & royal*
bright & cold.　　　　　*russets.*

Now, they pick more pears, filling the large wicker baskets. The large Cadilliac from France (now called the Catillac), with its yellow flesh, was a plentiful bearer, 'one of the best fruits for baking yet known', according to Miller's *Gardeners Dictionary*. They picked more apples, too. At different points, Gilbert mentions the tangy-scented white pippins, 'golden-rennets' (Golden Reinettes) and royal russets, with their bright red cheeks. The apples and pears would last over the cold months, stored in wooden crates in a dark outhouse. In the depths of winter, you could still breathe the scent of autumn fruit. Many tasks were now done with winter in mind. Carrots and parsnips were kept in cellars, sometimes covered in sand to stop them shrivelling. Potatoes could be kept there, too, covered with earth, or they could be left outside and dug into clamps, pits insulated with straw or leaves and covered with soil.

An aside: in one letter to Thomas Pennant, Gilbert described how a local farmer, ploughing up a dry, chalky field, found a water rat in a nest of grass and leaves, with over a gallon of potatoes (about five pounds) stowed at one end of its burrow,

> on which it was to have supported itself for the winter. But the difficulty with me is how this *amphibius mus* came to fix its winter station at such a distance from the water. Was it determined in its choice of place by the mere accident of finding the potatoes which were planted there; or is it the constant practice of the aquatic-rat to forsake the neighbourhood of the water in the colder months?

Or was it an 'aquatic-rat' at all? It seems more likely that the nest belonged to a vole, nosing out, as Gilbert said, a lucky heap of abandoned potatoes.

Friday 28
51. 29 7/10¼. NW.   *Dug-up potatoes, & carrots.*
Grey, sun, pleasant, cool. *Swallows, & martins.*
          Vast halo round the moon.

Tomorrow is Michaelmas – the feast of St Michael and All Angels – honouring the saint who battled Lucifer and protects against the demons of the dark. Close to the autumnal equinox, Michaelmas marks the end of harvesting and the coming of the real autumnal cool. And it's another Quarter Day, when rents become due and people move houses, when labourers are laid off or hired, when goose fairs are held and goose feasts enjoyed. Michaelmas daisies, covered with butterflies, glow in the sunshine – a farewell to summer.

One Michaelmas visit was especially striking. In early 1770, Gilbert had ended a letter to Pennant by noting that although 'foreign animals fall seldom in my way', he had something to tell him about the 'moose-deer'. This was a female moose, he explained in the next letter, that he had managed to see on Michaelmas Day 1768, among the 3rd Duke of Richmond's menagerie at Goodwood – a famous collection, put together by the 2nd Duke, including tigers, lions and leopards, vultures and eagles, wolves and bears, monkeys and raccoons. After weeks of rain, Gilbert had ridden the twenty miles from Selborne on a fine, dry day, but when he arrived at Goodwood, he found, to his intense disappointment, that the moose had just died. Its body was now hanging, legs down, in a harness in an old greenhouse, 'slung under the belly and chin by ropes', already bloated and stinking.

It must have been hard to brave the smell, but Gilbert managed it. He measured the moose's height, 'from the ground to its withers', amazed at the contrast between the long legs and short neck, an imbalance that would, he thought, have made it very difficult for the animal to graze. He noted its huge nostrils and wide lip – which, 'travellers say, is esteemed a dainty dish in North America' – and he would have stayed to measure the strangely long tibia, too, 'but, in my haste to get out of the stench, I forgot to measure that joint exactly . . . I should have been glad to have examined the teeth, tongue, lips, hoofs, &c. minutely, but the putrefaction precluded all further curiosity.' He must have breathed deeply when he closed the door.

Over time, the Duke had four moose, and these were often cited in a heated contemporary debate. In the 1760s, the surgeon William Hunter, who was interested in comparative anatomy and the development of species, had been exploring the idea, then highly controversial, that it was possible for a whole species to become extinct – an apparent contradiction of a settled Divine design. One example under consideration was the prehistoric elk known as the 'Great Irish Elk', whose skull and huge antlers – 12 feet across – had been discovered in an Irish peat bog in 1697. Some naturalists, however, including Pennant, believed the American moose was a survival of the same species. To explore this, when General Guy Carleton, governor of Quebec, presented a young bull moose to the Duke of Richmond in 1770, Hunter commissioned George Stubbs – known for the anatomical accuracy of his paintings of horses – to paint 'an exact resemblance'. Since the Duke's bull moose was only a yearling and had no antlers, only small, bumpy horns, Hunter asked Stubbs to include the antlers of a full-grown male, which Carleton had also presented to him. The theory was that if the Canadian moose had different horns to the Irish elk, the gap between the species would be clear.

A painting was not enough to persuade the sceptics, but the question was settled more definitively in 1773, when Carleton sent the Duke another animal, this time a mature bull moose with fully grown antlers. As these were very different to those found in Ireland – they were nowhere near the same size – it seemed that the Irish elk was indeed an extinct animal. This, in turn, raised new questions: why do some species become extinct? What did the fact of extinction say about the development of life on Earth?

The female moose that Gilbert saw had no antlers (though the artist Eric Ravilious included them when he imagined the greenhouse scene), but he was alert to this debate, asking if his description resembled any moose that Pennant had seen, 'and whether you think still that the American moose and European elk are the same creature'. Pennant stuck to his guns and firmly declared that they were.

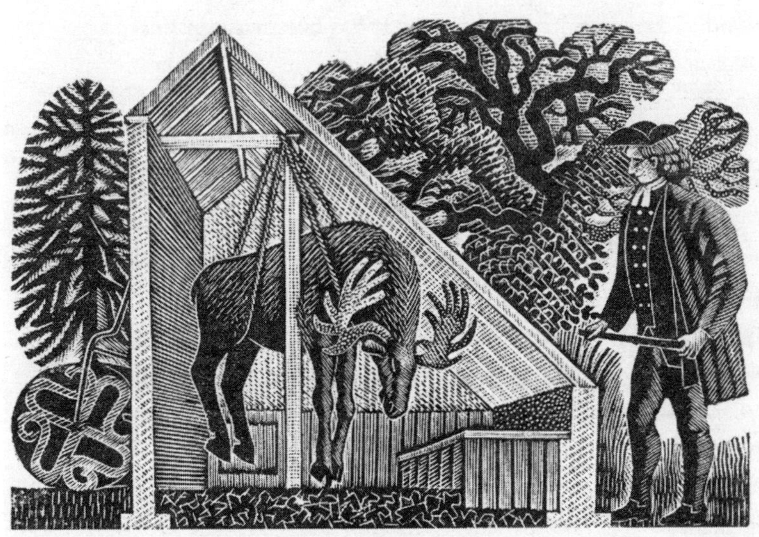

'The Goodwood moose' by Eric Ravilious, from *The Natural History of Selborne* (1938).

The moose question was related to another contemporary debate: how had animals become scattered around the globe? Some thinkers stuck to the biblical idea that all species were created in one blow, their nature fixed for all time, and that they had spread out after the Flood. Pennant, for example, argued in his book *Arctic Zoology* that the animals left the Ark on Mount Ararat and migrated through Asia and across the Bering Strait to the Americas, 'driven by a divinely-implanted instinct'. Linnaeus also imagined a single, but different, point of creation: a high mountain on an island in the tropics, cleverly designed with a wide variety of climatic zones so that creatures were suited to live in particular places; from there, they spread out as the primeval seas receded. The Comte de Buffon, by contrast, rejected these narratives, proposing that animals had emerged in the north, during a hotter epoch in the Earth's history, before drifting south.

Gilbert's stance on such speculation is clear. Responding to a question from Pennant as to 'animals peculiar to America, viz. How they came there, and whence?' he stands back. It is, he says, 'too puzzling for me to answer; and yet so obvious as often to have struck me with wonder'. He finds little help in what has been written so far:

> Ingenious men will readily advance plausible arguments to support whatever theory they shall chuse to maintain, but then the misfortune is, every one's hypothesis is each as good as another's, since they are all founded on conjecture.

Brooding on time, it's now thought that the passerines – the small perching birds – evolved around 50 to 60 million years ago, from therapod dinosaurs dating back over 150 million years. Birds flew across oceans and steppes long before any humans walked the land.

Saturday 29
51. 29 8/10½. SW. *Swallows, & martins.*
Grey, pleasant & still. *Grapes delicate.*

The swallows and martins still linger, but Selborne is thinking ahead. The pigs are now beginning to be fattened for Christmas, and Gilbert plans for the long, dark evenings, buying wine and port from London, decanting it and sharing it with Richard Yalden, and trying out his own home-made wines. Each September, he made elderberry wine – a costly affair, given the price of sugar: one year, after pressing the berries, he added 36 pounds of sugar to 18 quarts of juice, making, he said, '29 Quarts of Syrop'. Cookbooks were full of recipes for wines, from elderflower to orange, lemon, raspberry, redcurrant and walnut. Gilbert also made raisin wine every year, stirring pounds of Malaga raisins into sugar syrup, adding yeast and letting the brew ferment, before straining it off. He also liked to add several pints of brandy, so the wine was like a very sweet sherry or liqueur – alarmingly strong.

Sometimes, though, there were upsets. In May 1783, on the day after he bottled some 'very fine' raisin wine, Thomas Hoar would wake him early, saying that wine was streaming under the vault door; he thought it had fermented and broken some bottles. Nonsense, said Gilbert, it couldn't ferment so fast. But Thomas came back, reporting that the stream smelled of brandy or rum. 'So I got up, and went into the cellar: when, woe is me, the shelf was fallen down and – *caetera desunt*.' The whole lot had gone.

OCTOBER

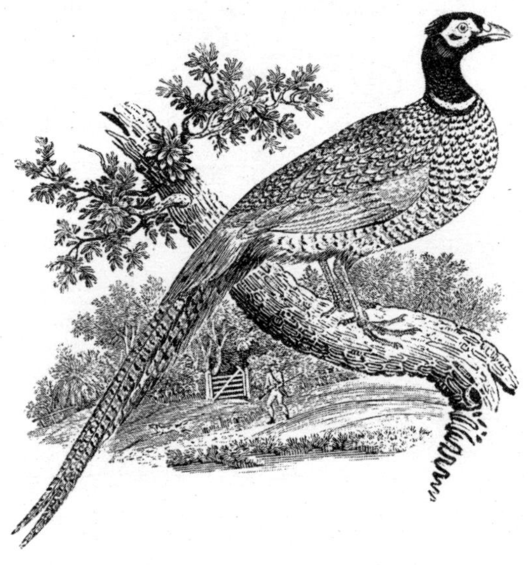

'The Pheasant' by Thomas Bewick, in *Land Birds* (1797).

I N O CTOBER, three years from now, Gilbert will write with astonishment: 'Hard frost, thick ice. In my way to Newton I was covered with snow! Snow covers the ground, & trees!!' This year, however, the month begins benignly. As he rides out with Thomas, Molly and his dogs, which are flushing out the game birds, his mind turns to his book. From time to time, he has been adding more stories to his letters to Pennant and Barrington, piled on his desk, and writing new 'letters' to expand the book still more. But in this autumn of 1781, he is concentrating on the second part, the *Antiquities of Selborne*. Thomas and Molly are helping him dig into the past, into the history of the village and the earth beneath. But the present presses on him, too, and glimpses of the future also suddenly flash up. In three years' time, in October 1784, a sign of things to come will reach Selborne, when Jean-Pierre Blanchard's balloon sails high across the village on a clear afternoon.

Monday 1

61. 29 8/10. sw.   *Good riding round Woolmere-pond within it's*
Fog, sun, hot, sweet day,   *banks, on the sand. [In a different hand.]*
moonshine.   *Many swallows.*

Gilbert doesn't write today's first entry. It's Molly who is proud of riding round Woolmer pond. She tells her brother Tom that she is riding every day in the beautiful weather, 'and I'll assure you, whatever you may think to the contrary that I am become quite a famous horsewoman'. She breaks off to take her morning ride, 'a very pleasant one round the inside of the banks of Wolmere pond which is at this time much shallower than usual. Indeed there has been much complaints for want of water in this part of the world and many people have been obliged to clean their wells out.'

One of those people cleaning out a well was Gilbert. Today, he adds a note:

Cleaned my well by drawing out about 100 buckets of muddy water:

there was little rubbish at the bottom. There were two good springs, one at the bottom, & one about three feet above. Nothing had been done to this well for about 40 years. The man at bottom in the cleaning brought up several marbles & taws that we had thrown down when children.

'Taws' were large, fancy marbles, made of stone and pottery, and only rarely of coloured glass, that Georgian and Regency children used in games of marbles. Layers of time peel back. Here were the children – Thomas and Ben, Henry and Francis and Rebecca, and Gilbert himself – leaning over the side and dropping their marbles, waiting to hear the plops and splashes as they hit the water deep below.

Tuesday 2
59. 29 6/10¾. W, NW. 17.   Gathered-in the wall-nuts.
Sun, grey, shower.
Full moon.

Gilbert had picked walnuts since he was a boy. The tree near the stable was usually barren, but the 'great tree' at the bottom of the garden always yielded several bushels of nuts, with some bunches containing from nine to fifteen walnuts each. As a 'bushel' was a measure of volume, the weight varied according to the different crops, but still, that was an awful lot of nuts.

Walnuts were another nourishing winter staple: for eating as they were; for grinding into flour for walnut bread; for preserving with sugar and egg whites or pickling in vinegar (Gilbert's household did their pickling in summer, when the walnuts were green). Ground up, soaked for a week in vinegar with shallots and then boiled with anchovies, mace and pepper, they made, apparently, an excellent 'catsup'.

At The Wakes, they also made catsup, or 'catchup', from mushrooms. Most of the mushrooms on the Hanger were the red-spotted fly agaric, which was to be avoided, but on the downs they found good field mushrooms, puffballs and fleshy boletus. One year, truffles were found 'in the deep, narrow part of the hill between coney-croft-hang-er, & the high-wood; & again on each side of the hollow road up the high-wood'. The truffler came regularly with his two little dogs, led on a string. Gilbert assumed he did well, as he was seen so often in the village, but marked him down as 'a surly fellow, & not communicative', a disappointment for a naturalist who liked to chat.

Other October harvests were berries, sloes and hips, and honey from the hive. Honeycombs sold for between 3 and 4 pence a pound; each year, a man from Chert, near Farnham, came over with a cart, 'to whom all the villagers round about brought their hives, & sold their contents'.

Wednesday 3
56. 29 8/10½. N.   *Bought a bay-Welch Galloway mare. Out of*
Sun, grey & pleasant.   *the horses that were offered me to try, there*
       were ten mares to one gelding.

Before he came to stay at Selborne this month, Thomas had bought a new horse. The 'aftergrass' that grows after the hay is cut, Gilbert told him, was long and lush, 'fetlock high', ready for his arrival. In the enthusiasm for riding, Gilbert himself buys a new mare, a Galloway, one of the large fell ponies, bred with Welsh ponies, that were used to cart loads from the Cumbrian lead mines. Tough and strong, Galloways could endure the harshest conditions – good for long rides.

Every time Thomas descends on The Wakes, he is a whirlwind of energy – in the garden, the village and the whole neighbourhood. 'Now your father, I know,' Gilbert writes to Molly, 'when at Selborne, loves to bustle about, and to have somewhat in pursuit.' On the Plestor, Thomas plants the sycamore to replace the fallen oak tree. In the meadow at The Wakes, he experiments with making 'fairy rings', marking concentric circles with hot water and trying different treatments within each one – oil of vitriol, saltpetre, 'Sal Tartar', wood and coal ashes – to see which will make the grass grow the deepest green ('The grass seems killed where the tea-kettle stood,' Gilbert writes drily). And as he has done

ever since the 1750s, and will do in years to come, Thomas comes loaded
with plants. In 1783:

> Brought down by Brother Thomas White from South Lambeth, &
> planted in my borders: – Dog's toothed violets – Persian Iris – *Quercus
> cerris* [Turkey oak], Double *ulmaria* [*Spiraea*] – Double *filipendula* –
> Double blue *campanula* – large pansies – double daisies – *Hemerocallis*
> – white fox-glove – Iron fox-glove – double wall-flower – double
> scarlet *lychnis* . . .

Thursday 4

55. 29 8/10. E, S.   *The frost killed the cucumber-plants.*
White frost, sun, soft   *No h: martins, nor swallows in the village, nor*
weather.   *grey sand-martins about the forest.*
                    Ld Stawel was fishing Wolmer-pond with a
                    long net drawn by ten men.

As the frost melts, they ride again to Woolmer, with Gilbert looking
out for the house martins and sand martins. The dry ground makes
the going easy. Not so for William Cobbett, riding this way half a century later. 'I got a boy at Selborne to show me along the lanes out into
Woolmer forest,' he wrote.

> The lanes were very deep; the wet malm just about the colour of
> rye-meal mixed up with water, and just about as clammy, came, very
> nearly up to my horse's belly. There was this comfort, however, that I
> was sure there was a bottom, which is by no means the case when you
> are among clays or quick-sands.

Untroubled by mud, Gilbert, Thomas and Molly ride east, past the
old oak woods of the Holt, where Queen Anne lay on the bank to
watch the keepers. Lord Stawel, whose fishing Gilbert notes, lived in
the Great Lodge in the middle of the Holt and was currently spending
a fortune on the house and garden, putting in pleasure grounds and an

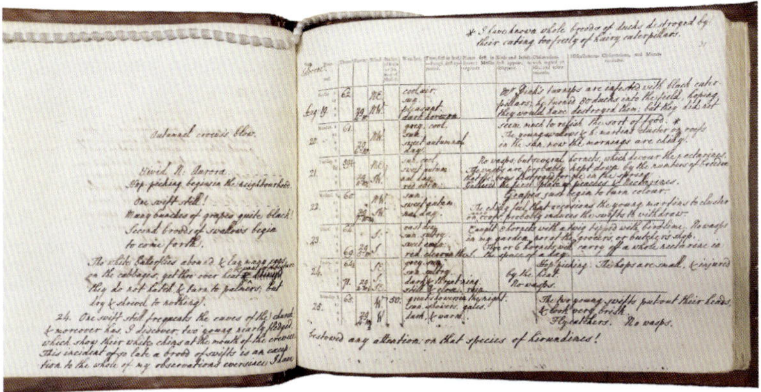

The Naturalist's Journal in late August 1781; a crowded page, including many notes about hops and swifts and ducks and hairy butterflies.

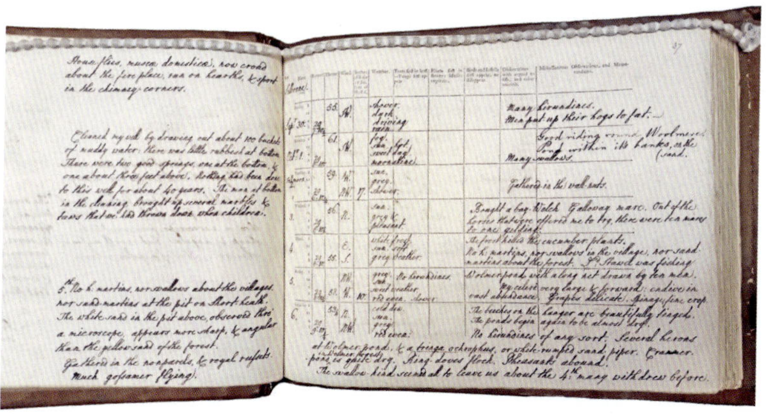

The Naturalist's Journal at the start of October – well-cleaning, pear-picking, herons on Woolmer pond.

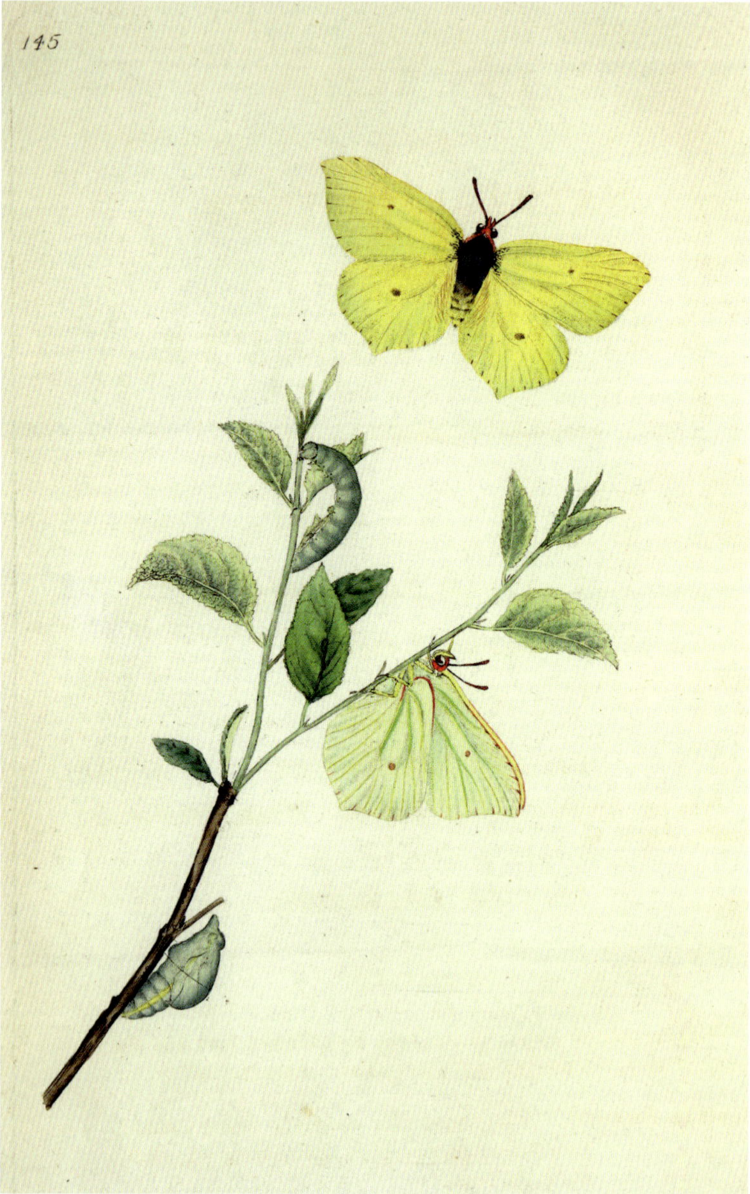

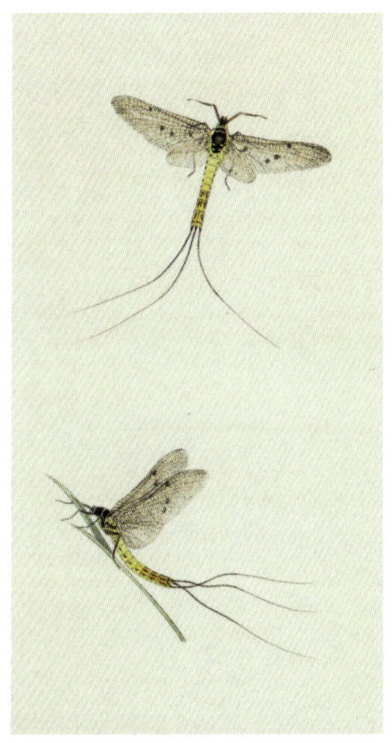

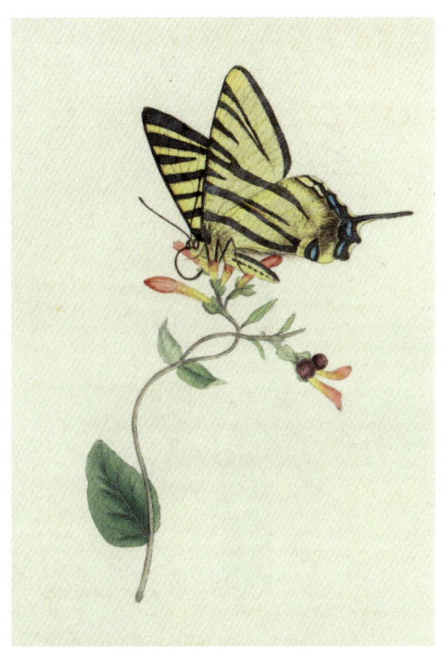

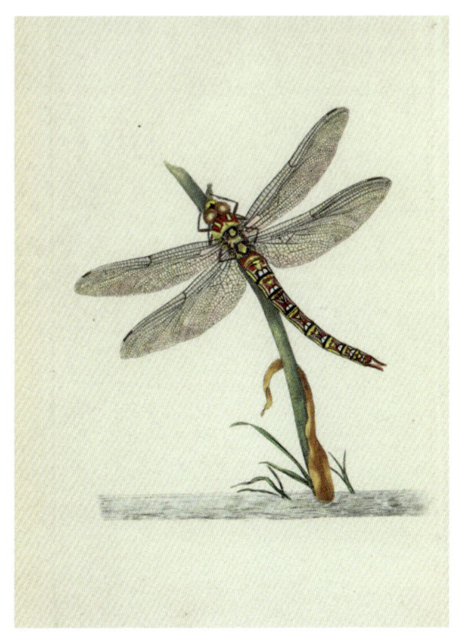

Four prints from Edward Donovan's remarkable *Natural History of British Insects*. Ten volumes were published between 1792 and 1801, and six more added by 1813.

'The Ephemeral Mayfly'

'The Scarce Swallowtail'

'The Common Dragonfly'

OPPOSITE
'The Brimstone Butterfly'

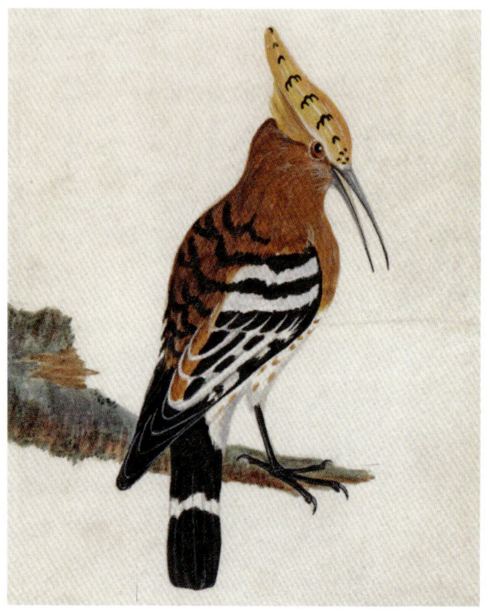

William Lewin,
Common Hoopoe (*c.*1780s).

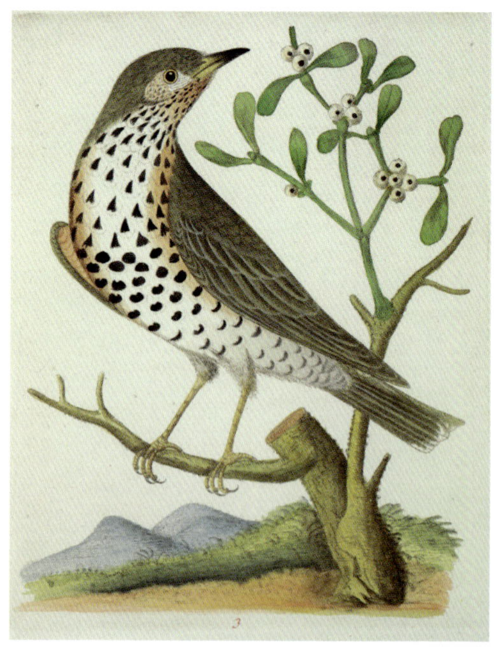

'Mistle Thrush and
Mistletoe' from
James Bolton's *Harmonia
Ruralis* (1794).

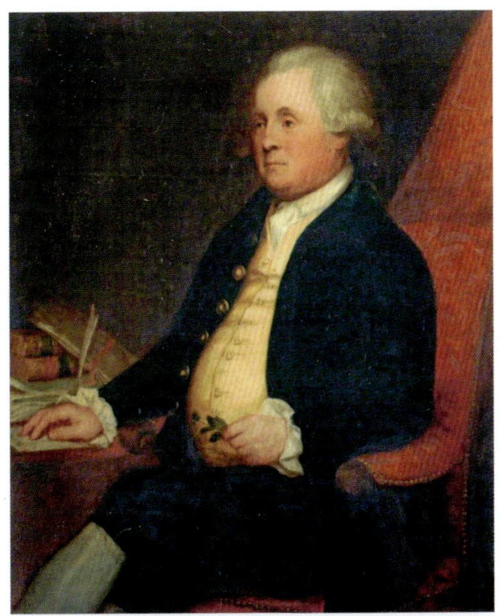

Thomas White in old age, holding a leaf to signal his interest in trees, with his paper and quill pen on the table. The artist and date are unknown.

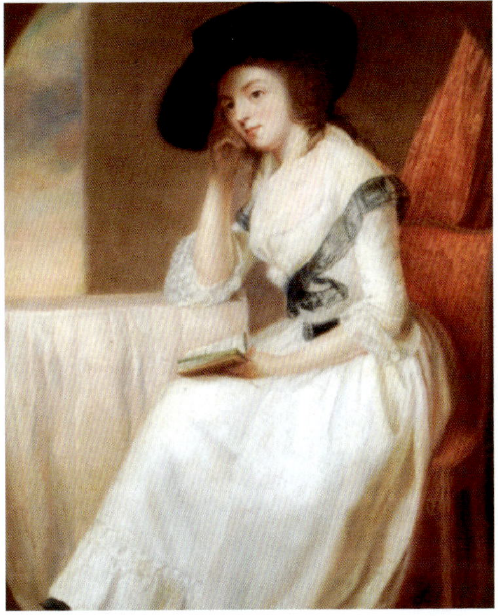

Molly White, artist and date unknown, but probably painted around the time of her marriage to her cousin Ben in 1785.

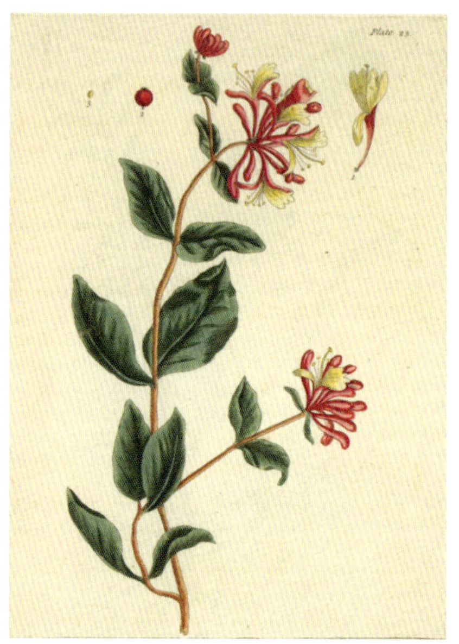

'Honeysuckle' by
Elizabeth Blackwell, from
her *A Curious Herbal*
(1780 edition)

'Entire Russola' by
James Sowerby,
in his *Coloured Figures
of English Fungi, or
Mushrooms* (1797).

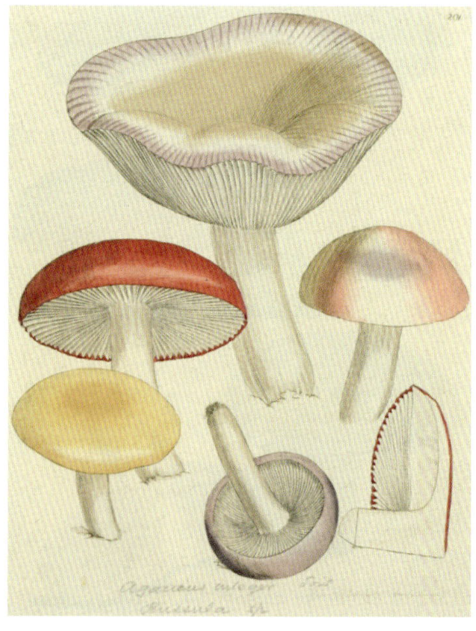

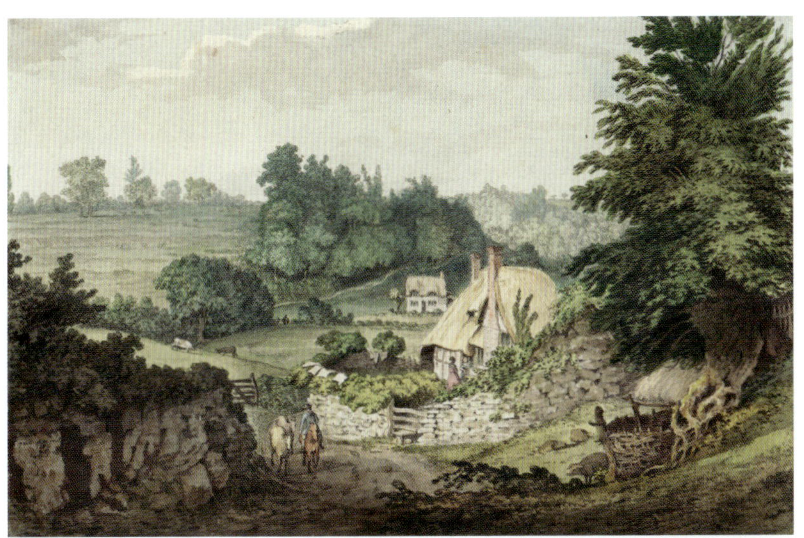

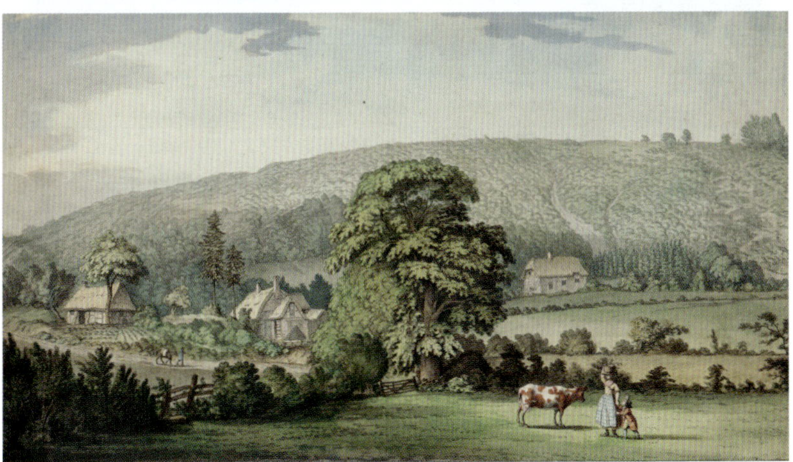

ABOVE Hieronymus Grimm, *Dorton* (1766). Looking down Hucker's Lane to Dorton, with the meadow of the Short Lythe in the background.

BELOW Hieronymus Grimm, *The Hanger* (1766). The view looks across to the scrubby south-east end of the hill, where Gilbert hoped the martins would stay in the winter. The Zig-Zag is on the extreme right.

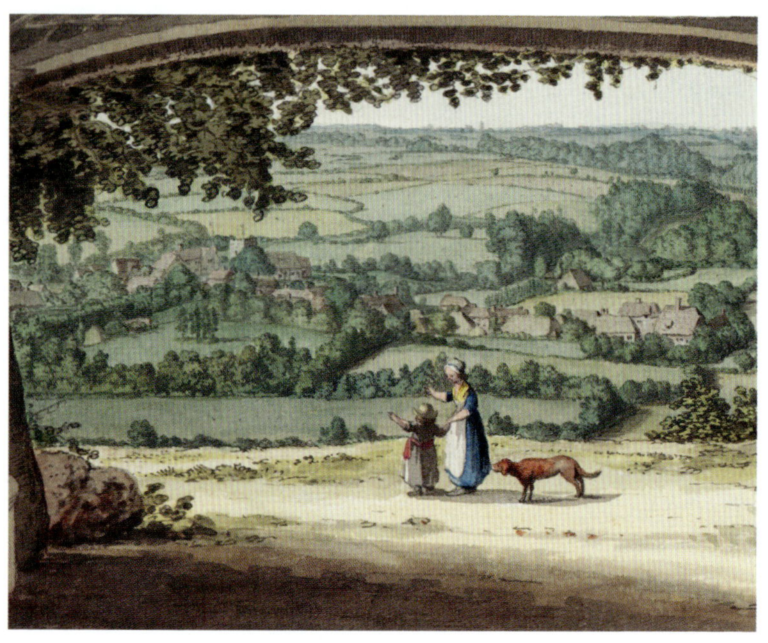

Detail of Hieronymus Grimm, *The View from Inside the Hermitage* (1776).
The little girl is looking towards Gilbert's quincunx of trees on Baker's Hill,
with The Wakes and the church behind.

ornamental lake. Stawel held the Holt and the forest through a grant from the Crown, which gave him the right to fish in Woolmer pond. But what were his men catching, thigh deep in cold water? The lake was full of eels, but there were also perch and carp and some mighty pike. One year, a pike weighing a hefty 24 pounds was caught, and 'in it's belly were 3 considerable carps'. Another pike, over three feet long, reached 30 pounds – or so, Gilbert writes, 'an eye witness tells me'.

Stawel was keen to exploit his rights, for timber as well as fishing. The government was currently desperately felling timber in Crown woods, especially oaks, to build ships for the navy. In 1784, a thousand oaks in the Holt would go under the axe. In the aftermath, Stawel, who laid claim to the branches left behind by the woodcutters, sued thirty-nine people from the local villages, demanding compensation for their carrying away 'all the lop and top', which they regarded as their right. Gilbert was in an awkward spot, not least because the husband of his niece Jane Clements was Stawel's attorney, and would later be his land agent. While he defended villagers' rights whenever they were challenged, he felt that this time they had overstated those rights and had cleared far too much away; one man had brought a team of horses and cleared forty stacks of wood. 'These folks, especially the females, are very abusive,' he told Molly, 'and set my Lord at defiance: for, they say, they can produce the will of one Alice Holt, wherein after bequeathing the Holt to the crown, she has given the lop to the poor of certain parishes.' There were rights on each side.

One starting point for the ride to the Holt and Woolmer Forest, beginning opposite The Wakes, was Hucker's Lane, which runs steeply downhill into the lush meadows of Dorton. Here, they could cross the Oakhanger stream to join the monks' old track from their granary, or 'grange' – now Grange Farm – to the Priory. Everywhere, like Grange Farm and the Priory, had its place in the village history, and Gilbert could talk about this to Molly and Thomas, who shared his love of the place and his interest in the literature, language and culture of

Anglo-Saxon and medieval England. It was Molly, for example, who arranged for the passage on Selborne from the Domesday Book be copied out for him for the *Antiquities*.

Woolmer pond, where they found Lord Stawel fishing, is where the *Antiquities* begins. Tradition, Gilbert writes in its opening 'Letter', held that the pond contained a great treasure, a belief boosted by finds of coins around its margins. In the drought of 1741, when Gilbert was a student and the pond was as dry and dusty as the surrounding heath, forest cottagers and labourers came with their spades and hoes, and 'instead of pots of coins, as they expected, they found great heaps, the one lying on the other as if shot out of a bag'. Sadly, the 'heaps' were not of gold or silver, but of hundreds of Roman copper coins, as well as medallions from the time of Marcus Aurelius and the Empress Faustina, a woman 'more celebrated for her beauty than her virtues'. The finders sold them to the local gentry – Gilbert bought several dozen – but many coins went unsold, even at low prices, 'and passed for farthings at the petty shops'.

How the coins came to be there remained a mystery. There was no Roman camp nearby, and surely no Roman town, Gilbert thought, 'because I have too good an opinion of the taste and judgement of those polished conquerors to imagine that they would settle on so barren and dreary a waste'.

Friday 5
58. 29 8/10½. NW, W. 10.   *No hirundines.*
Grey, sun, sweet   *My celeri very large & forward: endive in vast*
weather, red even: *abundance. Grapes delicate. Spinage, fine crop.*
shower.   *No h: martins, nor swallows about the villages,*
    nor sand-martins at the pit on Short-heath.

The white sand in the pit above, observed thro' a microscope, appears more sharp, & angular than the yellow sand of the forest. Gathered in the nonparels, & royal russets. Much gossamer flying.

Between inspecting the vegetables and grapes and picking more apples – the russets and nonpareils are his good 'keeping apples' – they ride again towards Woolmer.

In August, Gilbert had seen sand martins in the sandpit on Shortheath, just north of the forest. There's no sign of the birds today, but he's intrigued by the sand itself. Through his microscope, he can see how this crystalline 'sharp sand', with more quartz, differs from the fine silica he had peered at in September. He was interested not only in finding good building sand, but in the deep history of the landscape itself. Geology was in its infancy – the word had been accepted only gradually after Diderot used it in his *Encyclopédie* in 1751 – but natural philosophers had long been arguing about the way the world's crust had been formed. Only a few still held to the biblical creation date of four thousand years ago. In 1778, in *Les Époques de la nature*, Buffon, who believed the Earth had begun as a molten mass and had spent years calculating how long different materials, like iron cannonballs, rock and glass took to cool, estimated the planet to be roughly 75,000 years old. Privately, he thought that given the fossil record and the aeons that it would take to build a chalk mountain from tiny marine organisms, it might be far, far older – at least 10 million years – but this was too shocking to announce to the world.

It was also becoming hard to accept that Earth's strata were formed by the biblical Flood, an idea put forward almost a century earlier by Thomas Barker's father-in-law William Whiston in *A New Theory of the Earth* (1696). The notion of a primeval ocean covering the Earth persisted, but the investigation of basalt outcrops in the Auvergne, suggesting extinct volcanoes, followed by similar finds across Europe – even in the English Peak District – had prompted an opposing idea: that the surface of the Earth was formed not by flood, but by fire.

Arguments between Neptunists, who stuck to the oceanic version, and Plutonists, who supported the volcanic theory, were aired at all the European scientific academies, including the Royal Society, and were widely discussed in journals. A different confrontation would follow: between writers influenced by Gilbert's contemporary, the great Scottish geologist James Hutton, who proposed that changes in the Earth's crust resulted from gradual, lengthy processes, and those who saw them as due to dramatic, violent cycles of devastation and reconstruction, a theory that would come to be called 'catastrophism'.

Gilbert did not comment on these ideas and debates. The only time he ventured something in this vein was in his flight of fancy about the South Downs, near Ringmer, which looked almost organic or 'vegetative', he thought, with their 'gentle swellings and smooth, fungus-like protuberances':

> Or was there ever a time when these immense masses of calcarious matter were thrown into fermentation by some adventitious moisture; were raised and leavened into such shapes by some plastic power; and so made to swell and heave their broad backs into the sky so much above the less animated clay of the wild below?

These downs are alive to him, like a huge creature rolling its shoulders, rising from the depths.

Exploring his own Selborne landscape, Gilbert held a kind of geological map in his mind, a key to the different habitats of plants, birds and other animals. On the top of the Hanger was grey clay and flint. Below this came a layer of chalk, then, further downhill, a layer of a more crumbly, grey chalk, stretching across his garden and the cartway. On the other side of the street, chalk gave way to 'a warm, forward, crumbling mould, called black malm', running eastwards to Oakhanger and the Holt, until it met the sandy soil of Woolmer. Like hundreds of enthusiastic amateurs, Gilbert examined the fossil record, too. Over the past decades, mining and canal digging had turned up new minerals and fossils, prompting more conjectures about 'the bowels of the earth'. The casts of ammonites that were uncovered when digging the Bostal were common, but Gilbert's prize find was a 'petrified fish', which, he

A YEAR WITH GILBERT WHITE

decided, after much research, was a bivalve that had lived in the Indian Ocean – a distant past, half a world away.

Saturday 6
53½. 29 9/10¼. N, NW.   *The beeches on the hanger are beautifully*
Cold dew, sun,   *tinged. The ponds begin again to be almost dry.*
grey, red even: *No hirundines of any sort. Several herons at*
    Wolmer-pond, & a tringa ochrophus, or white-
    rumped sand-piper. Crammer-pond in Wolmer-
    forest is quite dry. Ring-doves flock. Pheasants
    abound.

He mentions the bronze-tinted beeches every autumn, sometimes rhapsodically, as on 12 October 1776, the year of Hieronymus Grimm's visit:

> The hanging beech-woods begin to be beautifully tinged, & to afford most lovely scapes, very engaging to the eye, & imagination. They afford sweet lights & shades. Maples are also finely tinged. These scenes are worthy of the pencil of a Reubens.

Those beeches are fiery as Gilbert, Thomas and Molly set off for Woolmer, where the great pond is a haven for wading birds: Gilbert mentions lapwings, snipes, wild ducks and teal, as well as the herons they see today, posing like statues, and the plump green sandpipers, with their long legs and beaks. Some sandpipers will stay here over winter, but most are resting on their way south, feeding happily here, bobbing in the mud, uttering their shrill, whistling cries.

In the trees, Gilbert hears the ring doves – wood pigeons – coo. Steely grey, with white patches on the side of the neck, they are every-where, taking off in a clatter, thumping on springing branches, mating as often as they can in their heavy, fluttering way. As well as scavenging for grain in the stubble, they nip at the cabbages and turnip tops. A few years later, he will write:

One of my neighbours shot a ring-dove on an evening, just as it was returning from feed, & going to roost. When his wife had picked & drawn it, she found it's craw stuffed with the most nice & tender tops of turnips. These she washed & boiled, & so sate down to a choice & delicate plate of greens, culled & provided in this extraordinary manner.

Although he no longer went out with his gun, his brothers and friends did, if not with huge success. Mr Yalden, Molly reported, fared badly, and although her uncle Ben killed a bird with his first shot, he hit nothing more. However, Rover, she said – the 'large and good for nothing' dog brought to Selborne from Fyfield in the spring, now a great favourite – set up a hen pheasant one morning and barked violently:

& it was ridiculous enough to hear the Bird scold at him: he is become so fond of hunting by himself that my Uncle has ordered a wooden Apron to be tyed round his neck whenever he means to keep him at home. At first he was rather disturbed at it, & is now much pleased with me when I release him as we are going to ride.

Rover was undeterred. Two years from now, Gilbert will write: 'Rover puts up pheasants every day.' And four years after that, he is still busy: 'Rover springs many pheasants.' (Rover had other roles, too. On 15 May 1788, Gilbert wrote: 'Sheared my mongrel dog Rover, and made use of his white hair in plaster for ceilings. His coat weighed four ounces.')

Sunday 7

30. 53. W, N.	*Not one hirundo to be seen.*
Cold dew, sun,	*Fleecy clouds, & beautiful gleams of sunshine.*
sweet weather.	*Rooks carry off the wallnuts from my trees.*

A note on the opposite page of the journal reads: 'The swallow-kind seemed all to leave us about the 4th: many withdrew before.' It's early for them to go. In other years, he's seen young martins in the nest in early October and watched them in the air for another month, 'playing all day long by the side of the hanger, & over my fields on Novr 3rd'. Once, he saw a single swallow on 4 October. 'What can this bird be doing behind by itself?' he asked, 'Why might they not all have staid, since this individual seems brisk, & vigorous?' But it wasn't a single bird. Two days later, just before it grew dark, a flight of about a dozen swallows darted over the house, as if, he said, they were going to settle in the Hanger. Or that was what he hoped.

In these fine days, when the swallows have vanished, the rooks and jays plunder his walnuts, often joined by nuthatches, 'rapping with their bills about the wallnut trees' and leaving the nuts on the ground, with holes bored into their shells.

Monday 8

31. 53. W, S. *Much gossamer. One cock ring-ouzel appears*
Grey, sun, sweet *still: few have been seen this autumn.*
weather. *Grapes delicate.*

The ring ouzels arrive on their journey south, and some autumns bring more unusual birds. 'One bunting in the northfield,' he had written in October 1776, 'a rare bird at Selborne.' He was sure that they overwintered in Britain. Dumpy little birds, streaky grey and brown, with pale-brown tails, corn buntings like open farmland and stubble, and their guttural, jangling cry ripples across the fields and downs. Gilbert had once seen 'several dozen', he told Pennant, in a severe frost on the downs near Andover and on the Sussex downs, but they were rare in the sheltered woodland around Selborne.

Every so often, he reports accounts of uncommon birds in other parts of Britain, like the spoonbills shot near Yarmouth in February 1775, which he thinks must have flown over from Holland. The most unusual birds he saw in Selborne were a pair of hoopoes, with their pink–gold-and-black crown and flaring black and white wings, which paraded around his walks 'in a stately manner' until the teasing of local boys scared them away.

Tuesday 9
30. 51. E.   *The grass was covered with cob-webs, which*
Deep fog, sun,   *being loaded with dew, looked like white frost.*
pleasant, red even:

Opposite his entry about this silvery, cobwebby morning, Gilbert adds: 'A grey hen was lately killed on that part of Hind-head, which is called the Devil's punch-bowl. This solitary bird has haunted these parts for some time.' Here's another rare bird.

A greyhen is the female black grouse, a pale, quiet bird, her grey plumage good camouflage for her nest in the heather. By contrast, the male – the blackcock – struts flamboyantly, a striking figure with bright-red eyebrows, black feathers and a fan-like white tail. Black grouse like the fringes of moors and forests, eating the buds and shoots of larch, birch and heather in spring, and haws and berries in autumn; this one was seen among the pine woods and gorse of Hindhead Common, just over the Surrey border. In *The Natural History of Selborne*, Gilbert remembered the occasional bird 'coming now and then to my father's table' when he was a little boy, but even then they were rare. The last 'pack', he said, writing in the 1770s, had been killed about thirty-five years ago:

> And within these ten years one solitary grey hen was sprung by
> some beagles, in beating for a hare. The sportsman cried out, 'A hen
> pheasant', but a gentleman present, who had often seen grouse in the
> north of England, assured me that it was a greyhen.

The greyhen is a reminder of his own past – his father carving the bird – and of a more distant time, when Woolmer Forest abounded with these birds. With each loss, Gilbert writes, 'another beautiful link in the chain of beings is wanting'.

Wednesday 10
49. 29 9/10. S, S.
Cold dew, sun, fog,
sweet autumnal
weather, grey.

My well rises. My hedges are beautifully tinged.
Wood-larks sing sweetly thro' this soft weather.
No swallows.

He often notes that woodlarks and skylarks sing all through the summer and autumn. But even these birds are at risk from hunters. 'Larks frolick much in the air,' he had written on 27 October 1776, 'when they are in that mood the larkers catch them in nets by means of a twinkling glass: this method they call *daring*.' To 'dare' meant to stun through terror, mesmerising the birds with flashing, reflective glass, so that they lay still until the men could throw a net over them and pin them down.

Thursday 11
48. 29 8/10. E, W.
Fog, sun, bright &
chill, dark.

A brood of swallows over Oakhanger-pond!
Dragon-flies copulate.

As the fog lifts, his spirits rise. Yesterday's note of 'No swallows' is overturned by the sight of a whole brood at the Oakhanger pools, where the dragonflies skim and mate. On their way there, Gilbert, Thomas and Molly have passed the ruins of the Priory, whose decline and fall Gilbert would describe so graphically in the *Antiquities*. Local people had carried off most of the stones long ago, to build houses and barns, but the Priory's history could still be read in its ruins, as well as in deeds, scrolls and documents. In July 1780, Gilbert told Ralph Churton that a large stone urn had been discovered there, perhaps a standard measure for corn. He looked back on this find with some chagrin: 'This vase I was going to procure, but found that the labourers had just broken it in pieces for way-mending.'

Friday 12
56. 29 8/10. NW, N.   *Farmer Parsons fetches a wagon-load of water*
Grey, grey & mild.   *from Dorton for brewing! Wells fail.*
                         No swallows about the village.

Saturday 13
53. 29 9/10. W.   *No swallows.*
Grey, sun, sweet   *On frequented roads the dust is very trouble-*
weather.   *some.*

The drought and dust continue. The ground is too hard this year for men to dig up more ancient stones. But the finds will keep coming. In October 1783, during another spell when Thomas and Molly are staying with Gilbert, men digging in the Priory's foundations will uncover a Doric capital and the base of a pillar, showing how grand and costly the church was. Like the urn, the broken pillar is destined to be used in patching up Selborne's roads and hollow lanes – the past beneath their feet.

Gilbert wrote happily in the *Antiquities* about these finds and others. John Mulso was right that this second part of his book would never be as popular as *The Natural History of Selborne*. It followed *The Natural History*, with 'Letters' to an unnamed addressee, and although it contained plenty of lists and dates and chunks of Latin, Gilbert tried to make it readable by pruning these. He lightened it, too, by filling it with anecdotes, like the story of Morris Ken, from the royal kitchen, who fell off his horse repeatedly in Woolmer Forest, making Edward II laugh so much that he gave Ken twenty shillings – 'an enormous sum' – as a reward. Gilbert tells this, he says, 'for the entertainment of my readers'. Similarly, recounting the Priory's history, he lists the main charters and gifts, but acknowledges that 'it would be tedious to enumerate every little grant'. Instead, he writes of his amazement (which he is sure will 'strike every thinking person with some degree of wonder') at the way that monasteries so skilfully wooed potential benefactors, swallowing whole areas, house by

                    A YEAR WITH GILBERT WHITE

house, field by field, until 'every precinct was drawn into the vortex'.

Telling these tales, he also digs into his own past. Writing of Woolmer, he remembers the stories about stray coins that 'old people' – like himself – heard from their fathers and grandfathers. Describing Selborne church, he copies his grandfather's memorial plaque, while his own childhood memories provide a link to traditions that stretch back to Tudor times:

> In the middle aisle there is nothing remarkable: but I remember when its beams were hung with garlands in honour of the young women of the parish, reputed to have died virgins; and recollect to have seen the clerk's wife cutting, in white paper, the resemblance of gloves and ribbons to be twisted into knots and roses, to decorate these memorials of chastity.

In Farringdon church, where he preached on Sundays, garlands of this sort still remained.

His memories seep into his prose. Writing of the church belfry (re-stuccoed this year, in 1781), he remembers how, when he was fifteen, the three old bells, which were 'loud and out of tune', were taken down and recast as four, and a new fifth one was added. 'The day of the arrival of this tuneable peal was observed as a high festival in the village,' he writes, and the treble bell was fixed upside down in the ground and filled with punch for all to share. Describing the hall in the vicarage where he was born, he adds: 'we remember a date, some time in the reign of Elizabeth; it was over the door that leads to the stairs'. At the manor house at Temple Farm, we see him peering at the walls with the same concentration that he gives to the nest of a harvest mouse:

> I have often looked for the lamb and flag, the arms of the Knights Templars, without success; but in one corner found a fox with a goose on his back, so coarsely executed that it required some attention to make out the device.

Describing the Plestor, which Adam de Guerdon – rebel, outlaw, then loyal follower of Edward I – gave to the Priory in 1271, as a 'Pleystow, *locus ludorum*, or play-place', he notes proudly, 'this village, even in Saxon times, could not be the most abject of places, where the inhabitants thought proper to assign so spacious a spot for the sports and amusements of its young people'.

Sunday 14

56. 29 9/10. SW.   *The greens of turnips wither, & look rusty.*
Grey, still & mild.   *Leaves fall.*

Today, turnips join the list of crops frizzled by the drought. The last really wet month was nearly two years before, in December 1779. In a note, Gilbert writes:

> The distress in these parts for want of water is very uncommon. The well at the Grange farm is dry; & so are many in the villages round: & even the well at Old-place in the parish of E: Tisted, tho' 270 feet, or 45 fathoms deep, will not afford water for a brewing . . . Most of the wells in Selborne-street are empty; & mine has only three feet of water.

The well at Old Place Farm, in East Tisted, a couple of miles south-west of Newton Valence, was over three times as deep as Gilbert's at The Wakes. Although 270 feet seems an extraordinary depth, borehole records show that this well – which had a wooden wheel to draw the water, worked by two dogs – may have been even deeper. Its difference to the well at Selborne is explained by the local geology. To get water, you need to dig or bore through the chalk, cutting across the vertical fissures or joints that let water flow from the aquifer. The upper greensand below the chalk provides a reasonable supply, but while the greensand is near the surface at Selborne, it dips towards the west, reaching a depth of 440 feet at East Tisted – hence the need for much deeper wells. It's a register of how bad things were that these deep wells

          A YEAR WITH GILBERT WHITE

were so low. Meanwhile, the dew ponds still had some water, and the Well Head spring flowed fast. Soon that stream would be their only source of water.

Gilbert feels time running on. Writing the *Antiquities* is taking far longer than he had hoped. It is now two years since he sat in his study, with Richard Chandler at his elbow, 'deeply engaged in Bishop Waynflete's Registers'. Chandler, a fellow of Magdalen, a classicist and antiquarian nearly twenty years Gilbert's junior, had been appointed as vicar of Worldham and East Tisted in 1779, and was an invaluable help with the *Antiquities*. In 1780, Chandler came again, ploughing through 'Bishop Beaufort's registers, from Winchester'.

This long labour irritated John Mulso, who felt that publication was being needlessly delayed by the 'Farrago of Antiquities, routed out of the Rusts and Crusts and Frusts of time'. Prodding Gilbert on, he reminded him that their old friend Tom Warton, with his two volumes of *The History of English Poetry*, had already 'given ye world two large Specimens of his old Bards and untuneable Harps. Go to!' This year, Warton published a third volume, largely focused on Elizabethan poetry, but also looking back to the thirteenth- or fourteenth-century tales in the *Gesta Romanorum* and to the romance of *Ywain and Gawain*. In 1782, the antiquary Joseph Ritson, then beginning his collection of folk songs and carols, would publish a blistering attack on Warton's inaccuracies, a barrage that continued up to and beyond Warton's death. Controversy and error are just what Gilbert wants to avoid. His constant checking of records is holding up his work, but his *Antiquities of Selborne* will never, he hopes, be found to lack evidence.

Monday 15
58. 29 8/10½. SW, NW.   *No swallows.*
Grey & still, & mild.   *Bright Aurora.*

My celeri is unusually large; & well blanched.
The mill at Hawkley cannot work one tenth of
the time for want of water.

Sometimes, however, excitement in the new overcame concern for the past. In two years' time, in the spring and summer of 1783, the Montgolfier brothers will send the first large hot-air balloons soaring over France, their passengers – who landed safely – being a sheep, a cock and a duck. The first manned ascents followed that autumn. The following year, on 15 September 1784, in front of cheering crowds, the Prince of Wales among them, Vincenzo Lunardi took off in his hot-air balloon from Chelsea, with a cat, a dog and a pigeon. Gilbert wrote impatiently to his niece in South Lambeth: 'Oh Molly! You don't tell us of the balloon, and the ascension of Mr Lunardi: did it not affect you, to see a poor human creature entering upon so strange and hazardous an exploit?' Pointing out surprises in the press, like the balloon allegedly being covered with ice, when the temperature below was above freezing, he sighed that he wished the newspapers would learn to write about weather instruments, and in particular thermometers, more precisely.

On 16 October that year, when Gilbert heard that the French balloonist Jean-Pierre Blanchard was planning a flight from London, he worked out that the wind that day would surely carry the balloon over Selborne. Dashing round the village, he 'exhorted all those who had any curiosity to look sharp from about one to three o'clock, as they would stand a good chance of being entertained with a very extraordinary sight'. He roused the people of Farringdon, too, in case the balloon floated further north. Crowds climbed the Hanger, while Gilbert went to dinner, leaving 'his hat and surtout ready in a chair, in case of alarm'. At twenty to three, the alert came. Grabbing his hat and coat, he ran to join a cluster of neighbours in the orchard. First, a small dot appeared in the sky, flashing in the westerly sun. Then he saw 'a dark blue speck at a most prodigious height', suddenly seeming to drop from the sky, 'hanging amidst the regions of the upper air, between the weather-cock of the tower and the top of the may-pole'. It seemed to move slowly, but then, 'in a few minutes',

it was over the may-pole; and then over the Fox on my great parlor chimney; and in ten minutes behind my great walnut tree. The machine looked mostly of a dark blue colour; but sometimes reflected

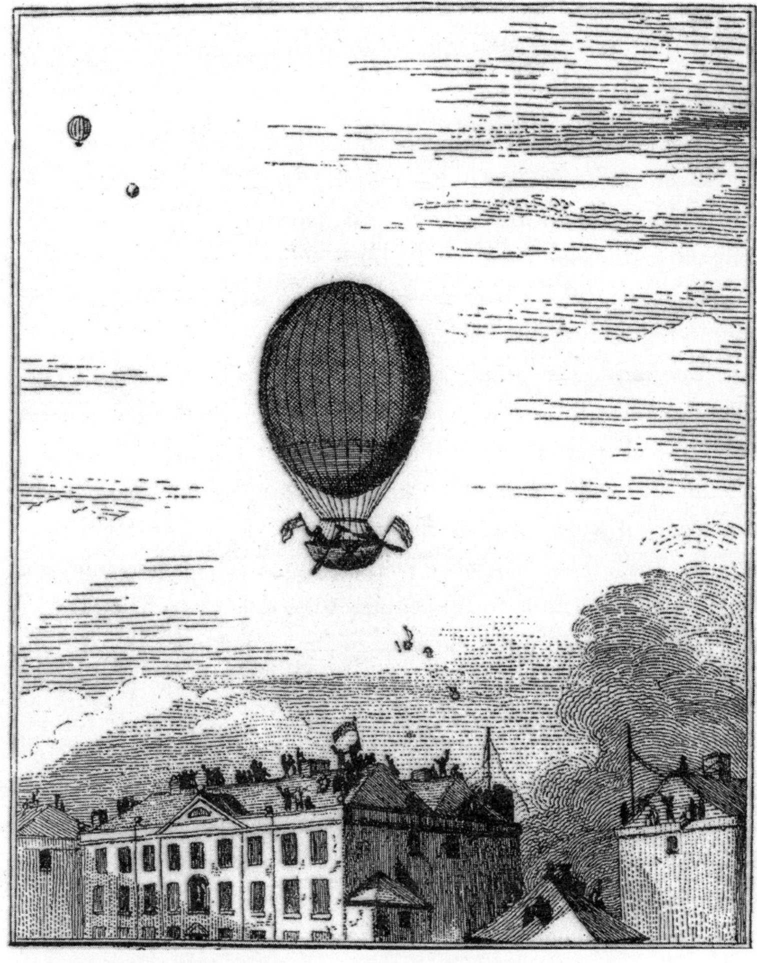

Excited crowds watch Blanchard's balloon taking off from the Royal Military Academy, Chelsea, on 16 October 1784.

the rays of the sun, and appeared of a bright yellow. With a telescope I could discern the boat, and the ropes that supported it. To my eye this vast balloon appeared no bigger than a large tea-urn.

Like Milton's 'belated peasant', who sees – or dreams he sees – the fairies dancing in the moonlight, he said, he felt his heart rebound with simultaneous fear and joy. He fretted about the passengers, 'lost, in appearance, in the boundless depths of the atmosphere', but at last, 'seeing with what composure they moved, I began to consider them as secure as a group of Storks, or Cranes intent on the business of emigration'.

As Gilbert tracks the course of the balloon, from the maypole on the Plestor, across the roof of his house and over the walnut tree in his garden, his gaze transforms the familiar landscape, as if he is seeing it from above, through the eyes of a bird. Only the image of balloon as tea urn and the affectionate thought of the long-legged birds on their autumn flight bring him back down to earth.

In the mid-1780s, people across Britain were fired with a zeal for balloon-making, at peril to haystacks everywhere. At Newton Valence, on 4 September 1784, Ben White's son Edmund made a small hot-air balloon out of thin paper, with a plug of cotton wool below, 'wetted with spirits of wine; & set on fire by a candle' to supply the 'buoyant air'. The candle fizzled out when he tried his balloon outside, but inside the vicarage it sailed up to the ceiling. A few days after the sighting of Blanchard's balloon, Edmund tried again, launching an air balloon from Selborne. 'It went off in a steady, & grand manner to the E., & settled in about 15 minutes near Todmoor on the verge of the forest.'

Wednesday 17
46. 30. NW.   *Greatham-mill can work but 3 hours in the day.*
White frost, sun,
bright & pleasant.

 A YEAR WITH GILBERT WHITE

Thursday 18
49. 29 9/10. NW.   *The beechen-woods grow very brown.*
Grey, still & mild.

Friday 19
51½. 29 8/10½. NW.   *On this ill fated day Lord Cornwallis, & all his*
Grey, sun & cold air.   *army surrendered themselves prisoners of war to the*
                                        united forces of France & America at York-town in
                                        Virginia.

Suddenly, we find one of his rare political entries. But this was a drastic day for Britain, and Gilbert went back and added the news when it hit the papers. Such a defeat seemed impossible, shocking, humiliating – unbelievable – but the signs had been there for some time. The previous year, French troops had landed at Newport, Rhode Island, to help the American forces, and in August 1781, the French West Indies fleet sailed to Chesapeake Bay, defeating a British fleet on the way and blockading the port of Yorktown, where Cornwallis was commanding the British army. Meanwhile, the American and French armies under Washington and Rochambeau joined forces and marched south to surround the town. On 19 October, realising that the British defences had been breached and food and ammunition were running out, Cornwallis surrendered. Seven thousand British soldiers were taken prisoner.

When the news reached the prime minister, Lord North, he reacted, it was said, as if he had been shot, pacing up and down and exclaiming wildly: 'Oh God! It is all over!' A furious George III refused to accept that the war was lost. But it was. The following March, North resigned. In the Treaty of Paris, drafted in November 1782, American independence was finally agreed. When the British government fell in 1783, Pitt the Younger stepped in as prime minister. But the impact stretched far beyond this. British imperial ambitions were now focused elsewhere: on the Caribbean, on India and on Asia. At home, furious outcries against the incompetent handling of the war led to renewed demands for reform, and for enquiries into government corruption and inefficiency.

All this was doubtless hotly debated in Gilbert's own family. In a few years' time, his nephew Thomas Holt White (the 'Tom' that Molly wrote to when he was at school) would be a thorough-going radical, a friend of campaigners, writing passionate articles arguing for universal suffrage and women's rights. If, in 1781, life in Selborne seemed unruffled, I'm sure Gilbert threw his arms up in despair at the ending of the American war – and then shrugged, as he did when difficult matters threatened.

Saturday 20
50½. 29 8/10. NW.   *Leaves fall very fast.*
Grey, sun, dark, &   *Endive very fine.*
harsh, bright.   *Grapes delicate.*

The focus shifts again, back to daily life, the garden and the trees. In a later autumn, he will write: 'The cat frolicks, & plays with the autumn leaves.' In the Plestor, boys kick heaps of leaves and toss them in the air.

The grapes are good. Normally, they show no signs of late ripening, but even then they can still be used. Next year, in 1782, Gilbert will write: 'We make tarts, & puddings with the crude unripened grapes. Gathered-in the Virgoleuse, & Chaumontelle pears, a good crop.' What were those tarts and puddings like, I wonder? Did they add the sweet pears to the sour grapes to offset their acid tang? The Virgoleuse pears, Gilbert notes years later, 'always rot before they ripen, & are eatable; yet when baked dry on a tin, they become an excellent sweetmeat'.

Sunday 21
51. 29 8/10. W.   *The distress for water in many places is great.*
Sun, bright & warm.   *Redwings appear.*

The winter thrushes arrive. The redwings, the smallest thrushes in Britain, are the first, flying in from Scandinavia, Russia and Iceland. They are easy to spot with their red–orange patches under their wings and white flashes over their eyes, and as they come, often migrating at night, you can hear them calling in the sky. Their arrival is a hinge between seasons. 'We saw several Red-wings among the bushes on the n. side of the common,' Gilbert writes one year. 'There were swallows about the village at the same time: so that summer & winter birds of passage were seen on the same day.'

Monday 22
51½. 29 9/10. N.   *Great fieldfare appears.*
Sun, bright & cold.   *Men continue to fetch peat from the forest.*

He expected the fieldfares, too, this week, often recording them between the 22nd and the 31st. In the fields, redwings and fieldfares forage together, working upwind, with each bird stopping now and then to stand and look around; if alarmed, they fly off downwind and form

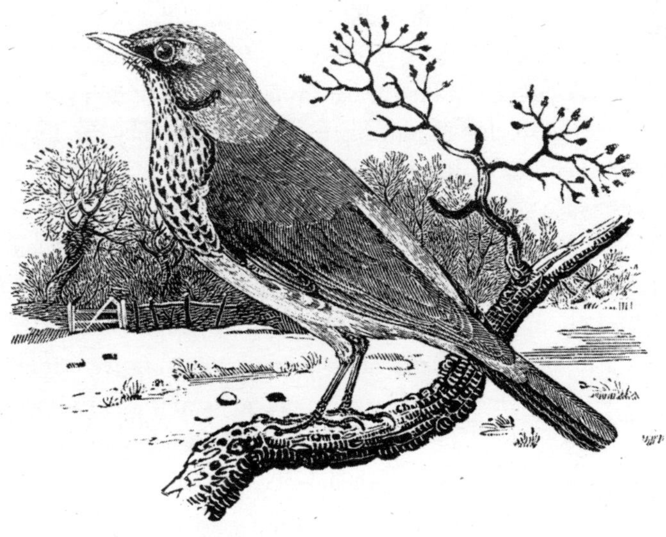

Thomas Bewick, 'The Fieldfare', in *Land Birds* (1797)

their group again. But the fieldfares stand out in these flocks: larger birds, with grey heads and warm-brown backs, black tails and creamy speckled breasts, they stand upright, hopping on the ground and chattering 'chk, chk, chk', as opposed to the redwing's mild 'tseep, tseep'. In the summer, they live mostly on worms and grubs, but now, as well as grain, they devour the berries of hawthorn, holly and yew, and fiercely defend their hoards of fallen fruit.

Gilbert always welcomed the fieldfares, but they puzzled him. Why didn't they breed here, like their fellow thrushes and blackbirds? And why, when they spent the days in the fields and trees and stripped the hedges for food, did they roost at night on the ground, not in the hedges? He deduced this from the way that he saw them come in at dusk

> and nestle among the heath on our forest. And besides, the larkers, in dragging their nets by night, frequently catch them in the wheat stubbles, while the bat-fowlers, who take many red-wings in the hedges, never entangle any of this species.

Some modern naturalists dispute his findings, holding that fieldfares do roost in thickets and hedges, like the redwings, but others agree that they are more often on the ground. Gilbert trusts to local knowledge. He talks to the larkers, and to the bat-fowlers who work along the hedges at night, waving torches of burning hay on poles so they can beat birds down with their broom-like bats when they fly towards the light.

Gilbert talks, too, to the peat cutters on the Woolmer heaths. The dry weather has helped them; after a wet summer they can sell only half their usual amount, which means that the poor thus lose their chance 'for laying in their forest fuel'. But although peat was a vital fuel and a money-maker, the ravages of peat-cutting were immense. In 1782, when 325 loads of peat were taken, as well as an astonishing 340,000 large squares of turf, the waters of Woolmer pond spilled into the cuttings and channels, and the lake changed shape entirely.

Tuesday 23
41. 29 8/10¼. N.   *Farmer Eames of Oldplace fetches his water from*
Frost, ice, bright &   *well-head!*
cold.   *Jupiter is now very low in the SW; at sun set.*

Wednesday 24
47. 29 7/10. SW, W.   *Many trees are naked.*
Frost, ice, dark &   *The tortoise is very torpid, but does not bury*
windy.   *itself. Grapes are delicate.*

As the trees become bare, Timothy slows down. He is usually quite perky in early autumn, but when the frost comes, as it does today, he retreats promptly at four o'clock to his bed under the wide leaves of the hollyhocks.

When I visit Selborne in October, I find sun and blue sky rather than frost and wind. I walk down the hill from Norton Farm towards the village, crossing the wheat fields, where the tussocky grass margins are sheltered by huge, spreading hedges. From here an old hollow lane leads down to Gracious Street. As I look up at the strata in the banks and the gnarled tree roots leaning out above me, I can see how water must cascade off the fields in a downpour. On one tree at The Wakes, Black Worcester pears hang in ranks, like a dusky chandelier, and other trees still bear the knobbed russet apples that Gilbert knew. It's so warm that I take off my coat and sit on the bench in a wild corner of the garden.

Gilbert's spirit is still felt in this village. My companion on the walk down the hill, Kate Faulkner, has been describing the conservation work that the local farm partnership is doing, inspired in part by *The Natural History of Selborne*: making surveys of harvest mice, creating open spaces for lapwings, cherishing wildflower meadows and ensuring different seeds are there for all the flocks that descend each winter. I think of Gilbert recording the richness of this place, when he compiled his *Flora Selborniensis* in 1766. His long note for 24 October is so vivid, mixing wild and garden plants, that I can't resist cramming it in here:

Plants naturally in bloom still:

Laurustine, Ivy, *arbutus*, great & less throat-wort, round-leaved *Campanula*, burnet-saxifrage, Hawkweeds several, round-leaved, & sharp-pointed, fluellin, blue Devil's bit, knapweed, wild-thyme, herb Robert, groundsel, hop-trefoil, soap-wort, yarrow, creeping tormentil, dwarf-cistus, chamomile, great basil, mallow, red pimpernel, small stitchwort, viper's bugloss, milkwort, dandelion, wild marjoram, white horehound, creeping mouse-ear, plowman's spikenard, cat mint, many foreign perennial asters, spotted arsmart, ragwort, marsh thistle, shepherd's purse, pansies, sweet scented *reseda*.

Then he added another list, almost as long, of 'Plants continued in bloom by accidents, such as a shady situation, the bite of Cattle, &c.', from mulleins and corn poppies to mouse-ear scorpion grass and the common daisy.

And what are 'creeping mouse-ear' and 'plowman's spikenard'? Ah, the mouse-ear is a relative of chickweed, staying green all winter, with little white flowers. And the spikenard is a tallish plant with purple stems and clusters of dull-yellow flowers. It was brought indoors because of its scent, to freshen the rooms and kill insects, and was boiled as a salve for wounds and bruises, like arnica. I learn something new all the time.

Thursday 25

50. 29 9/10. NW.
Sun, dark & cold.

The upland villages are in great distress for want of water. Acorns abound, & help poor men's hogs. Grass becomes very scanty.

'Distress' is a strong word, but a drought that means you can't water your cattle or plant the winter wheat can spell disaster, bringing hardship and hunger. One small consolation is that the oaks are heavy with acorns – food for the pigs. 'The crop of acorns is so prodigious,' Gilbert will write two years from now, 'that the trees look quite white with them; & the poor make, as it were, a second harvest of them, by gathering them at one shilling per bushel.' Women and children go acorning,

A YEAR WITH GILBERT WHITE

and the birds do, too – rooks and jays, and once, he remembered, turkeys, galumphing ponderously on the boughs.

Friday 26
30, 49. N.   *Men sow their wheat in absolute dust.*
Sun, bright & chill.   *My vines cast their leaves.*
                                              Bror T: & M: went away.

The vine leaves drop, and Thomas and Molly head home to South
Lambeth. Their rides to Woolmer are over for this year, but their long
conversations about the forest spill into Gilbert's book. At the end of
the year, he will tell Molly that in his account of Woolmer Forest for
The Natural History, he has added a note to his description of the cottages built of iron-hard bog oak, from trees long buried in the peat.
Some old people assured him, the note says, that on a winter's morning
they could discover these trees, deep in the bog, by noticing how the
hoar frost lay longer on particular places. He has looked up Hales's
Haemastaticks, which says that snow lies longest over old drains and
pipes, because they slow down the thawing effect of the warm earth.
'Might not such observations be reduced to domestic use,' Gilbert asks,
by allowing the discovery of old drains and wells near houses, 'and in
Roman stations and camps lead to the finding of pavements, baths and
graves, and other hidden relics of curious antiquity?'

In the introductory letters to *The Natural History*, he used trees, in
particular, to link Selborne to a wider national story. In Letter 2, he
writes of a small wood called Losel's, which had oaks of 'a peculiar
growth and great value'. They grew so close together that they reached
50–60 feet in height, with tapering trunks and no large side branches.
In the early 1750s, when timber was needed to mend a bridge at Hampton Court, these trees were just what were wanted, and the woodcutters
moved in. But one tree stood out. 'In the centre of this grove there stood
an oak,' he begins, as if in a folk tale. It was shapely and tall, but at
one point the trunk swelled out, and on this bulge a pair of ravens had

nested for so many years that it was known as 'The Raven-tree'. Boys tried again and again to reach the nest,

> But, when they arrived at the swelling, it jutted out so in their way, and was so far beyond their grasp, that the most daring lads were awed, and acknowledged the undertaking to be too hazardous. So the ravens built on, nest upon nest, in perfect security, till the fatal day arrived in which the wood was to be levelled. It was in the month of February, when those birds usually sit. The saw was applied to the butt, the wedges were inserted into the opening, the woods echoed to the heavy blows of the beetle or mallet, the tree nodded to its fall; but still the dam sat on. At last, when it gave way, the bird was flung from her nest; and though her parental affection deserved a better fate, was whipped down by the twigs, which brought her dead to the ground.

Effortlessly, with the neatness of a parable or fable, making us feel the rasp of the saw and the relentless blows of the mallet, Gilbert shows how a landscape is shaped by public needs, how a distant event like the repairing of a bridge can dictate the fate of a single bird – bringing her 'dead to the ground'. And how her spirit lives on.

Sometimes, the history inscribed in a landscape can't be deciphered easily. In his journal for this week, Gilbert includes a long note recording one of his brother Thomas's projects. On Selborne down, he says, 'are many long tumuli', which look like graves, although the country people think they are old saw pits:

> My Bror Tho: ordered two to be dug across; one of which produced nothing extraordinary; while in the other was found a blackish substance: but how, & in what quantity it lay, & whether it consisted of ashes & cinders, or of *humus animalis*, we had no opportunity to examine from the precipitancy of the labourer, who filled up the trench he had opened without giving proper notice of the occurrence.

The workman, fed up with digging, had no time for antiquarian whims. But Thomas was right to be curious. There are tumuli everywhere around. When the Woolmer barrows were excavated in the early nineteenth century, nothing was found except 'charcoal, ashes, calcined bones' and fragments of an urn, but later excavations nearby uncovered a wealth of Bronze Age weapons and ornaments – the 'Selborne Hoard'.

Saturday 27

47. 29 7/10½. NW, W. *My well sinks, & is very low.*
Dark & mild, moist, *The tortoise begins to dig into the ground.*
& foggy. *Mr Yalden fetches water from Well-head.*
The bat is out this warm evening.

The wells are nearly dry, and Richard Yalden has to go to the Well Head spring, which never seems to fail. There's no water for brewing, for watering horses, sheep and cattle. As the grass does not grow, the cows' milk dries up and the price of butter soars.

The tortoise starts to dig his winter hole, something Gilbert had watched with fascination for years. 'It scrapes out the ground with its fore-feet, and throws it up over its back with its hind,' he had told Barrington, 'but the motion of its legs is ridiculously slow, little exceeding the hour-hand of a clock; and suitable to the composure of an animal said to be a whole month in performing one feat of copulation.'

While Timothy digs, a bat flitters in the gloaming, hunting for insects, as if summer had never gone. 'The bat is out. Beetles hum,' Gilbert writes one year. In a mild season, he notes, many little insects, especially crane flies, 'continue still to sport & play about in the air, not only when the sun shines warm; but even in fog & gentle rain, & after sunset'. Ants run up and down the gate posts, 'without seeming to have anything to do'. One October, he finds a '*Sphinx atropos*, or death's head-moth, a noble insect, of a vast size: it lays it's eggs on the Jasmine. When handled it makes a little stridulous noise.'

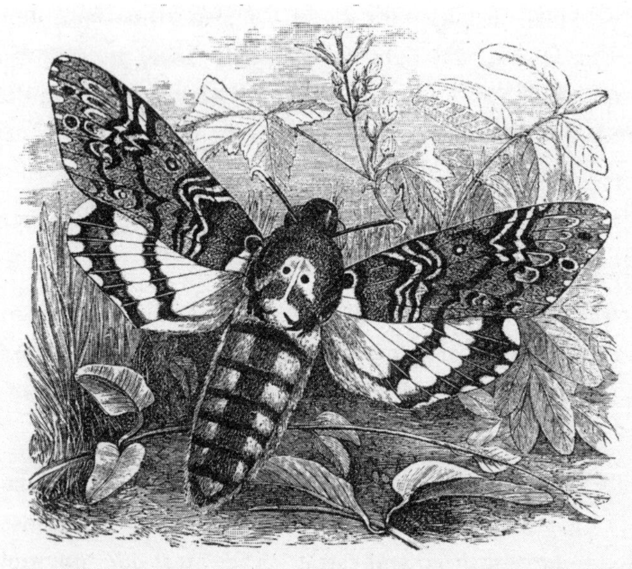

'Death's Head Hawk Moth', in *Cassell's Natural History* (1880).

Sunday 28
51. 29 3/10. W.   *Turnips suffer much for want of rain.*
Grey, sun, soft air,   *Woodcocks are come.*
heavy clouds, showers
about, bright.

The woodcocks fly in their thousands from Norway and Sweden, Finland and Russia, coming in a rush before the frost, around the time of the full moon before Halloween.

Woodcocks are shy birds. They like damp, mixed woods where there are open spaces nearby. All day, they hide deep in the bushes, camouflaged by their beautiful mottled brown feathers, skittering into the open only when someone startles them by walking or riding close by. At dusk, they come out to feed in the fields and heaths, digging for worms and beetles with their long, straight beaks. To his irritation, although he often opened up the stomachs of snipes and woodcocks,

          A YEAR WITH GILBERT WHITE

Gilbert could never quite find out what they ate, discovering only a sort of sludge, peppered with gravel. Their habit of lying motionless also intrigued him. Perhaps, he thought, it was exhaustion after their long flight from the north:

> One thing I used to observe when I was a sportsman, that there were times in which woodcocks were so sluggish and sleepy that they would drop again when flushed just before the spaniels, nay just as the muzzle of a gun that had been fired at them: whether this strange laziness was the effect of a recent fatiguing journey I shall not presume to say.

Sluggish or not, they were notoriously hard to flush out of hiding, and it was a great moment when a hunter bagged one. When Mr Richardson, of Bramshott, killed a large, plump female on boggy ground, Gilbert wrote: 'This bird was sent to London, where as the porter carried it along the streets he was offered a guinea for it.' A woodcock was a prize, not won by beginners unless through sheer luck. In the autumn of 1780, Ben's son Richard was staying at The Wakes. Shooting could be addictive, and Richard, Gilbert told Sam Barker,

> was quite transported beyond himself with the pleasures of shooting; and after walking more than a hundred miles, killed *one woodcock*; which ill-fated bird took the pains to migrate from Scandinavia to be slain by a cockney, who never shot a bird before!!! Pleasure is a most arbitrary matter! The pains my nephew took in his new pursuit would have been a great misery to many.

Misery to the woodcock, too.

Monday 29

47. 29 ½/10. W, NW.
Grey & still, heavy
clouds, small rain,
bright.

From the scantiness of grass I have given for some time. 9: pr pd for butter; a price here not known before.
Heavy clouds to the NE.

Tuesday 30
39. 29 ¾/10. N. | *Leaves fall very fast.*
Frost, ice, grey & cold, | *The tortoise retires under ground, within his*
clouds, cold showers. | *coop.*

Timothy turns his back on the frost and takes to the earth – or so Gilbert thinks. The previous year, Gilbert had watched him dig into the light soil by the fruit wall, throwing the earth over his shell completely, 'leaving only a small breathing hole near his head'. He had found a place, Gilbert thought, where he could 'enjoy the warmth of the sun, & where no wet can annoy him: a hen-coop over his back protects him from dogs &c'. In 1782, Timothy will choose this spot again. Gilbert will watch him place himself in the sun under the fruit wall, cleverly tilting his shell against the wall to get the full warmth on his back, 'yet this poor reptile has never read, that planes inclining to the horizontal receive more heat from the sun than any other elevation!'

Wednesday 31
38. 29 4/10. W, SW. 6. | *The water is so scanty in the streams, that the*
Frost, ice, grey & cold, | *millers cannot grind barley sufficient for mens*
bright & frosty. | *hogs. Dairy-farms cannot fill the butter-pots of*
 | *their customers.*

Will it ever rain? He reads in the *St James's Chronicle* of the extreme heat in Hungary, where husbandmen can only work in the night and all the snow that has covered the Carpathian Mountains for more than a century is entirely melted. Whether in Hungary or Hampshire, the vagaries of the weather, and their impact on farms, on animals and birds, are part of Gilbert's natural history. If the wells, ponds and rivers are exhausted across the world, how will anyone survive?

NOVEMBER

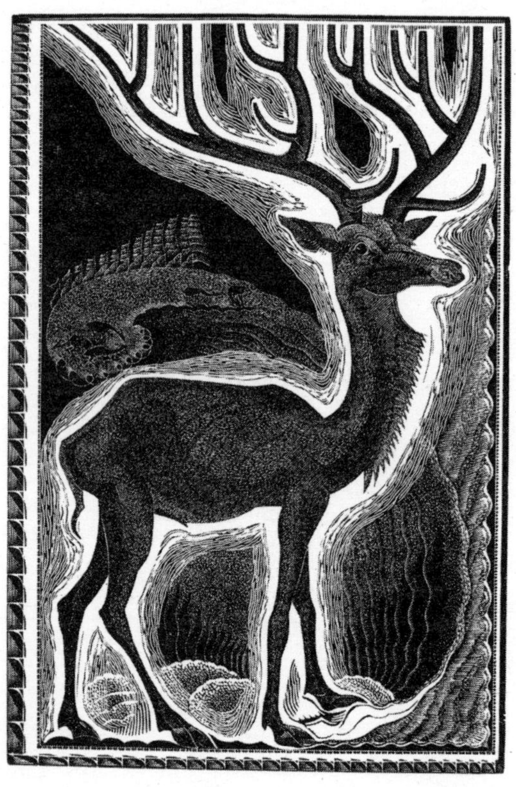

'The Deer' by Gertrude Hermes (1932), an illustration for a proposed *Natural History of Selborne* that never appeared. The prints were published in 1988.

IN THE OLD CHURCH calendar, November began with All Hallow-tide, bridging the end of harvest and summer and the start of winter darkness. This was the time when the borders between the worlds of the living and the dead were thin. October closed with Halloween, when people came to the churchyard, believing the dead would walk; the first of November was All Saints' Day, the day to remember the martyrs in heaven and the triumph over death; the next day was All Souls, when parishes remembered their dead of the past year. This feast overlapped with the Celtic Samhain, before sliding into Bonfire Night – as much a festival of fire defying the dark as of Protestants gloating over the death of the Catholic Guy Fawkes.

Soon, Gilbert writes, it will be dark within doors a little after three o'clock. He stacks his wood, orders thick stockings and brushes down his heavy, wide coat, 'cut high behind but with a turn down collar'.

Thursday 1

44½. 29 4/10½. sw.
Grey, sun, bright &
mild, small showers,
bright, mackarel sky.
Full moon.

Much wheat-land not sown yet; because men are afraid to sow their corn in the dust. Some water still in the pond on Selborne down: & the pond on Newton-farm, over the hedge, is more than half full.

It's still too dry to sow winter wheat, so there's no need for scarecrows to stop the wild geese devouring the early green shoots. But in this brisk weather, birds arrive in vast flocks, swirling, rising, settling – red-wings, fieldfares, linnets, yellowhammers.

Finches are everywhere. Greenfinches fill the lanes, feeding, Gilbert thinks, on the seeds of viper's bugloss. Flying over from Scandinavia, flocks of chaffinches double the resident population. These are 'hen chaffinches', writes Gilbert, underlining 'hen'. Many of the males stay abroad, defending their nesting sites; Linnaeus gave them the Latin name *Fringilla coelebs*, 'bachelor' birds, as the flocks he saw overwinter-ing in Sweden were all male. Occasionally, Gilbert spots bramblings, or 'snow-flecks', with their orange and white breasts. They, too, were migrant finches from Scandinavia and Russia. 'It is very amusing and strange,' he writes, 'that such a short-winged bird should delight in such perilous voyages over the northern ocean!' They are less common than chaffinches around Selborne, but they feed on the beech mast and seeds of knotgrass in the stubble, 'the great support of small, hard-billed birds in the winter'.

He looks out for more winter migrants, like the stock doves that flood in to feed on the acorns, beech mast and turnip tops. These smaller, silver- grey pigeons, with their iridescent green necks, the last winter birds of passage, he thought, 'leave us all to a bird in the spring, & do not breed in these parts: perhaps not in this island'. His 'perhaps' is significant. He really was not sure. Writing to Thomas Pennant on 30 November 1780, he wondered if the pigeons' habits in winter were different to those in summer. In fact, they don't disappear, but breed in woodland, in the holes of trees; they are just more visible when they come out into open farmland in winter.

Friday 2
50. 29 3/10. SW. 34. 22.   Showers, showers, showers, grey & still.

At last, there is a little rain to measure. Starlings run and feed in the fields near Newton Valence and join the rooks wheeling overhead. When he writes of these rooks, Gilbert's prose takes flight:

> The evening proceedings and manoeuvres of the rooks are curious
> and amusing in the autumn. Just before dusk they return in long
> strings from the foraging of the day, and rendezvous by thousands
> over Selborne-down, where they wheel round in the air, and sport
> and dive in a playful manner, all the while exerting their voices, and
> making a loud cawing, which, being blended and softened by the
> distance that we at the village are below them, becomes a confused
> noise or chiding; or rather a pleasing murmur, very engaging to the

                    A YEAR WITH GILBERT WHITE

imagination, and not unlike the cry of a pack of hounds in hollow, echoing woods, or the rushing of the wind in tall trees, or the tumbling of the tide upon a pebbly shore.

In the last gleam of day, they fly back to the deep beech woods.

Describing that evening chorus, Gilbert adds a memory, unusually sentimental:

> 'We remember a little girl', who as she was going to bed, used to remark on such an occurrence, in the true spirit of physico-theology, that the rooks were saying their prayers; and yet that child was much too young to be aware that the scriptures have said of the Deity – that 'he feedeth the ravens who call upon him'.

Was that Molly?

Saturday 3
45. 29 5/10. W.   *The air abounds with insects.*
White frost, cloudless,   *Flies come-out in the windows.*
sweet sunshine,   *Hogs, in eating acorns, chew them very small,*
red even: *& reject the husks. The plenty of acorns this*
                                             year avails the hogs of poor men, & brings
                                             them forward without corn.

Each year, cottagers turn their pigs into the Hanger, where they eat the beech mast and sometimes, if they are lucky, find truffles. The pigs look undiscriminatingly greedy as they snuffle and snort, but Gilbert sees that they are actually quite fussy, separating the acorn from its cup and chomping the nut into tiny pieces. They can, however, be a nuisance. 'No hogs have annoyed us this year in my outlet,' Gilbert writes with relief next year. 'They usually force-in after the acorns, nuts, beech & maple-mast; & occasion much trouble.'

Sometimes they were also fed potatoes. Fattening their pigs in this way, 'poor men,' Gilbert writes, 'killed very large hogs at little expense'.

In midwinter, they will be slaughtered, and every bit of them used, salted or smoked, from the head to the trotters. Sausages, ham and bacon are standbys, and even the ears can be pickled. In the later 1780s, with his sister-in-law Barbara firmly in charge, Gilbert often writes of salting and pickling, a mighty task: 'Tubbed half an hog, weighing 8 score: put half a bush: of salt, & two ounces of salt petre. The pork was well trod into the tub, & nicely stowed.'

Sunday 4
43½. 29 7/10. NW, NE.   *White frost, sun, sweet day.*

The old right of pannage – the freedom of cottagers to let their pigs graze in the woods – went unchallenged. Magdalen kept an eye on its land holdings and held its manorial courts each year, but it didn't seem anxious about the hogs, or even about game. In late autumn, when the rutting season was nearly over, hunters sometimes drove deer into the village street, where the dogs joined the chase. Later in this decade, in November 1788, the royal huntsmen came down with their hounds to hunt a famous stag long known to be in Hartley Wood, near Oakhanger. Hundreds came to see the animal being driven out, but the royal hounds failed to find it, and locals sneered at their 'lack of address and spirit'. It turned out that the stag had been there all the time:

> For as Harry Bright was lately pursuing a pheasant that was wing-broken in Hartley-wood he stumbled up on the stag by accident, & ran in upon him as he lay concealed amidst a thick brake of brambles, & bushes.

Monday 5
52, 55½. 29 2/10. SW, 78.   *The air is very warm, & the dew on the outside*
Rain, rain, rain.   *of the windows.*
        Grapes delicate still.

Rain at last, to everyone's relief. 'Our grapes are good still, and not quite gone. We eat of them twice every day at this time,' Gilbert tells Molly. He puts the success down to 'the concurring circumstance of a hot summer, a dry autumn, & a failure of wasps'.

Bonfire night passes without comment, although towns and villages everywhere were alight with fires, burning effigies, firecrackers and rowdy games. Gilbert's brother Henry dashes back from Weyhill fair to Fyfield this year to enjoy 'Bonfire, seven sky-rockets, four J's in a box and five roman candles'. Perhaps Selborne is quiet. Yet Gilbert rather liked it when things in the village turned a bit wild, or at least odd, like the time when Mrs Burbey's respectable farmer cousin came to stay and sleepwalked out of the window, waking to find himself naked in the cartway, nightcap in hand. Or the sight in January 1784, when, after a mad dog went on the rampage, '17 persons from Newton farm went in a waggon to be dipped in the sea, and also an horse', as a supposed protection against rabies.

Newton Great Farm seems rather unlucky. The year before that excursion to the sea, a 'young mad-headed farmer' arrived, with four friends, to marry Farmer Bridger's daughter. They paid the bellringers and got them all drunk, and drank in the Compasses inn for the whole of the next day, leaving a planned dinner at the farm to grow cold. The village was in uproar. 'Mrs Butler, hearing that her son was fighting, fell into fits and continued delirious two days,' while the bride's sister and sister-in-law fled to their rooms in fear. Eventually, the bride, 'who wept a good deal', was swept off to Berkshire. Selborne had seen nothing like it, but what made the most impact was the free booze:

> The common people all agree that the bridegroom was the most of a gentleman of any man they ever saw. He told the folks at the inn that whenever the next sister was married, he would come and spend ten guineas.

Fallen leaves squelch underfoot. Perhaps fed up with the damp, the kindly, bustling Barbara White, now well settled in at The Wakes, frequently goes over to the vicarage to chat with Mrs Etty. The vicarage was a fount of news and was often full of visitors. From time to time, Mrs Etty's cousins, formerly the beautiful Battie girls, arrived in their married grandeur. Anna was now Lady Young, married to Sir George, an admiral; Kitty's husband, John Rashleigh, was a commissioner for Greenwich Hospital; while Philadelphia was married to Sir John Call, who had been a famous engineer in India and a high sheriff of Cornwall, but was now an MP. But perhaps the three sisters looked across the road at The Wakes and the Hanger, from time to time, and thought of those shepherdess parties twenty years ago.

If the Battie sisters brought a touch of society glamour, the Ettys' son Charles, sailing with the East India fleet, linked Selborne to far-off dramas and exotic places. In August 1783, when his ship *The Duke of Kingston* caught fire off Ceylon, Charles would be the only man saved, clinging to wreckage, pulled naked from the sea by sailors from another vessel in the convoy, the *Vansittart*. The next year, coming back from Madras via the Cape of Good Hope, he brings treasures: the skins of two humming birds, ostrich eggs, shells from Mozambique and turtle eggs from Ascension Island. Best of all, are two tortoises from Madagascar, which, Gilbert wrote excitedly, 'appear to be *Testudo geometrica*, Linn: and the *Testudo tessellata* Raii'. Both tortoises, though they were brisk and well in London, must have been badly bumped during the coach ride to Selborne. They died within two days, 'but not before the female, a very grand personage, had laid an egg'.

Wednesday 7
45. 29 4/10. W, NW.
Grey, cold & dark,
& blowing.

John Hale has cleansed the pond on the down,
& carried out a large quantity of mud.
Men sow wheat: the ground works very fine.

Farmers can now sow in the rain-softened ground. On this week's blank page, Gilbert notes how farming in Selborne has improved in the last twenty years, in particular when it comes to wheat: 'Not that they plough oftener, or perhaps manure more than they did formerly; but from the more frequent harrowings & draggings now in use, which pulverize our strong soil, & render it more fertile than any other expedient yet in practice.' Today, this 'pulverising' is frowned upon: better to adopt a 'no-till' approach, sowing the seeds in drills, avoiding disturbance to the soil structure and harm to the beneficial worms, fungi and bacteria.

Thursday 8
44. 29 8/10½. NW.
Sun, mild & pleasant.

The tortoise came out of his coop, & has buried
himself in the laurel-hedge.

When my great parlor is kept close shut-up, it is not at all affected by condensations on the wainscot or paper tho' the hall & entry are all in a float.

It looked as though Timothy had gone to ground until spring. But he was restless, Gilbert told Molly, and 'not liking his quarters, on Nov. 8 he lifted up his coop, and came forth, and has buried himself again in the laurel-hedge, where he will probably be lost in the profoundest slumber during the uncomfortable months of winter'. The following year, Gilbert would set up the rejected hen coop by the fruit wall again, noting with satisfaction: 'Timothy the tortoise sleeps in the fruit border under the wall, covered with a hen coop, in which is a good armful of straw. Here he will lie warm, secure & dry. His back is partly covered with mould.'

Gilbert is still checking for the arrival of the less common birds. One is the reed bunting, which 'forsaking the reeds, & waterside in the winter, roves about among the fields, & hedges'. Another is the grey crow. This was a striking hooded crow with a sleek grey back and black head, a north-country bird. He is faintly piqued this month when Molly tells him: 'My uncle Benj. says he has seen the *grey* crow on Selborne-Common: we are in doubt whether it is in your list of birds.' Of course it was. 'I have, in my time,' he responds, 'seen two *grey* crows in Selborne parish.' He had seen two in November 1773, flying over the garden to the Hanger, and two years later, he claimed to have seen three, calling the bird as rare at Selborne as the carrion crow in Sweden.

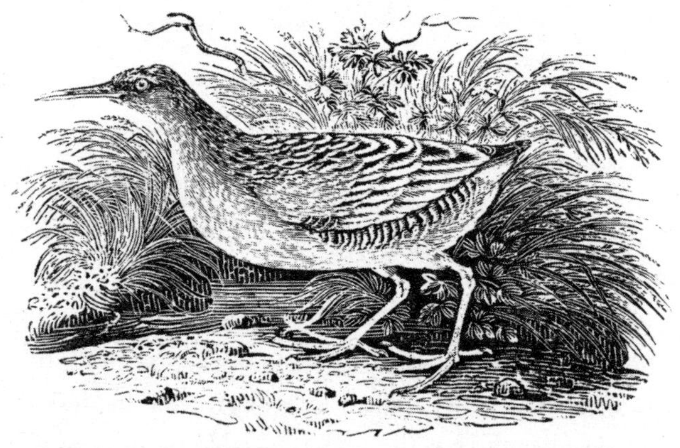

'The Water Rail' by Thomas Bewick, in his *A History of British Birds.*
Vol. II: Water Birds (1804).

The most unusual incomer, when he looked back, was a water rail, shot in the sedge of a pond in November 1774. 'This was the first of the sort that ever I heard of in these parts,' he wrote excitedly. 'I sent it to London to be stuffed & preserved. A beautiful bird.' It is indeed beautiful, with its brown back and barred chest, and is smaller than its relatives, the moorhen and coot. It runs among the reed beds, poking in the mud with its long red beak and sometimes using it like a dagger, aggressively stabbing small mammals or birds. Water rails are rarely seen because they are so nervous, freezing, or dashing into the rushes when disturbed, moving between their feeding and breeding grounds at dead of night. But since Gilbert was examining a bird that had been shot, he missed out on hearing its call: a mixture of explosive grunts and screams, said to be like a squealing piglet – a startling sound in the wetlands.

Saturday 10

50. 29 6/10. SW. 18.   *The dew is on the outside of the windows.*
Dark & wet, & warm,   *Planted two rows of lettuces close under the*
fog, dark & wet.   *fruit-wall to stand the winter.*

Hares eat down the pinks, & cloves in the garden: & yet sportsmen complain that the breed this year is very small; alledging that dry summers, tho' kindly for partridges, are detrimental to hares.

It's warmer outside than in, a good day to be in the garden. It took Gilbert a while to realise that it was hares who were munching his pinks; in previous years, he had just blamed 'some animal'. Accepted wisdom holds that dry summers are good for hares as they can have three or four litters, and the leverets thrive better than in cold, wet years. But now, in 1781, when water is so scarce that the grass is thin and meagre, the hares are skinny and small.

The oldest native hares, in Britain since before the Ice Age, are the mountain hares, which turn white in winter and are to be found in the north of Scotland. Until the 1770s, Gilbert knew nothing of these, and when he heard of them from Thomas Pennant, he was delighted, 'for the quadrupeds of Britain are so few, that every new species is a great acquisition'. The brown hares arrived in the Iron Age. Originally from the Asian steppes, they like grasses and arable lands, moving between crops, feeding at night and resting by day, and crouching as still as stones in their forms – shallow dips in the ground where they nest – when danger threatens. Although their numbers have plummeted since Gilbert's time, mostly due to changes in farming, they are often spotted at dusk and dawn on the open land around Selborne. To give them the vital winter cover they need, local farmers are providing wide field margins with long grass and planting wildflower plots to interrupt blocks of cereals. They would not need to eat Gilbert's pinks.

Sunday 11
55¾. 29 2/10½. SW. 58.   *Rain all night.*
Rain, dark & warm,   *My well rises.*
rain.

'The house martins have disappointed us again, as they did last year, with respect to their Novemr visit for one day,' he writes in a long note against this week. He skims through old journals to check, finding that in early November 1777 and 1779, they had appeared along the Hanger for the whole of one day, after disappearing for some weeks. He found it hard to accept that birds that were nestlings only a couple of weeks before could suddenly fly off to the tropics, and still hoped that the martins might hide over the winter in the scrub. He could not bear to let them go.

Monday 12
51½. 29 2/10. W.   *Grey, mild & still, sun, grey, red even:*

As he walks the lanes, now and in years to come, the hedges are covered with the wispy, feathery seed-heads of the wild clematis known as 'Old Man's Beard' or 'Traveller's Joy'. 'The downy seeds of travellers joy,' Gilbert notes, 'fill the air, & driving before a gale appear like insects on the wing.'

Today, he writes to Molly. Her visit with her father, he says, was far too short, and he brings her up to date with the news. As the evenings were getting darker, the energetic Mrs Yalden had taken the Bostal and the Zig-Zag in hand, marking the way between Newton vicarage and the tops of both paths with sticks. Then she had got together 'a cartful of chalk and a carter, and ordered him to lay lumps of chalk all the way', setting up posts over the whole down, 'so that Mr Etty who used to say he would not go over the common by himself for £50, might now venture for half the money'.

Village news followed. Old Larby's wife is getting iller every day. Poor Mrs Berriman, already described as out of her wits, 'continues to be the most unfortunate of women, for now she has lost *all* her clothes'. Soldiers had been billeted nearby, and when they left, two village girls – as entranced by military glamour as Lydia in *Pride and Prejudice* – set off to follow them, raiding Mrs B's wardrobe on the way, so that 'they might cut a figure in their new way of life'. When Robert Berriman chased them down and brought them back, he found nothing on them and gave up in despair, 'after much trouble and expense'.

After the end of the American war, while wounded, battered and dispirited men were trailing home, other British soldiers were setting off to fight the Dutch in the West Indies and Ceylon, and the French and different Indian states in India. Many were billeted near Selborne as they made their way to Portsmouth. In 1782, Highland soldiers – an astonishment in their kilts and plaids – would be quartered in Selborne and Oakhanger. Their regiment, the 77th Atholl Highlanders, had been founded recently in order to take on garrison duty at home and free experienced regiments to fight in America. Their terms had specified service only until the end of the American war, but suddenly they were told to join Lord Howe to help relieve Gibraltar, which was being besieged by the Spanish and French. Driven off course after duty in Ireland, they had landed in Devon and were making their way across land to the port.

'These sans-breeches men make an odd appearance in the S. of England,' Gilbert told Molly. To Mary Barker, he wrote admiringly that the Scots were very quiet, 'never known to steal even a turnip, or a cabbage, though they lived much on vegetables, and were astonished at the dearness of Southern provisions'. They were not always so quiet. Gilbert does not mention it, but once they arrived in Portsmouth and were told that they were embarking for India, not Gibraltar, the Highlanders mutinied. Soon the whole regiment was disbanded.

Wednesday 14
29, 52. SW. 85.   *One vast shower.*
Rain, rain, rain,
dark, rain.

Thursday 15
50. 28 7/10½. SW. 79.   *Vast rain in the night, with strong wind.*
Sun, grey, & windy,   *My well is risen near six feet.*
shower, bright aurora.   *Thomas begins to dress the vines, The crop of*
                             grapes is just over; having lasted in perfection
                             more than ten weeks.

He peers into the well at The Wakes. He measures the amount it rises and falls by the turns of the winch that pulls up the bucket; three or four turns mean five or six feet. When it begins to rain, if he leans over the edge, he can hear the spring and see it bubbling at the bottom as it begins to fill the well. 'Thus will three or four inches of rain replenish my well, deep as it is, after it has been very low, & foul, & almost dry for several months.'

The last grapes are finished, and now rain and wind are stripping the remaining leaves from the trees, sending them hurtling across the sky. In Cumbria, too, as I write and think about that Selborne autumn, the bronze leaves of the beech across the road lie in a great circle round the trunk, like a skirt flung off, the tree a ghost of its summer self. The sheep huddle in a clump, backs to the gale. Gilbert tells me something obvious, which I had never noticed:

> When horses, cows, sheep, deer, &c: feed in wind, & rain, they always keep their heads down the wind, & their tails to the weather: but birds always perch, & chuse to fly, with their heads to the weather to prevent the wind from ruffling their feathers, & the cold & wet from penetrating to their skins.

In Selborne in 1781, November feels bleak, despite the pale sun and glorious aurora. Gilbert turns to James Thomson's 'Autumn', adding his own emphasis:

> Fled is the *blasted* verdure of the fields;
> And, *shrunk* into their beds, the *flowery* race
> Their *sunny* robes resign. E'en what remain'd
> Of *stronger* fruits falls from the *naked* tree:
> And woods, fields, gardens, orchards, all around
> The *desolated* prospect *thrills* the soul.

The old English word *thyrlian*, from which 'thrill' derives, means 'to pierce like an arrow', 'to penetrate and shock', not 'to delight or excite'. For Thomson, autumn is principally a time of loss. One year, Gilbert made a note of this loss with regard to his trees. First to lose its leaves was the walnut, next the mulberry and the ash, and then the horse chestnut. Among the fruit trees, apples and peaches could stay green until the end of November. And while the taller beeches were often bare by late October, younger trees or beech hedges turned a deep chestnut colour and kept their leaves until the new ones pushed them out in the spring. Nothing is altogether 'desolate'.

Indoors, out of the gale, crickets are on the hearth. In 1780, Gilbert
had heard them crying faintly in the chimney; when they appeared,
the cats pounced fast. In 1790, in a long note, he will write that many
of them are minute, smaller than fleas, and clearly only just hatched.
Used to the constant kitchen fire, he thinks, they lack any sense of the
seasons and produce young when other crickets and insects are dead, or
'laid up for the winter, to pass away the uncomfortable months in the
profoundest slumbers, & a state of torpidity'.

The house crickets are always 'alert and merry: a good Christmas
fire is to them like the heats of the dog-days'. They are also perpetually
thirsty,

> being frequently drowned in pans of water, milk, broth, or the like.
> Whatever is moist they affect; and therefor often gnaw holes in wet
> woollen stockings and aprons that are hung to the fire: they are
> the housewife's barometer, foretelling her when it will rain; and are
> prognostic sometimes, she thinks, of ill or good luck; of the death of a
> near relation, or the approach of an absent lover.

They are hungry, too, eating yeast, salt and crumbs. In summer, they
fly out of the windows and over the roofs, moving, he says, beautifully, '*volatu undoso*, in waves or curves, like wood-peckers, opening and
shutting their wings at every stroke, and so are always rising or sinking'.
But in winter, if they reach huge numbers, they become pests, flying
into candles, dashing in your face. They could become 'like Pharoah's
plague of frogs, – "in their bedchambers, and upon their beds, and in
their ovens, and in their kneading-troughs"', only got rid of by the drastic expedient of blasting their hiding places in crevices and crannies
with gunpowder, or tempting them, like wasps, with beer traps, 'for,
being always eager to drink, they will crowd in till the bottles are full'.

Saturday 17
46½. 28 9/10½. SW.   Antirrhinum Cymbalaria *flourishes, & blows.*
Grey, small rain, sun,
bright.

His purple toadflax covers the wall. One night of fierce frost, and it
will scrumple up and die. The same goes for his nasturtiums and other
'Indian flowers'.

Sunday 18
42. 29 1/10½. E, NW.   *Frost, ice, sun, still & pleasant, red even:*

He goes to Farringdon to take the service, as he has done for so long.
But next year, in March 1782, William Roman, the vicar for whom
Gilbert was curate, will die, and change will threaten. Gilbert was staying in South Lambeth on one of his annual London visits when he
heard the news. He hurried back to Selborne, knowing that he might
lose his curacy, as there were rumours that the living was to go to a
young man of about seventeen who intended to live in the parish and
would not need him. But the wrench was not immediate, and Gilbert
would carry on as curate for some time before he left the church, with
its ancient yews, for good, closing the heavy door behind him.

His last entry in the Faringdon parish register would not be until
1 January 1785. That was a dark new year, with snow on the ground,
and his final week was sad: 'John and Anne, the twin, new born,
children of Sarah Bone, a single woman, were buried Dec. 30, 1785.
Paupers.' He had baptised the twins the day before. He never com-
mented harshly, as some clergy did, on illegitimate births, but this was
a reminder of how hard village life could be.

Gilbert also helped Andrew Etty in Selborne church from time to
time. But in the bitter spring of 1784, when the snow drifted high over
the hedges, Etty would struggle home from Alton and collapse in a de-
lirium. He died from his fever two days later. Gilbert took the funeral

service, signing himself as 'curate *pro tempore*'. The Ettys had been his friends for over twenty years, and the loss hit him hard. Months later, he told his sister Anne Barker: 'I miss poor Mr. Etty every day: he was a blameless man, without guile.' He dedicated his *Antiquities* to him, and in his chapter on the church, after copying his grandfather Gilbert's memorial, he included the inscription on Etty's plaque, with its emphasis on his humility and his kindness towards the poor and sick.

Then came another blow. In early June 1784, three months after Etty's death, Richard Yalden fell ill. He rallied at the end of August 'and talks much of shooting', but his health collapsed over the winter and he died on 5 March 1785. John Mulso wrote to Gilbert with sympathy and concern: 'For God's sake take Care of yourself and live as long as ever You can . . . I fear You are all plunged again into Sadness.'

The new vicar of Selborne, Revd Taylor, came on a visit with his glamorous new bride, and was generally liked. But as he had no plans to live in the village, Gilbert became Selborne's curate again, after a gap of twenty-six years. This also meant that Mrs Etty could still rent the vicarage, and she would live there with her daughters until she eventually moved away in 1788.

Meanwhile, Richard Yalden's living in Newton Valence went to Gilbert's nephew, Ben's son Edmund – not a very good neighbour at first, Gilbert thought, as he was 'so taken up with various courtships' that he was hardly there at all. But Edmund eventually married and settled in. The walk up the Zig-Zag and the Bostal was as busy as ever.

Monday 19
41½. 29 7/10½. NW.   *Planted two Cypresses in the garden.*
Grey, still, & agreeable.   *They come from S: Lambeth.*

The cypresses were a touch of Italy in Hampshire, brought by Gilbert's brother Thomas. They grew tall over future years as the lives of the White family developed in new ways. The deaths of Gilbert's old friends were followed by more changes. In June 1785, Molly married her cousin Benjamin, five years her senior. They had grown up together in South Lambeth, and Benjamin – confusingly, another 'Ben' – was now managing his father's bookshop in Fleet Street. Gilbert was delighted, but it was still a jolt. He wrote to Molly that December, in mock anger at Ben whisking his favourite niece away from a visit to The Wakes, 'yet I hope to live to see the day when she will be permitted to make me a much longer visit'. He signed off:

> Hoping, an other year, to find you a more dutiful niece, and less dutiful wife, I remain with true affection
>
> Yr loving uncle,
>
> GIL. WHITE

He was joking, but not altogether. He worried that they would never be so close again. Yet, if anything, things were even better. It was common at the time to send children to the country to live with their relations: the babies to thrive with a wet nurse, the children to grow up in the cleaner air. Ben and Molly's first son, yet another Ben, born in late summer 1786, would indeed be sent down to Selborne. Two more boys, Tom and Glyd, would follow.

The year after Molly's marriage saw a flurry of weddings. First, tying the Yalden and White families together even more firmly, if that was possible, Gilbert's brother Ben married Richard Yalden's widow Mary (Ben's first wife, Anne, had been Richard's sister).

Gilbert's favourite nephew Sam Barker also got married, having amused Gilbert with details of his courtship: 'Her name is Haggitt, a young woman of gentle manners and long black eye-lashes, and of course, you know, everything that is agreeable, &c. &c. &c.' 'You speak like a Turk,' responded Gilbert, with regard to the eyelashes. 'Now you talk of ladies, can you repeat "Pretty, pretty Peggy Haggit" three times in a breath?'

His letters in the mid-1780s are full of children, including the large Clements clan from Alton, the children of his niece Jane, Ben's daughter. 'Little Tom Clements is visiting at Petersfield,' he tells Sam Barker, 'where he plays much at Cricket: Tom bats, his grand-mother bowls, and his great-grandmother watches out!!'

The new family members were keeping pace with nature. On 16 May 1790:

One polyanth-stalk produced 47 pips or blossoms. Mrs Edmund White brought to bed of a boy, who has encreased the number of my nephews & Nieces to 56. The bloom of apples is great: the white pippin, as usual, very full . . . The dearling in the meadow is loaded with bloom . . . This year it bore 10 bush. of small fruit.

The last marriage, in January 1793, will be that of Gibraltar Jack, or 'Dr John'. His wife Louisa Neve is, Gilbert says, a small woman and a good musician who 'can shoulder a violin'. She brought Gilbert's nephews and nieces to a final total of sixty-two.

Tuesday 20
40½. 29 6/10½. S.   *Phalaenae fly under hedges.*
Frost, ice, grey & still.

He often noticed the moths at dusk. 'Strange that those nocturnal *lepidopterae* should be so alert,' he wrote in November 1775, 'at a season when no day-papilios appear, but have long been laid-up for the winter! . . . *Phalaenae* appear about hedges in the night time in mild weather the winter thro'.' Each November, he sees moths everywhere, as well as spiders, wood lice, gnats, crane flies and 'slippery jacks' – long narrow 'click beetles' that arch their back with a 'snap' and leap as far as six feet to get out of danger. All these come out on mild days.

Wednesday 21
49. 29 2/10. S. 50.   *Finished dressing the vines. The new wood was*
Dark & brisk gale,   *small, & not highly ripened; so it was laid-in*
rain, rain.   *the shorter. It covers the walls regularly.*

By now, the trees on the Hanger are almost bare, although the hedges are dotted with colour – rose hips and sloes, crab apples and haws – and sprinkled with mosses and lichens. 'Mosses begin to grow, & look vivid, & will begin to blow in a few weeks,' Gilbert writes in late November 1785. But what does he mean by 'begin to blow' (to flower)? Mosses are bryophytes, ancient non-flowering species. In a dry summer, they can shrivel and become dormant, resuming their life cycle when the rain comes with new, bright growth. Some male plants bear sex organs, and perhaps Gilbert means these, as they do look like tiny flowers on some species. They also produce 'capsules', where the spores are formed, and these stand out, waving gently in autumn and winter, when other flowers fade away. In this sense, I suppose, they can 'blow'.

In Borrowdale, notoriously the wettest place in England, we are surrounded by ancient woods – Great Wood, Johnny Wood, High Wood. These Atlantic oak woods, temperate rainforests, remnants of a forest that once stretched from Scotland to Wales, are famous for their mosses, liverworts and lichens, and in late autumn, the moss-covered boulders between the trees are dazzling emerald, shimmering in the sunlight filtering through the bare branches. Mosses have been on our planet for millions of years, surviving ice ages and droughts. I marvel at their variety and delicacy, at the patterns they form and their deceptive softness.

Grasses die and wither, seeds ripen and fall. But if the cycle pauses, it does not stop. There's new life here, too. Tiny spears of new wheat shiver, and one year Gilbert will find that Baker's Hill is completely covered with horse beans, already four or five inches high, springing up through the grass and moss, planted, he thinks, by the jays. Even the worst ravages, like Magdalen's felling of beeches at the top of the Hanger in 1785, can, he hopes, be mended. On 22 November 1786, he writes in his journal: 'I sent a woman up the hill with a peck of beech-mast, which she tells me she has scattered all round the down amidst the bushes & brakes, where there were no beeches before.' He asks Thomas Hoar to sow beech nuts in the hedges, and his brother Thomas scatters acorns and ash seeds and plants furze on the bare parts of the Hanger. Those trees will be green long after Gilbert has gone.

Magdalen's tree-felling left the earth depressingly bare, and dragging the felled trunks down the hill cut deep gouges, which were known as 'slidders' or 'sliders'. But all was not lost. 'When old beech-trees are cleared away,' Gilbert noted,

> the naked ground in a year or two becomes covered with straw-berry plants, the seed of which must have lain in the ground for an age at lest. One of the slidders or trenches down the middle of the hanger, close covered over with lofty beeches near a century old, is still called strawberry slidder, tho no strawberries have grown there in the memory of man. That sort of fruit, no doubt, did once abound there, & will again when the obstruction is removed.

The earth has its own hidden modes of revival.

Friday 23
42. 29 ½/10. S.   *Dark & blowing, rain, rain.*

Saturday 24
44½. 29 5/10. N, NE.   *Cascades fall from the fields into the hollow*
48, 2.   *lanes.*
Rain, grey & mild, fog.

After the rain of the day before and overnight, the towering banks of the lanes are like waterfalls. People sigh and take the long way round. The lanes look like Grimm's 'grotesque and romantic' scene of the waterfall in Silkwood, with its steep banks above.

But soon there will be changes. When his brother Thomas and Molly and the twins Tom and Henry arrive in November 1784, Gilbert writes briskly in his journal: 'Came via Newton lane, & down the

N. field hill; both of which have had much labour bestowed on them, & are now very safe. This is the first carriage that ever came this way.'

Sunday 25
42. 29 7/10. E, SE.   *As the fog cleared away, the warm sun occasioned a*
Fog, wh: frost, sun,   *prodigious reek, or steam to arise from thatched soft*
& bright.   *roofs. In the evening picturesque partial fogs come*
    rolling-in up the Lithe, from the forest.

This is the last Sunday before Advent, and the collect for the day, from the *Anglican Book of Common Prayer*, begins: 'Stir up we beseech thee, O Lord, the wills of thy faithful people.' As Gilbert told Ralph Churton in 1788: 'there is an old maxim, which poor dear Mrs Etty used to use', that once this collect 'had been read and passed over, the festival of Xtmass came creeping upon us before we could be aware'. Like Mrs Etty, people saw the text as a herald of Christmas – the day became popularly known as 'stir up Sunday', when housewives and cooks raided the spice cupboard and set about making their Christmas puddings and cakes. It's still called this, though not so many of us, I'm sure, roll our sleeves up quite as fervently as people did in the past.

In 1781, the day is marked not by snowy Christmas weather, but by fog and sudden warmth. The thermometer has leapt up 8 degrees, from 44° to 52°F (7° to 11°C). It's sunny enough to make damp thatch steam. The air is full of vapour. Evening mists float up the valley from the Lythe, and the smoke from cottage chimneys and other fires drifts low above the ground. In a later year, in the same week, he notes: 'The smoke of the new lighted lime-kilns this evening crept along the ground in long trails: a token of a dry, heavy atmosphere.'

Monday 26
42½. 29 6/10½. S.   *Planted against the fruit-wall three well-trained*
Frost, sun,   *trees, that are to begin to bear fruit next year.*
mild, & grey.

viz: 1 Peterboro' nectarine: N:E: end: 1 Montaban peach: 1 red Magdalen peach. Against the scullery, 1 Elrouge Nectarine. These trees came from Mr Shiell's nursery at Lambeth, & cost 7s 6d on the spot. They have healthy wood, & well-trained heads. Planted a Virginian creeper against the wall of my house next the garden.

The planet Venus now is visible at Selborne over the hanger.

In November, there's still time to plant bare-root trees and shrubs. Thomas White sends a load down from South Lambeth, bought from James Shiell, who was known for his fruit; he even cultivated pine-apples and had a glasshouse of the latest kind.

Venus shines brightly now, rising in the south-east long before dawn and remaining in the sky all day, although lost in the sunlight. Jupiter, too, is at its brightest and shines all night. So if Gilbert is up early, he can see both planets at once. He has become a keen sky-watcher. Earlier this month, on Saturday 10th, he had written in a note: 'The wintry & huge constellation, Orion, begins now to make his appearance in the evening, exhibiting his enormous figure in the E.' He likes this strong hunter, his belt and sword, club and shield marked out by stars. 'That great straddle-bob Orion,' he tells Sam Barker, likes to 'bestride my brew house in winter.'

Tuesday 27
47. 29 4/10½. S. *Began to use some of the advertised Celeri,*
Grey, mild & still, *which, I think, is crisper & finer flavoured*
still & moist. *than any sort that I have met with.*

Wednesday 28
29 7/10. N. 29. *This month proved a very wet one, more so*
Rain, rain, rain. *than any month since Decemr 1779: in which*
 fell 6 inc: 28; in this 6. 18.

Gilbert is now in Oxford, spending a week here before the election of the new provost of Oriel on 5 December. When the previous provost, Dr John Clarke, died in late November, Gilbert's brother Thomas and Molly saw this in the papers, and Molly wrote to her brother Tom: 'we wish we could elect my Uncle Provost of Oriel, but I fancy he would make some objections, was it in our power'. The main objection would be to leaving Selborne.

Friday 30

No temperature, no weather, no entry for today – has he left his journal behind?

DECEMBER

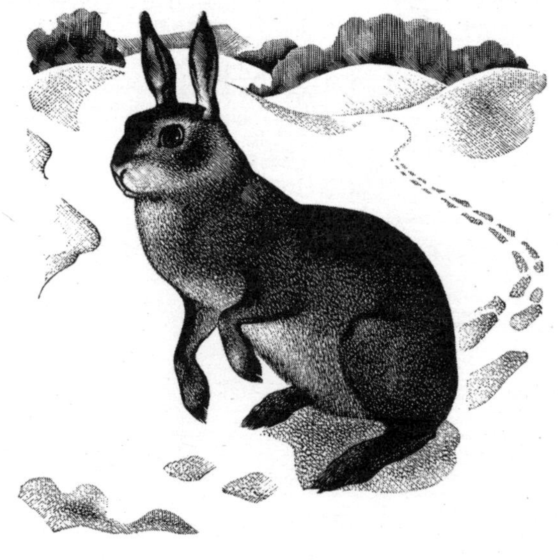

'Hare in the Snow' by Agnes Miller Parker, in H. E. Bates's *Through the Woods* (1936).

GILBERT MAKES NO entries for the first week of this month, when he is in Oxford, apart from a couple of brief notes about Selborne's rainfall, probably reported by Thomas Hoar. Even when he comes home, he doesn't seem to venture out much. The birds he mentions are either indoor species – neighbours' bullfinches in cages – or ones described by his sportsmen friends. Is he in his study, surrounded by papers, adding more details to the *Antiquities* and his letters for *The Natural History of Selborne*? It will be almost the end of the decade before his book is finally wrenched out of his hands.

Tuesday 4
Rain, 30.

Today, Molly writes to Gilbert, anticipating his return from Oxford. All her letters show her alert, speculative turn of mind and her easy ability – very like her uncle's – to turn from gossip about family and friends to Anglo-Saxon names of the months or variant readings of Latin phrases. Her learning amused Barbara White. 'Mrs J White smiles to see you quote Latin so boldly,' Gilbert wrote once.

Knowing how Gilbert disliked the winter gloom, Molly's letter turned to spring, sparking his own wandering response about such things as the Anglo-Saxon name for April. This was 'Eostre' in Bede's list, from Goster, the goddess of dawn, whose festival comes at Easter, the spring equinox. Molly sends him a lovely quotation from Chaucer's 'The Floure and the Leaf' about young oak leaves shining in the early-morning sun. Poets had often noted the varying shades of autumn, he replies, but Chaucer, in her quotation, is the only one, he thinks, who noticed 'the different colours of leaves at their first coming out in the spring'.

They write about the grey crow on the common and the local terms for trees. Molly suggests that he should add to his local names '*Merise*, a small bitter Cherry says the French dictionary (perhaps from *Amarus*)'. 'You are certainly right,' responds Gilbert, 'respecting *Merise*, a bitter cherry: hence no doubt comes our provincial word, *Mery*, or more probably *Meris*, the S. being dropped.' Then he turns happily back to salt fish, worsted stockings, low wells and poor Dame Larby lying ill (when she died, he contributed to her funeral expenses). Poetry and housekeeping, birds on the common, Chaucer and village life inter-twine.

Wednesday 5
Rain, 35.

That's all. He's set off for home again. He writes no entry at all for Thursday the 6th – St Nicholas Day, the start of the Christmas season.

But a year ago, on 6 December, he had been busy at home, planting out 'Sweet-Williams, vine, goose-berry cuttings, honey-suckle cut-tings, & several crab-stocks grafted from a curious & valuable green apple growing at South Lambeth'.

Friday 7   *ALTON*
                 The weather was dark, still, & foggy, all the time
                 that I was absent, & the wind mostly NE: *&* E.

Saturday 8
39. 29 3/10. E.   Rain, rain, rain.

He adds a note:

> George Tanner's bullfinch, a cock bird of this year, began from it's
> first moulting to look dingy; & is now quite black on the back,
> rump & all; & very dusky on the breast. This bird has lived chiefly
> on hemp-seed. But T: Dewey's, & – Horley's two bull-finches, both
> of the same age with the former, & also of the same sex, retain their
> natural colours, which are glossy & vivid.

The last two birds were also fed hemp seed. So, he concludes, the idea that this particular seed blackens bullfinches 'does not hold

                    A YEAR WITH GILBERT WHITE

good in all instances; or at least not in the first year'. He's correcting a deduction he made many years before, when a single example persuaded him that hemp seed was to blame for the bird's discolouration. Today's qualified conclusion shows that he's prepared to change his mind when new evidence suggests his reasoning has been wrong.

The bullfinch's colour was a matter of concern to his bird-keeping neighbours – natural history at its most local and intimate. Keeping birds was popular among all classes. In grand mansions, parrots and mynah birds carolled from Chippendale-designed cages that looked like miniature Taj Mahals and mock Versailles. In cottages, common songbirds sang from wicker cages that were hung in the window or set on a table, and which were often carried from room to room while a housewife cleaned – portable music. But keeping birds did not appeal to Gilbert: it would make him too anxious, he said. Writing to Daines Barrington about the caged birds Barrington kept, he explained that much as he would like to get a blackcap for him, 'I am no bird-catcher; and so little used to birds in a cage, that I fear if I had one it would soon die for want of feeding'.

The image of the caged bird gathered multiple meanings in the late eighteenth century. Sometimes it was used as an emblem of domesticity, of nature tamed, of a 'woman's place' in the home. Often, too, the ability to be moved by the bird's song was cited as an illustration of fashionable 'sensibility' and depth of feeling. Elsewhere, the caged bird appears as a straightforward symbol of incarceration, as embodied by the starling in Sterne's *Sentimental Journey* (1768), which cries, 'I can't get out – I can't get out.' Some parts of Barrington's paper 'Experiments and Observations on the Singing of Birds', which appeared in the Royal Society's *Philosophical Transactions* in 1773, might well have made Gilbert uncomfortable, like his observation that wrens die quickly when caged, or that the nightingale is so sulky when first confined that it refuses to eat and has to be 'crammed', and 'it is also necessary to tye his wings, to prevent his killing himself against the top or sides of the cage'. Gilbert liked his birds to fly free, agreeing perhaps with Philip Miller's praise of orchards, which 'harbour a constant Aviary of sweet Singers without wires'.

Sunday 9
41. 29 3/10¾. E. 35.   *Hares continue to eat all my pinks, which they*
Dark & still, small   *have now near destroyed.*
rain, dark & moist.

He is in despair about the hares. 'Hares make sad havock in the garden,' he groans again, two years later; 'they have eat-up all the pinks; & now devour the winter cabbage-plants, the spinage, the parsley, the celeri, &c. As yet they do not touch the lettuces.' A decade on, they are still there: Thomas Hoar will find one hiding under a cabbage leaf, catching her just as she begins to nibble the tops of the pinks.

Other garden inhabitants are stirring. On mild days, Timothy emerges, looking rather disconsolate, as if he wants a better place to dig himself in. Often, Gilbert is not quite sure precisely where he is. 'Timothy is buried we know not where in the laurel hedge,' he will write in 1784. But in some years, he can relax, knowing that his tortoise is content: 'Timothy has laid himself up under the hedge against Benham's yard in a very comfortable, snug manner: a thick tuft of grass shelters his back, & he will have the warmth of the winter sun.'

Monday 10
39. 29 4/10. E.   *Yellow-water-wagtail.*
Grey & still, sun, grey. *My well is shallow, & does not rise.*

Gilbert's yellow bird is probably a grey wagtail. The 'yellow' ones, delicate little birds with long black legs, are summer visitors from Africa, found mostly in the eastern and midland counties. The only kind that definitely stay here are the grey wagtails. But whichever bird he sees, he cherishes the whole wagtail species for being faithful to Hampshire: 'Wagtails, all sorts, remain with us all the winter.'

                    A YEAR WITH GILBERT WHITE

He once watched wagtails join swallows and martins in chasing off a hawk, but in his journals, he sees them more often running by the stream to catch insects, bouncing on the ground and shaking their tail, which 'bobs up and down like a jaded horse'. Long ago, when he started to include birds in his *Garden Kalendar*, he had noted acutely: 'The water wagtail seems to be the smallest English bird that walks with one leg at a time: the rest of that size and under all hop two legs together.' Most small birds hop, he writes, 'but wagtails and larks walk, moving their legs alternately'.

Tuesday 11

38. 29 4/10. E, NE. Antirrhinum Cymb: *continues to blow.*
Frost, ice, sun, soft *Trenched some ground in the meadow for carrots.*
& still, red even: *The planet Venus now makes a splendid appearance*
    over the hanger.

The icy morning isn't fierce enough to kill the toadflax, but he looks for patches of frost in the garden and on the hill. Country people, he says, 'who are abroad in winter-mornings long before sunrise', talk of how the ground is free of frost in places where the fog lingers, but if the air is clear, it freezes hard. Although it's cold today, with a shivering easterly wind, the ground remains soft. He's plotting next year's crops, sending old Larby out to dig.

From his bedroom window looking over the garden he watches Venus shine above the Hanger. This gives him pleasure all winter. Early next February, he will write to Molly:

> Venus was so resplendent last night, and is again this evening, that
> she casts a beautiful pale light on the walls of my chamber, &c.,
> and shows distinctly the shades of the window-frames, and the
> lead between the panes of glass, or, to speak as an astronomer, she
> *shadows* strongly.

Wednesday 12
38, 41. 29 5/10½. NE.   *Larby now digs & double trenches a weedy*
Grey, & mild,   *spot in the great meadow. The ground is black,*
deep fog.   *& mellow, & fit for carrots, for which it is*
    intended.

Double digging, two spades deep, is a fashion of the past. Trenching is even deeper – three spades' depth. It's looked at askance now because it disturbs the soil structure and disrupts valuable microbes and fungi. But I remember my father digging a long, deep trench, clearing the soil into a big heap at the edge, forking the bottom and adding manure. Then he dug another one alongside it, pushing the soil from the new trench back onto the manure in the first – and so on, across the plot, filling the final line with the soil from the first. So Larby has a lot of work to do, breaking up the rich meadow soil to make it light and crumbly – good for carrots.

In the areas where Gilbert grew crops, his men ploughed up the wheat stubble in December 'to prepare it for barley, & grass-seeds'. In the garden, they had to tackle a host of tasks before the frost set in: trimming the vines; carrying used dung from the cucumber beds to spread on the meadow; covering the tender asparagus and artichoke shoots with compost and leaf litter. Work never ceased, but it was worth it for the promise of next year's crops, flowers and fruit.

Thursday 13
42. 29 4/10¾. E.   *My well sinks, & when much water is drawn,*
soon Fog, grey & mild,   *grows foul.*
rain.

Although it rained hard a few days ago, the water levels fluctuate, and Gilbert's lament for rain continues, as it will do year after year, even in icy winters. 'Most of the wells in the street are dry!' he will exclaim in December 1788. 'Among the rest my own is so shallow as not to admit the bucket to dip!' Yet at the same time, the earth is soft enough for moles to work, heaving up their hillocks.

Throughout his journals over the years, the birds continue to sing their winter songs: dunnock and mistle thrush, great tit and coal tit, linnet, robin and wren. 'Wrens whistle all winter,' he noted in 1770, 'much more than any English bird in a wild state.'

Friday 14
46½. 29 4/10. SE.   *Trees condense the vapour, & drip much.*
Warm, deep fog.   *The dew lies on the outsides of the windows.*
                            Walls sweat much.

In heavy fog, the countryside is blotted out and the damp runs in streams down the trees. Fog could work magical transformations. 'Beautiful, picturesque, partial fogs along the vales, representing rivers, islands, & arms of the sea!' he will write in 1789. In London, that year's fog, thickened by smoke and fumes, would last well into January, so thick, Gilbert will learn, that men fell into rivers and carriages overturned in ditches. Some years later, Charles Lamb would maintain that you almost had to swallow a good London fog, rather than breathe it. To get the genuine brand, he advised his readers, 'please to ask for the "true London particular," as manufactured by Thames, Coal Gas, Smoke, Steam, & Co.'.

Even mild fogs, however, brought problems, misting windows and making outside walls sweat. Insulation was poor, and Gilbert was understandably worried about his new parlour. In 1779, he had found to his horror that everything was damp: 'the grate, the marble-jams, the tables, the chairs, the walls are covered with dew'. With an almost audible sigh, he realised there was nothing he could do, except to keep the doors and window shutters closed and hope for the best.

Saturday 15
48, 50, 51. 29 2/10. S, SE.   *Grey, sun, soft, clouds, & rain.*

In his note for the week, he writes: 'Some of my friends have sported lately in the forest: they beat the moors & morasses, & found some jack & whole snipes, most of which they killed, with a teal, a pheasant, & some partridges. The flight of snipes is but small yet. There is now, I hear, a flight of woodcocks in the upland coverts.'

There's a faintly nostalgic tone here, as if he wishes he, too, were out beating coverts. Wildfowl were always there in the 'morasses', or marshes, of Woolmer Forest in a mild December. As he had described them years ago, with psalm-like beauty: 'they lie in the great waters by day & feed in the streams & plashes by night'. In one great frost, the keeper tells him that sometimes there were flocks of five hundred ducks together, but when the lake froze hard – the ice so thick that it would bear a wagon – every bird disappeared.

The most unexpected December water bird was found in 1774, not in Woolmer, but in Selborne, on the Gracious Street ponds: '*Mergus serratus*, the Dun-diver, a very rare bird in these parts . . . shot in James Knight's ponds just as it was emerging from the waters with a considerable tench in it's Mouth.' This was a goosander, a large, handsome 'saw-bill' duck (its bill has a serrated edge for catching fish). Admiring its rust-coloured neck and crest, Gilbert turned to John Ray's account, finding that the male and female birds differed so much that some writers made them two species. This particular bird was a female, 'called in some parts the sparlin-fowl . . . the female Goosander'. The male is equally striking, a streamlined white and black, with a bottle-green head and red beak. The bird's appearance in Selborne was unusual enough for Gilbert to write a long, full entry in his journal.

Much later, in 1789, he wrote to Ralph Churton:

If you had stayed three days longer at Xmas we had made a staunch ornithologist of you for life; for a young farmer brought us in two rare water-birds, a *Gooseander* and *Dun-diver*, a drake and a duck of

      A YEAR WITH GILBERT WHITE

the genus *Mergus merganser* Linn. The beauty of the colours, and the curious formation of the parts would have struck you with wonder; and would have obliged you to reflect on the wisdom of God shown in the works of Creation; and perhaps in no instance more, than in that of the birds of the air!

Sunday 16
51, 51½. 29 4/10. SW. *Flies, & some butter-flies come out.*
Sun, soft, bright   *Beetles hum.*
& pleasant.

As Gilbert noticed, when the temperature reached 50°F (around 10°C), the insects ventured out. Gnats streamed from the hedge-tops, bees crept out of their hives and a few butterflies appeared, shivering their wings to stay warm. On such days, red admirals, which don't become completely dormant in winter, take to the air, while tortoiseshells and peacocks that have been sheltering, torpid, in sheds, dense ivy or woodpiles, rustle and stir. Long ago, Gilbert had noted that a peacock 'appears within doors, & is very brisk'.

When resting, many butterflies, with their dark mottled underwings, look like old leaves or scraps of bark. Once awake, they sip from old fallen fruit and winter flowers. But what flowers are there for them to settle on? When Gilbert wanders around the lanes and the Hanger now, he is not seeking plants in bloom, but seedlings to transplant into the garden – mulleins, foxgloves, stinking hellebore. Mistletoe clings to the boughs of his medlar tree and sometimes the garden walks are strewn with its berries.

The medlars and all the orchard fruits have been carefully stored. The only ripe fruit now is in the hot houses of the rich. Long ago, Gilbert had admired the way that the pineapples – or 'pines', as he calls them – grown in the hot house at Sir Simeon Stuart's grand old home at Hartley Maudit were being cut for eating in December. A decade from now, in 1792, Selborne's vicar, Christopher Taylor, will present him with a pineapple, which, Gilbert will say, rather half-heartedly, is, 'for the season, large, & well-flavoured'.

Monday 17
50½. 29 4/10. SW.   *Heards well is now dry: it is of a vast depth.*
Grey, sun, mild, small
scud, soft, & still.

Nothing stops his concern for water. At the start of September 1792, when news of massacres in France will fill British newspaper readers with horror, wells will still be at the top of his mind: Heards well, on Goleigh Hill, south of Newton Valence, which he mentions today, will continue to be of particular interest. That summer, he roped his nephew Edmund in to measure its depth and that of the one at nearby Goleigh Farm. Heards was 212 feet to the water and 250 feet to the bottom, they found, while that at Goleigh was shallower, 166 feet to the water and six more to the bottom:

> A stone was 4½ seconds falling to the water of Heards well; & 4 seconds to the water of Goleigh . . . Deep, & tremendous as is the well at Heards, John Gillman, an Ideot, fell on the bottom of it twice in one morning; & was taken out alive, & survived the strange accident for many years.

Tuesday 18
50½, 51. 20 3/10½. S.   *Earth-worms lie-out on the turf during these*
Dark, moist, & warm,   *moist, mild nights.*
rain.

The worms are busy. 'Many in copulation,' he had noticed five years before. 'They are very venerous, & seem to engender all the year.' When the icy weather comes, these worms will bury deep below the level to which the frost penetrates and curl into tight knots. If they get frozen, they die. But their eggs, cleverly cocooned, survive to hatch in the spring.

'Mrs White and Mr and Mrs Etty, who have been gossiping all the morning with Mrs Clements,' Gilbert tells Molly in a letter today, 'bring some imperfect accounts of good news both from India and off Brest. God grant that they may be true!' The friends had been discussing scattered reports from India of British victories against Hyder Ali and his Dutch and French allies, and even more significant rumours of naval manoeuvres nearer home. Since the summer, when French and Spanish ships had loitered in the Channel, the British had been blockading the port of Brest, in order to pin down the French fleet. Today's good tidings may have been rumours of the Battle of Ushant, which had taken place on 12 December. But news arrived slowly and Gilbert did not add any mention of this to his journal until Christmas Day.

Gilbert had also been conferring with Mrs Etty and other neighbours about sending orders for their winter supplies to Molly in London. This year and next, he asks her for 'half a hundred of good salt fish, to be sent down by Earwarker the carrier'.

The 'good Iceland cod fishes' were a staple, but not always free from mishap. One year, the fish arrived in a leaky barrel, and when the brine trickled out onto the kitchen floor, Gilbert told Thomas Hoar to take it to the cellar. Thomas picked it up by the iron hoops around the tub and got to the cellar stairs, 'when off came the hoops, down fell the barrel, out flew the head; in short the stairs from top to bottom became one broken wet scene of barrel-staves and codfish!' The lingering smell must have been terrible.

Thursday 20

50. 29 7/10. W. 7.   *Sun, soft & pleasant.*

The winter solstice has come. Gorse bushes flare like candles on the shortest day. Every year around this time, from 1770 onwards, Gilbert has recorded the birth of lambs at Farmer Lassam's Priory Farm. This seems strange to me, as I think of lambs coming in spring; in most breeds, the ewes will take the ram only in the autumn, after Michaelmas, and up here in Borrowdale, the ewes come down from the fells in November for tupping. But Lassam's Dorsetshire ewes are unique in their ability to take the ram at any time of year, so tupping can be brought back to August or September, with lambs in December or January. Some farmers had developed winter lambing so that they could send the sheep and lambs out to manure the barley fields before a spring sowing. But Lassam is probably simply aiming at the Easter market – lamb and mint sauce.

It's too cold for lambs to be born in the fields, so they build thatched pens in a special fold near the farm and feed the ewes on winter crops like turnips, or on linseed cake. Caring for the ewes, helping with tricky births and feeding milk to the weaker lambs is hard in midwinter. Lassam faces a crisis one year, when his ewes begin to lamb, but, Gilbert will say, 'His turnips are frozen as hard as stones.'

When Gilbert looked back through his journals, he found plenty of mild days in the week before Christmas, when gnats rose in columns from the laurel and the thrushes and robins sang. But in other years, harsh winds blew and trees were silvered with ice. There was, for example, the fierce December of 1767, when 'there were considerable falls

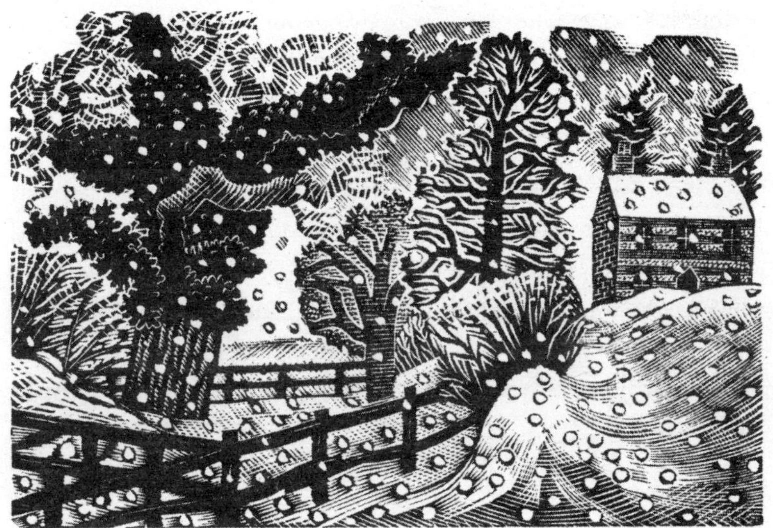

Eric Ravilious's illustration for 'considerable falls of snow', from *The Natural History of Selborne* (1938).

of snow, which lay deep and uniform on the ground without any drifting, wrapping up the more humble vegetation in perfect security'.

In one of the introductory letters that he added to *The Natural History of Selborne* in the 1780s, Gilbert gives a tumbling list of the feeding habits of birds in harsh weather – a good example of his 'watching narrowly'. Wagtails, he says, haunt shallow streams near the spring heads, 'where they never freeze', wading through the water to find the chrysalises of caddis flies and other insects; dunnocks pick up crumbs and sweepings from gutters; robins and wrens haunt outhouses and barns, searching for spiders and flies; and all the small, soft-billed birds poke around in the nooks and crannies of branches, fences, buildings, rocks and rubbish, hunting for the chrysalises of moths and butterflies. Among the tits, only the delicate long-tailed tit stays in the wood, while the others – great tits, coal tits, blue tits and marsh tits – come to the houses. In deep snow, he once watched a great tit, while it hung with its back downwards (to my no small delight and admiration), draw straws lengthwise from out the eaves of thatched houses, in order to pull out the flies that were concealed between them, and that in such numbers that they quite defaced the thatch, and gave it a ragged appearance.

The blue tit, meanwhile, picks bones on the dunghills and 'is a vast admirer of suet, and haunts butchers' shops'; as a boy, Gilbert had seen twenty or more caught in mousetraps baited with suet or tallow. But, he says, they will also peck at old apples and 'be well entertained with the seeds on the head of a sun-flower'. The smallest birds defy the harshest frost.

Sunday 23
51. 29 4/10½. S.   *Dark & moist, dark & blowing.*

It is windy, but nothing compared to some Christmas gales. On 23 December 1790, after a week of strong winds, roaring across the village and tearing thatch from the roofs, Gilbert will write with some excitement:

Thunder, lightening, wind, rain, snow! A severe tempest . . . Vast damage in various parts! Two men were struck dead in a wind-mill near Rooks-hill on the Sussex Downs: & on Hind-head one of the bodies on the gibbet was beaten down to the ground.

Monday 24
52, 53. 29 4/10⅓. SW.   *Soft & mild.*
30. Rain, rain, sun
& clouds.

Everyone, even the poor of the parish, brings green boughs into their houses, carrying in great bundles or filling their carts with holly, ivy and mistletoe, adding rosemary for remembrance. Holly and ivy decorate the church, their green scorched brown in some icy winters. In the eighteenth century, everyone in Selborne would have known the old carols, like the 'Holly and the Ivy' and the 'Coventry Carol'. New ones, too, would soon become standards: Nahum Tate's 'While Shepherds Watched Their Flocks by Night', Isaac Watts's 'Joy to the World', John Wesley's 'Hark! The Herald Angels Sing' and John Reading's setting of 'Adeste Fideles'. And a popular, loudly roared version of 'God Rest Ye Merry Gentleman' would have gone down well at Selborne's two pubs, the Compasses and the White Hart.

Over in Fyfield, where the catering was always substantial for Henry's large family and his pupils, this particular Christmas Eve is chaotic. 'Shelves behind ye kitchen fell with 21 cheeses,' Henry writes in his diary, 'providential escape, no one hurt, weight sufficient to have broken the ablest head.' And later: 'Cheese almost eaten by mice coming along ye ceiling to hanging shelf & not observed in time: stopped holes in ye ceiling to keep mice from cheese.'

Tuesday 25

49. 29 7/10¼. sw, s.	*A gardener in this village has lately cut several*
Sun, bright,	*large cauliflowers, growing without any glasses.*
& pleasant.	*The boys are playing in their shirts.*

Christmas Day. The church bells ring, and Gilbert takes the service and gives his Christmas sermon. His usual text was from St Luke: 'And the Angel said unto them, fear not; for behold I bring You good tydings of great Joy, which shall be to all people.' Gilbert stresses the identity of the Angel's hearers, themselves part of a farming community, 'poor, but good and harmless person, some diligent and careful shepherds'. From this, he makes the point 'that no person should think the worse of himself or any other upon the account of the meanness or poverty of his birth, since the circumstances of no person's coming into the world could be meaner than those of the Son of God'.

In his journal, however, he writes nothing about the Nativity or his clerical role. Instead, he expresses amazement at a fellow gardener's cauliflowers and notes, as he goes to take the service at Farringdon, that it's warm enough for the village children to throw off their coats. Next Christmas Day, he will see this again: 'The boys at Faringdon play in the churchyard in their shirts. They did so this day twelvemonth.'

For some years now, he has celebrated Christmas with the Ettys and the Yaldens. 'I reckon You have pure hospitable Christmas Doings in *your* three Neighbourly Families,' wrote John Mulso. 'Be jovial & refresh your Hearts, & forget not in your Cup your old & faithfull friend.' Now Barbara White is there too, while Gilbert's niece Jane Clements and her family come over from Alton, and his Oxford friend Ralph Churton is staying, and they have music, play cards, gossip, eat and drink. Inviting Churton in 1780, Gilbert wrote that the country-side was now 'shorn of its tresses and much in dishabille; but we still have pleasant footpaths, wild views and chearful neighbours. I will give you some roast-beef, plum-pudding, and other Xstmass-cheer.'

There was plenty of Christmas cheer from now until Twelfth Night, from balls and plays at grander houses – 'We have lately had some Dramatic Performances at the Deanery,' Mulso wrote from Winchester one year, 'where My Children shone very much' – to village feasts and competitions. Writing to Molly in 1785, Gilbert will tell her of a handbill declaring 'that there will be shot for at the Red Lion at Oakhanger a good fat porker, yards for inches, at a card . . . and also two boar-pigs to be bowled for'. Another bill announces that at Farringdon, a good watch, worth a guinea, 'is to be *played at farmering for*: he that *wins the farm* the three first times to have the watch'. But I still can't find out how 'farmering' was played.

Wednesday 26
48. 29 2/10¼. SE. 45.   *Much wind in the night.*
Dark & windy, rain,
rain, rain.

A little later, Gilbert went back to write opposite Christmas Day: 'On this day Admiral Kempenfelt fell in with a large convoy from Brest,

     A YEAR WITH GILBERT WHITE

& took a number of French transports.' This was the Battle of Ushant on 12 December, when a small British squadron under Admiral Kempenfelt, commanding the *Victory* – later Nelson's flagship at Trafalgar – had intercepted a French convoy setting out from Brest to the Caribbean with troops and supplies. Fifteen French merchantmen were captured, and the rest of the fleet, scattered in the gale, returned to Brest.

Gilbert's notes of events were scattered and random. There will be no note, for example, against 14 July 1789, the day of the storming of the Bastille, apart from an account of a woman from the Hanger bringing a fern-owl's nest and 'Benham skims the horse-fields. Rasps come in: not well flavoured.' At first, like many British people, Gilbert thought the overthrow of the absolutist *Ancien Régime* in France, Britain's old enemy, was a positive step, but he was shaken by the sense that even the most stable-seeming structures could topple. 'Surely,' he wrote to Churton,

> we live in a most eventful and portentous period; when wars, devastations, revolutions, and insurrections crowd so fast upon the back of one another that a thinking mind cannot but suppose that providence has some great work in hand! But of all these strange commotions, the sudden overthrow of the French despotic monarchy is the most wonderful – a fabrick which has been now erecting for near two centuries, and whose foundations were laid so deep, that one would have supposed it might have lasted for ages to come; yet it is gone, as it were, in a moment!!

He writes with some astonishment, too, against the journal entry for 21 September 1792: 'On this day Monarchy was abolished at Paris by the National Convention; and France became a republic!' And then, on 21 January 1793, opposite 'Thrush sings, the song thrush: the missle-thrush has not been heard,' he will add a note:

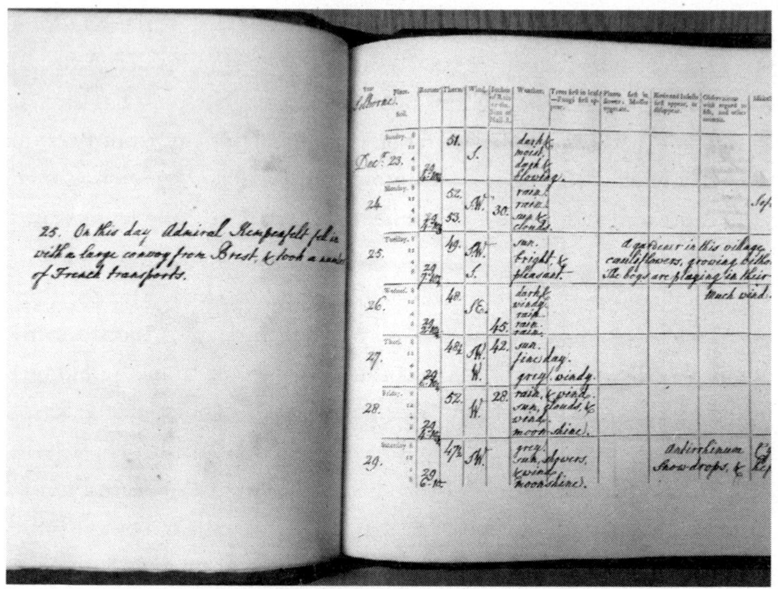

A quiet Christmas week in *The Naturalist's Journal*, with news of naval conflict off Brest.

On this day Louis 16th late king of France, was beheaded at Paris, & his body flung into a deep grave without any coffin, or funeral service performed.

The lack of coffin and service seem more horrific, somehow, than the death itself.

Thursday 27
48½. 29 6/10¼. SW, W. 42.   *Sun, fine day, grey, windy.*

On 27 December one year, when the ground is white with snow, Gilbert cuts into the hay rick that he made in the hot, dry months and is rather disappointed to find it 'without much scent, & consists more of weeds than grass. The summer was so dry that little good grass grew 'till after the first crop was cut.' Nonetheless, even the slightest waft of scent is a taste of summer past, and summer to come.

               A YEAR WITH GILBERT WHITE

Friday 28
47½. 29 6/10. SW.   *Rain & wind, sun, clouds & wind, moon-*
shine.

He is a naturalist, even indoors. One Christmas, he watched the black ants bustling around the kitchen hearth. Another year, in the quiet days before new year, he was fascinated by a house fly that had 'lengthened his life' – they usually live about a month – in the warmth of the parlour, relaxing like an old gent in the evening. 'He usually basks on the jams of the chimney within the influence of the fire after dinner,' Gilbert wrote, '& settles on the table, where he sips the wine & tastes the sugar, & baked apples. If there comes a very severe day he withdraws, & is not seen.'

Saturday 29
47½. 29 6/10. SW.   Antirrhinum Cymb: *in bloom.*
Grey, sun, showers,   *Snow-drops & hepaticas blow.*
& wind, moonshine.

The first of the next year's flowers have arrived early. Snowdrops spear upwards, and hepaticas – or 'pennywort', relatives of buttercups and anemones, plants that love chalky soil – shine like blue jewels in sheltered corners. He had looked out for these ever since compiling his *Flora Selborniensis*: 'Hepaticas in bloom all the frost,' he wrote in 1766. And his toadflax is still flowering away.

Sunday 30
47. 29 1¾/10. S. 43.   Helleborus foetidus *blows.*
Dark & mild, showers
& wind. Full moon.

On the last Sunday of the year, he goes across to Farringdon, looking up at the rooks and the old yew tree, seeing the stinking hellebore on his way.

Monday 31
45. 29 3/10¾. NE, S.   *Grey, showers, wet.*

New Year's Eve, wet and grey. He writes to Molly, promising to send
the next batch of worsted stockings for her father Thomas, asking about
the salt fish and hoping for 'more hints, quotations, and anecdotes' for
the *Antiquities*. Then he tells her that Uncle Will, 'coming down in
great glee from Newton to Selborne', had taken a shortcut down the
slider below the hermitage. The slippery ground hurried him on so fast,
Gilbert went on,

> that he fell with his head on a stump and cut his forehead sadly.
> He was stunned with the fall, and lay senseless for some time. I was
> shaving when he came in, and seeing at my elbow a courier with his
> hand full of letters, and all over dirt and blood, could not imagine at
> first who he was.
>
> Yr loving unkle,
> GIL. WHITE.

That's his last word for this year . . . But I can't leave him here, open-
mouthed, shaving brush in hand. Perhaps I can tip over into next year,
when the first week's entries are full of promise?

January 1782
Tuesday 1: Winter aconites blow.
Thursday 3: Mezereon blows. *Viola tricolor*, red lamium, & grounsel
blow. Hazel catkins open.
Sunday 6: Bees come out of their hives. Gnats play about . . .

CODA

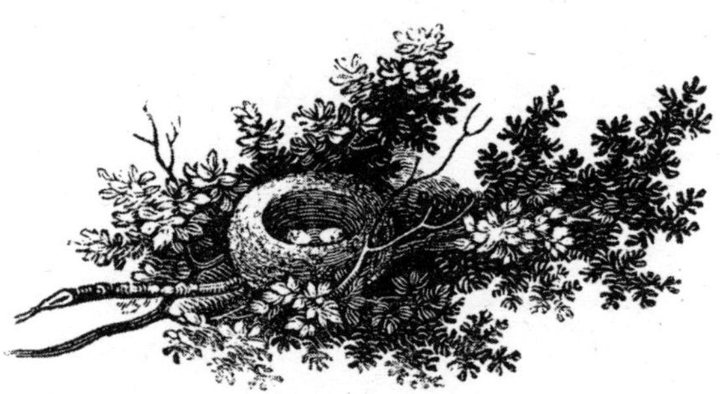

'Bird's Nest', Thomas Bewick.

GILBERT HAS ELEVEN more New Years ahead of him; eleven and a half more years of his journal. He sees his house fill up with family, counting nephews and nieces into the next generation. He plants his garden, records the Selborne crops and chronicles the ups and downs of village life. And always he watches the birds.

In the 1780s, he would continue to write and rework his *Natural History of Selborne*. There was always something to add: the anecdotes of the field crickets; the doings of Timothy; the goldfish at Fyfield; worms, butterflies, winter arrivals . . . He had kept copies of his letters to Thomas Pennant and Daines Barrington, always planning to make use of them. But when he went through them, he realised that these correspondences alone would not amount to the kind of local history that he dreamed of. For one thing, once he cut out the informal chat, such as accounts of visits from family and friends, and excised the overlapping passages where he had written much the same to both men, he was left with large gaps. He saw, too, that having often said that his concern was with 'the life and conversation of animals', his letters had concentrated largely on birds, and he needed more on all the other creatures. To fill the gaps, he looked back through his journals for material and wrote new 'letters'. Fifteen were supposedly to Pennant – around half the number originally written – and forty to Barrington. Then he interspersed these with the ones that he had actually sent.

At the same time, he edited, expanded and recast the original correspondences. Longer letters were split up. One to Pennant, for example, originally written in February 1772, became three separate letters: on winter flocks, November swallows at Newhaven, and an affectionate account of Timothy at Ringmer. He shifted and rewrote passages, altered dates (often for no clear reason) and added anecdotes and notes, many of them referring to discoveries that took place years after the date of the original letter. In one case, Letter 26 to Pennant, dated 12 May 1770, the printed text starts with a genuine letter about migrant birds, then includes a new section about the pairing of birds, before moving on to cats' fondness for fish (based on a journal entry made after seeing goldfish at Fyfield in 1782), and finally records the discovery of a male otter, shot by a stream near the Priory. The otter was recorded in his journal in October 1784 – fourteen years after the date of the supposed letter. At least once, Gilbert included letters to other people altogether. One, allegedly to Barrington, dated 3 April 1776, is actually a copy of a letter to his brother John, written the previous August.

He had help with the fiddly work of writing and rewriting, cutting and pasting, with Gibraltar Jack and Sam Barker among those who copied out the reworked manuscript at different times. Then, in the 1780s, he gave shape to the book as a whole. First, he wrote the nine new letters that open the book and set the scene. Then, working right up until the book was at the printer, he added six concluding letters on Selborne's climate. For these, he looked back to his journal entries on the weather, and its extremes of ice and snow, drought and floods, calm and storm. The book that began with soil and stone ended with the sky and the winds, the elements that no one could control.

Gilbert knew that he must eventually take the plunge and publish, and his family encouraged him, cajoling him and boosting his confidence. Molly and her husband Ben, who moved from South Lambeth to the Fleet Street shop, were intimately involved, but Ben White senior was also important. In July 1787, John Mulso, scolding Gilbert for his diffidence, insisted that he must consult his brother on spreading the word about the book, as Ben's experience and reputation 'in giving a Ton & a Currency is of vast Importance'.

By then, Gilbert had surrendered much of his text. But he was still tinkering, sending Molly a letter to be inserted before the last three or four about the weather, and promising just one more. Then he added: 'But that I may not be wanting in the most momentous part of my *Natural History* permit me to add, that your son is perfectly well and jolly, and much disposed to eat my roasted apples; and promises another double tooth.' While they looked after his 'brat', he looked after theirs, watching the little boy as he crawled and walked and talked. 'The *learned pig* is very intelligent,' Gilbert wrote a few months later, describing young Ben's astonishment at meeting Jane Clements, solemnly looking her up and down, wide-eyed at the ostrich feathers nodding on her hat. Gilbert loved the children and laughed at Molly's second son Tom, too. When Tom was three, Gilbert wrote that he 'talks much of mum's martin's nest; but complains that the young *poop* on the pavement'.

He still kept his early plan for an expanded journal of a year in some part of his mind. In the final paragraph of *The Natural History*, he wrote that he had wanted to add an 'Annus Mirabilis, or the Natural History of the Twelve Months,' but he had put this aside, he said, after the Unitarian doctor and writer John Aikin, whom Gilbert's brother John had known at Blackburn, published *A Calendar of Nature* for young people in 1785.

He had to accept that the book was finished, if not quite relinquished. In early January 1788, he told Sam Barker: 'I have been very busy of late; and have at length put my last hand to my Nat Hist and Antiquities of this parish. However I am still employed in making an Index; an occupation full as entertaining as that of darning of stockings, though by no means so advantageous to society.' Ralph Churton was with him at The Wakes, working on an index for the *Discourses on the Four Gospels*, by his friend and benefactor Thomas Townson. 'So that my old parlor,' Gilbert wrote, 'is become quite an *Index manufactory*.'

The result was idiosyncratic:

August, the most mute month respecting the singing of birds
Boy, an idiot, his strange propensity; eats bees, &c.
Castration, its strange effects
Cats, house, strange that they should be so fond of fish
Dispersion of birds, pretty equal, why

Echoes occasioned by the discharge of swivel guns

Herissant, Monsieur, mistaken in his reason why cuckoos do not use
   incubation

Tortoise, a family one

Worms, earth, no inconsiderable link in the chain of nature,
   some account of . . .

Molly was soon correcting the proofs of *The Natural History*, with
Gilbert fretting over his marking of italics, especially for the names of
birds, and asking her to get her father Thomas to check the barometer
readings. The *Antiquities* prompted more anxious reminders. Should the
letters be addressed to anyone? Please could they put '*sic*' in the margin
for 'very bad Latin' or 'strange uncouth spelling' and remove the note
on '*foxhunting* parsons; they must do as they like best'? (His note on
the fourteenth-century injunction against the monks joining 'noisy tu-
multuous huntings' ran: 'If the bishop was so offended at these sporting
canons, what would he have said to our modern fox-hunting divines.')

In March, Gilbert told Molly: 'Two sheets more, I conclude, will
comprize all the *Natural History*.' But it was too late. The text was set,
and hardly any of Gilbert's last-minute corrections appeared in the first
edition. Indeed, his additions to two Barrington letters – one about the
blossoming of plants, and the other about two Chinese dogs brought
back by Charles Etty – were included at the end of the whole volume,
after the *Antiquities*.

Gilbert could do nothing more. In July, Mulso wrote to congratu-
late him: 'I rejoyce excessively at your being now committed to the
Press.' He knew that Gilbert was full of 'Frights & Fears'. 'But I will
put You in great Heart,' he went on, telling him that James Chelsum,
chaplain to the Bishop of Winchester,

> told me that he had *seen your Book*, that it seemed a very promising
> Performance, & likely to get into great Favour, that it was well put
> forth & decorated with very pleasing Prints & Views . . . What would

you have more in your prae-existing State? This is but your Embrio Glory: your material & Substantial happiness & Enjoyment is to come.

Ben had clearly let some early proofs filter out. But Gilbert was not reassured. He felt, he told Churton, 'in no small squeeze . . . like a school boy who has done some mischief, and does not know whether he is to be flogged for it or not. As you were accessory to making me an author, you must defend me if I am attacked unreasonably.' The book was printed. The large engraving of Hieronymus Grimm's view from the Short Lythe made a superb fold-out frontispiece, and a few other engravings were chosen, including a vignette of Henry White as the hermit on the title page. All Gilbert could do now was wait.

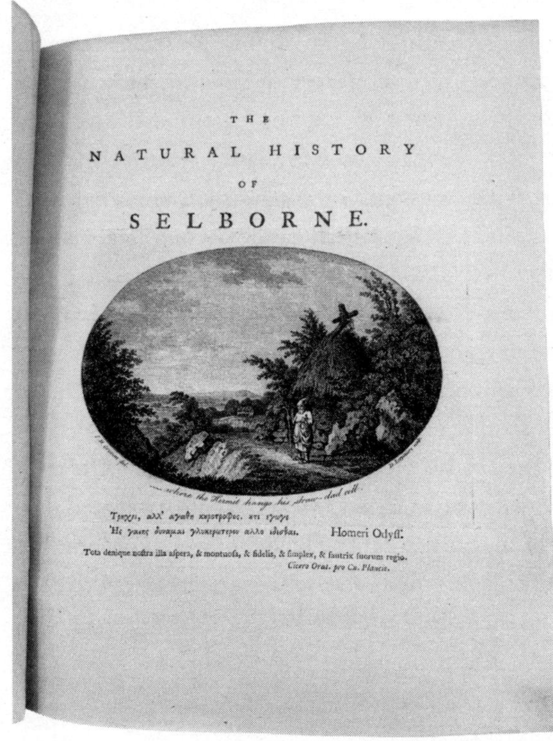

The title page of the first edition of *The Natural History of Selborne* (1789), with Henry White as the hermit.

THE YEAR 1789, the year of the French Revolution, also saw a quiet revolution in natural history, with the publication of three books: Erasmus Darwin's extraordinary long poem *The Botanic Garden*, Thomas Bewick's *A History of Quadrupeds* and Gilbert White's *The Natural History of Selborne*. It was a tipping point in spreading new ways of seeing and thinking about the natural world.

Although 1789 was technically the publication date, Bensley, the printer, delivered the sheets of Gilbert's book to Ben's bookshop, the Horace's Head, in late autumn 1788, and early copies were bound for family and friends. Mulso was delighted to finally see the work of his 'well-beloved friend'. He even praised the *Antiquities* that had worried him so much: 'you have given to them such a Grace in your Manner of treating the Subject, as would give a Pleasure & a Hunger of reading to a Man not an Antiquarian'.

On 3 December, Henry White wrote in his journal: 'Hamper from London containing ye *Natural History of Selborne*, presented by ye Author.' It was, he thought, a very elegant quarto with 'splendid Engravings' and curious investigations. But Henry was not there to celebrate with Gilbert when messages of congratulations came in at new year. On 27 December 1788, he died suddenly of a heart attack at Fyfield. He was fifty-five. The whole family, as Gilbert said, were plunged into 'deepest sorrow and trouble'. Gilbert, Thomas, Ben and Ben junior all sent money and scurried to care for the children, the youngest of whom was only six. Luckily, Henry's oldest son Sampson was able to take over his father's living at Upavon and curacy at Fyfield. As he was followed in time by his brother Charles, this meant that their mother Elizabeth could stay on at Fyfield vicarage with her daughters. Years later, the oldest of the girls, another Elizabeth, would become the second wife of Gibraltar Jack – one of several marriages between the White cousins, keeping the family circle close.

Soon after the publication of Gilbert's book, Thomas White wrote a two-part review (suitably restrained, as the author's brother should be), which appeared in the *Gentleman's Magazine* in January and February 1789. Then, in April, an astute account appeared in *The Topographer*, recognising the book as

> the result of many years' attentive observations to nature itself, which are told not only with the precision of a philosopher, but with that happy selection of circumstances, which mark the *poet*. Throughout therefore not only the understanding is informed, but the imagination is touched.

In Fleet Street, Gilbert's nephews Ben and John would publish a second edition, edited by John Aikin, in 1802, and a third in 1813. Slowly, this idiosyncratic book came to seem in tune with both the Romantic poets' sense of humanity's closeness to nature and the scientific value of precise observation in the field. Wordsworth read *The Natural History* 'with great pleasure' as a schoolboy; Coleridge annotated a copy of the 1802 edition – perhaps belonging to Southey – correcting Gilbert's views on instinct but hoping that his note 'will not be considered as lessening the value of this sweet, delightful Book'. Charles Darwin remembered how 'from reading White's Selbourne I took much pleasure in watching the habits of birds & even made notes on this subject. In my simplicity I remember wondering why every gentleman did not become an ornithologist.'

In the mid-nineteenth century, as new editions followed, appreciation shifted from Gilbert's observations to the place itself, the 'sequestered retreat'. Selborne was set apart, the *New Monthly Magazine* declared in 1839, 'from increasing commerce and population, from factories and filiations, manufactures and Methodism, genius and gin, prosperity and pauperism'. The view of Gilbert as secluded and innocent lingered long, before being slowly replaced by a recognition of his revolutionary approach and his energy and vivacity. For Edward

Thomas, in 1917, *The Natural History* 'overflowed with a new spirit – a spirit of minute and even loving enquiry into the life and personality of animals in their natural surroundings . . . it had style, or whatever we like to call the breath of life in written words'.

That judgement holds. As Virginia Woolf wrote in 1939:

His observation of the insect in the grass is minute: but he also raises his eyes to the horizon and looks and listens. In that moment of abstraction he hears sounds that make him uneasy in the early morning: he escapes from Selborne, from his own age, and comes winging his way to us in the dusk along the hedgerows.

He speaks to us still as both an acute empirical observer and a consummate stylist, an unexpected combination imbued with a personal voice that is key to the book's strangeness, and to its lasting appeal. When we brush aside sentiment and pastoral myth, we can see Gilbert White as an inspired, meticulous naturalist and brilliant writer. His study of the 'conversation of animals' was a pioneering step towards ethology, the examination of behaviour, which combines field studies with laboratory work on anatomy, instinct and learning. Long before the word was used, he was an 'ecologist', alert to the way plants and creatures are dependent on particular habitats, land use and climate. He spoke to everyone, not just to scholars, encouraging us all to look closely at the natural world. One of his twentieth-century editors, James Fisher, described him as 'the man who started us all birdwatching', while the naturalist Stephen Moss adds that Gilbert White and his admirers – Thomas Bewick, George Montagu and John Clare – 'found a connection between human beings and nature at the very moment when a dislocation between man and the natural world was beginning to occur'.

At a time of loss of species, rising seas, melting glaciers and ravaged forests, he reminds us powerfully of the vital, delicate balance and interconnectedness of all life, from parasitic plants to humans sowing wheat, magpies eating ticks off sheep's backs and worms improving the soil. Furthermore, he taught people how to discover this on their own, particular, local patch. It is an approach that anticipates 'citizen science' – for example, the RSPB's 'Garden Birdwatch' or the 'Big Butterfly Count'. And he showed, above all, that while there's no place for sentiment with regard to nature, there is plenty of room for feeling and for 'wonder'.

GILBERT KNEW THAT he had written something worthwhile, although it could never be complete. He was pleased with the response, hoping that 'as the world has been so indulgent to my book', it might even sell well enough to repay its editors – his brother Benjamin, nephew Ben and Molly – 'for the trouble and expense they have bestowed on the publication'. In December 1790, Mulso assured him that 'it is every where spoke of, and with the highest Praises', and that their old friend Jo Warton was 'excessively pleased with it'. The book that Mulso had feared he would never see was finally out in the world. But the old friends would not meet again: Jenny Mulso died that month, and her husband followed her in September 1791.

Gilbert was pleased to receive admiring letters, like the one from George Montagu, who was compiling a dictionary of British birds. He liked to hear that people were asking for the book in the Horace's Head and wrote proudly to his new friend Robert Marsham in August 1792: 'My book is gone to Madras, and several to France, and one to Switzerland, and one copy is going to China with Lord Macartney: but whether some Mandareen will read it, I know not.' His correspondence with Marsham, prompted by the book, was a great joy of his last years, covering a host of topics, from the trees they both loved to butterflies and bugs, tortoises and hunting dogs, elections and Boswell's *Life of Johnson* – and, of course, fern-owls, swallows, martins and swifts. 'I concur with you most heartily,' Gilbert wrote, 'in your admiration of the harmony and beauty of the works of the Creator! Physico-theology is a noble study, worthy of the attention of the wisest man!'

Marsham was eighty-two in 1790, but he was as keen and curious as Gilbert. 'Sir, I conclude that you are right, & that I was mistaken about the amours of the toad,' he admitted happily. 'Frogs, you know, generally leap or jump; now the people we talk of, only walk and creep; and I thought that I had particularly observed their swelled bellies.' Their exchange became a real epistolary friendship. 'You will, I hope, pardon my neglect, & write soon,' Gilbert ended one letter in December 1791. 'O, that I had known you forty years ago!'

WITH THE BOOK behind him, Gilbert continued to write in his *Naturalist's Journal*, sometimes even more fully than before, making notes on lime trees and squirrels, men bringing mackerel to the door, his bantam hens flying over the roof in surprise at the snow. He recorded family visits and trips to stay with Thomas and Ben. Now and then, abrupt notes would break into his ebullient entries, as on 1 February 1793: 'The Republic of France declares war against England and Holland.' That month, he is sowing radishes and carrots, wheeling dung and planting cabbages. As the spring comes, he visits Ben's new house at Marelands, on the other side of the oak woods of the Holt, describing redwings and starlings in the meadow, and deer and brimstone butterflies in the woods. In Selborne, there is thick ice in March, but soon the chiffchaff is heard in the Lythe and an early nightingale sings by James Knight's ponds. Timothy comes out and wanders round the garden, and a fern-owl chatters in the Hanger. In late May, 'My weeding woman swept up on the grass plot a bushel-basket of blossoms from the white apple-tree: & yet that tree seems still covered with bloom.' Barbara White makes rhubarb tarts and pudding, 'which was very good'. Molly and young Ben come to stay, the house martins build and the wells – as always – dry up.

On 12 June 1793, a day of bright sun followed by a golden evening, he writes: 'Cut eight cucumbers. Mrs Clement & children left us. Many swifts.' On 13 June: 'Cut ten cucumbers. Provence roses blow

   A YEAR WITH GILBERT WHITE

against a wall. Dames violets very fine. Ten weeks stocks still in full beauty.' Then, on the 14th, Mulso's son John arrives. He is Gilbert's last visitor, and his departure the next day is the last entry in *The Naturalist's Journal*.

The next day, Gilbert wrote to Marsham, saying that he had been troubled since the cold spring by a cough and 'wandering gout', a series of aches and pains 'that have pulled me down very much, & rendered me very languid & indolent'. A fever set in. The doctor came from Alton and gave him 'anodyne draughts' for the pain. He died on 26 June 1793, in his room looking out across the garden to the Hanger. He was buried, as his will specified, in Selborne churchyard, 'in as plain and private a way as possible without any pall bearers or parade'. He had asked for his coffin to be carried by 'six honest day labouring men' with large families, to whom he left a sizeable ten shillings each for their trouble. His grassy grave is at the back of the church, with a low headstone bearing his initials 'G.W.' and his dates. The carving is now almost invisible.

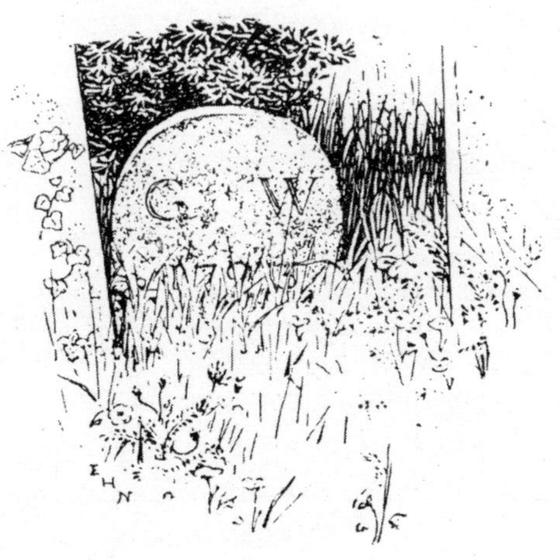

Gilbert White's grave. Illustration by E. H. New,
in *The Natural History of Selborne* (1900).

WHITE FAMILY TREE

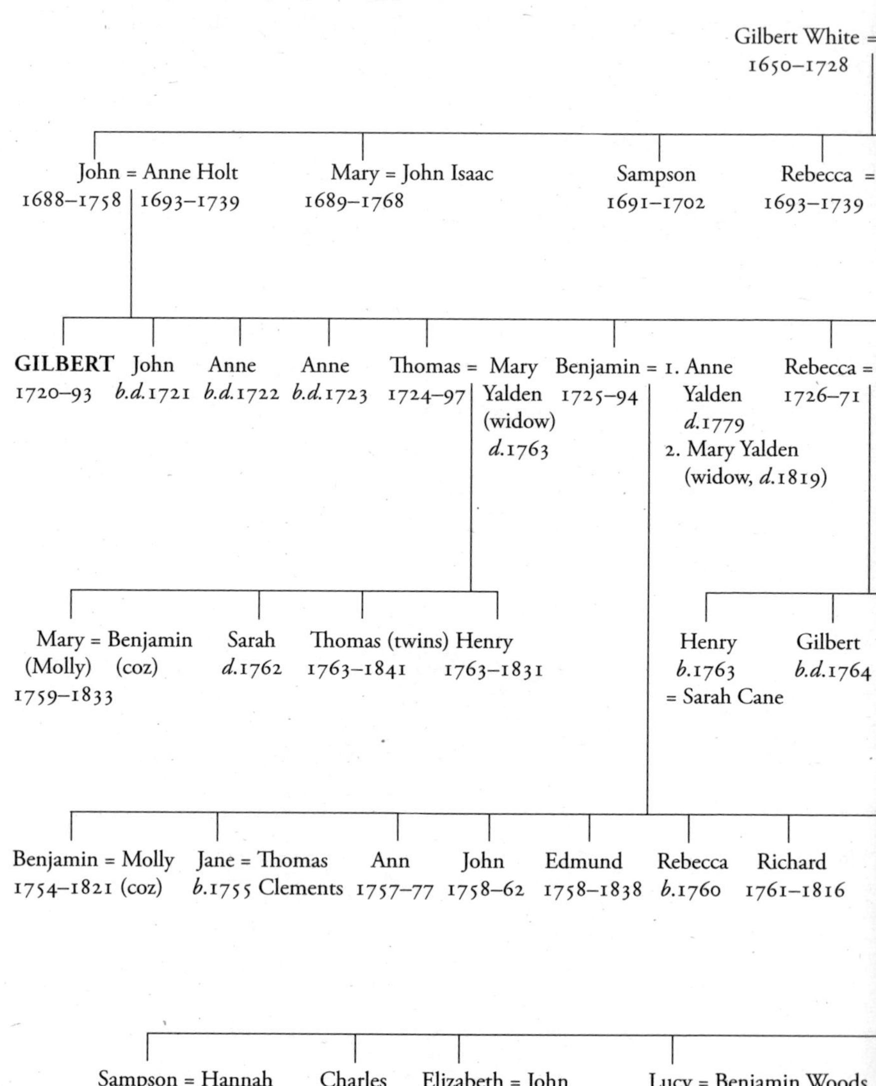

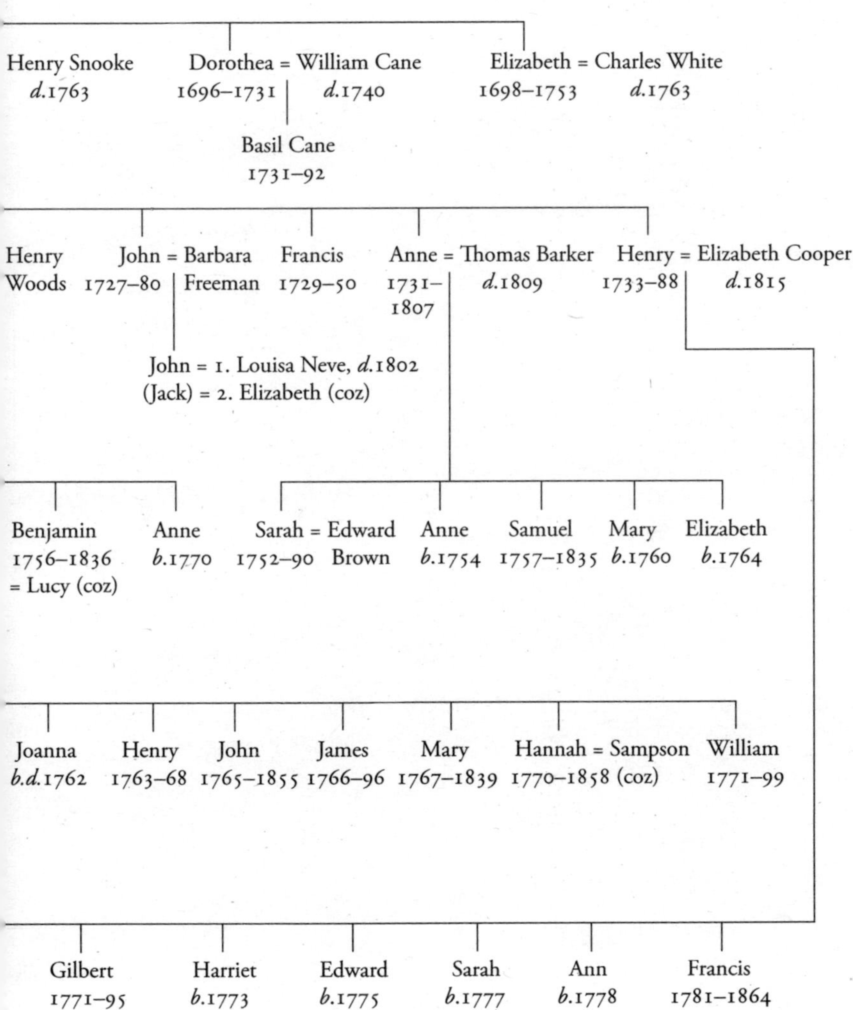

Rebecca Luckin
1664–1755

Henry Snooke
d.1763

Dorothea = William Cane
1696–1731   d.1740

Elizabeth = Charles White
1698–1753   d.1763

Basil Cane
1731–92

Henry Woods

John = Barbara Freeman
1727–80

Francis
1729–50

Anne = Thomas Barker
1731–1807   d.1809

Henry = Elizabeth Cooper
1733–88   d.1815

John = 1. Louisa Neve, d.1802
(Jack) = 2. Elizabeth (coz)

Benjamin
1756–1836
= Lucy (coz)

Anne
b.1770

Sarah = Edward Brown
1752–90

Anne
b.1754

Samuel
1757–1835

Mary
b.1760

Elizabeth
b.1764

Joanna
b.d.1762

Henry
1763–68

John
1765–1855

James
1766–96

Mary
1767–1839

Hannah = Sampson
1770–1858 (coz)

William
1771–99

Gilbert
1771–95

Harriet
b.1773

Edward
b.1775

Sarah
b.1777

Ann
b.1778

Francis
1781–1864

ACKNOWLEDGEMENTS

One of the great pleasures in writing this book has been working at the Gilbert White House in Selborne, and I owe particular thanks to the archivist, Kimberley James, for her warm welcome, and her tireless unearthing of material. I would also like to thank the head gardener, Keith Oakley, for helping me to understand the garden and the techniques of Gilbert White's day, and for teaching me to scythe, and Heather Vine for identifying the vines and annuals grown there mentioned in the *Garden Kalendar*.

Many people have helped me on my way. My first thanks go to Richard Mabey, whose books have been an inspiration, and whose encouragement and insight have been so heartening. I would also like to thank Richard and Polly for their hospitality, including a true 'Gilbertian feast'. I am grateful to the following people for their assistance: Francesca Greenoak, editor of the 1986 edition of the Journals; Brycchan Carey for his work on parson naturalists and Gilbert White; Stephen Moss, for generously checking my descriptions of birds; Steph Holt of the Natural History Museum, for information on bats; Kate Faulkner of Norton Farm, for explaining the work of the Selborne Land Partnership; David G. Bate of the British Geological Society, for information about wells and dew ponds; Marion Raynor of the British Bryological Society for explanation of mosses; Gavin Bowie for details of sheep farming and cereal crops; Ollie Douglas and Tim Jerome of the Museum of English Rural Life for researching the 'farmering game'; and Tim Russell for his personal permission to use the work of Gertrude Hermes.

I owe particular thanks to Zoë Stansell at the British Library, for her invaluable help when Special Access Manuscripts were not accessible after the cyber attack, and Will Beharrell and Andrea Deneau of the Linnean Society Library, which is a source of treasures as well as a magical place to work. My thanks too, to Zoë Hill of the Houghton Library, Harvard; to Rob Petre, Archivist of Oriel College, Oxford, and to the staff of Hampshire Records Office, Winchester. I also owe a great deal to the individual naturalists and societies who share their knowledge on the web: I have thanked several in my notes but would have liked to name many more.

Many thanks are due, as ever, to my warmly reassuring agent, Zoë Waldie, and to Melanie Jackson in New York, and to Jonathan Galassi of Farrar, Straus and Giroux for his long-standing friendship and support. At Faber, I am hugely grateful to my keenly perceptive editor, Alex Bowler, and to Kate Ward, with whom I have now worked for many years, and whose patience, grace, and genius for making books beautiful, never ceases to amaze. Thanks, too, to Ian Bahrami for his meticulous copy-editing, to Anne Rieley for proofreading, Sarah Ereira for the index and Emily Faccini for the lovely maps.

Among my friends, my warm thanks go to Alison Samuel, who makes me laugh and whose advice I always take without fail, and to John Barnard for his sympathetic support. I could not tackle anything without Hermione Lee as my first reader. Her presence, as I hope she knows, is beyond thanks. And above all, I have enjoyed exploring Gilbert White's world with Steve, from reading the diaries and watching the birds, to getting lost in wandering Hampshire lanes. This book is for him.

A NOTE ON THE TEXT
AND ILLUSTRATIONS

The text follows Gilbert White's entries in individual volumes of *The Naturalist's Journal*, 1768–93 (BL Add. MS 31846–31851; Volume III, 1781–83, is BL Add. MS 31848). Other journal quotations are from the *Garden Kalendar*, 1751–67 (BL Add. MS 35139), and *Flora Selborniensis*, 1766, the manuscript of which is owned by the Selborne Society, London. I have kept the original spelling and punctuation, including Gilbert's use of 'it's' as a possessive, but like Francesca Greenoak in the three-volume edition of *The Journals of Gilbert White* (1986), I have italicised scientific names. Greenoak's edition has a useful glossary–index, giving scientific and common names.

Quotations from *The Natural History and Antiquities of Selborne* follow the first edition of 1789; the copy manuscript, with additions and corrections, is in Gilbert White's House, Selborne, and can be viewed online. I have followed Paul Foster (*NHS*, 1993) and Anne Secord (*NHS*, 2013) in correcting typographical errors and using Arabic rather than Roman numerals.

Most of the illustrations date from within fifty years of Gilbert's life, including several from *The History of British Birds. Vol. I: Land Birds* (1797) and *Vol. II: Water Birds* (1804) by Thomas Bewick, who admired Gilbert and cites him often, and whose wood engravings are a visual equivalent to Gilbert's patient, loving attention to detail. I have also included a few later illustrators to show how artists responded to *The Natural History*, particularly during the wood-engraving revival of the 1930s and '40s. For a survey, see Simon Martin, *Drawn to Nature: Gilbert White and the Artists*, from the 2021 exhibition at Pallant House, Chichester.

ILLUSTRATION CREDITS

I am grateful to the following for allowing the reproduction of images, and I owe particular thanks to all the institutions who have now put works of art for which there are no copyright restrictions into the public domain. All efforts have been made to identify copyright holders. I apologise if there are any omissions and would be glad to learn about any copyright information that should be included in future reprints or editions.

Plate sections: Bridgeman Images: James Sowerby, 'Persian Iris', James Bolton, 'Mistle Thrush'; British Library, London: Gilbert White, *The Naturalist's Journal*; Cleveland Museum of Art: George Brookshaw, *Pomona*; Gilbert White's House, Selborne: portraits of Thomas White, Molly White; Houghton Library, Harvard University: Hieronymus Grimm watercolours; Linnean Society Library, London: Elizabeth Blackwell, 'Cucumber', Edward Donovan, insects; Yale Centre for British Art: Philip Reinagle, 'Tulips', William Lewin. 'Hoopoe', James Bolton, 'Nuthatch', Elizabeth Blackwell, 'Honeysuckle'.

ABBREVIATIONS AND SOURCES

AB	Anne Barker	
BW	Benjamin White	
DB	Daines Barrington	
GW	Gilbert White	
JM	John Mulso	
JW	John White	
MW	Mary (Molly) White	
RC	Ralph Churton	
RM	Robert Marsham	
SB	Sam Barker	
TB	Tom Barker	
THW	Thomas Holt White	
TP	Thomas Pennant	
TW	Thomas White	

Archives and data

BGS	British Geological Society
BL	British Library, London
BTO	British Trust for Ornithology
GBIF	Global Biodiversity Information Facility
GWH	Gilbert White's House, Selborne, Hampshire
Houghton	Houghton Library, Harvard University
HRO	Hampshire Record Office, Winchester
Linnean	Linnean Society Archives, London
NHM	Natural History Museum
Oriel	Oriel College Archives, Oxford
RSPB	Royal Society for the Protection of Birds
SLP	Selborne Landscape Partnership

Key Sources

This is a very select list, related directly to Gilbert White's work. All other books, articles, websites etc. are listed in full on their first appearance in the Notes.

Antiquities – Gilbert White, *The Antiquities of Selborne in the County of Southampton*, ed. W. Sidney Scott (1950)

Barker – Thomas Barker, *The Weather Journals of a Rutland Squire: Thomas Barker of Lyndon Hall*, ed. John Kington (1988)

Bell – Thomas Bell, *The Natural History and Antiquities of Selborne*, 2 vols (1923; volume 2 contains correspondence, accounts and other material)

Coulson – Louis Coulson, *To Edify and Delight: The Sermons of Gilbert White of Selborne* (2011)

Foster – Paul Foster, *Gilbert White and His Records* (1988)

FS – Gilbert White, *Flora Selborniensis. With Some Co-Incidences of the Coming, & Departure of Birds of Passage, & Insects; & the Appearing of Reptiles* (1766). Linnean Society Archive, SS/3, Tray 1/3. Transcribed in Greenoak, Vols 188–222

GK – Gilbert White, *Garden Kalendar*, 1751–1773. BL Add. MS 35139. 18–186

Greenoak – *The Journals of Gilbert White*, 1754–1793, ed. Francesca Greenoak, 3 vols (1986)

LL – Rashleigh Holt-White, *The Life and Letters of Gilbert White of Selborne*, 2 vols (1901)

Mabey – Richard Mabey, *Gilbert White* (1986, 1999 edns)

Mulso – Rashleigh Holt-White (ed.), *The Letters of Gilbert White of Selborne. From His Intimate Friend and Contemporary, the Rev John Mulso* (1907)

NHS – *The Natural History and Antiquities of Selborne* (1789)

NHS (1993) – *The Natural History of Selborne*, ed. Paul Foster

NHS (2013) – *The Natural History of Selborne*, ed. Anne Secord

NJ – *The Naturalist's Journal*, 1767–1793. BL Add. MS 31846–31851. Volume III, 1781–3, Add. MS 31848.

Phil. Trans. – *Philosophical Transactions of the Royal Society*, London

NOTES

3 'to give a frame': as Anne Secord notes (*NHS* (2013), xv), the nine introductory
letters may have been suggested by the appearance of the first number of *Bib-
liotheca Topographica Britannica* in 1780, which included 'Queries for the better
Illustrating the Antiquities and Natural History of Great Britain and Ireland',
reflecting the tradition of questions applied to parishes by antiquaries, including a
description of 'soils, topography, scenery, history and statistics of a parish'. Secord
also notes other suggestions from this source that are followed in the text of *NHS*,
including records of 'echoes' and local superstitions.

4 'The parish of Selborne': *NHS*, TP 1, n.d.

– 'first I must mention': *NHS*, TP 3, n.d.

5 'who know the name and habitat': Elizabeth Gaskell, *Mary Barton*, Chapter 5.
See Anne Secord, 'Elizabeth Gaskell and the Artisan Naturalists of Manchester',
Gaskell Society Journal, 19 (2005), 34–51.

6 'to have lived before the Fall': James Russell Lowell, 'My Garden Acquaintance',
My Study Windows (1871).

7 'Think only of my knowing': JM to GW, 26 Dec. 1773, M 247.

8 'one single straggling village street': *NHS*, TP 1, n.d.

– 'Finish'd a paved foot-path': *GK*, 18 Dec. 1762.

– 'the Hanger': *NHS*, TP 1, n.d.

9 'reposing herself on a bank': *NHS*, TP 6, n.d.

9 'the straggling street': Virginia Woolf, 'White's Selborne', *New Statesman and
Nation*, 30 Sept. 1939, in *The Captain's Death Bed and Other Essays* (1950).

– 'We abound with poor': *NHS*, TP 5.

10 'In a list at the start': MS of *NHS*, GWH. This list is initialled 'TW', for GW's
brother Thomas, who also collected statistics of birth and mortality in London
parishes in the early 1780s, writing about them for the *Gentleman's Magazine*. See
also GW, 'Answers to the Several Questions Respecting the Parish of Selborne,
1788', Houghton; Parish relief, Selborne Vestry Accounts, HRO 32M66 PUI.

– 'The more people understood those laws': see Katherine Calloway, *Natural Theology in the Scientific Revolution: God's Scientists* (2014), 71–94.

12 'our great naturalist': *NHS*, DB 7, 8 Oct. 1770. For Willughby, see Tim Birkhead,
The Wonderful Mr Willughby: The First True Ornithologist (2019).

– 'Ray's studies': *Historia Plantarum*, 1686. Ray's ideas in *The Wisdom of God as Mani-
fested in the Creation* (1691) and *Physico-Theological Discourses* (1693) were carried
forward by his pupil and biographer William Derham, in *Physico-Theology; or a
Demonstration of the Being and Attributes of God from His Works of Creation* (1713).
For context, see Patrick Armstrong, *The English Parson-Naturalist: A Companionship
Between Science and Religion* (2000), and also Stephen Moss, *A Bird in the Bush: A
Social History of Birdwatching* (2005).

12 'Far as Creation's': Alexander Pope, 'An Essay on Man: Epistle I, Part VII'
(1733). For a succinct analysis of the distinction between physico-theologists and
materialists with regard to the Chain of Being, see Diana Donaldson, *Picturing
Animals in Britain, c.1750–1850* (2007), Prologue and 29–35.

– 'not subjected': *NHS*, DB 4, 19 Feb. 1770.

13 'bare descriptions': *NHS*, DB 10, 1 Aug. 1771.

14 '*Axioms*, whereby the Cause': Hooke, 'A Method for Making a History of the
Weather', in Thomas Sprat, *The History of the Royal-Society of London, for the
Improving of Natural Knowledge* (1667), 173–9. Hooke's columns included wind,
temperature, humidity, pressure, clouds, illnesses, thunder and lightning, and
tides. See Jan Golinski, *British Weather and the Climate of Enlightenment* (2007),
29, 82–4, 115.

– 'Other initiatives': in 1723, John Jurin, secretary to the Royal Society, suggested
that people should send journals to create a pool of information; from this, doctors could draw conclusions about weather and illness, and farmers could decide
when best to plant.

– 'The weather of a district': *NHS*, DB 61, n.d.

– 'abrupt, uneven country': *NHS*, DB 10, 1 Aug. 1771.

– 'the cleverly organised *Naturalist's Journal*': the first set, in 1767, was published
anonymously by W. Sandby. Benjamin White persuaded DB to put his name to
the Preface. Foster, Chap. 8, n. 19, 184. After the weather data, the columns were
headed 'Trees first in leaf – fungi first appeared'; 'Plants first in flower: Mosses
vegetate'; 'Birds and insects first appear, or disappear'; 'Observations with regard
to fish and other animals'; 'Miscellaneous Observations, and Memorandums'.

15 'You are more able': 23 Aug. 1756, *Mulso*, 111.

– 'like a setting-dog': *NHS*, DB 15, 8 July 1773.

– 'I have minuted these birds': *NHS*, DB 15, 8 July 1773.

16 'No doubt their spines are soft': *NHS*, TP 27, 22 Feb. 1770.

17 'We are reading a poet': GW wrote formal poetry, too. For his technical understand-
ing, see Robert Hardy, 'Gilbert White and the Natural History of Virgilian Echoes',
The Classical World, vol. 95, no. 2 (2002), 163–9, and Brycchan Carey, 'The Literary
Gilbert White', *Birds in Eighteenth-Century Literature, 1700–1840* (2002), 173–92.
Carey makes the point that these trios of lines often feel very like a Japanese haiku, a
form that GW was unlikely to know.

– 'My world seems to be so enormous': Ronald Blythe, *Desert Island Discs* (2001).

18 'heath-cock': *NHS*, TP 6, n.d.

– 'but in former times': *NHS*, TP 44, 30 Nov. 1780.

– 'Of thunder': John Milton, *Paradise Lost*, Book II, where the fallen angels salute
Satan. White misquotes; it should be 'as the sound'. With the migrating pigeons
came small blue doves, or *rockiers*, the wild rock dove now limited to the coasts
and islands of Scotland.

January

21 'The only authentic portraits': flyleaf of vol. II of Alexander Pope's *Iliad* (BL Add.
MS 388), portrait signed 'T.C.'; a smaller portrait in vol. V is signed 'Portrait of
G:W: penned by T:C:'. This is probably Thomas Chapman, senior proctor when

White was junior proctor in 1752, who also appears in the list of chess scores, written inside vol. II, dated 26 March 1746. See June E. Chatfield, 'Likenesses of the Revd. Gilbert White', *Proceedings of the Hampshire Field Club Archaeological Society*, vol. 39 (1987).

– 'Jack is very tall': GW to JW, *LL* II, 4.
– 'little red room': GW to AB, 2 Sept. 1778, *LL* II, 28.
– 'a fine ribbed one': GW to MW, 7 Dec. 1782, *LL* II, 87.
– 'half a pound': GW to MW, 7 Jan. 1784, 8 Aug. 1783, *LL* II, 111, 102.
22 'half-bound': GW Accounts, GWH, White MS, AGW, 10. Other accounts show cheaper copies, costing only 1s 6d, but by 1787, Ben's price for a new copy had risen to 7s.
– 'Galileo's pupil Torricelli': in 1648, Descartes and Pascal added a scale, and Pascal's brother-in-law Périer took the barometer to the top of the Puy de Dôme, proving that the pressure declined with altitude. In 1660, Boyle and Hooke noticed a link between changes in the weather and pressure, and by 1670, clockmakers were beginning to make barometers for scientific use. They included Daniel Quare and Thomas Tompion, followed by Jesse Ramsden and Peter Dollond.
23 'Some barometers had a "wheel" attached': http://www.christies.com/features/ barometers-collecting-guide-12271-1.aspx. Nicholas Goodison, *English Barometers 1680–1860: A History of Domestic Barometers and Their Makers* (1968, rev. 1999).
– 'Tom Barker's barometer': Barker, 26–7. This was designed by the royal clock-maker, Daniel Quare.
24 'The US still uses Fahrenheit': in the UK, the Met Office began publishing temperatures in both scales in 1862, turning to Celsius only from 1970. For a quick conversion, subtract 30 from the Fahrenheit reading, then divide by 2; for greater accuracy, take away 32, then divide by 1.8.
– 'Gilbert keeps one thermometer indoors'; Jan. 1782 observations, TW, *Gentleman's Magazine*, vol. 53, no. 1 (1783), 186; also Bell II, 143.
– 'Frost begins to come in a door': *NJ*, 8 Jan. 1770, 20 Jan. 1772. The frost of 1768 is noted in *NHS*, DB 61. See also Peter Rowntree, 'Daily Observations of Outdoor Temperatures in England in the 1770s and Early 1780s', Royal Meteorological Society, *History Newsletter*, 1 (2014), 26–30.
– 'There *was* a time': GW to MW, 17 April 1779, *LL* II, 35.
– 'A strong funnel': Asit K. Biswas, *History of Hydrology* (1970), 193, quoting John Dalton, 'Experiments and Observations to Determine Whether the Quantity of Rain and Dew Is Equal to the Quantity of Water Carried Off by the Rivers and Raised by Evaporation; With an Enquiry into the Origin of Springs', *Memoirs of the Literary and Philosophical Society of Manchester*, 5 (1802), 346–7.
25 'Theories about springs and rivers': Robert Plot, *De Origine Fontium* (1684), and John Woodward, *An Essay Toward a Natural History of the Earth and Terrestrial Bodies, Especially Minerals: As Also of the Sea, Rivers, and Springs: With an Account of the Universal Deluge: And of the Effects That It Had Upon the Earth* (1695).
26 'is the hardest thing': *NHS*, DB 28, 8 Jan. 1776.
– 'These prognostics of weather': *A Collection of English Proverbs* (1670; 2nd edn 1678).
27 'linnets congregate': *NJ*, 9 Jan. 1769.

27 'the most numerous': Phil Gates, 'Look Beneath the Leafy Lasagne', *Guardian*, 5
Jan. 2024. See his blog, https://cabinetofcuriosities-greenfingers.blogspot.com.

28 'A young woman': Burials, Farringdon, All Saints Parish Register, 7 November 1769,
HRO.

29 'The Selborne Yew': *Antiquities*, Letter 5.

– 'older than Stonehenge': Fiona Stafford, 'Seeing the Wood for the Trees', lecture at
Wordsworth Grasmere, 20 July 2024.

30 'craftsmen carved the wood': Richard Mabey took two yew logs to Norfolk, sculpted
into forms that evoked the feeling of 'something still more deeply interfused' in
Wordsworth's 'Tintern Abbey'; Richard Mabey, *Nature Cure* (2006), 5, 166–74,
and *Turning the Boat for Home* (2019). Also Fiona Stafford, 'The Selborne Yew', 6
November 2020: https://www.euromanticism.org/the-selborne-yew.

31 'removed the hovels': *Antiquities*, Letter 6.

– 'teaching the poor children': Gilbert White snr's will, *Antiquities*, Letter 6.

– 'he qualified as a barrister': John White was admitted to the Middle Temple on
26 November 1707 and called to the bar on 15 May 1713. He had chambers in
No. 1 Elm Court, keeping a formal interest until his death.

32 'children arrived like clockwork': other children: John, b. Sept., d. Dec. 1721;
Anne, b. Oct., d. Nov. 1723; Thomas, b. Oct. 1724; Benjamin, b. Sept. 1725;
Rebecca, b. Sept. 1726; John, b. Sept. 1727; Francis, b. March 1729 (in East
Harting, Sussex, where Anne's family owned a farm); Anne, b. April 1731; Henry,
b. June 1733.

33 'Took up the yellow lilies': *GK*, 21, 22 Sept. 1757.

– 'he added narcissi': *GK*, 24, 29 Nov. 1757.

– 'Their sap contains proteins': University of Cambridge Botanic Garden website:
https://www.botanic.cam.ac.uk/the-garden/gardens-plantings/snowdrops.

34 'Weathervanes like this': A. Needham, *English Weathervanes* (1953).

– 'If I had not interposed': GW to MW, 17 April 1779, *LL* II, 34.

35 'Much Snowfall': HRO 33M66/P17, diary of Richard Yalden, vicar of Newton
Valence.

– 'My apples, pears': *NJ*, 11 Dec. 1784.

38 'sentinel' . . . 'small manor house': Mark Cocker, *Crow Country* (2007), 113, 116.

– 'A rook should be shot': *NJ*, 4 Feb. 1775.

39 'As intense frost': *NJ*, 29 Jan. 1776, at South Lambeth.

– 'three Warton children': Joseph (Jo), 1722–1800; Jane, 1724–1809; Thomas,
1728–1790.

– 'Jane, who wrote anonymously': her work included a conduct book, *Letters
Addressed to Two Young Married Ladies, on the Most Interesting Subjects* (1784), and
the novel *Peggy and Patty, or, The Sisters of Ashdale* (James Dodsley, 1783), which
was unusual for its working-class heroines.

40 'a list of the books': Oriel, MPP/W 6/2/1, first page of notebook.

– 'Firm, unremitting': James Thomson, 'Summer' (1727), in *The Seasons* (1730).

– 'The loosen'd ice': James Thomson, 'Winter' (1726), in *The Seasons* (1730).

41 'Nature! great parent!': ibid.

– 'take the pains to examine': *NHS*, DB 35, 20 May 1777.

– 'a small and despicable link': a 2022 study suggests that with the use of pesticides,

inorganic fertilisers and more frequent drainage and ploughing, earthworms have declined by over a third in the UK in the last twenty-five years. James Pearce-Higgins,
BTO, and Ailidth Jones, British Ecological Society Annual Meeting, 19 Dec. 2022.

42 'with marble sculptures': the story was told by the plantsman William Baxter in
the 1830s. Richard Mabey, *Flora Britannica* (concise edn), 171–2. For botanical
details, see https://frustratedgardener.com/2019/04/14/plant-profile-ivy-leaved-
toadflax.

44 'within sight of some window': *NHS*, DB 44, n.d.

45 'majestic mountains': *NHS*, DB 17, 9 Dec. 1773.

– 'A flock of wild Geese': *LL* I, 31. In 1742, Gilbert spent three months at Whitwell: GW to SB, *LL* II, p. 159.

– 'I heartily wish': 13 Dec. 1750, *Mulso*, 43–4.

– 'The Barkers had four girls and a boy': Barker children: Sarah, b. 1752; Anne, b.
1754; Sam, b. 1757; Mary, b. 1760; Elizabeth, b. 1764.

– 'without the least complaint': GW to MW, 4, 8 Aug. 1783, *LL* II, 102, 107.

46 'a bittern had been shot': *NJ*, 14 Jan. 1774. The others were shot in Emshot (by
Richard Yalden) and Greatham.

47 'Gilbert's favourite authorities': Ray's edition of Willughby's *Ornithology*, quoted
in Tim Birkhead, *The Wonderful Mr Willughby: The First True Ornithologist*
(2018), 237.

– 'after a brief revival': in 1997, only eleven males were recorded; in 2022, there
were around 228 booming males. See RSPB and BTO websites.

48 'The living was almost a family fiefdom': the Yaldens, *LL* I, 21, 74. Edmund snr,
vicar, 1717–46; Edmund jnr, 1746–61; Richard, 1761–85.

– 'We have this winter': GW to AB, 25 Dec. 1778, GWH, AGW 8.

49 'many elegant lessons': AB and girls stayed from 6 Sept. to 14 Oct. 1782. See GW
to MW, RC, 4 Jan. 1783; GW to Mary Barker, 22 Jan. 1783, *LL* II, 89–90, 92.
The quote is from Gassendi's life of the Provençal naturalist Nicolas-Claude Fabri
de Peiresc.

50 'come forth of the ground': Gerard, *A Catalogue of Plants Cultivated in the Garden
of John Gerard, in the Years 1596–1599*, Chap. 373: 'Of Winter Wolfs-Bane'.
Named *Eranthis hyemalis* in 1807.

– 'settering': https://bugwomanlondon.com/2015/12/09/wednesday-weed-stinking-
hellebore.

– 'good women': *NHS*, DB 41, 3 July 1778.

– 'Soft day': *NJ*, 25 Jan., 4 Feb. 1769.

52 'woodlark', 23 Jan. 1770. He sent DB a list of birds in the order of their first
singing. *NHS*, DB 2, 2 Nov. 1769.

February

55 'My Uncle White': MW to THW, 17 March 1783, Houghton MS Eng. 731
(246).

– 'six guineas a year': account book, Oriel College, MPP/W 6/2/1.

– 'but such as may be': Edward Bentham, *Introduction to Moral Philosophy* (1745).

– 'the toil': Gibbon, *Memoirs of My Life and Writing*, quoted in Walter Johnson,
Gilbert White, Pioneer, Poet and Stylist (1928), 43.

56 'spent his allowance': all items from his account book, Oriel, MPP/W 6/2/1.
   For the account books as early examples of meticulous recording, see Foster, 12,
   and Jill Atkins and Warren Maroun, 'The Naturalist's Journals of Gilbert White:
   Exploring the Roots of Accounting for Biodiversity and Extinction Accounting',
   Accounting, Auditing and Accountability Journal, vol. 33 (8) (2020).
 — 'The Doctrine of the SCREW': Thomas Warton, *Companion to the Companion*
   (1760). Poems for *The Student*, 1750: 'A Panegyric on Oxford Ale', 'The Pleasures
   of Being Out of Debt'. See also Mabey, 36, 38.
58 'Saw several empty nutshells': *NJ*, 23 Feb. 1775.
59 'Spiders, woodlice': *NJ*, 11 Feb. 1775.
60 'pipistrelle species': there is no way of knowing whether Gilbert was looking at
   the common pipistrelle or the soprano pipistrelle, as the differentiation was made
   only in the last few decades, thanks to the advances in bat detection and radio
   tracking. Both are present at Selborne. With thanks to Steph Holt of the NHM.
 — 'Foxes begin now': *NJ*, 13 Feb. 1778.
61 'Agnes Miller Parker': this is an individual print, but Parker made ten wood
   engravings to accompany extracts from the Nonesuch edition of *NHS* (1938), in
   The Saturday Book (1941–2); Simon Martin, *Drawn to Nature: Gilbert White and
   the Artists* (2021), 66.
62 'This is the person': Mabey, 57.
63 'had been eight Years': Swift, *Gulliver's Travels* (1726), Part III, Chap. 5. See
   Anne Secord, 'Hotbeds and Cool Fruits: The Unnatural Cultivation of the
   Eighteenth-Century Cucumber', *Medicine, Madness and Social History: Essays in
   Honour of Roy Porter*, eds Roberta Bivins and John Pickstone (2007).
 — 'paid Farmer Parsons': account book, GWH, AGW 10.
64 'To raise the prickly': William Cowper, *The Task* (1785), Book III, 'The Garden'.
 — 'No person shall be permitted': *Wiltshire and Salisbury Gazette*, March 1784. The
   prize for a brace raised from seed was 'a piece Plate of one Guinea and a Half value'.
   https://www.wiltshiremuseum.org.uk/?artwork=devizes-annual-cucumber-feast.
 — 'large well-grown cucumbers': *NJ*, April 1763.
 — 'Molly White is very well': GW to AB, 30 March 1775, *LL* I, 285.
65 'Mrs Etty's niece': Mary Souter m. Nicolls Raynsford of Brixworth Hall, 5 Feb.
   1781. Her journey from India: GW to MW, 17 April 1779, *LL* II, 35.
 — 'they would be troubled': GW to MW, 6 Feb. 1781, *LL* II, 66.
66 'Sea-gulls, winter mews': *NJ*, 3 Nov. 1777, 26 Nov. 1776, 15 Nov. 1783.
67 'when Noah sent one out': Stephen Moss, 'Dodo, Eagle, Sparrow . . . The 10
   Birds That Changed the World for Ever', *Observer*, 19 Feb. 2023.
 — 'Bear's foot': *FS*, 23 April 1766.
 — 'in the deep stony lane': *NHS*, DB 41, 3 July 1778.
68 'Oft in this season': James Thomson, 'Autumn' (1730), in *The Seasons* (1730).
69 'I never heard or read': GW to SB, 26 March 1781, *LL* II, 67, with extract from
   John Reinhold Forster: *Observations Made During a Voyage Round the World on
   Physical Geography, Natural History, and Ethnic Philosophy* (1778), 120. BW had a
   share in Forster's volume of Antarctic genera.
 — 'I shall read Longinus': John Wooll, *Biographical Memoirs of the Late Revd. Joseph
   Warton* (1806), vol. I, 9.

70 'Concerning Enthusiasm': Anthony Ashley-Cooper, Lord Shaftesbury, 'A Letter Concerning Enthusiasm, to my Lord *****' (1708), included in his *Characteristics of Men, Manners, Opinions, Times* (1711).

— 'We have had for these three days': *Northampton Mercury*, 19 Feb. 1781, and *Gentleman's Magazine*, Feb. 1781.

71 'A hard-trotting horse': 11 Feb. 1781, *Mulso*, 295.

— 'dropping in to Hogarth's studio': 11 April 1750, *Mulso*, 33.

— 'I was at ye Races': Aug. 1744, *Mulso*, 3.

— 'Busser': 17 July 1749, *Mulso*, 20.

72 'I gather': 29 May 1750, *Mulso*, 35.

— 'I will imitate You': 11 Feb. 1781, *Mulso*, 296.

— 'peculiar way of shrugging': Georgiana White (Benjamin White senior's grand-daughter), 'Gleanings', Houghton MS Eng. 731 (67).

74 'Harry and his wife': GW to SB, 1 July 1776, *LL* I, 322.

— 'eldest son of a baronet': Foster, 166, n. 9.

— 'in the publick papers': JW to GW, 10 Jan. 1759, *LL* I, 110–12.

75 'my South country correspondent': BL Add. MS 35138, GW to TP, 28 Nov. 1768.

— 'John responded eagerly': for the letters from JW in Gibraltar, see Foster, 115–28, and transcriptions in Foster, 'The Gibraltar Correspondence of Gilbert White', *Notes & Queries* (1985), vol. 32, nos 2–4; and later letters, 1770–7, in Bell II, 3–94, including Latin correspondence with Linnaeus, 1771–4.

— 'Mr Lee, the botanist': GW to JW, 25 Jan. 1771, *LL* I, 196.

— 'The old arch-naturalist': GW to TP, 19 March 1772, *LL* I, 208.

— 'Giovanni Scopoli's pioneering studies': Giovanni Scopoli (1723–88). His studies of the Carniola region (now in Slovenia) included *Flora Carniolica* (1760), *Entomologia Carniolica* (1763), and *Anni Historico-Naturales*, on birds (1769–72).

— 'Your butterfly-like insect': GW to JW, 26 May 1770, *LL* I, 178–80. For the modern names, see the GBIF website: https://www.gbif.org.

76 'There is endless room': *NHS*, DB 5, 12 April 1770. For observations, GW uses the word 'autopsia', not related to autopsy at death, but meaning 'eyewitness'. From the Greek *auto* ('self') and *opsis* ('sight').

77 'with that relish': GW to JW, 1 Oct. 1773, *LL* I, 228.

— 'all the Georgics through': GW to JW, 29 April 1774, *LL* I, 251.

— 'I should wish': 12 Jan. 1774, *LL* I, 238.

78 'to give him balm tea': Mabey, 131.

— 'He is now a real service': GW to JW, 4 Feb. 1774, *LL* I, 240.

— 'As to Jack's': GW to JW, 12 Aug. 1775, *LL* I, 288.

— 'The ivy': *NJ*, 14 Feb. 1774.

79 'The dry pith of ivy berries': RSPB.org, 'Birds and Berries'. *Guardian* gardening blog, Kate Bradbury, 19 Feb. 2015.

— 'get a chaplaincy in a Regiment': 7 Sept. 1745, *Mulso*, 9.

— 'How does Tom Mander's System': 27 Oct. 1746, *Mulso*, 16.

80 'popping and snapping': 21 Aug. 1747, *Mulso*, 17.

— 'As an electrician': GW to JW, 30 Jan. 1776, *LL* I, 300.

— 'You live a scambling': 30 Aug., 6 Oct. 1750, *Mulso*, 39, 41.

81 'Molly's son Glyd': Glyd White (1790–1869), ordained 1813; Coulson, xi.
82 'Lazarus was the starting point': Linnean, SS3. The text is from John II, verse 33. Transcribed in 2011 by Mich Maroney, https://commonground08.wordpress.com/category/gilbert-white. Other sermons are held in GWH, Houghton MS Eng. 731 (68, 169–88), and HRO 16M97/1/12–16.
83 'Perhaps it was through him': flyleaf inscription: 'Gil. White, Oriel College, Oxon – Given to me by Mr Alexander Pope on my taking the degree of B:A – June 30, 1743 – 6 volumes'. For Hales, see D. G. C. Allan and R. E. Schofield, *Stephen Hales: Scientist and Philanthropist* (1980).
– 'whole mind seemed': GW to RM, 25 Feb. 1791, *LL* II, 230–1.
84 'to find that I had escaped': GW to SB, 26 March 1781, *LL* II, 68.
85 'Mountain-wine, very old': accounts, Bell II, 316–17.
– 'a feather-topped grizzle wig': account book, 16 April 1752, Bell II, 317.
86 'round China-turene': Bell II, 323.
– 'Our Girls are clear': 27 Jan. 1753, *Mulso*, 65.
– '& to the saving of my Heart': 6 Dec. 1755, *Mulso*, 105–6.
87 'We can make You a Bed': 23 Aug. 1756, *Mulso*, 110.
– 'Gilbert had around £250 a year': the Bank of England calculator estimates this as £35,498 in 2024, around the same as the UK average income (https://www.bankofengland.co.uk/monetary-policy/inflation/inflation-calculator). Government bonds: GWH, account books, 13.5, and HRO 16M97/1–2. GW's account books and receipted bills are divided between GWH, AGW 10, A13.5, and 1HRO 16M97/1/1–5, 16M97/12/2, 99M91.
88 'half-year's petticoats': account books, GWH, AGW 10.

March

91 'Ben . . . had flourished': Ben White's career began as partner to John Whiston, Tom Barker's uncle, in 1745.
– 'there stood a confounded': 29 Jan. 1752, 11 March 1753, *Mulso*, 57, 67.
– 'Ben took a long lease': Ben White held a twenty-one-year lease on the Vauxhall Escheat. It was renewed by his trustees when he died in 1794 and held by his estate until 1821. 'Vauxhall and South Lambeth: Vauxhall Escheat', in *Survey of London: Volume 26, Lambeth: Southern Area* (1956), 73–80.
– 'has furnished in a splendid manner': GW to AB, 7 Feb. 1776, *LL* I, 306.
92 'Respects over the way': GW to MW, 2 Nov. 1778, *LL* II, 32.
– 'selling stock': correspondence of 1746–7, GW and TW with father John and family attorney Mr Butcher, Houghton MS Eng. 731. Gilbert's maternal grandmother left money inherited from her family to her widower, Revd Thomas Holt, who bequeathed it to his half-brother, also Thomas Holt.
– 'began to sell his stock': GW to AB, 7 Feb. 1776, *LL* I, 305.
– 'Gilbert estimated around £300 each': GW to JW, 30 Jan. 1776, *LL* I, 301.
– 'he wrote articles': Arthur Sherbo, 'Thomas Holt White [T. H. W.] (1724–1797), Naturalist and Literary Critic', *ODNB*. TW contributed twenty-five letters between 1769 and 1790. See Emily Lorraine de Montluzin, 'Attributions of Authorship in the *Gentleman's Magazine*, 1731–1868: An Electronic Union List', https://bsuva.org/bsuva/gm2/GMintro.html.

93 'the Society's *Transactions*': joint papers in *Phil. Trans.*, LXIX (1779)–LXXXIII (1793).
  – 'Thermometer placed in a shade': TW, *Gentleman's Magazine*, vol. 53, 1 (1783), 186.
  – 'was the first plant described': *Curtis's Botanical Magazine*, 1, Table 1 (1786).
  – 'commonplace book': GWH, A10.1.
94 'London Botanical Garden': Curtis thanked TW and DB for their 'generosity and public spirit', to which 'the garden in great degree owes its existence', *Gentleman's Magazine*, 69/2 (1799), 636; Thomas White, *ODNB*. Curtis was an expert on grasses, and Thomas sent turf from Hampshire and Sussex. Other supporters were John Coakley Lettsom and William Fothergill.
  – 'a very friendly man': GW to SB, 20 March 1776, *LL* I, 313.
  – 'the warm thick slobber': Seamus Heaney, 'Death of a Naturalist' (1966), in *New Selected Poems 1966–1987* (1990).
  – 'The frogs have began': John Clare, *The Natural History Prose Writings of John Clare*, ed. Margaret Grainger (1983).
  – 'The frog croaks loud': 'Dyke Side', *John Clare: Poems of the Middle Period*, eds Eric Robinson, David Powell and P. M. S. Dawson, vol. 5 (2003), 379.
95 'the copulation of frogs': *NHS*, TP 17, 18 June 1768.
96 'These gardens are famous': British History Online: *The Environs of London*, vol. I, Surrey (1792), and *Victoria County History, Surrey*, vol. IV (1912).
97 'You may smile': GW to MW, 9 April 1781, *LL* II, 69.
99 'The uplands glow': *FS*, 28 April 1766.
  – 'The old name "pilewort"': see http://www.livingfield.co.uk/medicinal/pilewort (James Hutton Institute, Dundee); Gerard is quoted in Geoffrey Grigson, *The Englishman's Flora* (1958).
100 'Rooks are continually fighting': *NJ*, 12 March 1775.
  – 'Some unhappy pairs' . . . 'Thus did the raven': *NJ*, 18 March 1775.
  – 'As soon as rooks have finished': *NJ*, 19 March 1775.
  – 'rooks, in the breeding season': *NHS*, DB 43, 9 Sept. 1778.
101 'Is it because rooks': *NHS*, DB 11, 8 Feb. 1772.
  – 'a booby of a carter': *NHS*, TP 15, 30 March 1768.
102 '*Testudo Graeca* of Linnaeus': at times, Timothy has been identified as an Algerian and a South American tortoise, but is now judged to be *Testudo ibera graeca*. His shell, given to the British Museum by Gilbert's great-niece Georgiana White, is in the Natural History Museum.
103 'seemed quite out of his element': *NJ*, 1 July 1780.
  – '& indeed it is a Subject': 28 Aug. 1765, *Mulso*, 200.
  – 'A Calendar of Flora': *FS* was edited in 1911 by Wilfred Mark Webb as *A Nature Calendar*.
105 'a copy of the Latin *Flora Anglica*': see Foster, 70. Hudson, a librarian at the British Museum, used Hans Sloane's herbarium to apply the new Linnaean classification.
106 'twenty-four bumblebee species': see https://www.bumblebeeconservation.org and the more technical BWARS (UK Bees, Wasps and Ants Recording Society) web-site. The early bumblebee is *Bombus pratorus*; the bumblebee that nests under-ground is *Bombus terrestris*. Both emerge in February/March. *Bombylius Medius*, a kind of bee-fly mimicking a bee, was identified by Linnaeus in 1758.

108 'I make no doubt': *NHS*, TP 16, 18 April 1768.

109 'now lying before me': *NHS*, TP 19, 17 Aug. 1768.

  – 'A further instance': *NHS*, DB 14, 26 March 1773.

110 'watch for wagons': *NJ*, 21 Aug. 1791.

111 'few antiquities': GW to JW, 29 April 1774, *LL* I, 250.

  – 'I fear the sweet': 22 July 1779, *Mulso*, 285–6.

  – 'mighty hunters': GW to SB, 2 Sept. 1778, *LL* II, 29.

112 'the fourteenth-century *Vision of Piers Plowman*': *Antiquities*, 90–1, Letter 17. White's footnote quotes Warton's *History*, vol. I, 29. See also TW, *Gentleman's Magazine*, November 1755; Arthur Sherbo, 'Samuel Pegge, Thomas Holt White and Piers Plowman', *Yearbook of Langland Studies* 1 (1987), 122–8.

  – 'Tom Warton's *History of English Poetry*': Warton also argued that the poems of 'Thomas Rowley', allegedly a fifteenth-century priest, were the work of the teenage Thomas Chatterton, who had killed himself in his London garret – probably accidentally – with arsenic and opium in 1770, a martyr in the eyes of the Romantics.

113 'pondering their derivation': *Antiquities*, Letter 2, n. 3.

  – 'the degree of dustiness': GW to SB, 26 March 1781, *LL* II, 68.

  – 'Mem. Sowed Radishes': *GK*, 16 April 1752.

114 'very subject': Philip Miller, *Gardeners Dictionary*, 754, listed under 'LEUCIOUM *luteum*' for 'stock Gillyflower'.

  – 'Sow'd three Rows': *FS*, 15 April 1752.

  – 'to see the gardens': to Blenheim, 5–6 June 1752; Stowe, 11–12 August 1752. Bell II, 319, 321.

  – 'cut into a Mathematical Figure': Joseph Addison, *The Spectator*, no. 411, 25 June 1712.

115 'We have not reformed': 13 Nov. 1754, *Mulso*, 92. The oil jars were installed in 1756; statue of Hercules, 1757–8; hermitage and obelisk, 1758; mount and wine pipe in meadow, 1759; ha-ha, fruit wall and sundial, 1761; alcove, 1762.

119 'an excellent fence': *NJ*, 24 Jan. 1761. After the ditch was dug in late 1759, it was left to settle for almost two years before the supporting wall was built.

  – 'stones of a sandy nature'. *NJ*, 25 July 1761.

120 'Breda Apricot': *GK*, 30 Dec. 1761.

April

124 '*The History of Selborne* is a grand book': Eric Ravilious to Helen Binyon, Jan. 1936, in Jeremy Greenwood, *Ravilious: Engravings* (2008), 63.

125 'The *Bombylius medius* abounds': *NJ*, 6 April 1774.

  – '"Grass lamb" and "house lamb"': William Ellis, *A Compleat System of Experienced Improvements, Made On Sheep, Grass-Lambs, and House-Lambs: Or, the Country Gentleman's and the Shepherd's Sure Guide* (1749).

126 '*Hirundo domestica!!!*': *NJ*, 13 April 1768.

  – 'The hirundines are': *NHS*, DB 15, 8 July 1773.

127 'of their retiring' . . . 'A Swedish naturalist': Alexander Berger, whose *Flora* was included in Stillingfleet's *Tracts*. *NHS*, TP 12, 4 Nov. 1767.

  – 'We must not' . . . 'a bird may travel': *NHS*, DB 9, 12 Feb. 1771.

– 'they were all on the wing' . . . 'I could not help': *NHS*, TP 23, 28 Feb. 1769.

128 'in the sheltered district': *NHS*, DB 55, 10 Oct. 1781.

129 'It has been my misfortune': *NHS*, TP 10, 4 Aug. 1767.

130 'I have received': GW to JW, 2 Nov. 1773, *LL* I, 233.

– 'a quaint and magisterial': *NHS*, TP 40, 2 Sept. 1774.

– 'new editions': third edn, 1770; fourth edn, 1776. BW paid £100 for permission to publish the second edn, and Pennant gave all profits to the Welsh Charity School, London.

– 'always quarrel': GW to JW, 29 March 1774, *LL* I, 244. For the 1790s, see 'Pennant and His Publisher', *Archives of Natural History*, 11 (1982), 61–8.

131 'If he survives': GW to TP, 8 Oct. 1768, BL Add. MS 35138, *LL* I, 160.

– 'perhaps the very best': Barrington, introductory notes to *The Naturalist's Journal*.

– 'the leaden mace': Horace Walpole, *Letters of Horace Walpole*, vol. IV, Letter 202.

132 'prevented them being': Mabey, 120–1; Barrington, *Miscellanies* (1781).

– 'Gilbert responded eagerly': *NHS*, DB 1 and 2, 30 June and 2 Nov. 1769. See Foster, 25.

– 'published a long essay': 'Essay on the Periodical Appearing and Disappearing of Different Kinds of Birds', *Phil. Trans.*, 62 (1772), 265–326. Received 29 November 1771, read April, May 1772.

133 'on haws, yew berries, &c.': *NJ*, 9 April 1774.

– 'not without some degree of shame': *NHS*, TP 25, 30 Aug. 1769.

– 'we may conclude': *NHS*, TP 38, 15 March 1773.

– 'on sides of small brooks': Sampson Newberry to GW, 14 June 1774, *LL* I, 253.

– 'immune systems': Royal Society, 'Recovery of Constitutive Immune Function After Migratory Endurance Flight in Free-Living Birds', *Biological Letters*, 19, 2 (Feb. 2023).

– 'If bees': *NJ*, note on blank page opposite 30 April 1774.

134 'Post Office officials recommended': GW to MW, 9 April 1781, *LL* II, 69. Post Office advertisement, February 1782, recommended 'first writing the name, date, and year at the end of the note and the letter and number at the other end. By this means each part will contain a sufficient specification of the whole and prevent any kind of difficulty in the payment of it at the Bank of England to the right owner, in case of the loss of the other part' (*Northern Echo*, 21 Nov. 2021).

– 'probably he put it': MW to THW, 17 April 1781, HRO 16M97/4/12 (205).

– 'called slugs': *NHS*, DB 35, 20 May 1777.

135 'slugs, which are': *NJ*, 20 April 1777.

– 'in shoals': *NJ*, 11 April 1774.

– 'Other birds arrive, including the cuckoo': for route and data, see BTO, 'Cuckoo Tracking Project, using PTTS (Platform Transmitting Terminals)', https://www. bto.org/community/blog/what-have-cuckoos-taught-us, 13 June 2022.

– 'a nurse': *NHS*, DB 4, 19 Feb. 1770.

136 'This proceeding': ibid.

– 'Philosophers have defined instinct': *NHS*, DB 56, copied by GW in a note in *NJ*, 10 July 1790.

– 'But . . . it also resembles the idea': e.g. theories and arguments about 'mental modules', spurred by Jerry Fodor's *The Modularity of Mind* (1983). For GW, see https://evolvingthoughts.net/2013/01/20/

gilbert-white-on-instinct-stepping-back-from-nature.

– 'Thus is instinct': *NHS*, DB 16, 20 Nov. 1773.

137 'several single ones': *GK*, 14 Dec. 1759.

– 'old-thatch in four': *GK*, 12 April 1765.

– 'have prevailed': *NHS*, DB 37, 8 Jan. 1778.

– 'Potatoes, brought to Europe': see R. N. Salaman, *The History and Social Influence of the Potato* (1985) and Rebecca Earle, *Feeding the People: The Politics of the Potato* (2018), 80–8.

138 'The quantity of potatoes': *NJ*, 3 Oct. 1787.

– 'investigate the laws': *NHS*, DB 40, 2 June 1778.

– 'before there were any enclosures': *NHS*, DB 37, 8 Jan. 1778.

139 'The productions of vegetation': *NHS*, DB 40, 2 June 1778.

140 'Francis Halliday': see GW to JW, 9 March 1775, *LL* II, 281.

– 'I could not believe': William Wilberforce, May 1789, quoted in Brycchan Carey, *The Unnatural Trade: Slavery, Abolition and Environmental Writing 1650–1807* (2024), 2.

142 'I observed a snail': John Clare, journal, 12 April 1825, in *The Natural History Prose Writings of John Clare*, ed. Margaret Grainger (1983).

143 'purple double stocks': *GK*, 16 April 1752.

– 'the largeness of': Philip Miller, *The Gardeners Dictionary* (1754).

– 'Why should it be thought': Acts 26:8, GWH, photocopy. Coulson, no. 13, 64–8.

144 'If we do but consider': Houghton MS Eng. 731.172. Coulson, no. 6, 38–41.

– 'All my apricots': GW to SB, 17 April 1786, *LL* II, 157.

145 'more backward': *NHS*, TP 29, 12 May 1770.

– 'but play and sport about': *NHS*, DB 16, 20 Nov. 1773.

146 'So it will be time enough': Paul Foster and Sarah Markham, 'Gilbert White Begins Work on the *Antiquities* of Selborne: Two Letters', *Proceedings of the Hampshire Field Club Archaeological Society*, 45 (1989), 157–66. GW met Loveday through Richard Chandler, an Oxford friend of Loveday's son John.

146 'what is usually called a mouse-colour': this quote and those that follow, *NHS*, DB 20, 26 Feb. 1774.

147 'Some few bank-martins': *NJ*, 28 March 1776.

148 'Gilbert wrote two papers': 'Account of the House-Martin, or Martlet', letter to DB, dated 20 Nov. 1773, read to Royal Society on 10 Feb. 1774, *Phil. Trans.*, 64, 31 Dec. 1774; 'Of the House Swallow, of the Swift or Black Martin, of the Sand Martin', letter to DB, dated 28 Jan. 1774, read 16 March 1775, *Phil. Trans.*, 65, 31 Dec. 1775. Edited and expanded versions in *NHS*, DB 16, 18, 20 and 21.

– 'makes me say that': GW to SB, 16 Nov. 1775, *LL* I, 295.

– 'Gilbert lent him copies': Foster, 'The Hon. Daines Barrington FRS – Annotations on Two Journals Compiled by Gilbert White', *Notes and Records of the Royal Society*, 41 (1986–7), 77–93.

– 'Mr Barrington wants': GW to SB, 7 Feb. 1776, *LL* I, 307.

– 'One early idea': GW to JW, 30 Aug. 1770. See Foster, 126–7.

– 'As matter flows in': GW to JW, 25 Jan. 1771, Houghton MS Eng. 731.

– 'it should be somewhat': GW to TP, 19 July 1771, *LL* I, 201.

149 'Out of all my journals': GW to JW, 29 April 1774, *LL* I, 250.

– 'lie in my cupboard': GW to JW, 29 March 1774, *LL* I, 244.

- 'his ingenious correspondents': *Philosophical Letters Between the Late Learned Mr Ray and Several of His Ingenious Correspondents, Natives and Foreigners: To Which Are Added Those of Francis Willughby*, ed. W. Derham (1718).
- 'candour and openness': *NHS*, TP 25, 30 Aug. 1769.
150 'The note of the white-throat': *NHS*, TP 40, 2 Sept. 1774.
- 'I am at a loss': *NHS*, TP 12, 4 Nov. 1767.
152 'I have left no room' . . . 'Therm: at 60': Thomas Gray to Thomas Warton, 22 April 1760 and *c*.20 June 1760; Thomas Gray Archive online, Letters. 0358, 0361. BL Egerton MS 2400, 130–4.
- 'In his copy of Linnaeus's': https://collections.etoncollege.com/etons-bard-thomas-gray-and-his-elegy. Marginal annotations: https://www.thomasgrayexhibition.com/gray-as-reader.
155 'should happen to come': GW to Joseph Banks, 21 April 1768, Bell II, 241.
- 'the same chatty . . .' GW to JW, 1 Sept. 1769, *LL* I, 231.
- 'the only naturalists': GW to TP, 1 Sept. 1769, BL Add. MS 35138. Richard Skinner was a fellow of Corpus Christi.
- 'from venison down to barley': John Lightfoot to GW, 27 Jan., 13 Sept. 1773, Bell II, 231–4.
156 'After an ineffectual search': *NHS*, TP 32, 19 Oct. 1770.
- 'he does not talk': *NHS*, TP 39, 9 Nov. 1773.
- 'an immense magazine': extract from W. Sheffield letter, GW to SB, 21 Dec. 1772, *LL* I, 210.

May

161 'All nature is so full': *NHS*, TP 20, 8 Oct. 1768.
- 'For, as no man can': *NHS*, TP 31, 14 Sept. 1770.
- 'every kingdom': *NHS*, DB 7, 8 Oct. 1770.
162 'plows with two teams': *NJ*, 7 June 1774.
- 'a molecule called luciferin': https://www.nhm.ac.uk/discover/the-glimmering-world-of-glow-worms.
163 'chearfull shrill cry' . . . 'large brawny thighs': *GK*, 20 April 1761.
- 'a long, sword-shaped weapon': *NHS*, DB 46, n.d.
165 'restored heathland': project 'Back from the Brink', 2017–21, led by the RSPB on heathland in Surrey and West Sussex. https://naturebftb.co.uk/projects/field-cricket.
- 'We have round this church': *NJ*, 25 May 1771.
- 'the common swift': Mark Cocker, *One Midsummer's Day: Swifts and the Story of Life on Earth* (1923).
166 'I opened a hen swift': *NJ*, 6 May 1780.
- 'raising their young': *NHS*, DB 21, 28 Sept. 1774.
- 'many years exact observation': *Phil. Trans.*, 65, 31 Dec. 1775, 266.
167 'I saw two swifts': *NJ*, 14 June 1776.
- 'swifts skim': *NJ*, 22 May 1788.
- 'Tryed an experiment': *GK*, 25 March 1758.
168 'I think there is no doubt': *NHS*, TP 10, 4 Aug. 1767
169 'There is one circumstance': ibid.

- 'horrid pests': *NHS*, TP 16, 18 April 1768.
- 'green plover': Patrick Galbraith, *One Last Song* (2022). https://granta.com/the-lapwing-act-patrick-galbraith. The BTO lists lapwings with the plover family *Charadriidae*.
- 'The lap-wing': *FS*, 24 April 1766.
- 'Green gooseberries': *NJ*, 8 May 1769. Sale banned under the Protection of Lapwings Act, 1928, and Wild Birds' Protection Act, 1954. Now on the Red List, the UK's breeding population has dropped by over 59 per cent since 1967 (BTO).
- 'Those that are': *NJ*, 11 May 1786

170 'I find now': ibid.
- 'The missel-thrush': *NJ*, 12 May 1780.
- 'Magpies beat': *NJ*, 18 May 1780.
- 'As you have seen Selborne': GW to RC, 8 May 1781, *LL* II, 70.

172 'the martin begins': *Phil. Trans.*, reused in *NHS*, DB 16, 20 Nov. 1773.

173 'When the house-sparrows': *NHS*, TP 29, 12 May 1773.
- 'very rudely': *NHS*, DB 21, 28 Sept. 1774.

174 'a wonderful and curious creature': quotations in this paragraph, *NHS*, TP 22, 2 Jan. 1769.
- '*only* in its flight': GW to TP, 2 Jan. 1769, BL Add. MS 35138, and see *NHS*, TP 23, 28 Feb. 1769.

175 'I have above twenty Acres': JM to GW, 28 June 1760, *Mulso*, 153.

176 'My family encreases': 7 Dec. 1763, *Mulso*, 183.

177 'Bror Harry's strong beer': *NJ*, 7 March 1775.
- 'Tasty': https://untappd.com/b/gilbert-white-s-brewery-garden-kalendar/4629468.

178 'The sycamore': *NJ*, 12 May 1776.

179 'a most lovely shrub': *NJ*, 4 July 1789.
- 'My white thorn': *NJ*, 31 May 1792.

182 'interfering landlord': until the Birkenhead Reforms and the Law of Property Act, 1925, Magdalen sent their president and bursar to hold annual manorial courts in the Great Tithe Barn at the Grange; Anthony Rye, *Gilbert White and His Selborne* (1970), 74, 156. Many properties on the Tithe Rent Charge Roll had 'Rights of Common on Selborne Hill', relinquished for £50 compensation, when Magdalen gave the Hanger and common to the National Trust in 1932. The Trust's other sites include Church Meadow and Long Lythe.

183 'Taken from the oldest records': parish register, HRO 32M66 PR1703. The beating of the bounds is recorded from 1721–83. See also https://www.stmary-schurchselborne.co.uk/registers.
- 'from time immemorial': note, 1789, parish register 1783–1812 (notes preceding Baptisms). 1793 enclosure threat, James White to GW, 12 Feb. 1793, *LL* II, 258–9; GW to BW, *LL* II, 261.

184 'Delicate harvest weather': *NJ*, 28 Aug. 1770.
- 'Turneps are all rotten' . . . 'Farmer parsons': *NJ*, 2 March 1771.
- 'Several fields of cone': *NJ*, 24 July 1773.
- 'Men stack their turneps': *NJ*, 25 Nov. 1777.
- 'There is in this year': *NJ*, 13 Aug. 1778.

185 'a quarter of meadow-grass-seeds': *NJ*, 8 May 1778.
— '"new" husbandry': this referred to both the rotation promoted in the 1730s by Townshend and Jethro Tull's rejection of fallowing in *The Horse-Hoing Husbandry* (1733).
— 'A knowledge of the grasses': GW to SB, 19 Aug. 1776, *LL* I, 328.
186 'Black-cap sings sweetly': *NJ*, 19 May 1770.
186 'The hanger': *NJ*, 6 May 1786.
188 'from John's book': he used the manuscript again, in *NHS*, DB 53.
— 'Take a chicken': *NHS*, DB 43, 9 Sept. 1778.
— 'Imagination cannot paint': *NHS*, DB 43, 9 Sept. 1778.
189 'turbulent animal' . . . 'From long experience': *NHS*, DB 33, n.d.
— 'there is a wonderful spirit' . . . 'These two incongruous animals': *NHS*, DB 24, 15 Aug. 1775.

June

193 'The grass-hopper lark': *NJ*, 28 May 1781.
194 'the grandeur of wildness': Samuel Johnson, 'William Collins', *Lives of the English Poets* (1781).
— 'warm in his friendships': *LL* II, 62–5; 'Memoirs of the Life of William Collins, the Poet', *Gentleman's Magazine*, vol. 51 (1781), 11–12. The letter is signed 'V', but someone who saw it alleged that it was in Gilbert's handwriting. His authorship remains doubtful.
— 'You are a Man': 1 Nov. 1769, *Mulso*, 218.
195 'On the same spot': *NHS*, 11 June 1786.
— 'His theme is': St John 14:151: 'If ye love me, keep my Commandments. And I will pray the Father, & he shall give you an other Comforter; that he may abide with you for ever: Even the Spirit of Truth.' See Coulson, 74. Last preached at Whitsun, 26 May 1793, a month before his death.
196 'the simple fact': https://sussexwildlifetrust.org.uk/news/european-hornets.
— 'my good friend' . . . 'base hoarhound, or downy woundwort': *NJ*, 20 Oct. 1767. This area, around Witney, is still the only place it grows in the UK.
— 'wth your Eyes fixed': 25 April 1766, *Mulso*, 202.
197 'Providence': see also Brycchan Carey, *Birds in Eighteenth-Century Literature* (2002), 173–92.
— 'this would be adding wonder': *NHS*, DB 4, 19 Feb. 1770.
— 'God moves in a mysterious way': first published in 1774, included in *Olney Hymns* (1779).
199 'Last night': MW to THW, 7 June 1780. HRO 16M/4/12/198.
201 'The air was crouded': *NJ*, 10 June 1771, followed by a reference to Scopoli's *Entomologia*.
— 'When day declining': 'The Naturalist's Summer-Evening Walk', *NHS*, TP 24, 29 May 1769.
202 'plants out the annuals': *NJ*, 10 May 1757, 13 April, 1, 10 May 1759.
203 'Crickets sing much': *NJ*, 4 June 1785.
— 'Now, it is paler': on 1 June, Venus sets three and a half hours after sunset; by the 30th, two hours (BBC *Sky at Night*).

204 'My bees when': *NJ*, 24 June 1777.
   – 'trail in unending clouds': Virgil, *Georgics*, IV, 557–9, trans. Kimberley Johnson (2009).
   – 'The subject, Sir': Samuel Johnson, *Table Talk* (1807 edn), 152–3.
   – 'Grapes are hermaphroditic': https://www.jordanwinery.com/blog/lifecycle-vine-yard-grape-flowers.
205 'We have lost poor Timothy': GW to MW, 22 May 1784, *LL* II, 121.
   – 'in the range of the meadow': GW to MW, 12 June 1784, *LL* II, 123–4.
   – 'Know then': GW to Hester Mulso, 31 Aug. 1784, *LL* II, 128.
206 'Martins begin building': *NJ*, 13 June 1776.
   – 'My Bro.r Thomas': *NJ*, 5 June 1782.
   – 'calls all the swallows': *Phil. Trans.*, 65, 31 Dec. 1775, 261–2.
207 'Long-horned bees': *NJ*, 9 June 1772, 2 June 1774, 14 June 1778.
   – 'Dragon-fly': *NJ*, 20 June 1776.
   – 'A vast insect': *NJ*, 26 June 1776.
208 'White butter-flies': *NJ*, 14 June 1778.
209 'Yes, I see you upon': 12 July 1763, *Mulso*, 176.
210 'cousin Basil Cane': Basil, the vicar of Ludgershall in Wiltshire, not far from Fyfield, was the son of Gilbert's aunt Dorothea and her husband William Cane.
   – 'A little Journal': all quotations from Kitty Battie's journal, 4 June to 4 Aug. 1763, are from *LL* I, 129–37.
211 'How you would have stared!': 29 June 1764, *Mulso*, 190.
212 'reduc'd, by ye departure': 28 July 1763, *Mulso*, 179.
   – 'no great Matter': JM to GW, 3 Oct. 1763, *Mulso*, 181–2.
   – 'When spouting rains': Bell I, 501.
214 'Just before they retire' . . . 'The swifts that dash': *NJ*, 25 June 1774.
215 'screaming parties': data collected by the RSPB (2022), '1921–Onwards, Swift Screaming Parties, UK', https://registry.nbnatlas.org/public/showDataResource/dr475. This includes records from projects including 'The Swift Inventory' (2009–15), 'Swift Survey' (2016–19) and 'Swift Mapper' (2020).
216 '1st Young redbreasts': *NJ*, June entries, 1769.
   – 'very jealous of their young': *NJ*, 23 June 1774.
   – 'A boy climbed this tree' . . . 'by it's hawk-like': *NJ*, 30 June 1781.
217 'the male honey-buzzard': ibid.
   – 'mentions the whetting': *NJ*, 8 July 1792.
218 '77 rows'. . . '40 hand-glasses': *NJ*, 14 June 1788.
219 'The progressive method': *Phil. Trans.*, 65, 31 Dec. 1775, 261.

July

223 'lack of insects': in 2024, the Butterfly Conservation's 'Big Butterfly Count' revealed the lowest number for years, due to a wet summer adding to the effects of climate change and pesticides: https://butterfly-conservation.org/emergency, 18 Sept. 2024.
   – 'ruminate and solace': *NHS*, TP 8, n.d.
224 'The heat overcomes': *NJ*, 11 July 1783.
   – 'You have a double Felicity': 8 July 1775, *Mulso*, 258.

          A YEAR WITH GILBERT WHITE

225 'The lateness of the Season' etc.: 26 March 1776, 1 June, 9 Oct. 1777, 21 Sept.
     1780. *Mulso*, 262, 270, 273, 294.
   – 'as a remedy for coughs': *NJ*, 25 July 1790.
226 'five young kestrels': *NJ*, 12 July 1775.
   – 'nightjar's eggs': *NJ*, 4, 14 July 1789.
   – '& then in a dubious' . . . 'hawking round': *NJ*, 27 Aug. 1792.
   – 'a hen Wood-chat': *NJ*, 7 July 1792.
227 'A pair of': *NJ*, 23 May 1787.
   – 'Butcher-bird': the BTO describes this as 'effectively extinct' as a breeding bird in
     Britain, with a mean of just four breeding pairs reported between 2015 and 2019.
     https://www.bto.org/understanding-birds/birdfacts/red-backed-shrike.
   – 'myriads of frogs': *NJ*, 7 July 1771.
   – 'Some of the little frogs': *NJ*, 10 July 1776.
229 'so daring and ravenous': *NHS*, TP 43, n.d.
   – 'Will: Tanner shot a sparrow-hawk': *NJ*, 23 July 1782.
230 'suffered all my life': GW to RM, 20 March 1792, Bell II, 278.
   – 'the want of that Ornament': 27 March 1776, *Mulso*, 262.
   – 'Mr Grimm, my artist': *NJ*, 8 July 1776.
   – 'everything curious': British Library blog: Brett Dolman, '"Everything Curious":
     Samuel Hieronymus Grimm and Sir Richard Kaye', eBLJ 2003; W. Hauptmann,
     Samuel Hieronymus Grimm, 1733–1794, A Very English Swiss (2014).
   – 'he has a vein of humour': GW to JW, 15 May 1776, *LL* I, 320.
231 'a grotesque and romantic': list of Grimm's pictures, GW to SB, 1 Nov. 1776, *LL*
     II, 3.
   – 'You are enjoying Yourself': 17 July 1776, *Mulso*, 266.
   – 'He first of all': GW to JW, 9 Aug. 1776, *LL* I, 326.
232 '*Hypopitys lutea*': *FS*, 7 July 1766. The argument continues as to whether it should
     still be classed under *Monotropa*, or have a genus of its own, *Hypopitys*.
   – 'Stinkhorns, or stinking morel': *FS*, 1 July 1766.
   – 'I thank you': 25 April 1766, *Mulso*, 202.
233 'The spirit of building': GW to JW, 2 May 1777, *LL* II, 8.
   – 'drowning weather': GW to TW, 16 July 1777, *LL* II, 10.
   – 'he splashed out': 'Bills relating to the building of my great parlor', *LL* II, 50–1.
   – 'looks very handsome': MW to THW (?1780), *LL* II, 52.
234 'The jasmine is so sweet': *NJ*, 17 June 1783.
   – 'about thirteen brace': *GK*, 15 July 1758.
235 '& have squab': *NJ*, 14 June 1776.
   – 'squeaking a little': *NJ*, 22 July 1774.
   – 'seem much at their leisure': *NJ*, 5 July 1774.
   – 'where they tumbled about': *NHS*, DB 21, letter dated 28 Sept. 1774, edited later.
236 'they settle on': *NJ*, 6 July 1785.
   – 'swifts dash & frolick': *NJ*, 18 July 1777.
237 '*Papilio machaon*': 'Insecta Lepidoptera, Papilio', Linnaeus, *Systema Natura*, 10th
     edn (1758), 461–2.
   – 'Today, the native subspecies': https://www.ukbutterflies.co.uk/species.php?spe-
     cies=machaon.

238 'Newfoundland codfish': Arthur Young, *Annals of Agriculture* (1793), 411–29.

239 '*anguis fragilis*': *NHS*, TP 17, 18 June 1768.

239 'A great flock': *NJ*, 12 July 1782.

240 'Downlands': Hampshire Garden Trust, research.hgt.org.uk.

241 'At 4 young': *NJ*, note, 29 July 1780.

242 'as rough as the sea': *GK*, 13 July 1765.

  – 'Thomas's thermometer': *NJ*, note opp. 18 July 1778.

  – 'Some people': *NJ*, 20 July 1778.

243 'The sun, "shorn of his beams"': *NJ*, 24 June 1783.

  – 'an amazing and portentous': *NHS*, DB 65, n.d.

  – 'very like Virgil's': Barker, 88.

  – 'excess / Of glory obscured': Milton, *Paradise Lost*, Book I, ll. 594–7; *NHS*, DB 65.

244 '& would pursue': the journal note is slightly expanded in *NHS*, 7, 8 October 1770.

  – 'Claire Oldham': see Robin Simon, *Drawn to Nature: Gilbert White and the Artists* (2021), 69–72.

245 'a water wagtail's nest': *NJ*, 22 July 1790. Three years later, a village boy, Daniel Wheeler, found yet another in a hedge-sparrow's nest.

  – 'rooks fly' . . . 'owl glides' . . . 'swifts pursue': *NJ*, 27 July 1787, 20 July 1768, 14 July 1783.

246 'is a very harmless': *NJ*, 3, 4 July 1776.

  – 'studies have shown': see, for example, M. F. Willson, D. A. Graff and C. J. Whelan, 'Color Preferences of Frugivorous Birds in Relation to the Colors of Fleshy Fruits', *Condor: Ornithological Applications* (1990), 545–55.

247 'This day': MW to THW, 29 July 1780, HRO 16M97/4/12 (200).

  – 'The two calendars': the Calendar (New Style) Act 1750 received royal assent in May 1751, and was applied in September 1752, changing the legal start of the year from Lady Day, 25 March, to 1 January.

  – 'comes forth every midsummer': *NJ*, note, 4 July 1778. For flying ants, see https://www.nhm.ac.uk/discover/when-why-winged-ants-swarm-nuptial-flight.html.

August

253 'You know my uncle': MW to THW, 19 Aug. 1782. HRO, Holt White Papers, 215.

  – 'your uncle dines': MW to TW, undated [1782], HRO, Holt White Papers, 250.

254 'has much straw': GW to MW, 1 Aug. 1781, *LL* II, 72–3.

  – 'Edmund had been briefly apprenticed': letter from Richard White, Nov. 1777, Selborne, White MS.

255 'Mrs J. White made Rasp': *NJ*, 29 July 1790.

256 'thatching': see the informative website 'Thatchinginfo.com' and https://thatchinginfo.com/thatching-ricks-stacks-in-britain. Also L. Brunt and E. Cannon, 'English Farmers' Wheat Storage and Sales in the Late Eighteenth and Early Nineteenth Centuries', *Economic History Review* (2021), 932–59.

257 'smoke & ferment': *NJ*, 5, 7 Nov. 1776.

259 'Gilbert watches the birds skim': *NHS*, DB 42, 7 Aug. 1778.

  – 'which, from its habits': *NHS*, DB 30, 3 April 1776; based on GW to JW, 12 Aug. 1775.

260 'these poor birds': GW to RM, 13 Aug. 1790, Bell II, 251.

– 'The night-moths': *GK*, 21 Aug. 1765.

– 'hide its head': *NHS*, TP 11, 9 Sept. 1767.

261 'not drinking': with thanks to Steph Holt, who considers these were probably Daubenton's bats, 'which collect insects directly from the water, making it look like they're dropping down to drink, and they often do so in large numbers'.

– 'dipping down': *NJ*, 1 Feb. 1785.

– '*vespertilio altivolans*': *NHS*, TP 26, 36, 8 Dec. 1769, Sept. 1771.

– 'the tragus . . . large glands': Bat Conservation Society; Mammal Society; cornwallmammalgroup.org/noctule. On attracting females to the roost, Steph Holt notes that there is some footage at https://www.facebook.com/reel/1169714747633728, 'and you can see that just as White mentions, the scent glands are close to the mouth'.

262 'Titlarks . . . not only sing': *NHS*, TP 39, 9 Nov. 1773. Listing birds that sing while they fly, GW uses the Linnaean name *Alauda pratorum*. Foster points out that the meadow pipit, which GW sometimes calls the 'small field lark', sings in ascent as well as descent. *NHS* (1993 edn), 275, n. 85.

– 'And God said': Genesis 1:26, King James Version.

263 'wantonly and cruelly': GW, 'Account of the House-Martin', *Phil. Trans.*, 64 (1774), 170.

– 'Rooks sometimes dive and tumble': *NHS*, DB 42, 7 Aug. 1778.

264 'hatching their young': *NHS*, TP 17, 18 June 1768.

– 'heavy and bloated': GW to JW, 12 Aug. 1775, *LL* I, 290.

– 'crowded with young': *NHS*, DB 31, 29 April 1776.

– 'This little fry': *NHS*, DB 30, 3 April 1776.

265 'And anyway, he added': GW to JW, 12 Aug. 1775, *LL* I, 290.

– '& as drawn off backward': *NJ*, note opposite last week of Sept. 1790.

266 'The person who brought': *NHS*, TP 10, 4 Aug. 1767. GW was in London, 18 April to 12 June.

– 'both of which': *NHS*, TP 12, 4 Nov. 1767.

267 'They never enter' . . . 'This wonderful procreant': *NHS*, TP 12, 4 Nov. 1767.

– 'the nests are made of leaves': Mammal Society.org, Harvest Mouse, *Micromys minutus*. See also Fiona Matthews et al., *A Review of the Population and Conservation Status of British Mammals* (2018), 26.

– 'burrow deep into the earth': *NHS*, TP 13, 22 Jan. 1768.

– 'they were just two inches': ibid. A third of an ounce is just over 9 grams.

268 'a survey by local farmers': in Selborne, only one was found between 1990 and 2014. Fearing the species was locally extinct, in 2014–15, the Selborne Landscape Partnership (SLP) carried out a survey, finding over 470 nests, prompting a project to develop hedgerow habitats. See SLP Report, and Kate Faulkner, 'In the Footsteps of Gilbert White', Game and Wildlife Conservation Trust, *Working Conservationists* (2018). In a nationwide survey, 2021–22, the Mammal Society found 1,500 nests from 900 searches.

– 'The wheat tans brown': John Clare, 'August', in *The Shepherd's Calendar*, eds Geoffrey Summerfield and David Powell (1984).

269 'To a thinking mind' . . . 'known to fail': *NHS*, DB 29, 7 Feb. 1776, citing *NJ*, May 1775.

– 'Wood Pond': https://gilbertwhiteshouse.org.uk/pond-mere-rune-flint, 28 Sept. 2019. I am grateful for detailed information from David Bate, British Geological Society, honorary research associate. Also, Edward A. Martin, 'Some Observations on Dew Ponds', *Geographical Journal*, 34, 2 (Aug. 1909); *Country Life*, 2 June 2006; SLP Report, 2023.

270 'what prodigious fogs': *NHS*, DB 28, 6 Feb. 1778.

– 'Short-heath': 'Short Heath Common Local Nature Reserve', Hampshire Countryside Service website. There is still a sandpit and quarry north of the common. After the introduction of field crickets in 1999, they are there in substantial numbers.

– 'mistle thrush families': Mark Cureton post, 23 Feb. 2022, birdwatching.co.uk.

271 'Yellowhammers': *NJ*, 27 Aug. 1768; 'stone curlews', 10 Aug. 1770; 'blackcaps', 4 Aug. 1772.

– 'In the list': *NHS*, DB 2, 2 Nov. 1769.

– 'For many months': *NHS*, DB 3, 15 Jan. 1770.

272 'is very loquacious': *NJ*, 16 Aug. 1771.

– 'suspended; in hot': *NHS*, DB 2, 2 Nov. 1769.

– 'His experiments': 'Experiments and Observations on the Singing of Birds', *Phil. Trans.*, 63 (10 Jan. 1773), 249–91. Earlier research by Baron von Pernau (1660–1731) also examined whether songs were innate or learned. See Peter Marler and Hans Slabbekoorn, eds, *Nature's Music: The Science of Birdsong* (2004); and Francesca Mackenney, *Birdsong, Speech and Poetry: The Art of Composition in the Long Nineteenth Century* (2022).

– 'sensory phase': articles abound, but see Richard Mooney, 'Birdsong', *Current Biology*, vol. 32, no. 20 (Oct. 2022). A clear summary is given by John Mitchison: https://bylinetimes.com/2022/09/16/the-upside-down-why-being-bird-brained-is-a-compliment.

273 'Spinach – ground hard': *NJ*, 3 Aug. 1786.

274 'sibilous, shivering noise': *NHS*, TP 10, 4 Aug. 1767.

– 'the reflection of the wall': *NHS*, DB 14, 6 March 1773.

– 'essay on the goldcrest': Chris Arthur, *Linnaean News*, 18 March 2024; https://www.terrain.org/2024/nonfiction/learning-to-see-goldcrests (11 Jan. 2024). For Ellen Thaler's research, see Tim Birkhead, *The Most Perfect Thing: Inside (and Outside) a Bird's Egg* (2016), 189–90.

275 'turnip sawflies': Michael Shrubb, 'Farming and Birds: An Historic Perspective', *British Birds*, 96(4) (2003), 158–77.

276 'several birds': *NJ*, 16 Aug. 1772.

277 '*Aut asper Crabro*': *Georgics* IV, 245 ('immiscuit' is misquoted as 'immis' in *NJ*, 19 Sept. 1780).

– 'very troublesome': *GK*, 26 Aug. 1754.

– 'broke up the arch': *NJ*, 26 Aug. 1783.

– 'with the raspings': *NJ*, 17 Sept. 1774.

– 'wool-carder': *NJ*, 1 Aug. 1773; 'Horseflies', 15 Aug. 1774; 'black weevils', 29 Aug. 1772.

– 'high copulation': *NJ*, 9 Aug. 1775.

280 'Not one wasp': *NJ*, 25 Aug. 1782.

281 'the whole air': *NJ*, 20 Sept. 1791.

282 'We held our *Harvest home*': 26 Aug. 1783, *Mulso*, 313.
284 'parasitic louse flies': following Linnaeus, Gilbert calls these *Hippoboscidae hirundinis*. The family *Hippoboscidae* contains many louse flies: swift louse flies are *Crataerina pallida*; those that prey on martins are *Crataerina hirundinis*. See Oxford University Swift Research Project; Mark D. Walker and Ian D. Rotherham, 'The Common Swift Louse Fly, *Crataerina pallida*', *Journal of Insect Science*, 10 (2010), 193; Royal Entomological Society, 'Keds, Flat-flies and Bat-flies', *Handbook for the Identification of British Insects*, vol. 10, part 7.
  – 'A fledg'd young swift': *NJ*, 17 Aug. 1782.

September

287 'From the latter part of July': *Phil. Trans.*, vol. LXXI, 1781. Reprinted in John Kington, ed., *The Weather Journals of a Rutland Squire* (1988), 157.
288 'We have, I should think': *NJ*, 8 Sept. 1775.
  – 'come in a door': *NJ*, 12 Sept. 1774.
290 'Vast flock': *NJ*, 5 Sept. 1782.
  – 'a kind of *black-bob*': *NJ*, 28 March 1790.
  – 'Mrs J. White': *NJ*, 18 Aug. 1792.
291 'A vast flock of ravens': *NJ*, 6 Oct. 1784.
  – 'But they grow alongside': William Cobbett, 11 Sept. 1826, *Rural Rides* (1830).
  – 'The great heats': GW to MW, 4 Sept. 1781, *LL* II, 73–4.
  – 'I just saved my credit': MW to THW, 6 Sept. 1781, HRO, Holt White Papers, 255.
  – 'shootings in my back': GW to Barbara White, Sept. 1780, HL 93, Mabey, 179.
292 'a whole band': GW to MW, 30 Sept. 1780, *LL* II, 55–6.
  – 'a fine romantic path': *NJ*, 27 Sept. 1780.
  – 'All people agree': GW to MW, 30 Sept. 1780, *LL* II, 56.
  – 'To say the truth': GW to SB, 23 Nov. 1780, *LL* II, 57.
293 'Though I have long ceased': GW to RM, 7 Aug. 1792, *LL* II, 245.
  – 'swarmed to such a degree': *NHS*, TP 6, n.d.
  – 'these he pleasantly': *NHS*, TP 29, 12 May 1770.
  – 'Shooting season but few partridges': *NJ*, 3 Sept. 1776.
  – 'Partridges innumerable': *NJ*, 2 Sept. 1779.
  – 'In the dusk of evening': *NJ*, 7 Sept. 1775.
294 'the international Red List': the list of species at risk of extinction has been produced by the International Union for Conservation of Nature (IUCN) since 1964.
  – 'The hop-planters': *NJ*, 14 Oct. 1786.
  – 'No other growth': *NJ*, 14 July 1787.
  – 'blow into flyers': *NJ*, 6 Sept. 1772.
  – 'two wagons': *NJ*, 8 Oct. 1782.
  – 'two days': *NJ*, 11 Sept. 1783.
  – 'Hops so small': *NJ*, 10 Sept. 1787.
  – 'Several women': *NJ*, 8 Oct. 1781.
295 'About 8000 people': *NJ*, 10 Sept. 1770.
  – 'quiet, pilfering': John Clare, 'The Gypsy Camp', in *John Clare: Selected Poems*, ed. Jonathan Bate (2003), 237.

– 'gangs or hordes' . . . 'brought with them from the Levant' . . . 'Last September': *NHS*, DB 25, 2 Oct. 1775.

296 'Gypsies are called': ibid.
– 'The creeping fogs': *NJ*, 17 Sept. 1777.

297 'been to the comic opera': MW to THW, n.d. May 1781. HRO, Holt White Papers, 242.

298 'the common little horsebean': Arthur Young, *The Farmer's Calendar* (1804), January.

299 'young housekeeper': GW to AB, 25 Dec. 1778, GWH. In September 1789, GW sent twelve plants of ladies' tresses from the Long Lythe to William Curtis's botanical garden.

301 'vast, swagging, rock-like clouds': *NJ*, 22 Nov. 1768.
– 'On sunny days': *NJ*, 18 Sept. 1772.

302 'The winters': see Tim Sparks et al., 'A Comparison of Nature's Calendar with Gilbert White's Phenology', *British Wildlife*, vol. 31, no. 4 (April 2020).
– 'One study': BTO, https://www.bto.org/our-science/publications/peer-reviewed-papers/uk-birds-are-laying-eggs-earlier.
– 'insects such as aphids': James R. Bell et al., 'Insects. Spatial and Habitat Variation in Aphid, Butterfly, Moth and Bird Phenologies Over the Last Half Century', *Global Change Biology*, vol. 25, no. 6 (June 2019).
– 'comes into leaf earlier': Tim Sparks, 'Spring into Action', https://www.rsb.org.uk/biologist-interviews/spring-into-action-2. Stephen Moss ('Climate Disruption to UK Seasons Causes Problems for Migratory Birds', *Guardian*, 16 May 2024) notes that earlier springs pose problems for wood warblers, redstarts and flycatchers, who feed on oak-moth caterpillars. Swallows have also been badly affected by the unpredictable weather patterns.

303 'he would need a lot of water': Michael Combrune, *The Theory and Practice of Brewing* (1762). See Sambrook, *Country House Brewing in England 1500–1900* (1996).

304 'Gilbert made about fifty gallons': 'An Account of Strong-Beer. A Chronicle of Strong-Beer and Raisin Wine', GWH MS.
– 'I only know that': GW to TB, 10 Jan. 1787, *LL* II, 163.
– 'sending the description': GW to JW, 9 March 1775, *LL* I, 280.

305 'I found the stubbles': *NHS*, DB 23, dated 8 June 1775. See Peter Marren and Richard Mabey, *Bugs Britannica* (2010), 111.

306 'prodigiously fond of music': MW to THW, 6 Oct. 1781, HRO 16M97/4/12/207.
– 'a heavy Hand': JM to GW, 29 Sept. 1781, *Mulso*, 299–300.

308 'Owls move': *NHS*, DB 7, Aug. 1778.
– 'snails, rats': *NHS*, TP 11, 9 Sept. 1797.
– 'the mansion': *NHS*, DB 15, 8 July 1773.

310 'musical friend': *NHS*, DB 9, 12 Feb. 1771; the cuckoo seemed to call in D, D sharp and once in C, but the nightingale's song was too rapid and varied to judge.
– 'went almost half a note': *NHS*, DB 10, 1 Aug. 1771.
– 'but the survivor': *NHS*, TP 29, 12 May 1770.

311 'its flesh is melting': Prudence Leith-Ross, 'Fruit Planted Around a New Bowling

Green at John Evelyn's Garden at Sayes Court, Deptford, Kent, in 1684/5', *Garden History*, vol. 31, no. 1 (spring 2003).

312 'Folkestone Beds': part of the Lower Greensand formation, Cretaceous period. BGS Lexicon; also https://pubs.geoscienceworld.org (1999).

– 'Hold Infinity': William Blake, 'Auguries of Innocence', *The Complete Poems* (1977).

313 'on which it was to have supported': *NHS*, TP 26, 8 Dec. 1769.

315 'foreign animals': *NHS*, TP 27, 22 Feb. 1770.

314 'ridden the twenty miles': see Alexandra Harris, *Rising Down: A Sussex Landscape* (2024).

– 'slung under the belly': *NHS*, TP 28, March 1770.

315 'a mature bull moose': Stubbs painted this as *The Duke of Richmond's Second Bull Moose* (1773), and Pennant published an engraving in *Arctic Zoology*, 1784, declaring, 'The Moose and the Elk are the same species', 18. See Helen McCormack, 'Pennant, Hunter, Stubbs and the Pursuit of Nature', in *Enlightenment Travel and British Identities: Thomas Pennant's Tours*, eds Mary-Ann Constantine and Nigel Leask (2017). The 'Great Irish Elk' has been identified as *Megaloceros giganteus*, the most recent remains dating from over 7,000 years ago in Russia.

316 'driven by a divinely-implanted instinct': see Tobias Menely, 'Travelling in Place: Gilbert White's Cosmopolitan Parochialism', *Eighteenth-Century Life*, vol. 28, no. 3 (2004), 59, 60; quoting Thomas Pennant, *Arctic Zoology*. For arguments on the dispersal of species, see also J. C. Briggs, *Global Biogeography* (1995), 2–3.

– 'animals peculiar to America': *NHS*, TP 24, 29 May 1769.

317 '29 Quarts': *NJ*, 28 Sept. 1761. He adds: 'Mem: two gallons & half of picked berries, moderately squeezed, produced about a gallon of juice.'

– 'So I got up': GW to MW, 13 May 1783, *LL* II, 100.

October

321 'Hard frost': *NJ*, 25 Oct. 1784.

– 'and I'll assure you': MW to THW, 6 Oct. 1781, HRO, THW papers, 207.

322 'several bushels of nuts': *NJ*, 15 Oct. 1776, 25 Oct. 1780.

– 'for preserving': John Farley, *The London Art of Cookery*, 1800; pickling, *NJ*, 25 July 1785.

– 'catsup . . . from mushrooms': *NJ*, 4 Oct. 1779.

323 'in the deep, narrow part': *NJ*, 22 Oct. 1783.

– 'a surly fellow': *NJ*, 21 Oct. 1790

– 'to whom all the villagers': *NJ*, 4 Oct. 1773.

– 'fetlock high': *NJ*, 3 Oct. 1781.

– 'buys a new mare': MW to THW, 6 Sept. 1781, HRO 16M97/4/12.

– 'Now your father': GW to MW, 8 Aug. 1783, *LL* II, 101.

– 'The grass seems killed': *NJ*, 7 Oct. 1786.

324 'Brought down': *NJ*, 14 Sept. 1783.

– 'I got a boy': William Cobbett, 7 Aug. 1823, *Rural Rides* (1830, 2001 edn), 115.

325 'in it's belly': *NJ*, 28 Dec. 1771.

– 'an eye witness': *NJ*, 19 Dec. 1777.

– 'These folks': GW to MW, 12 June 1784, *LL* II, 123; added this to *NHS*, TP 9, describing Woolmer and the Holt.

326 'the Domesday Book': copy in an unknown hand, White MS, Selborne.
 – 'instead of pots of coins' . . . 'more celebrated' . . . 'and passed for farthings' . . .
  'because I have too good': *Antiquities*, Letter 1, 19–20.
327 'In August': *NJ*, 14 Aug. 1781.
 – 'fine silica': the quarry here today produces silica sand for use on turf and quartz
  sand for building and cement. Tarmac Kingsley Sand and Gravel Quarry, Borden.
 – 'estimated the planet': *Les Époques de la nature*, https://www.geolsoc.org.uk/
  Geoscientist/Archive/April-2018/Buffon-the-geologist. See Martin J. S. Rudwick,
  *Bursting the Limits of Time: The Reconstruction of Geohistory in the Age of Revolu-
  tion* (2005).
328 'vegetative': *NHS*, DB 17, 9 Dec. 1773.
 – 'a warm, forward, crumbling mould': *NHS*, TP 1, n.d.
 – 'the bowels of the earth': see Jenny Uglow, *The Lunar Men*, Chaps 13 and 25.
 – 'petrified fish': *NHS*, TP 3, n.d. Authorities consulted by GW included the seventeenth-century zoologists Martin Lister and George Rumphius, and d'Argenville's
  La Conchyliologie (1742).
330 'One of my neighbours': *NJ*, 12 Dec. 1789.
 – 'large and good for nothing': MW to THW, 6 Oct. 1781, HRO 16M97/4/12/207,
  also 206.
 – 'Rover springs many pheasants': *NJ*, 16 Oct. 1783, 20 Oct. 1787.
 – 'Sheared my mongrel dog': *NJ*, 13 May 1788.
331 'playing': *NJ*, 2 Oct. 1773.
 – 'What can this bird': *NJ*, 4 Oct. 1775.
 – 'rapping with their bills': *NJ*, 22 Oct. 1776.
 – 'One bunting': *NJ*, 25 Oct. 1776.
 – 'several dozen': *NHS*, TP 13, 22 Jan. 1768. Buntings, too, are Red List birds,
  casualties of intensive farming.
 – 'spoonbills shot': *NJ*, 12 Feb. 1775.
332 'in a stately manner': *NHS*, TP 11, 9 Sept. 1767.
 – 'coming now and then': *NHS*, TP 6. The black grouse is now the fastest-declining
  bird in the UK.
333 'the Oakhanger pools': these ponds are still great places for dragonflies. See South
  Downs National Park websites, and https://yateleycommoncountrypark.word-
  press.com/category/shortheath-common.
 – 'This vase I was going to procure': GW to RC, 3 July 1780, *LL* II, 49.
334 'an enormous sum' . . . 'In the middle aisle': *Antiquities*, Letter 2.
 – 'it would be tedious': *Antiquities*, Letter 7.
335 'loud and out of tune': *Antiquities*, Letter 4.
 – 'Describing the hall': *Antiquities*, Letter 4.
 – 'I have often looked': *Antiquities*, Letter 9.
336 'Pley-stow, *locus ludorum*': *Antiquities*, Letter 10.
336 'The well at Old Place Farm': see British History Online. Borehole records show
  the depth as 170.68m (557ft), compared to The Wakes at 27.43m (90ft): British
  Geological Survey, Borehole Index. A nearby well at Rotherfield Park reached
  284ft.
 – 'To get water': I am grateful to David G. Bate for explaining this.

337 'deeply engaged': GW to RC, 17 Nov. 1779, *LL* II, 38.
  – 'Bishop Beaufort's registers': GW to RC, 3 July 1780, *LL* II, 50.
  – 'Farrago of Antiquities': JM to GW, 21 Sept. 1780.
  – 'with his two volumes': Tom Warton, *History of English Poetry*, three vols (1774, 1778, 1781). Eighty-eight pages of an incomplete fourth volume were published after his death (1789).
338 'Oh Molly!': GW to MW, 24 Sept. 1784, *LL* II, 134.
  – 'exhorted all those': *NJ*, 16 Oct. 1784.
339 'in a few minutes': GW to AB, 19 Oct. 1784, *LL* II, 134–6.
340 'zeal for balloon-making': see Richard Holmes, *The Age of Wonder* (2008), 133–62.
  – 'wetted with spirits': *NJ*, 4 Sept. 1784.
  – 'It went off': *NJ*, 21 Oct. 1784.
341 'Oh God!': quoted in Nathaniel William Wraxall, *Historical Memoirs of My Own Time. Part the Second, from 1781 to 1784* , ed. Henry Wheatley (1904), 398.
342 'Thomas Holt White': drafts of his articles fill the Commonplace book, shared with his father, Selborne, GWH, A10.1.
  – 'The cat frolicks': *NJ*, 3 Oct. 1783.
  – 'We make tarts': *NJ*, 10 Oct. 1782.
  – 'always rot': *NJ*, 10 Oct. 1791.
343 'We saw several Red-wings': *NJ*, 13 Oct. 1787.
344 'fieldfares stand out': BTO, 'Identifying Redwing and Fieldfare'.
  – 'and nestle': *NHS*, TP 27, 8 Dec. 1769. Larkers caught the birds in nets; bat-fowlers, similarly, shone a light to get the birds to fly out of the bushes into nets, and then hit them down with sticks, or 'bats'.
  – 'more often on the ground': animali.bio/fieldfare.
  – 'for laying in their forest fuel': *NJ*, 7 Oct. 1792.
  – 'loads of peat': 'The Royal Forest of Woolmer', www.Simonknott.co.uk, Woolmer Forest Conservation Society.
345 'local farm partnership': SLP Partnership 2023. The 2023 *Annual Report for Natural England's Agri-Environment Evidence Programme*, published on 7 Aug. 2024, summarising the findings of seven research projects, showed that on eco-friendly farms, there were on average 53 per cent more butterflies and 25 per cent more breeding birds.
346 'The crop of acorns': *NJ*, 12 Oct. 1783.
347 'rooks and jays': *NJ*, 30 Oct. 1770, 8 Oct. 1773; 'turkeys': *NJ*, 17 Oct. 1775.
  – 'Woolmer Forest': GW to MW, 31 Dec. 1781; *NHS*, TP 6, GW note 10.
349 'antiquarian whims': see similar entry on TW's excavations, *NJ*, 15 Sept. 1782, and GW to RC, 4 June 1783, *LL* II, 91.
  – 'charcoal, ashes': *Antiquities*, Appendix A, article by Lord Selborne, 1874. There are tumuli at Newton Valence and East Tisted, at Blackmoor and Greatham, at Hartley Mauditt, near West Worldham, and near Oakhanger and Woolmer Forest. For bowl barrows, see, L. V. Grinsell, 'Hampshire Barrows: Part III', *Hampshire Field Club and Archaeological Society Papers and Proceedings*, 1939. For 'the Blackmoor Hoard' or 'Selborne Hoard' (held in GWH; British Museum; and Metropolitan Museum, New York), see Jennifer Wexler, https://blog.micropasts.org/2014/11/17/

things-that-go-bump-in-the-night-the-selborne-blackmoor-hoard-the-significance-
of-lba-weapon-hoards.
  – 'It scrapes out': *NHS*, DB 13, 12 April 1772.
  – 'The bat is out': *NJ*, 29 Oct. 1778.
  – 'continue still to sport': *NJ*, 26 Oct. 1774.
  – 'without seeming to have': *NJ*, 24 Oct. 1784.
  – '*Sphinx atropos*': *NJ*, 11 Oct. 1777.
350 'To his irritation': *NHS*, DB 3, 15 Jan. 1770.
351 'One thing': *NHS*, DB 9, 12 Feb. 1771.
  – 'This bird': *NJ*, 1 Oct. 1777.
  – 'was quite transported': GW to SB, 3 Nov. 1780, *LL* II, 58. Woodcock are now on
    the Red List, although shooting contributes. The season is 1 October to 31 Janu-
    ary, but the group Wild Justice is campaigning to move its start to 1 December.
352 'leaving only': *NJ*, 13 Nov. 1780.
  – 'yet this poor reptile': *NJ*, 17 Oct. 1782.

November

354 'Gertrude Hermes': the prints were published in 1988 by the Gregynnog Press in
    Wood Engravings by Gertrude Hermes, Being Illustrations to Selborne, introduced by
    William Condry.
355 'cut high behind': GW to MW, 3 Feb. 1788, *LL* II, 179.
  – 'Greenfinches fill the lanes': *NJ*, 27 Nov. 1769.
  – 'hen chaffinches': *NJ*, 29 Nov. 1788.
  – '"bachelor" birds': Carey Davies, 'Days Like These Have Inspired Great Art', *Guard-
    ian*, 23 January 2023.
356 'It is very amusing': *NHS*, TP 26, 8 Dec. 1769.
  – 'leave us all': *NJ*, 24 Nov. 1770.
  – 'The evening proceedings': *NHS*, DB 59, n.d.
357 'cottagers turn their pigs': *NJ*, 12 Nov. 1786.
  – 'No hogs': *NJ*, 18 Nov. 1782.
  – 'poor men': GW to TB, 10 Jan. 1787, *LL* II, 164.
358 'Tubbed half an hog': *NJ*, 31 Jan. 1788.
  – 'For as Harry Bright': *NJ*, 1 Nov. 1788.
359 'Our grapes': GW to MW, 13 Nov. 1781, *LL* II, 76.
  – 'the concurring circumstance': *NJ*, 4 Nov. 1781.
  – 'Bonfire': HW's journal, 6 Nov. 1781, BL Add. MS 43814.
  – 'Mrs Burbey's respectable': GW to MW, 20 Sept. 1785, *LL* II, 147.
  – '17 persons': GW to MW, 7 Jan. 1784, *LL* II, 111.
  – 'young mad-headed farmer': GW to MW, 20 Feb. 1783, *LL* II, 96–7.
360 '*The Duke of Kingston* caught fire': GW to RC, 30 March 1784, *LL* II, 115.
  – 'he brings treasures': *NJ*, 13 June 1784.
  – 'appear to be': *NJ*, 17 July 1784.
  – 'but not before the female': GW to MW, 16 Aug. 1784, *LL* II, 130.
361 'not liking his quarters': GW to MW, 13 Nov. 1781, *LL* II, 76.
  – 'Timothy the tortoise': *NJ*, Nov. 1782.
362 'forsaking the reeds': *NJ*, 28 Nov. 1771.

–   'My uncle Benj.': MW to GW, 4 Dec. 1781, *LL* II, 77.
–   'I have, in my time': GW to MW, 19 Dec. 1781, *LL* II, 78.
–   'He had seen two': *NJ*, 16 Nov. 1773; 'two years later': *NJ*, 29 Nov. 1775.
–   'This was the first of this sort': *NJ*, 4 Nov, 1774. For water rails, see the Yorkshire Wildlife Trust blog, 3 Feb. 2023, https://www.ywt.org.uk/wildlife-explorer/birds/wading-birds/water-rail.
363 'for the quadrupeds': *NHS*, TP 26, 8 Dec. 1769.
–   'brown hares arrived': https://www.gwct.org.uk/media/208618/conserving-the-brown-hare.pdf; for Selborne, see 'Brown hare', SLP Report 2023.
364 'The downy seeds': *NJ*, 23 Nov. 1788.
365 'a cartful of chalk': GW to MW, 13 Nov. 1781, *LL* II, 75.
366 'These sans-breeches men': GW to MW, 14 Dec. 1782, *LL* II, 88.
–   'never known to steal': GW to Mary Barker (niece), 22 Jan. 1783, *LL* II, 93.
–   'Thus will three or four inches': *NJ*, 23 Nov. 1790.
367 'When horses, cows . . .': *NJ*, 16 Nov. 1775.
–   'Fled is the *blasted*': James Thomson, 'Autumn', in *NJ*, 20 Nov. 1783.
–   'One year, Gilbert made a note': *NJ*, 14 Nov. 1776.
368 'alert and merry': *NHS*, DB 47.
369 'Indian flowers': *NJ*, 11 Nov. 1772.
–   'Etty would struggle home': GW to MW, 6 April, 18 April 1784.
370 'curate *pro tempore*': Selborne parish register, 12 April 1784.
–   'I miss poor Mr. Etty': GW to AB, 19 Oct. 1784. *LL* II, 117, 120, 137.
–   'and talks much of shooting': GW to MW, 12 June, 31 Aug. 1784, *LL* II, 123, 132.
–   'For God's sake': 19 March 1785, *Mulso*, 322–3.
–   'so taken up': GW to SB, 17 April 1786, *LL* II, 155.
371 'yet I hope to live': GW to MW, 1 Dec. 1785.
–   'Her name is Haggitt': SB to GW, 18 July 1786.
–   'You speak like a Turk': GW to SB, 1 Aug. 1786, *LL* II, 158–60.
372 'Little Tom Clements': ibid.
–   'who can shoulder a violin': GW to RC, 26 Jan. 1793, *LL* II, 256.
–   'Strange that those nocturnal': *NJ*, 25 Nov. 1775.
–   'click beetles': https://www.wildlifetrusts.org/wildlife-explorer/invertebrates/beetles/coppery-click-beetle.
373 'look like tiny flowers': these antheridia look like flowers in *Mnium hornum* (swan's-neck thyme moss) and in some other species. My thanks to Marion Raynor of the British Bryological Society for her clear explanation. https://www.britishbryologicalsociety.org.uk/learning/some-common-bryophytes/common-woodland-floor-mosses.
–   'horse beans': *NJ*, 17 Nov. 1792.
374 'plants furze': *NJ*, 19 Sept. 1789.
–   'When old beech-trees': *NJ*, 19 July 1789.
–   'Came via Newton lane': *NJ*, 23 Nov. 1784; also GW to MW, *LL* II, 139.
375 'there is an old maxim': GW to RC, 3 Dec. 1788. The traditional Christmas pudding, often thought to be a Victorian innovation, was apparently brought to Britain at the time of George I's arrival, in 1714.

375 'The smoke of the new lighted lime-kilns': *NJ*, 22 Nov. 1788.
376 'glasshouse': Richard Weston, *Tracts on Practical Agriculture and Gardening* (1773).
— 'That great straddle-bob': GW to SB, 17 April 1786, *LL* II, 157.
377 'we wish': MW to THW, 4 Dec. 1781, *LL* II, 76. The new provost would be Dr John Eveleigh.

December

381 'Mrs J White smiles': GW to MW, 30 April 1783, *LL* II, 99.
— 'the different colours': GW to MW, 19 Dec. 1781, *LL* II, 78.
— '*Merise*, a small bitter': MW to GW, 4 Dec. 1781, *LL* II, 78.
— 'You are certainly right': GW to MW, 19 Dec. 1781, *LL* II, 78.
382 'Sweet-Williams': *NJ*, 6 Dec. 1780.
383 'correcting a deduction': *NHS*, TP 15, 30 March 1768.
— 'I am no bird-catcher': *NHS*, DB 5, 12 April 1770.
— 'it is also necessary': DB, 'Experiments and Observations on the Singing of Birds', *Phil. Trans.*, 63 (10 January 1773), 249–91.
384 'harbour a constant Aviary': Philip Miller, *Gardeners and Florists Dictionary* (1724).
— 'Hares make sad havock': *NJ*, 18 Dec. 1783.
— 'Timothy is buried': *NJ*, 2 Dec. 1784.
— 'Timothy has laid himself up': *NJ*, 8 Dec. 1791.
— 'Wagtails, all sorts': *NHS*, TP 39, 9 Nov. 1773.
385 'bobs up and down': *NHS*, TP 40, 2 Sept. 1774.
— 'The water wagtail': *GK*, 30 Aug. 1765.
— 'but wagtails and larks': *NHS*, DB 42, 7 Aug. 1778.
— 'who are abroad': *NJ*, 21 Dec. 1775.
— 'Venus was so resplendent': GW to MW, 9 Feb. 1772, *LL* II, 81.
386 'to prepare it for barley': *NJ*, 20 Dec. 1777.
— 'Most of the wells': *NJ*, 18 Dec. 1788.
387 'Wrens whistle': *NJ*, 29 Dec. 1770.
— 'Beautiful, picturesque': *NJ*, 3 Dec. 1789.
— 'please to ask for': Charles Lamb, 'London Fogs', *Works of Charles and Mary Lamb*, ed. E. V. Lucas, 8 vols (1903–5), vol. 4, 436.
— 'the grate': *NJ*, 2 Dec. 1779.
388 'they lie in the great waters': *NJ*, 8 Dec. 1770.
— 'In one great frost': *NJ*, 27 Dec. 1784.
— '*Mergus serratus*' . . . 'called in some parts': *NJ*, 9 Dec. 1774.
— 'If you had stayed': GW to RC, 20 May 1789, *LL* II, 196.
389 'appears within doors': *NJ*, 30 Dec. 1769. For winter butterflies, see https://www.hiwwt.org.uk/blog/hiwwt/winter-butterflies; and Butterflyconservation.org.
— 'Gilbert had admired the way': *NJ*, 22 Dec. 1768.
390 'for the season': *NJ*, 10 Dec. 1792.
— 'A stone was 4½ seconds': *NJ*, 3 Sept. 1792.
— 'Many in copulation': *NJ*, 3 Dec. 1776.
391 'Mrs White and Mr and Mrs Etty': GW to MW, 19 Dec. 1781, *LL* II, 78.
— 'half a hundred': GW to MW, 14 Dec. 1782, *LL* II, 87.

391 'good Iceland cod': GW to MW, 26 Dec. 1785, *LL* II, 149.
 – 'when off came the hoops': GW to MW, 9 March 1785, *LL* II, 141.
392 'lambs in December': *NJ*, 22 Dec. 1784.
 – 'Some farmers had developed winter lambing': see Gavin Bowie, 'Re-Defining
   Farming Practices on the Hampshire and Wiltshire Chalklands, 1250–1850',
   Proc. Hampshire Field Club Archaeol. Soc., 70 (2015), 136–54 (Hampshire
   Studies, 2015).
 – 'His turnips are frozen': *NJ*, 22 Dec. 1784.
 – 'there were considerable falls': *NHS*, DB 61, n.d.
393 'feeding habits': *NHS*, TP 41, n.d.
394 'while it hung' . . . 'is a vast admirer': ibid.
395 'Shelves behind ye kitchen': HW, 24 Dec. 1781, Diaries of the Rev. Henry White,
   BL Add. MS 43814.
 – 'And the Angel said': Christmas sermon, Houghton MS Eng. 731.175. Coulson
   no. 15, 69–74. First preached when he was briefly curate of Selborne in 1751.
   Text is St Luke 2:10–11. GW's alternative text was Matthew 1:21: 'And she shall
   bring-forth a Son, & thou shalt call his name Jesus: for he shall save his people
   from their Sins.' Houghton MS Eng. 731.182. Coulson no. 28, 124–8.
396 'I reckon': 10 Jan. 1773, *Mulso*, 240.
 – 'shorn of its tresses': GW to RC, 7 Dec. 1780, *LL* II, 59.
 – 'We have lately': 7 Jan. 1776, *Mulso*, 261.
 – 'there will be shot for': GW to MW, 26 Dec. 1785, *LL* II, 150.
397 'we live in a most eventful': GW to RC, 4 Dec. 1789, *LL* II, 210.
398 'The lack of coffin': see also GW to RM, 21 Dec. 1793: 'You cannot abhor the
   dangerous doctrine of levelers and republicans more than I do! I was born and
   bred a Gentleman, and hope I shall be allowed to die such.'
 – 'without much scent': *NJ*, 27 Dec. 1785.
399 'the black ants': *NJ*, 24 Dec. 1778.
 – 'He usually basks': *NJ*, 27 Dec. 1787.
 – 'Hepaticas in bloom': *FS*, 25 Jan. 1766.
400 'more hints': GW to MW, 31 Dec. 1781, *LL* II, 79.

Coda

403 Overlapping passages: see Mabey, 203–4. Letter to John White, see *NHS* (1993),
   Introduction, xxi.
 – 'the conversation of animals': *NHS*, DB 10, 1 Aug. 1771.
 – 'three separate letters': see Mabey, 203, but the long letter of 8 Feb. 1722 is to
   Barrington, not to Pennant. This became *NHS*, DB 11, 12 and 13, dated 8 Feb.,
   9 March and 12 April 1772.
 – 'Letter 26 to Pennant': *NHS*, TP 26, 12 May, 29 May 1770; Foster, 151.
404 'nine new letters': these began as final invented letters 'to Barrington' and were
   moved to the front.
 – 'eventually take the plunge': Mabey, 202, suggests GW's decision may have been
   influenced by the publication of the *History and Antiquities of Hawsted* by Sir
   John Cullum, Suffolk clergyman and antiquary. GW told Marsham that he
   admired Cullum, 'an agreeable, worthy man and a good antiquary': GW to RM,

7 Aug. 1792, Bell II, 287.   – 'in giving a Ton': 23 July 1787, *Mulso*, 337.
— 'But that I may not be wanting': GW to MW, 26 Nov. 1787, *LL* II, 172–3.
405 'The *learned pig*': 26 Feb. 1788, *LL* II, 172, 178–9.
— 'talks much of': GW to MW, 14 Sept. 1791, Houghton MS Eng. 731 (149).
— 'expanded journal of a year': GW to TP, 19 July 1771, *LL* I, 201.
— 'John Aikin': Aikin (1747–1822) knew John White in Blackburn. A prominent
Unitarian doctor and writer, his *Calendar of Nature, Designed for the Education
and Entertainment of Young Persons* (1785) was dedicated to his sister, the edu-
cational writer Anna Letitia Barbauld. After GW's death, the White family gave
his papers to Aikin, asking him to fulfil GW's hope of recording a year. Aikin
published *A Naturalist's Calendar* in 1795, giving dates of entries by month, but
not years. He also edited the second edition of *The Natural History*, in 1802.
— 'I have been very busy' . . . 'So that my old parlor': GW to SB, 8 Jan. 1788.
— '*Discourses on the Four Gospels*': Townson's *Discourses* appeared in 1788. He had
looked after Churton as a boy when his parents died, paying half his expenses at
Oxford.
— 'August, the most mute month': a selection made by Andrew Green. 'Indexing
Gilbert White', 10 Nov. 2018, https://gwallter.com/books/indexing-gilbert-white.
html.
406 'correcting the proofs': GW to MW, 26 Nov. 1787, *LL* II, 171–3.
— 'very bad Latin': GW to BW jnr, Feb. 1788, *LL* II, 178.
— '*foxhunting* parsons': GW to MW, 26 Feb. 1788, *LL* II, 180.
— 'If the bishop': *Antiquities*, Letter 14, n. 1.
— 'Two sheets more': GW to MW, 13 March 1788, *LL* II, 181.
— 'I rejoyce excessively': JM to GW, 21 July 1788, *Mulso*, 341.
407 'in no small squeeze': GW to RC, 4 Aug. 1788, *LL* II, 185.
— 'The large engraving': as well as Grimm's view of Selborne from the Lythe,
these illustrations included his prints of the hermitage, south and north views
of Selborne church, Temple manor house and the Plestor, plus Gilbert's fossil
'Mytilus, Crista Galli' and the long-legged stilt, *Charadrius himantopus*.
408 'you have given to them': JM to GW, 15 Dec. 1788, *Mulso*, 344.
— 'Hamper from London': Dec. 1788, BL Add. MS 43814.3; *LL* II, 187.
— 'deepest sorrow and trouble': GW to TB, 8 Jan. 1789, *LL* II, 192.
409 'with great pleasure': the quotations from Wordsworth's letter to Francis
Wrangham (1808), Coleridge's annotation (7 July 1810), Darwin's 'Recollections
of My Mind and Character' and the *New Monthly Magazine* (vol. 29, 1830) are
taken from Anne Secord's edition, *NHS* (2003), 242–3.
— 'new editions': see Edward A. Martin, *A Bibliography of Gilbert White* (1970). For
his mid-nineteenth-century reputation and influence, see Mary Ellen Bellanca,
Daybooks of Discovery: Nature Diaries in Britain, 1770–1870 (2007), 78–107.
410 'overflowed with a new spirit': Edward Thomas, *A Literary Pilgrim in England*
(1917), 115.
— 'His observation of the insect': Virginia Woolf, 'White's Selborne', *New Statesman
and Nation*, 30 Sept. 1939, included in the *Captain's Death Bed and Other Essays*
(1950).
— 'ethology': derived from post-Darwinian studies, the term was coined in 1902,

while 'ecology', coined in 1866, examines the relationship of organisms to their physical environment.

410 'started us all birdwatching': James Fisher edited *NHS* in 1941.
 — 'found a connection': see Stephen Moss, *A Bird in the Bush: A Social History of Birdwatching* (2004), 9–10.
411 'local patch': British books concerning local neighbourhoods published in the last twenty years include Stephen Moss, *A Sky Full of Starlings* (2008); Jeremy Mynott, *Birdscapes* (2009); Dominic Couzens, *A Patch Made in Heaven* (2012); and Mark Cocker, *Claxton: Field Notes from a Small Planet* (2015) and *Further Field Notes* (2020).
 — 'as the world has been': GW to RC, 20 May 1789, *LL* II, 196.
 — 'it is every where spoke of': 15 Dec. 1790, *Mulso*, 349.
 — 'My book': GW to RM, 7 Aug. 1792, *LL* II, 244.
 — 'I concur with you': GW to RM, 7 Aug. 1792, Bell II, 287.
412 'Sir, I conclude': RM to GW, 31 Aug. 1790, Bell II, 257.
 — 'You will, I hope': GW to RM, 19 Dec. 1791.
413 'wandering gout': GW to RM, 15 June 1793, *LL* II, 268.
 — 'in as plain': GW's will, quoted in *LL* II, 272.

Etty, Mrs: cousins (Battie sisters), 210, 360;
  friendship with Barbara White, 360,
  391; husband's death, 369–70; news
  from abroad, 391; orders for Christmas
  supplies, 391; tutoring Molly, 64;
  view of 'stir up Sunday', 375; wedding
  anniversary, 210; Zig-Zag debate, 292
Etty family, 48, 237, 391, 396

Farringdon (Faringdon): All Saints church,
  28, 335; churchyard, 27; Gilbert's role
  as curate, 27–8, 143–4, 369; Gilbert's
  journey from Selborne, 28; Gilbert's
  sermons, 28, 37, 81–3, 143–4, 195, 281,
  335; hop gardens, 278; Manor Farm,
  257; parish register, 28, 144, 369;
  vicarage, 37; vicars, 83–4, 369; yew
  trees, 28, 29
fieldfares, 343–4, **343**, 355
flea beetles, 275
flies: bat feeding on, 260; birds feeding on,
  125, 188, 220, 227, 272, 394; caddis, 75,
  166, 393; flesh flies, 154, 273; houseflies,
  59, 399; wasps feeding on, 288
Flora Selborniensis, 14, 50, 103–5, 152,
  345 399
flycatchers: feeding, 246; migration, 150,
  168, 195, 282, 301–2; nests, 195, 274;
  spotted, 168, 195, 215, 240, 274
fog: after volcanic eruption, 243;
  dampness, 387; dew ponds, 269–70;
  frost and, 385; insect behaviour, 349;
  London, 387; migrating swallows,
  127–8; November, 375; picturesque,
  296, 375, 387; sainfoin cutting, 208;
  September, 297
Forster, Johann Reinhold, 68–9
Fort family, 254
fossils, 4, 10, 110, 132, 327, 328
foxes, 60, **61**, 406
French invasion threat, 200
French Revolution, 390, 397, 408
French wars, 365–6, 391, 396–7, 412
frogs and tadpoles, 12, 17, 94–5, 217, 227,
  412
frost: damage to cucumber plants, 324;

damage to trees and plants, 168, 369;
  first frosts in September, 311; fog and,
  385; freezing drought, 34, 37; frostbite,
  17, 35; fruit trees in bloom, 105, 119;
  January, 23–4, 26–7, 39; May, 187;
  October, 321; response of tortoise, 345,
  352

Garden Kalendar: Gilbert's first journals,
  14, 30, 44; including birds, 385;
  January's work, 30; new notebook, 103;
  note on brewing, 177; note on field
  crickets, 163; note on snails, 135; notes
  on hayricks, 224; notes on melons, 142
Gaskell, Elizabeth, 5
George III, King, 6, 104, 341
Gerard, John, 50, 99
Gibbon, Edward, 55–6
glow-worms, 162, 201–2
gnats, 41, 126, 389, 392, 400
goatsucker, 174, 259, **259**, 260, *see also*
  nightjar
goldcrest, 274
goldfinches, 272, 291
Goldsmith, Oliver, 182
goosander, 388
gooseberries, 72, 169, 173–4, 213, 253
Gordon riots, 199–200
Gould, William, Revd, 248
Gracious Street, Selborne: floods, 46, 198,
  242; Gilbert's route to Farringdon, 28;
  hop gardens, 278; lane to, 345; ponds,
  25, 46, 162, 201, 227, 261, 388
Grange Farm, 8, 198, 257, 325, 336
grapevines: care of, 62, 187, 366, 386;
  flowering, 204–5; flycatchers' nest, 195,
  274; grapes, 151, 215, 249, 258, 278;
  last grapes, 366; leaves, 258, 347; pests,
  187–8, 287–8; planting, 382; pruning,
  211, 213; 'Sweet-water vine', 120; uses of
  grapes, 342, 359
grasses, 103, 138, 185, 363–4, 373
Gray, Thomas, 152
Great Chain of Being, 12, 95, 262
greenfinches, 169, 355
greyhen (female black grouse), 332

Grimm, Hieronymus: career, 230–1;
character, 230–1; commissioned by
Gilbert, 230–2; *Dorton*, 234; *Hawkley
After the Earthquake*, 234; *Haymaking*,
234; *The Hermitage*, 231, 306; scene of
the Plestor, 231; *Selborne from the Short
Lythe*, 231, 407; stay with Gilbert, 230–1,
300, 329; *Waterfall in the Hollow Stream
Bed*, **286**, 374; working method, 231
gypsies, 295–6

hail, 65, 120, 198, 283
Hale, John (butcher), 162, 279
Hale, John (farmer), 183, 208, 257, 361
Hale, John (nurseryman), 120
Hales, Stephen, 83–4, 167, 269, 347
Hampton, Goody, 62, 134
Hanger, the: beech wod, 186; Bostal path,
see Bostal; fern-owl, 412; flooding,
46; geology, 328; Gilbert's poem, 212;
Hercules figure, 115; hermitage, *see*
hermitage; honey buzzards, 216–17;
house martins, 364; landscape, 8; marsh
tits, 57; mezereon, 104; mushrooms,
322; pigs, 357; pond, 269; ravens, 66–7;
'slidders', 374; tree-felling, 373–4; view
of, 21, 249; wood pigeons, 18; Zig-Zag
path, *see* Zig-Zag
hares, 36, 363–4, **380**, 384
harvest: acorns, 346–7; barley, 175; bean,
297–8; berries, 323; dates, 209, 302, 313,
355; fallows, 288; fine weather, 249, 254,
255; 'harvest home' celebration, 282;
hay, 162, 175; honey, 323; hops, 9, 302;
pasturage after, 9; vetch, 297–8; wheat,
184, 238, 239, 242, 245, 266
harvest mouse, 16, **252**, 266–8, 345
Hasselquist, Frederik, 156
hawthorn, 179, 344
haymaking, 209, 211, 217–18, 224
hayricks, 144, 218, 223–4, 398
heat, 107, 198, 223–4, 283
hedgehogs, 16
heliotrope (sundial), 43–44
hellebores, 67; stinking (*Helleborus
foetidus*), 49–50, **51**, 67, 389

Henry, David, 185
hens and chickens, 188, 229, 412
hepaticas, 399
Hermes, Gertrude, **354**
hermitage: churn-owl vibrations, 174;
construction, 118; descriptions of, 212–
13; hermit, 211, 231, 407, **407**; parties
at, 209–10, 211, 298; slider below, 400;
view from, 209, 231, 306
herons, 264, 329
Herschel, William, 106
Hill, John, 115, **118**, **180**
hirundines, 126–8, 224, 258, 281, 289–90
Hoar, Thomas: bees, 203; brewing, 303;
care of tortoise, 101; care of vines, 187,
366; cellar disasters, 317, 391; character,
62, 173–4; clothing, 88; finding a hare,
384; hearing, 58; jobs, 62, 173–4, 181,
187, 204, 213, 234, 254, 273; nursing
Jack, 77–78; relationship with Gilbert,
62, 381; sowing beech nuts, 374; wages,
87
Hoare, Farmer, 226
holly, 99, 344, 394–5
hollyhocks, 62, 219, 228, 241, 345
Holt, the, 9, 324–5
Holt, Thomas, 92
honey buzzard, 216–17, 229
honeysuckles, 179, 195, 208, 232, 246–7
Hooke, Robert, 14
Hooker, William, 120
hoopoes, 331–2
hops: aphid pests, 176, 294; date of
harvest, 302; drying, 281; failures,
294–5; farmers, 161–2; flowers, 246–7;
frost damage, 168; gardens, 9, 295;
Gilbert's suggestions, 283; growth, 157,
268, 294–5; hail damage, 198, 283; heat
damage, 280, 294; home-brewed beer,
177, 303–4; kilns, 279, **280**, 295; lack
of rain, 268–9; picking, 9, 278–9, **279**,
282–3, 294–5; poles, 58, 157, 278, 296;
Romany pickers, 295–6; sale of, 139,
278; tying, 157, 162
Horace, 40, 77
Horace's Head bookshop, 91, 254, 408, 411

Nash, John, **2**, **214**, **309**

The Natural History of Selborne: account of adder dissection, 264–5; account of field crickets, 163–4; account of gossamer fall, 305–6, **307**; decision to write, 76; description of barn owls, 308–9; editions, 409; ending, 243, 404; first edition, 193, 406; frontispiece, 407; illustrations, **2**, **90**, **214**, **222**, 230–1, **244**, **252**, 306, **315**, **354**, **393**, 407, **413**; index, 405; influence, 345, 410–11; introductory letters, 347, 393, 404; last greyhen, 332; letters, 3, 149–50, 193, 321, 403–4, 406; manuscript, 10, **160**, 404; opening, 4, 8, 404; planning, 112, 148–9, 193; poems, 193; popularity, 3, 334, 411; proofs, 406, 407; publication, 3, 140, 225, 260, 405–8; readership, 3, 4, 38, 124, 142, 409–10, 411; responses to, 224–5, 409–12; reviews, 409; social and political background, 6–7, 48, 72–3, 140, 182–3, 199–200, 257–8, 341–2, 365–6, 391, 396–7; structure, 3; style, 3, 304–5, 347–8, 410; theology, 197–8; title page of first edition, 407, **407**; writing and rewriting, 3, 193, 224–5, 229–30, 381, 393, 403–6

Naturalist's Journal: design and publication, 15, 22, 35, 131, 242; Gray's use of, 152

Naturalist's Journal: Gilbert's use of, 5, 15–16, 22, 36, 106, 123, 412; illustrations of Gilbert's entries, **54**, **398**

nectarines: blossom, 105, 119; care of, 204; eaten by hornets, 276, 279, 283, 287; fruit, 151, 283, 291; picking fruit, 276, 287; Red Roman Nectarine, 120

New, E. H., **413**

Newberry, Sampson, 133

Newton Great Farm, 273, 355, 359

Newton Valence: balloon making, 340; barley harvest, 268; Grimm's visit, 231; temperature, 35; vicarage, 35, 48, 340; water supply, 175; White family background, 31, 372; Yalden family, 35, 48, 268, 297

nightingales: arrival, 135, 144, 412; caged, 383; nests, 186; song, 153–4, 193, 216, 272, 412; young, 216

nightjar, 174–5, 226, 258–60, **259**, *see also* goatsucker

Noar Hill, 8, 31, 133, 212

Norton Farm, 8, 67, 198, 345

nuthatch: feeding, 4, 36, 58, 331; noises, 26–7, 95, 272

Oldham, Claire, **90**, **244**

Oriel College, Oxford, 44, 55–6, 79, 85–7, 377

owls, **2**, **11**, **309**; barn (white), 15, 308–10; brown, 308; chasing swallows, 4, 220; churn-, 174, *see also* goatsucker, nightjar; fern-, 174, 193, 258–60, 264, 397, 411, 412, *see also* goatsucker, nightjar; hooting, 308–9; hunting, 245, 308; shot as pests, 310; tawny (wood), 308

Pallas, Peter, 266

Parker, Agnes Miller, **61**, **141**, **380**

Parsons, Farmer, 63, 162, 184, 334

partridge, 47, 292–4, 363, 388

peaches: blossom, 105, 119, 152; care of, 204; fruit, 151, 270, 283, 291; leaves, 367; Noblesse variety, 120; pests, 277; picking fruit, 287; planting trees, 375; varieties, 376

pears: blossom, 151, 152; picking fruit, 310–1, 312; storage, 35, 312; uses, 342; varieties, 310–11, 312, 342, 345; windfalls, 310

peas, 62, 139, 215, 298

peat: ashes from, 97; bog oak, 347; carting, 63; cutters, 226, 344; dust, 137; Irish bog, 314; right to dig from the forest, 182, 343

Peiresc, Nicolas-Claude de, 49

Pennant, Thomas: *Arctic Zoology*, 316; background and character, 129–30, 131; *British Zoology*, 129, 130, **171**, 174; Gilbert introduced to his work, 111; letters from Gilbert, 3, 75, 108, 123, 127, 130, 148–9, 156, 161, 193,

    A YEAR WITH GILBERT WHITE

vistas, 14, 115–18; well, 175, 242, 273, 300, 321–2, 336, 349, 364, 366, 384, 386; wine cellar, 24, 317
walnuts, 322, 331
Walpole, Horace, 131
warblers, 135, 150, 216, 276; leaf, 108; willow, 108–9, 168; wood, 109; *see also* chiffchaff, whitethroats
Warton, Jane, 39
Warton, Joseph (Jo): career, 39, 87; education, 56–7; *The Enthusiast*, 69; friendship with Collins, 56–7, 193–4; friendship with Gilbert, 39, 56–7, 411; friendship with Mulso, 56–7, 411; poetry, 57, 69; view of *Natural History*, 411
Warton, Thomas, Revd, 39, 69
Warton, Thomas (Tom, son of above): career, 39, 87; education, 56; *Five Pastoral Eclogues*, 69; friendship with Gilbert, 39, 337; friendship with Mulso, 337; *History of English Poetry*, 112, 337; letters from Gray, 152; poetry, 57, 69
wasps: eaten by birds, 227; feeding, 78, 177, 178, 276, 287–8, 299; killed by village boys, 177–8, 276; nests, 178, 277, **289**; queens, 178, 276; relationship with bees, 288; traps for, 178, 277, 368; vanished, 279, 359
water levels: mill wheels, 38, 338, 352; ponds, 25, 46, 65, 157, 242, 266, 268–70, 273, 299, 321, 326, 329, 337, 355; springs, 25, 46, 198, 299, 337, 345, 349; streams, 25, 266, 306, 352; *see also* wells
water rail, 362–3, **362**
watercress, 61, 201
weather: freakish, 243; proverbs, 26; records, 14, 35, 131, 151–2, 242, 260; unpredictable, 242; *see also* barometer, fog, frost, hail, heat, rainfall, snow, storms, thaws, thermometer, wind
Well Head spring, 25, 226–7, 299, 337, 345, 349
wells: cleaning out, 321–2; depth, 25, 273, 306, 336–7, 390–1; dried-up, 306, 336, 387, 390, 412; Selborne houses and farms, 25; water for brewing, 177, 303,

336, 349; water levels, 175, 242, 273, 287, 294, 299, 300, 333, 336–7, 349, 364, 365, 366, 384, 386
Wells, Nathan, 80
wheat: Battersea Field, 95–6; beer, 177; blighted, 232, 239; bread, 139; crop, 184; crop rotation, 184; drought effects, 37; flowering, 213; harvest, 238, 242, 245, 246, 254, 266; housed, 184, 245, 254, 260, 262; mildewed, 239; new shoots under hedges, 287; prices, 183; ricks, 162, 256–9, 262, 266–7; ripples in the wind, 227; Selborne farming, 361; sheaves, 266–7; smut disease, 237–8; sowing, 162, 184, 347, 355, 361; spikes, 194, 203; stooks ('shocks'), 255; stubble, 246, 254, 329, 344, 386; turning colour, 219, 238, 268; varieties, 184; wagons loaded with, 110
Whiston, William, 45, 327
White, Anne (Holt, mother of Gilbert), 31–2, 55
White, Anne (sister of Gilbert), *see* Barker
White, Anne (sister of Gilbert, died in infancy), 32
White, Anne (sister of Richard Yalden, first wife of Ben White, sister-in-law of Gilbert), 48, 91, 114, 371
White, Barbara (Freeman, sister-in-law of Gilbert, Mrs J. White): battle with cockroaches, 290; Christmas celebrations, 396; husband's death, 74; life at The Wakes, 255, 290, 296, 358, 412; marriage, 74; move to Blackburn, 76–7; relationship with Gilbert, 255, 291, 358; relationship with Molly, 381; social life, 360; son, 74, 77, 303
White, Ben (brother of Gilbert): bookshop, 75, 91, 110, 371; brother Henry's death, 408; career, 91; character, 91, 225; childhood, 32, 322; children, 91; gardening and farming, 218; Gilbert's visits, 84–5, 91, 98, 110, 233, 253, 412; life in South Lambeth, 84–5, 91–2, 218, 233; marriages, 49, 371; new house in the country (Marelands), 98, 412;

of intelligence and feelings in animals
and birds, 109–10; views on diet, 138–9;
views on migration, *see* migration; views
on politics and social issues, 6–7, 72–3,
139–40, 199–200, 257–8, 341–2, 391,
396–8; weather readings, 22–5, **54**;
wine making, 317; *see also Antiquities
of Selborne, Flora Selborniensis, Garden
Kalendar, The Natural History of
Selborne, Naturalist's Journal*
White, Gilbert (grandfather of Gilbert),
31, 178, 182
White, Glyd (great-nephew of Gilbert),
81, 371
White, Henry (Harry, brother of Gilbert):
birth, 32; Bonfire night, 359; brewing,
177, 235; career, 73–4; childhood, 322;
death, 408; dressed as hermit, 211, 231,
407, **407**; education, 85; experiment
with owls, 310; Fyfield home and school,
73, 201, 214, 218, 233, 235, 395, 408;
Gilbert's visits, 201, 235, 253; marriage,
73; party at hermitage, 210, 211; post
from Gilbert, 134; pupils, 73, 140, 395;
rain gauge, 93; relationship with Battie
sisters, 210–12; social life, 210–12
White, Henry (nephew of Gilbert), 55, 64,
253, 374
White, James (nephew of Gilbert), 183
White, Jane (niece of Gilbert), *see*
Clements
White, John (brother of Gilbert): career,
74, 76; childhood, 32; correspondence
with Linnaeus, 75; death, 74; debts, 74;
digging 'Zig-Zag' path, 115; education,
74; father's death, 74; health, 77, 255;
helping to write the *Garden Kalendar*,
142; letters from Gilbert, 21, 75–6, 80,
129–30, 148, 193, 231, 233, 265, 304,
404; letters to Gilbert, 74, 103, 127,
146, 156, 173, 193; life in Gibraltar,
74–6; marriage, 74; move to Blackburn,
76, 77, 405; ordination, 74; return to
England, 76–7; sending specimens from
Gibraltar, 75, 155, 187; son, 21, 77–8;
writing *Fauna Calpensis* (natural history

of Gibraltar), 76–7, 110, 188, 304
White, John (father of Gilbert): career,
31–2; character, 31, 305; children, 32;
death, 74, 79; father's death, 32; father's
will, 31; garden, 30, 33; Gilbert's care
of, 33, 55, 86; Gilbert's memories of,
305, 332; illness, 33, 86; life at The
Wakes, 32–3, 175; marriage, 31–2; sister
Elizabeth's marriage, 44; well, 175;
wife's death, 33, 55
White, John ('Gibraltar Jack', nephew of
Gilbert, son of John): appearance, 21;
birth, 74; career, 78, 255, 303; education,
77; marriages, 372, 408; relationship
with Gilbert, 77–8, 254, 303, 404
White, John (nephew of Gilbert, son of
Ben), 218, 409
White, Louisa (Neve, niece of Gilbert),
372
White, Mary (aunt of Gilbert), *see* Isaac
White, Mary (widow of Richard Yalden,
then second wife of Ben White, sister-
in-law of Gilbert), 371
White, Mary (widow of Will Yalden, then
wife of Thomas White, sister-in-law of
Gilbert), 48, 64
White, Molly (niece of Gilbert):
appearance and character, 64–5;
brothers, 55; education, 64; involvement
in publication of *Natural History*, 404,
406, 411; letter to father, 253; letters
from Gilbert, 24, 64, 92, 97, 134, 144,
205, 254, 291, 323, 325, 338, 347, 359,
361, 365, 366, 371, 381–2, 385, 391, 396,
400, 404–5, 406; letters to brother Tom,
199–200, 233–4, 247, 253, 321, 342,
377; letters to Gilbert, 49, 64, 134, 254,
362, 381; London life, 297; marriage,
370–1; mother's death, 64; move to
Fleet Street, 404; research for Gilbert's
Antiquities, 111, 321, 325–6, 400; riding,
297, 321, 324; shopping for Gilbert, 21,
391; sons, 81, 371, 404–5, 412; visiting
Gilbert, 296–7, 299, 321, 324, 329, 330,
334, 347, 374, 412
White, Nanny (niece of Gilbert), 91, 254

 A YEAR WITH GILBERT WHITE

A YEAR WITH GILBERT WHITE